CW00853577

A
FUNNY KIND
OF
EDUCATION

Ross Mountney

About the author

Ross is a passionate parent, home educator, writer and ex-teacher. Whilst she and her husband home schooled their children she tried to rid herself of all things teacherish, as she found it was irrelevant to education. Now that her kids have moved onto Uni and beyond she attempts to educate the dog who is not impressed!

Visit her at http://rossmountney.wordpress.com/

By the same author
'Learning Without School. Home Education'
A guide for parents wanting to home educate
Jessica Kingsley Publishers

Cover by Charley: http://www.flickr.com/photos/53677850@N07/

Dedication

To our two amazing children who have inspired our lives so much and made this book possible.

And to gratefully acknowledge the support from dear friends and home educating families who have shared our journey and those special few who have supported me through the publication of this book.

Copyright Ross Mountney 2012

All rights reserved. No part of this publication may be reproduced or transmitted in any form or by any means, including electronic or mechanical, information storage or retrieval systems, without prior permission from the author.

Oh my god, we've gone and done it now!

The rush of adrenalin hit me the second I was awake enough to think. It was probably brought on by an overdose of excitement. But it could equally have been fear. I was out of bed in an instant.

I'm such a wretched morning person usually death seems more inviting than leaving the duvet. But today was different. Today sucked me out of bed like I'd won the lottery because today was unique. Today was the start of a new adventure.

We'd withdrawn the children from school and they were going to learn at home full time; we were a Home Educating family.

I mustn't panic.

I groped for the kettle in a fog of thinking. The joy and terror fought for supremacy as I made tea; difficult as my hand was shaking from being so hyper. I tried to calm my breathing between sips, failing miserably as my mind did whoopsies.

Yet despite the doubt about doing the right thing, despite the worry about the kids missing out by not being in school, despite the collywobbles over such a monumental decision, the overriding feeling of hope and unimaginable possibility surged through me as the caffeine kicked in.

How long this will last who knows? I might be gagging to send them back to school next week. Although I don't think so somehow...I think it'll last longer than a week.

But just for now, just for this moment, just for this day, there was a sense of happiness, a sense of rightness along with the panic. And best of all, as the girls staggered down all warm and sleep tousled, there was the return of those wonderful smiles which had been absent from their faces from the minute they started school.

It was the loss of those smiles that creased us the most after the girls went to school. The loss of the giggling; our eldest, Chelsea, was virtually born giggling. Her grandma is just as bad and the two of them giggling is so infectious it's almost knicker wetting. But over the four years she has been at school we've watched that giggling replaced by the seriousness of a hunched old woman with a mega life burden on her shoulders.

We'd always presented school as the next positive stage in our family journey. I was writing articles about it at the time and Chelsea posed outside the school gate for a picture all happy and proud and grown up. Looking back now it seems such hypocrisy.

The positivity wore off along with the smiles and the good health and was replaced with constant illnesses, constant infections and constant nits. Nits were rife – not that the school ever wanted to admit to it. I got so sick of nit combing Chelsea's waist length hair I sent one to the head teacher to ask if he'd like to try wearing one himself or do something about it. He didn't take me up on either offer. Finally impetigo scabbed her beautiful face; the result of continual reinfestation.

But nits were the least of the problems. It was the total and absolute disappearance of Chelsea's happiness and health, magically restored in the holidays, which set us to ask the question; is this necessary just for her to become educated?

When Charley started three years later the problems got worse and worse. Except it only took a year for our suspicions to become face-slappingly obvious. School was snuffing out her happiness, her personality and the worse thing of all, her enthusiasm for learning.

"I hate learning," she suddenly announced at the grand old age of five. My god, she'd got another ten years of it at least. We couldn't let it stay like this, could we?

We had talked about Home Educating but when I suggested it was crunch time to Charles I thought he was going to turn round, open the cupboard door, climb in and hide. He stood there, hovering, clearly not knowing what on earth to say. As usual, I filled the huge gaping silence by gabbing on.

"Well, we've got to do something. We can't stand by and watch both our kids have their personalities totally crushed by school not to mention their desire to learn wiped out. And it's not as if switching to the other local school is going to solve anything. They've got just as many problems."

More silence. He fiddled with the cupboard latch wearing the kind of look he might have when going for testicular surgery. I perched on the table and gabbled on.

"I mean look at them; Chelsea's constantly ill with infections and she's totally miserable and unhappy which is probably why she's always ill. Charley can't stand the noise and hubbub and there's no way she's going to cope with the boring stuff when she needs to be doing practical things – she's already being kept in for not doing things that are totally inappropriate for her. They'll be sticking some awful label on her soon and she's only five, for goodness sake."

"I know. I hate to see it too," Charles said, standing there looking like a dejected dog clearly hoping that the problem would have just gone away by now.

"But you don't see the most of it actually, that's the thing; in the mornings when the girls say they're ill but I know the real reason is it's just they hate it. And I have to keep convincing them that they need to go because school's important and it's good for them to go, when actually I think most of what goes on there is a whole load of shite!" I was that angry I'd be foaming at the mouth soon.

"I know, I know! You're right. It can't go on." His face was cloudy and grey with concern.

"So what are we going to do? What on earth are we going to do?"

He actually turned away then and undid the latch. Typical man I thought, hide away from the issue and it's not as if this is the first time we've talked about the girls' schooling. But I was wrong; he wasn't climbing in the cupboard he was only getting out the potatoes. He tipped them into the bowl in the sink and started peeling. This way he had his back to me and I couldn't see his face but I sensed he was stewed up when he spoke.

"I just feel worried I wouldn't know what to do if we Home Educated. It's alright for you; you've worked in school. My experience was only when I went and that was pretty dire," he said.

"Exactly, and look what happened. School totally failed you and now it could do exactly the same to our kids. You want that to happen? Besides, you know when I was working in schools much of what I saw going on there I felt was bad for kids. I don't want them continually subjected to that, do you?"

"Course not! I just worry that it'll mostly be on your shoulders while I'm at work."

"I know that. But, I'm not expecting you to know what to do. I don't either and I know most of it would be up to me, but anyway we'd be in it together – we'll learn together and with your work schedule you'll have time at home to be involved. From what I know most Home Educating parents enter into it from the same point, they have to learn as they go along. It's a new journey for all of us."

"But do you think we can do it?" He stopped peeling to think. He could never multitask.

"Well, it's got to be better than what's happening to them now. I reckon the girls will be far happier and consequently learning a hell of a lot more from being Home Educated than from being in school right now. I mean look at them, they're not the happy little people they used to be. They can't learn if they're miserable and they're just miserable all the time and falling out. They never used to be like that."

"I know. I hate it. It's like our real kids have disappeared." He'd hit the nail on the head with that remark. The truth of it rattled round the silence. The potatoes were nearly finished. He was going to have to face it in a minute.

I took in a deep breath. "Well perhaps we could just give it a try. It's not forever. But I don't really think we have an alternative, if we're both agreed we don't want it to go on like it is."

He chucked the last potato in the pan and turned round.

"I certainly don't want it to go on like this." A hopeful grin spread across his face as he looked at me. "Do you think we could?"

"What choice have we got, if we don't want the kids to hate education as they're learning to?"

"Perhaps we should then." He wiped his wet hands on his jumper. "It's got to be worth a try."

We stared at each other and both started grinning, as if a little seed of something new, naughty, but still to be treasured was growing. We clamped our arms round each other and hugged in celebration, his damp hands on my shirt. Least I think we were hugging; we might have been just clinging to each other in terror.

*

The deal was clinched on Wednesday.

Monday and Tuesday had been bad days for Charley. She'd come home crying twice – and she doesn't cry easily. First off she was teased cruelly but hadn't dared say anything. Second day she'd been 'lost' at the end of the day sending me into a complete panic.

I was standing in the playground waiting as I always did. Children streamed out of the school, greetings were made, families drifted away. Still no Charley. Ten minutes later, everyone gone, I was still standing there, the sense of alarm now so fierce I was about to stride into the school whether they liked it or not. Normally they didn't like it – they kept parents out of the school as much as they possibly could. Made me wonder what they had to hide.

As I moved towards the entrance the teacher came out leading Charley sobbing with fright and distress. I had never seen her so distraught.

"Whatever's happened?" I asked.

The teacher got her answer in first.

"She got left behind, silly girl. I found her in the cloakroom."

"I – I – I couldn't f – f – find my bag," Charley sobbed out. "I was left o – on m – my own."

"Silly girl," said the teacher again, looking very guilty. How I didn't slap her I don't know. She was very young, she was inexperienced, she didn't know about kids at all. I didn't even feel my child was safe.

I swept Charley up into my arms, turned my back on the teacher and carried her to the car. Held her a minute whilst I calmed her and the convulsions stopped and reassured her that I would always find her wherever she was and this would never, ever happen again, and helped her strap in. Chelsea was at home with another infection and she and Charles were wondering what had taken us so long.

When we got back I let them stare at children's TV for a while and told Charles what had happened. We both felt enough was enough. That was that, they were not going back.

That evening, rather than running round the table whooping for joy and throwing the school skirts in the air as I felt like doing, I put on my most sensible parent voice.

"Your dad and I have been thinking".

They ignored us.

"We think it best you continue your education at home for the time being."

Two pairs of eyes switched from the telly and locked into mine.

"You mean, not go to school?" asked Chelsea, sneezing suddenly. I had my suspicions it was school that had that effect. It got up her nose so much.

"Yes."

"What? No more school?" asked Charley, her tear tired eyes brightening.

"Yes. I mean not go to school, just for now. You'll do all your work at home, if you prefer. What do you think?"

The glimmer of developing hope in their faces said it all.

It only took a second before Charley exploded. She flung herself off the settee, lobbed herself at me and clasped her arms tight round my waist. She pressed her face into me and the desperation in her voice was shocking.

"Oh, thank you mummy, thank you, thank you."

I could hardly speak for the emotion constricting my vocal cords.

"Are we allowed to do that?" Chelsea asked, ever the conscientious nine year old. How she suffered in school with her teacher pleasing.

"Yes, darling. You're allowed to learn at home if it suits you better. And we think it will at the moment."

Then I saw the beginnings of that old familiar smile. Tired looking and drained from her infection, but familiar; a glimpse of something that used to be. She came and joined in the cuddle.

"I'll work hard, I promise," she said.

"And I will too, I'll work ever so hard," added Charley.

That's not what I wanted them to worry about.

"Well, we'll sort all that out soon enough, you just need to get well for now," I said. Just get rid of all those awful scabs off your face, I was thinking. They were crusted round Chelsea's nose, mouth and eyes with her latest infection. And as for Charley; she needed to get rid of the scabs in her spirit. We left them to talk excitedly.

Charles and I couldn't keep the excited smirks off our faces either. Or was it nerves twisting up our lips?

Sipping my tea slowly – no school routine to attend to – the anticipation was immense. I imagined the world of learning opening up beyond us with a myriad of possibilities. I thought of all the wondrous things there are in the world to discover, to explore, to find out about. I thought about all the things the kids already did at home, had done pre-school, which taught them so much; all their experimenting, their creative activities, their joy in books and stories, their curiosity which drove their desire to learn. All the things they learnt outside school, from the places we went, the things we did in our holidays. There was so much to do and see, feel and experience. Why couldn't their learning just continue like this? The world is so full of wonder I want to show them it all. I want their education to grow and blossom like plants in a fertile soil. And to make a better job of providing the soil than school's done. I want to reinstall their joy in learning about the world. Surely I'm more excited than nervous?

*

My legs trembled a bit as I took in the deregistration letter.

"Is she ill again?" asked the Teaching Assistant seeing Chelsea wasn't with me. Still feeling a bit wobbly about the magnitude of what we were doing I wasn't brave enough just then to explain or discuss our decision so I edited the truth; after all, she was genuinely poorly.

"Yes, she's got another infection."

"Aw! I hope she feels better soon. Tell her I'll miss her."

She was a terribly sweet lady and I knew she thought the world of Chelsea. She once told me at a parent's evening that if she had a daughter she would want her to be just like ours. I guess she probably told that to all the mums. But then I watched another mum screaming at her monstrous kid and thought; perhaps she didn't.

"Thank you," I said. Then another thought struck me. "Chelsea seems to be ill an awful lot these days. Do you think she's happy at school?"

The TA thought a moment before answering.

"I don't know. But I have noticed she doesn't seem to have that lovely smile anymore." That's the saddest thing I'd ever heard – we'd definitely made the right decision.

I handed my letter in at reception and had to prevent myself from skipping back down the path and out the school gates kicking my heels with relief and excitement.

On second thoughts, perhaps I should have just gone for it!

*

On our first day of freedom we grouped ourselves round the kitchen table. I didn't really want them to be doing much. I just wanted to give them some space to get school out of their system and to get well. But they had other ideas and got lots of books out. I was thinking we'd do some creative things. They wanted to do some 'work', i.e. writing and maths.

Then we read a story about Henry VIII. We looked up how to make paper because it came up in conversation and we decided to have a go at it ourselves sometime. They got their own things out to do in the afternoon. The girls were engaged, happy and motivated. It was so easy.

Could learning really be this happy? The potential seemed mind blowing. We could learn like this all the time at any time. It was like learning without a clamp on.

"Had a good day?" asked Charles when he got home and had happy cuddles the minute he got in the door. The usual greeting lately had been something grunted from glazed faces in front of the

TV.

"I can't believe how much you can get through in a day."

"You'll have to slow down or you'll exhaust them," he joked.

"It's just so great to see them happy," I said.

"Yea, I know what you mean." We looked at them. You could see it. You could see it through their whole bodies. An ease that used to be there before school rubbed it all away with the prospect of the dull days ahead. Did a person have to suffer dullness just for an education?

Early days or not; I'm sure they don't.

On our first Monday of our first week of our life without school I was still in a state of trance-like excitement. It was Monday and *no school*! I hadn't had such joy about anything since they were born.

I had a permanent sense of holiday even though I knew it wasn't. Even though I knew there would be worry and planning and decisions and strange challenges like explaining to the lady at the swimming pool why our kids weren't in school.

That aside it felt like the world was at our fingertips. The world was our school. Our curriculum was our life. Our approach would be tailor made. Possibilities seemed as broad as exploring space.

Taking them for a swim was like having our own private pool. Just a few old folks swimming sedately up and down with wrinkly arms and rubber swathed heads. Even some of the men. Those without the rubber smelled of extreme hairspray. Although it was a bit weird without any young people in there, sinister almost.

The afternoon had the girls doing some beautiful art. It's almost as if their inspiration, their creativity, their motivation to do other things than just watch the telly has suddenly been reignited.

I saw that and regretted not doing it years ago even though there is still a mass to sort out.

Aside from all the education stuff there's the pressing consideration of how I'm going to manage my time so I can still write while Charles is out at work full time, even though his full time is condensed so there are times he's home. Just when I was getting some of my life back after small childhoods had gobbled up a few years they're at home again.

But it's worth it. It's worth it to see those school bonds fall away from them. The bonds that constricted their personalities. The bonds that constricted their joy of learning. The bonds of time restrictions, place restrictions, subject restrictions that squeezed their desire to learn about things until it ceased to breathe.

My god you can still even learn while sitting on the toilet.

"Mu-um," yelled Charley through the toilet door to an accompanying tinkle.

"Yes, darling?"

"How does the wee get in there?"

A short biology lecture at nine o'clock at night. It's still learning! The possibilities blow me away the more I think about the potential to learn all the time if you're allowed to. And if you're happy.

*

It's all very well being happy but I know there are some other things I must sort out pretty damn quick:
- Contact with others
- Getting hooked up to the World Wide Web – the millennium may be approaching but it's still so antiquated out here the web's only just arrived.
- What we're going to do - i.e. some kind of educational plan.
- What we're going to tell folks – that seems the most daunting of all.

*

"Not in school today?" said the lady in W H Smiths as she bagged up our new books.

It's very, very bizarre being out and about in term time in the day with the girls when all other children are in school. We get looked at as if we were committing some kind of horrendous crime having our children out in public on weekdays like they're not fit to be seen or something.

"No, they don't go to school. They're Home Educated." I smiled at her, helpfully.

The smile was not returned. "Oh!" She took the money from my hand being careful not to touch my skin as if she was afraid she might catch something.

"No school today?" asked the lady in the bakers where we went to get a sticky bun and a hot drink and make a decision about going back for some more of the books we'd seen.

"No, they're Home Educated. They don't go to school." I smiled again.

Hysterical laughter was the response this time as if I'd just told her a cracking joke. I looked at the girls and they looked at me. I suspected they were beginning to feel as freakish as I did. We needed to have a chat about this when we got home.

"Out of school early?" asked the librarian when we eventually got there later. After what had gone on before I felt like shouting 'No, piss off and mind your own business', but I behaved myself and rephrased it.

"No. We're home schoolers."

"Oh well done. We have another home school family in sometimes. I expect you know them."

I was that shocked and relieved at her response I found myself gawping at her in surprise.

"No, we've only just started actually. I don't suppose you know who they are, do you?"

"No, sorry dear, I couldn't give out personal details anyway. But we do have some contact details of organisations, if that would help."

I managed to turn my gawp into a smile of gratitude. We took the details of 'Education Otherwise' and came away with an immense feeling of relief that perhaps we aren't so freakish after all.

*

"What we doing today mum?" Chelsea asked me brightly.

That's a completely different start to the day than school mornings. Then it had been a painful drag to get them out of bed. A struggle to get some breakfast inside them. And a decision to be made as to whether they were well enough to go or not.

The morning conversations would generally go like this:

"My head hurts."

Or "I don't feel well. I'm all stuffed up."

Or "I feel sick."

Or "My head's itchy."

Now they were out of bed, dressed, keen, busy, got new workbooks out and asking me difficult questions before I've even had time to prise open my eyelids and brain with an injection of caffeine. It stays like that all day until they drop into bed willingly come evening, thank god.

I'm not sure I'll be able to stand the pace. But Charles and I are so thrilled to have our kids back we can hardly believe the transformation.

*

I'm hatching a bit of a plan. As plans go it's fairly flexible. That's how we want to keep their learning; as flexible as their needs are.

I intend to do some basic skills practice with them in the mornings, literacy and numeracy skills, plus some science, stuff like that.

In the afternoons we'll do creative/inventive/experimental stuff, play, meet others, outings, physical activities, do things that they're interested in. And goodness, how they are interested. In everything. And I suddenly see that *everything* is worth learning about. The possibilities are infinite. They expand beyond our normal boxed in subject boundaries and the whole of life looks potentially educative. How could I not have seen it before?

I couldn't believe what they did today. They started enthusiastically on their maths books at eight thirty when I can hardly think straight let alone do maths. I know these books are a novelty and it will probably wear off but it's still amazing. We had a long discussion about the maths they were doing and why and how it relates to their everyday lives. Charley was doing some exercises about time in her book so we got the clock down and played with that and worked out what time we were having a break, lunch, going swimming etc. After which she understood it so well she filled in all the exercises in the book easy-peasy.

Then we watched a history programme which promoted loads more discussion about conditions for children working in Victorian times. And I told them about the Victorian school room at our local museum and we made a plan to visit it.

After lunch (during which there was a long discussion about nutrition – I think I'm becoming an education fanatic) we went off for another swim, practising times tables in the car by making it into a game. Definitely a fanatic. Reading later, then some TV and chilling really because I was totally whacked out by then.

I could not believe it but they went back to those maths books later in the evening leaving me feeling concerned I'm breeding two terrible swots.

And here was me worrying they wouldn't learn anything. I'm going to have to make a much bigger plan.

*

Telling people what we're up has been a similar experience to telling them I was about to give birth to an alien. People can be really strange when they know there's aliens in their midst. And I suppose Home Educating is pretty alien to most people.

Some folks are like the lady in Smiths and clearly recoil, obviously not wanting to be contaminated by anything catching like radical thinking.

Some folks are downright bloody snooty; "Well I hope it works out for you" in a tone that clearly suggests it won't.

Someone said, "But they need to be in school because they just soak up learning during those primary years." Obviously they thought our kids were not going to do any learning whatsoever, even though over the past few days they've probably done twice as much as they would in a school week.

My god, do people think none of us learn anything outside of those school gates?

Some people are just silent. They don't know what to say. I am quite shocked at the lack of support even from some of those who are closest. You soon find out who your friends are. My best friend said "Wow! That's so brave. I just wish I had the courage to do it too."

The children's only surviving grandparent, my mum, was the best of all, but then she is quite an extraordinary lady. She lives in a dated old cottage on the coast down the road from us and has a key ring that says 'the more people I meet the more I love my dog' which pretty well sums her up. And she has a capacity for contentment a Zen monk would envy.

"Well, that's marvellous," she said when I told her what we had decided. "I will always remember meeting a family when we lived in London whose children went to Summerhill School. The children may have been a bit forward, which some adults find hard to cope with, but I just remember thinking how well spoken and intelligent they were."

"Thanks mum." My mum and I are the greatest. We've always been close. We're like a bun and a cherry. She's the bun; squidgy and sweet.

"Tell you what, they could come to me for an afternoon a week if you like. We can do painting or cooking or have stories. Whatever you want. Then you'll get a bit of a break for your writing. Or just to rest and have time off. What do you think? But I don't want to interfere, just tell me what'll help."

"That would be really good, aw, thanks mum. Everyone else just seems a bit negative."

"Well, they're just narrow minded stick-in-the-muds." She burst into laughter – she doesn't need much provocation. "No, they just don't understand and people are negative when you're doing something they can't conceive. I'd love to have the girls, whenever you want."

"Well, they'd love coming," I said, thinking that's because they can get up to all kinds of mischief that they can't do at home. Not to mention eat lots of chocolate and biscuits.

"I'll look forward to it then, send them tomorrow if you like."

"Well, I'll bring them down in the afternoon and we'll talk about it some more."

I felt much more positive after that conversation. I felt a lot less like an alien too. It's not that weird is it?

*

Mum only lives about a mile and a half down the lane. The girls and I cycled down together and after a quick chat (various instructions) I left them to it and pedalled off on my bike for some exercise. Throughout my life I've always relied on exercise in the natural world to keep me sane. Looks like I'm going to need it more than ever.

The wind rushed through my hair like cleansing fingers massaging worries away. The land was bathed in that soft apple light that autumn does absolutely best. And the air was filled with the sweet scent of moist earth newly turned from the plough.

I cycled along smiling like someone with a guilty secret. Around us was this beautiful world and I just wanted to show every little bit of it to the girls. I wanted to show them that learning about it is beautiful too. That learning can be full of fun and full of love and not the dull, dreary days shut inside that they'd come to expect through schooling. I will take them places; museums, galleries, nature reserves, cities, exhibitions, zoos. We will enjoy real life relationships across a wide spectrum of society, not those unnaturally cloistered within the confines of age groups.

They will be respected.

My legs turned the pedals as my mind turned the ideas. Our first week of Home Educating was through and it's been like living along the Yellow Brick Road. Education has become a golden opportunity in our lives now as it truly should be, instead of the awful drudgery it had become.

I must have pedalled five miles without noticing. That's how I want their learning to be.

"What's that mum?" asked Chelsea looking over my shoulder at my pack from Education Otherwise.

"It's a load of information about the other Home Educators there are. I expect we'll be able to make lots of new friends," I said.

"Cool."

It had a newsletter and a contact list and lots of useful information. The contact list is a whole booklet – hundreds of names – of families who are Home Educating. A whole community of other aliens. Nice to know there really are other people as weird as me.

There are people to talk to and numbers I can ring if I want help with specific issues like filling in Local Authority forms or Home Educating teens. My goodness, fancy Home Educating teenagers - do people do that?

When I read the newsletter I saw that they do. It contains some articles by people who have been doing it for years.

I found the section which lists the families that are local to us. We live so rurally that travelling miles a day is as natural part of our life as the Tube is to Londoners. I shall have to pluck up courage and call them. Cold calling is not something I've ever done before but, hey ho, we're all learning new skills now.

*

I haven't seen the girls this happy since they were toddlers and life was just one big exciting adventure.

"Mum, what's an art school?" Chelsea asked me as I tucked her in. She has made the most dramatic turn around. Her infectious giggling is back and her whole face is lifted somehow. Even better, she seems truly well and all the sores off her face have cleared up.

She thrives on all the creative activities she now has time to do.

"Why, darling, where did that come up?" I said stroking the beautiful hair laid out across the pillow.

"I was reading about a girl who went to art school."

"Well, it's a kind of school for older children where they do art all day."

"Wow. That's so cool. Could I go to art school when I'm older?"

"Yes, if you wanted to."

"I think I would."

"If you like, you can art all day now some days."

Her beam widens even more.

She has ambition. At nine! And it suddenly struck me; I hardly ever saw any original artwork that they did in school. All I saw was test results. English this. Maths that. Never anything truly creative. I don't call colouring in worksheets that creative. Just think if she had to go another nine years without doing the creative projects she really needs to do. How stifling that would be.

Even more worrying, I also failed to see any true aspirations for the children in school other than teachers aspiring to put ticks on required government records.

We must have made the right decision. I wouldn't mind if all she did was be creative for the next five years. I'm sure maths and English would come into it somewhere. Perhaps that's what they mean by autonomous education in that article in the pack I was sent.

*

The first drawback to Home Education came today.

"Look at these," said Charles. He handed me a whole sheaf of forms from the Local Authority.

"Great!" I said. They looked as appealing as tax returns.

"We don't have to fill them in do we?"

"Apparently not, but we have to tell them something. I'll leave it a while till I've thought it through."

"They don't seem appropriate to what we want to do at all."

"No they're not," I said.

The forms asked about subjects and learning rooms and tests and work schemes. The whole point of Home Educating was to lift some of those learning boundaries that schools have to stick to and allow the children's development, mental, physical and spiritual, to blossom in the way that suits them best. To find approaches that will best enable them to do this. To educate beyond school boundaries.

I didn't realise I thought that until I saw the ridiculous forms. I now realise it's what I've been thinking for years. In fact that's probably the reason I chucked in teaching in the first place. Because the National Curriculum placed so many restrictions on children, teachers and learning that it narrowed what should be a broadening experience down to a single track. A single blinkered track at that.

I remember having a conversation with someone once.

"But going to school will surely broaden the children's lives," he said.

"It's strange, but the way it's going, with more and more testing and pre-set targets and prescribed curriculum I can only see it becoming narrower," I replied.

"Education is so important," he said.

"I agree totally. But schooling and education are two completely different things."

It took him a while to see that. I guess we've taken the girls out of school so we can pay attention to their education rather than their schooling.

Later when Charles was reading to the girls in bed I read the forms through again; 'Who's going to be teaching our children? Where will the teaching take place? What qualifications do we have? Outline your curriculum and the subjects you will cover. Describe your educational philosophy.'

Perhaps it was the terror but I felt facetious answers hatching; we won't be 'teaching' them we're just encouraging learning; the learning will take place within the context of the whole world; their curriculum will be life and we got their education right up till the age of five. And as for our educational philosophy? How many pages do they want?

I think I'd better think this through more thoroughly. I put them on the side in the kitchen where they'd get the least amount of glue and coffee damage.

*

I keep looking at the names in the contact book of those who live nearest to us. I don't want accusing of isolating my kids as well as being weird.

I wondered if the kids miss the buzz of school and their friends. They don't seem to. They continue with so many evening group activities they don't seem bothered.

"Do you miss the children at school, darling?" I asked Charley whilst she was busy trying to dismantle our old video player. Investigating things has always been a huge part of what she does – sometimes without our permission.

"No. Sam stabbed me with a pencil."

"What? That's awful. You never told me."

She stopped unscrewing and looked at me, face all school serious again.

"He said he'd do it again if I told."

"So you didn't tell anyone. Not even the teacher?"

"No. She just shouted all the time. I didn't like her. She would have shouted at me if I said anything and told me to sit down." She picked up the hammer.

This conversation made me think about one of the other questions on the LA form; 'What social contact will you be providing for your children?'

Better social contact than they receive in school, I thought.

*

"What we need is a stick," I said whilst we were trying to do measuring. Charley looked worried.

"To measure with. Then you can see how much a metre is," I added. Anyone would think I was going to beat her with it.

We were having a great morning. I'd been helping Chelsea do some estimation and Charley wanted to do a chart too. But she didn't exactly get the idea of appropriate estimations and just said any old number. Then I realised she didn't really know what a centimetre and metre looked like. She needed to see it, to feel it, to experience it in order to know it.

We went out to the shed together, got a stick, measured it to a metre and sawed it off, then calibrated it with centimetres.

She loved it. She was busy measuring for ages; the table, the telly, the cat. We also made a tiny one centimetre stick and various parts of the cat got measured again until a threatening flick of the tail and a growl dissuaded her from any more investigations. Now Charley's better than her dad at estimating metres as he's stuck in feet and inches.

And I had the mind blowing insight that we could adapt all their learning and tailor them to exactly suit their needs. It could nearly all be experiential like that – if I just have the ideas.

We spent ages in the Victorian classroom at the museum playing schools that afternoon. Ironic really! Quite a lot of cane wielding went on. The lady in the tea shop gave us a nice smile and did not say 'not in school today' which endeared her to me enormously.

The evening saw them making up the craft kits we bought at the museum. And all during dinner everything on the table got measured too. I'm beginning to see that Home Education never ever stops. It's going to be awesome – if I can keep up.

*

"Hi, I hope you don't mind me ringing, I got your name from the Education Otherwise contact book and wanted to talk to someone about Home Educating." I'd finally plucked up courage to cold call another local home schooler.

"Oh, yes, how can I help?" said a pleasant voice on the other end.

And off we went. She was so nice it was easy to talk to her for ages. She has two children, similar ages to ours and has been Home Educating for several years. She told me that they visited their local group regularly and all about the families there. We made a date to meet next week.

It was such a successful phone call I just wished I hadn't been such a sissy and done it sooner.

That gave me the courage to ring up the Education Otherwise helpline and ask what to do about these forms that keep shouting at me from the kitchen dresser where I was trying to ignore them and hope they'd go away.

I spoke to another really helpful lady. Their family had been Home Educating for years and her children were teenagers now. She gave me lots of useful advice about contact with the LA like knowing your rights, being clear about your ideas and what you want to do, and having a plan even if it is broad. She agreed that the forms were totally inappropriate if you wanted to use a less schoolish approach to your children's learning and said that I don't actually have to fill them in (relief!). But I do need to be clear about what I want to do with the children and I should put all this in a letter. I also needed to mention that I intended to remain flexible in my approach, changing often as you would expect the children's needs to change as they grew. (Good point). And that I should also request some time to settle into our Home Educating and that we will not be making any plans yet and will get back in touch after that time. (Another good point, putting me back in charge).

I came off the phone buzzing. It's like there's been this whole hidden community existing in what seems like a parallel universe, all working along their brave and open ended pathways and I never knew they were there.

*

We've found another drawback to the girls not being in school. Charles and I can't slink upstairs and make love when he's at home in the afternoons. Oh well, I'm sure we'll find a way round it.

Autumn beamed seductively across the land and suddenly we could take full advantage of it; we could go out whenever we want to, whenever the sun shone, whenever we wanted exercise. No need to keep learning confined indoors.

I don't always remember we have this flexibility stuck as I am in school schedules. But then I have a light bulb moment.

"Come on girls, it's too good to stay in today, let's go to the beach."

"But I haven't finished my writing yet," said Chelsea, also stuck in the routine of four years in school.

"We can finish it another day. Today is an outdoor learning day."

Charley had no problem with it. Her wellies were on before Chelsea had even closed her book. We collated a picnic together and set off.

I had that sense of almost criminal delight again at the thought of all the other children cloistered in school when we were able to be so spontaneous. Then I felt sad for them – they should be out too on such a day.

We walked out onto the vacant sands where there was hardly a soul about. The holiday makers had dwindled, no children screaming for ice-creams, no falling out over buckets and spades, no parents telling the kids to F off as seems obligatory in holiday time. No smell of rancid chip fat. Just the odd retired couple and dog walker bagging up poo.

We studied our charts and books and spotters guide to the beach. We ate our gritty picnic. Carefully packed away our rubbish after observing that the tide line is full of plastic rather than sea treasures. Then the girls amused themselves.

Chelsea got out her book on fashion design, spread herself and her accessories elegantly on a blanket and lay reading. Charley busied herself with a hole, the sand, the sea and spent hours just dribbling sand heaps into surreal sculptural shapes.

Both girls were utterly content. Me too. When I see the children outside I think; this is what they should be doing. Looking and learning, engaged, exploring and discovering their world. Being observant, analysing, speculating, discussing, questioning, all those important thinking skills the teachers don't have time for in a class.

I was still glowing from the feeling of something being right that has been wrong for a long time. I almost felt uneasy about it. Shouldn't we really be in a classroom reaching the next target, enabling the teacher to put the next tick in a box somewhere? Should we really be enjoying ourselves? Can learning be this easy?

And what about the future?

Sod the future! Who knows what will happen. This just feels right. I can't explain it yet – but I'm sure I'll think of something. All those years I spent teaching kids in classrooms knowing much of it wasn't right. It wasn't what the kids needed. Didn't work for many of them. And I'd even go so far as to say that many of the schools were the wrong place for the kids to be. It felt wrong.

This feels right.

I watched them. Even while they were relaxing here on the beach the girls were using and developing skills, experiencing things, thinking. I am confident it is doing them good. I may not know the psychology or the philosophy of it. But I know it feels right. That's good enough for me.

The girls helped unpack the car when we got back and then crashed out and picked sand from under their toenails. I snatched a quiet cuppa. The sea air had left me with a strong urge to close my eyes, but I fought it with trying to work out what to have for supper. My mind's been so full of the children's needs I hardly have time to think of anything else. And my eyelids suddenly weighed at least a kilogram each. How did that happen?

When Charles got back and we'd eaten our very exciting supper of baked spuds and cheese which was all I could think of, we sat talking and I realised that I felt exhausted.

It wasn't a physical exhaustion really. More emotional. With all the excitement of our new adventure I'd been on such a high, it couldn't possibly be maintained, plus there are still very real issues to be worked out. The one uppermost in my mind and also another very big snag about Home Educating that I hadn't faced full frontal; how was I ever going to get time to myself and time to write?

We talked about it while we cleared up together.

"Well, the way my shifts run, with my thirty seven hours packed into only four days out the house, you'll have some time to work when I'm here," he said. "Perhaps I could do the swim and take them on other trips too, stuff like that."

That sounded reasonable.

"Okay. And maybe I could go back to my early morning writing and research time now that we don't have to turn out for the school run. I could do that whilst the girls are still in bed," I said.

It seemed to be the only answer. I'm not an early bird. Mornings are torture for me – always have been. But it was better than not being able to write at all.

"Yes. And if your mum had them one afternoon like she said she was going to that's a bit more isn't it?" he added. "And perhaps you could just go out for coffee with a friend sometimes when I'm here too, get a break away from the kids – give them a break from you!" he grinned at me. I flicked a piece of grated cheese at him. But I could feel my sanity returning as we talked and planned, which was a good thing for all our sakes.

*

Today was a benchmark. I discovered that I'm not the only person in the whole world who thinks school is not always right for all children. For years I've held it in me like a dirty secret, slightly shaming in my professional capacity as a teacher. Now I know I'm not alone.

"Learning doesn't have to be difficult," said Gen the home schooling mum I'd rung last week. We sat and chatted whilst Chelsea and her daughter were upstairs and Charley and her son were outdoors. "It's just schools have made it so by the systems they use and by forcing the kids to pass tests all the time."

I could have hugged the woman. I cannot believe what a relief it is to have someone else's words endorse what I've been thinking for years.

She told me how they educated by allowing their children to choose their activities and not worry too much what they did as long as they were busy. Through these activities various learning concepts inevitably arose and that was the time to learn about them. This way the children remained engaged. They used a few workbooks to formalise and practise the things they learned and to keep on a parallel with the National Curriculum, just in case the children ever wanted to go to school. Their learning seemed so happy and relaxed and easy, it was wonderful to hear about it.

I asked her about the forms from the Local Authority.

"I didn't fill mine in," she said. "They're just not appropriate for Home Education really. I wrote a long letter stating what I intended to do, that I would be educating the children from their interests and would be flexible to their needs. Kids' needs vary enormously, to state you were going to do one thing and stick to it irrespective of their needs would be failing them in my view."

I looked at her in amazement. "So what was the LA's response to that? Have you had a visit from them?"

"Yes, we've had several and they always seem completely satisfied with all the things the children had done and with our approach."

"I feel a bit daunted by the prospect."

"Don't worry. You sound as if you know exactly how you want to work things. And anyway, you need to put them off for a while and explain you need time to settle to home schooling and for the kids to get school out of their system."

"They certainly need to do that. Although I can already see it happening. We can't believe how changed they are. More like their old selves."

"Yes, mine were too. We asked to be left alone to adjust for a while and the LA were perfectly reasonable about it. Everyone starts out a little daunted. You just need to work to the kids really."

It all made perfect sense to hear her talking. Made me feel easier too. And less guilty. Funny how having the kids out of school made me feel guilty. Bit like when seeing a policeman makes you feel you're doing something wrong.

The girls came down to show us the outfits they'd made for the dolls. Chelsea hadn't played with her dolls since she'd been at school – she didn't want to seem babyish.

"That's so nice to see," I smiled at my new friend.

"Yes, I agree. I think they learn so much just through playing like this and parents don't realise, they think learning only happens in lessons. It's sad that once they're at school they think they can't play any more because it's childish. It's such a shame because their play just gets more and more sophisticated and becomes hobbies and develops skills all the time."

It was so obvious once she'd said it. I loved this woman.

There was one tricky moment when the two youngsters came in covered in mud. Typical of Charley – she's no water baby, she's a mud baby. I've tried to divert her onto other things but it's no good. She just loves the feel of it, building with it, sculpting with it, 'cooking' with it. I've resigned myself to it – it's clearly something she has to do and I guess I'll understand the purpose one day. She is to mud as Chelsea is to art materials although I can imagine more uses for art. Perhaps I'm just retarded.

I looked at the state they were in and held my breath. Was there a piece of his clothing that wasn't splattered?

Gen just laughed.

"Goodness, these two have been having some fun, haven't they?"

"We've been cooking," explained Charley.

"Sorry. I should have warned you he might get mucky outside," I said.

"No problem," she said. "I always carry spare clothes in the car, he can change later. Just go back out and enjoy it," she said to him. They disappeared again.

"We don't have anywhere like this at home, we live on an estate. He'll love it out there," she added, smiling happily.

I put the kettle on again. I needed some tea to get over the happy shock that I'd met someone normal. She needed more tea I'm sure to compensate for the barrage of questions I was asking.

The next set was about managing time. She had a strategy for that too; respect.

She said, "I just set times when the children are not to bother me. After all, they have times when they're doing things and they don't want me to bother them. And I point out that it's the same in return. I have times when I don't want bothering either, when they have to sort themselves out and not pester me, or just wait to do something. It's about respect really. I respect them and I ask them to respect me."

"But don't they press you for attention?" I asked handing her a fresh cuppa.

"Sometimes, but generally not. They get lots of my attention anyway through Home Educating. So they don't need to clamour for my attention all the time like other kids do who hardly see their parents. And it's important to encourage them to be independent too. They just get used to it – if you keep practising," she laughed obviously seeing I was totally gobsmacked by all this reason.

She made it sound so easy. I was still glowing with positivity long after they'd gone, long after Charley found his muddy socks in the garden.

*

I tried what Gen had suggested. I picked my moment carefully; I'm not a complete idiot and I was determined for it to work. Both the girls were absorbed in something, Chelsea was making a collage – well, some of it was on the paper anyway. Charley was creating a little town with Lego and chatting away to herself in various characters. It was like listening to a Soap Opera.

"I'm just going upstairs with my books for half an hour and I want you to carry on with what you're doing and if there's anything you want I'll sort it when I come down. Okay?"

They hardly looked up.

"Okay, mum," said Chelsea, still scattering lentils on the floor.

I hovered. "That means I don't want you to disturb me but get on by yourselves, do you see?"

"Okay mum," said Chelsea again, looking at me now to see if there was something she'd missed as I was clearly expecting more. She couldn't see it so she turned back to intently pick lentils off her glue covered fingers.

Still I hovered. Could I leave them? Was I neglecting their education? Was I being a bad mother?

Don't be such a twit, go read your book.

I sat in the bedroom with the book open, not reading, not relaxing, listening for some devastating mishap going on downstairs.

All sounded quiet – just as I'd left it. I stared at the open page and saw not words but every imaginable scenario of chaos, destruction and death that could possibly happen in half an hour. Less than half an hour. I could only stand the tension for twenty minutes. I didn't want to read anyway, did I?

"Everything okay?" I asked when I'd leaped down the stairs two at a time.

Charley was still telling herself stories with the Lego which was now a complete empire. Chelsea had completed the collage and was picking lentils up off the floor and putting them back in the jar for cooking.

They looked at me as if I was an idiot for expecting it not to be. Perhaps I am. Perhaps I'll have to practise this time off as Gen said – not to get the kids used to it but to get me used to it instead.

I had to have chocolate to get me over the trauma.

I'd managed to start my early morning writing routine. Funny, but all I seem to be able to write about is education. I think I might have OCD.

I also did a bit more when the girls were with mum. They loved going and always come back with gorgeous things to eat, or wonderful paintings or creations. And plenty of strange stains down their clothing with added pet hair.

The minute they arrived back from hers I could hear the giggling as they clambered out of the old truck she drives. Three sets of happy faces, twinkling, fun-filled eyes, straggly hair and a disconcerting sense of having got up to mischief came through the door. If it wasn't for the wrinkles you would think there was no difference between their ages. How I am filled up with love for all three of them.

"Look what we made, mum." Chelsea showed me a tin of sticky delights.

"We'll have a cup of tea and test them shall we?" I said reaching for the kettle. Mum plopped down on a chair and Charley climbed on her lap immediately. Chelsea drew up beside her.

"Thanks for having them mum. Are you tired out now?" I said. She smiled her lovely smile at me.

"Not at all, it's great fun," she said, squeezing them both and making them giggle. They beamed up at her and I could almost taste the sweet happiness that flowed between them. Or maybe that was just the cloud of icing sugar that came off Charley when she moved.

Tea made I was just about to tuck into the sticky things they'd made when Charley said,

"We found a mouse in the kitchen." My mouth hovered.

"Dead, I hope?" I asked. I tried not to look hesitant and took a bite.

"Oh, yes, it was completely dried out," said Chelsea.

"I'm surprised the cat didn't eat it," said Charley stuffing all hers into her mouth.

"Well, the cat isn't allowed in the cupboards," said mum indignantly, as if her hygiene was of unquestionable standards. It isn't. And since the cat seems to be allowed everywhere else it's a wonder it isn't in the cupboards too. Mum brushed crumbs off her round tummy.

I tried not to let my imagination put me off the sumptuous delights and ignored the occasional pet hair in my mouth and the grime under the Charley's fingernails. She must have got that after she finished cooking – surely?

*

I decided that in order to help me achieve the things I want to do, as well as the things the children need to do, I need lists. Lists give me some security; make me feel like I know what I'm about.

I have a special jotter on my desk where I write down my own personal 'to do' list and look at it in spare moments during the day. It reminds me there is life outside Home Educating. Usually I'm so busy enjoying the Home Educating and the exciting and unexpected routes it takes us down I forget all about my list. Then I pass it by on my way to fetch something and see that I had a writing project, an outing with a friend and a new book to read lined up for this week that are still just that; lined up. Oh well, they can be 'carried forward'. I'm getting more 'carried forwards' than things crossed off. Even worse this week's list also has; complete and send forms to LA. It's now several weeks since I received it I really ought to do it. That's if I still find them and they're not too tea stained.

Not doing it today though. The technician came to finally get us hooked up to the internet.

After the whirring and buzzing as it 'dialled up' our first

experience of the World Wide Web was a pair of massive bosoms.

We'd all clustered round the computer the minute the technician had gone, all desperately excited to try it out.

"Can I have a go? Can I have a go?" Charley was the keenest, always loving anything with buttons to press and gadgets to investigate.

"Why should you have first go, I want a go?" said Chelsea.

I hadn't even had a go myself yet and had no idea what we were up to.

"Perhaps mum should have a go first, until we know what to do," said Charles, the most afraid of new technology out of the lot of us.

"We'll do it together," I said.

"What do I have to do?" asked Chelsea sitting down in front of the keyboard before Charley could. Charley squeezed onto the chair beside her and stared at the keyboard in drooling anticipation.

"Well, you type in whatever you want to find out about in this box here."

"What shall we look up?" she asked. The whole world at our fingertips and we couldn't think of anything.

"Dinosaurs," offered Charley.

"No, they're boring, I know, I'll look up my favourite clothes shop. All the shops have a website now." Chelsea started typing.

Her typing was painstakingly slow. But it was only one short word she had to type. Unfortunately the name of her favourite shop was Tammy.

Tammy is also the name of a prostitute whose breasts are the biggest I have ever seen. They are the biggest breasts any of us have ever seen and we were glued to them as we all sat waiting to be stunned by the wonders of the World Wide Web. Stunned we certainly were. In fact, I think Charles had actually stopped breathing.

Apparently Tammy was prepared to cater for all sexual preferences...and I don't know how much of the rest of the explanations the girls were able to read as I blundered about trying to remember how to shut the page down.

"Well, she hasn't even got any of the clothes I like on," said Chelsea in scorn.

"Why is she naked?" asked Charley.

Charles walked off sniggering and left me to deal with it, the coward.

"I don't think that was the right website, darling, maybe we'll look at it another day when I can sort it out a bit better. Maybe the shop hasn't got a website yet." I fumbled about with excuses making a mental note to sort out the child protection facility. Perhaps there's a mum's embarrassment protection facility too.

"Her bosoms are much bigger than mums," I heard Charley say as we walked away from it.

The computer man did leave us some brilliant educational CD Roms though. He was very interested in our Home Education and keen to help.

"These are not like a lot of them which are rubbish – little better than babysitters" he told us.

I've already investigated some of those. They're sold under the title of 'educational' but are nothing more than cheap mind numbing entertainment. Some of them are probably even less educational than Tammy's breasts.

The programmes he left were really good. They explored maths, English and science and were great. I could leave the children using them in complete confidence.

I couldn't wait to get on the web myself when the girls had gone to bed and there's no danger of anyone overseeing my boobs in all senses of the word.

I'll add it to my 'to do' list.

*

At last I've got my letter to the LA drafted. I quite surprised myself.

I started all formally, thanking them for their letter. But then went on to release an enormous amount of pent up educational opinion that's been festering away for years;

'We are unable to fill in your enclosed form because it is inappropriate to our Home Education situation and the education we plan to provide for our children.

We plan for the education of our children to be centred around their needs, for the most part autonomous, deriving from their own interests and daily pursuits, at times democratic, where their learning is shared, helped, broadened and encouraged by our parental input. Our aim is for happy confident, self motivated children who take pleasure in learning. We hope to provide a stimulating environment in which they may do this, both in the home with materials, books television, computers, and in the community and further afield with trips to libraries, visits to places of interest, field trips and activities which encourage an interest and curiosity about their daily lives and environment, all of which are sources of learning and educational opportunity.

We see learning as an integral part of our children's daily lives and not separate from it or segregated into subjects. Therefore it is not timetabled or structured; this would be unnecessarily inhibiting. It may take place from the minute they wake to the minute they sleep, over meal times, social times, unusual times, any time, by discussions and questioning, conversations, investigations and research, not necessarily in a formal procedure. We see it therefore as mostly spontaneous and unplanned. Thus we can take advantage of the purest receptive moments when learning potential is at its peak.

We are quite confident that contact with family, friends, social events, clubs and activities of this nature provide our children with plenty of social interaction.

Having said all that I'm sure you must appreciate that our children have to recover from the numbing effects of school, which has damaged their learning potential, and it may take us some time to settle into our Home Education. We look forward to this with enthusiasm and excitement.

We hope this fulfils your requirements. We will be happy to answer any queries you may have about our educational provisions when we see you. Do please let us know when you would like to visit.'

Phew! That should take them a while to digest, especially looking up all the words in the dictionary like I had to. Thank god for spell check.

It sounds so as if I know what I'm doing even I'm impressed. I just hope they are too.

*

Had a lovely outing - without the children for once as per my list. I took mum over to our favourite tea shop nestled among the folding Wolds and we sat and had uninterrupted chat. Maybe the first since this adventure started.

We ended up talking an awful lot about the girls though.

"It's lovely having them round to do things with, they're such bright little things aren't they?" she said squeezing her happy tummy into a corner seat.

"They certainly are. And they love coming. But I hope it's not a bother mum."

"Not at all darling. They'll keep me young. Otherwise it's too tempting to sit by the fire reading all afternoon," she beamed. She always had such an enviable capacity to enjoy her life.

"Nothing wrong in that," I said.

"The cat who sits on my knee all afternoon certainly doesn't think so," she beamed at me again and studied the cakes. Her hand wobbled a bit like it always did when she was excited.

I realised as we talked that she is getting older and changes are inevitable. I've been so wrapped up in the girls ever since they were born that I hadn't appreciated to what extent that had happened. And her wonderful energy, positivity about life and disposition masks the fact she is eighty two. Only her dwindling hearing gives it away and the fact that she talks very loudly as if she thinks everyone else's hearing is as poor as hers.

I don't mind at all, it's just that it's usually the other people in the teashop that she's talking about.

I need yet another occasional entry on my personal 'to do' list; spend time with my mum.

Every new Monday is still a joy. No groaning, no dread on a Sunday night, no boring routine to return to, as you never know what the day will turn up.

Chelsea giggles more and more like she used to. And the worry frown no longer appears on Charley's face. It's more a frown of concentration as her intrigue in finding out is exercised daily.

I am confident that their learning has developed and grown and expanded since they 'came out'. They are emerging like butterflies from a chrysalis.

I'm trying not to feel too smug since this Monday is a double joy as all the other children go back to school after half term and we don't have to. Fantastic that we don't, sad for the others.

It is only now that we are Home Educating that I realise there are NO children out and about in term time. Obvious really, but I never gave it a thought before. So when we're spotted, because Home Educating is so rare, people naturally assume we're playing truant and it's still hard not to feel that we are. The ironic thing though, as I'm fast learning, is wherever we go, whether it's shopping or other errands, taking the car to the garage, giving mum a lift to the surgery, there are still things to talk about and learn.

We talk why, how, what's a budget, what's discounts and percentages, why we don't buy loads of biscuits and sweets even though we like them, where places are, what's nutritious, how to keep our bodies healthy, which organs do what, what people do, why I absolutely won't buy the latest sugary poison filled drink the manufacturers are promoting as healthy. It's all learning. The list is exhaustive.

But learning out in public also has its drawbacks. It takes twice as long. And can be extremely embarrassing.

"Look mum, that lady's trolley is full of biscuits and cakes, is that why she's so fat?"

Or, "Is that man wearing underpants like dad does?" The stranger must have overheard because he immediately crossed his legs.

And sometimes the comments from the public make me want to spit venom.

We were in the lift with an elderly couple. Our arms were full of shopping and library books and some new art materials.

"Why aren't you in school today?" said the old guy looking directly and accusingly at the girls, completely bypassing me.

Before I can say anything Chelsea answered.

"We're Home Educating," she announced proudly. I was proud of her too. I'd never heard her say this to anyone. But the miserable bugger put her down immediately.

"Shopping on the curriculum, is it?" he sneered. Chelsea's face fell.

I felt like ramming his words down his throat with his false teeth. But instead I just said as dismissively as I could,

"Yes, you can learn an enormous amount just through shopping." And whisked the girls out of the lift without even looking at him. Snide little shit.

How can people be so offensive to little kids? We discussed it in the car on the way home. I have no qualms in letting the children know that not everyone deserves the respect that we would like to give. Respect is a two way thing.

It would have been a lot easier to say some folks are just Tossers. But I didn't think that would be educationally sound.

*

Practised my 'out of bounds' session again today. I left the girls content in their rooms and went into mine with notebook and pen. Managed not to spend all my time listening and fretting. I sipped tea and scribbled my notes and no one disturbed me. I emerged half an hour later so full of love for them I was nearly bursting. So took them for the promised swim.

"Not in school today?" asked the receptionist.

"No we're Home Educators," I said wondering how long we'd be going through this routine. Perhaps I should wear a badge.

"Have a good swim," she said choosing not to comment.

We'd timed it wrong and got tangled up with a school in the changing room. The hubbub was terrible, until the teacher came in and shouted at the top of her voice.

"Will you stop shouting," which we thought was rather ironic. My two were visibly cowed in her presence.

She spent most of their lesson shouting at them to listen to the Instructor who couldn't get her instructions out because of the teacher shouting. The school kids spent most of their time standing still in the water listening and shivering. And the rest of the time standing on the side shivering waiting for their turn. After half an hour of this they all trouped back to the changing rooms again still shivering, teacher still shouting. Then it faded away and there was this sense of calm descending even on the life guards who looked less like naughty schoolboys themselves.

The swim instructor padded past in her flip flops and smiled down at us conspiratorially.

"It's a bit quieter now, isn't it?" she said.

I smiled back. So did the girls. That sure makes a nice change from 'not in school today' or the git in the lift.

*

There's been a parallel universe existing all along where the children are out and about in the world, where the parents and children have a different respect for each other and for learning, and education is enjoyable. Where rules are unwritten yet binding through invisible threads of care and love. Where all ages and all backgrounds just mix together easily without the constraints of how old you are, what colour your hair is, what you're wearing or what group you're in. And now we're part of it as we join the other Home Educators.

We met at the local park and playground with a picnic. The girls just disappeared with the others like we'd known them for years.

I was keen to ask why others were Home Educating. The stories of school experiences were worrying, distressing and in some cases shocking.

"He was made to stand up in front of the whole class in shame because he had wet himself and the reason he did that," one mum said, "was that he was too afraid of the teacher to ask if he could go to the toilet. He's only five for goodness sake, they're supposed to be building trust."

I was really shocked. "Did you say anything?" I asked.

"Course I did. But the school virtually made out that my child was lying and I was lying. Anyway they already had me down as an interfering parent because I'd asked if Shaun could have water instead of milk to drink as milk makes him sick. But they didn't like that either."

Shaun came running up. A bright boy of around seven with a smiling open face. And full of respect for his mum I noticed.

"Mum, can I go to the sandpit?"

"Okay, darling. Is anyone going with you?"

"Yes. She is." He pointed to Chelsea. She smiled, obviously feeling important with the duty of looking after.

"Is that okay?" mum asked me.

"Yea, fine."

Charley ran over.

"Do you want to go with Shaun and Chelsea to the sand?" I asked.

She nodded eagerly.

"I'll look after her," said Shaun and took Charley's hand. The three of them went off happily together.

"Sweet boy," I said to Shaun's mum.

"Yea. We've got our old Shaun back. It was horrible when he was in school. He became so cross and aggressive. And he hardly ever seemed to laugh."

"That sounds familiar," I said.

"Mine just went dead quiet, hardly spoke and began to wet the bed at night. He hadn't done that since he was a baby," said another mum.

"How is he now?" I asked.

"He's fine. Back to his normal self. He's there, look."

I looked across to see a happy lad hanging upside down on the monkey bars chatting intently to Chelsea who'd rejoined them. "I think he's taken a shine to her," laughed his mum.

Chelsea was chatting back and laughing and I could tell she seemed completely at ease with these kids.

"They all just seem to get on so well," I said.

"Yes, we mostly find it's like that in the home school groups we go to," said Shaun's mum. A dad joined in the conversation.

"Well, they don't have to compete with each other, do they? Or do each other down. Or fight for teacher attention. Or worry about getting things wrong and getting laughed at, or going to the loo and looking stupid. No one's going to sneer at them because they can't read or don't know what four fours are. Ours have become totally relaxed since they came out of school, and seem to learn everything twice as fast."

Another lady joined in.

"Mine have never been to school so they've never experienced class dynamics but one of mine remarked to me that the kids at Cubs seem very different from the Home Educated children he knows. I asked him how different and he said he wasn't sure really but they just seemed unkind to one another which he didn't get."

"Oh, that's typical," said Shaun's mum. "Shaun had a friend stop playing with him because he didn't go to school. His mum wouldn't let him any more."

"Really?" That shocked me.

"Are you surprised," laughed the dad. "They wouldn't want their kids asking if they could learn out of school too, would they?"

I hadn't thought of that.

We chatted for the rest of the afternoon. I hardly saw the girls except when they came to snatch a drink or another sandwich. Same with all of them. I don't think I'd ever seen a bunch of kids play together for so long without conflict. Actually, the parents did pretty well too.

I noticed that most of the children in this group were boys. When I mentioned it the dad took up the soap box again.

"Yes, it's the boys that the education system really fails. Girls take to sitting and doing writing and stuff so much more easily. But the boys need far more physical activity and they're cutting back on that in schools all the time. Plus the fact the staff are so obsessed with SATs and stuff, it gets worse and worse."

The more I thought about it, the more I realised he was right.

On the way home, two tired, relaxed, happy children melted quietly down in the back of the car.

"Good time?" I asked.

"Brilliant," said Chelsea. Charley was too tired to answer and just shut her eyes.

I buzzed from meeting all the other families at the Home Education group meet. It was such a warm, supportive and heartening social experience; a complete contrast to the school gate where cliques could rule, competition was as contagious as the black death and arms were folded like a shield to repel contact with anyone remotely weird i.e.; not fitting in the clique.

I could never understand this as weren't we all parents, aren't we all human, all in the same club? Perhaps I'm not human. Perhaps it's just an illusion. Funny, but it's usually their dad that the girls think is from another planet.

Okay, so weird I may be, but now thanks to my new found home school community at least I'm not weird on my own. It's great for the kids to have that too. Although, I don't think it's really dawned on the girls how unusual it is for them to be learning out of school despite the random comments from the people we meet. Kids are so much more accepting – that's when the adults stop trying to influence them all the time and let them think for themselves.

*

Least the ladies in the local shop have got used to us now. Probably thanks to one of them who has cleaned for mum for years and has become very close to her. I know mum and her sit and chat for ages over coffee – probably longer than the cleaning takes – and mum would probably have been telling her all about our decision to Home Educate.

She stopped us by the baked beans.

"Hello, there, hello girls," she said, smiling warmly at them, stopping counting for a moment.

The girls smiled back and said hello.

"Your grandma's been telling me you learn at home now. That's nice isn't it? Are you enjoying it?"

The girls nodded enthusiastically. She looked at me with her open honest face.

"Well, I wish you all the best with it. It's a very courageous decision."

I glowed with the positive feedback. It's a bit rare. She must have discussed it with the other ladies because they now give the girls special smiles and help them when they pay for their own things at the counter. We feel more special than weird at times.

*

The time raced on – so it is when you're enjoying yourself. It disappeared faster than the biscuits. It was well into November and I didn't know how that happened. We got through so much yet there was always so much that we still wanted to do. We had more meetings with the group and I was managing to get some writing done when the girls were with Charles or mum.

Chelsea was producing some lovely artwork again. School pressure and stress seemed to have wiped it out. But while we were drawing I soon noticed Chelsea sighing, getting crosser and crosser, rubbing out and generally getting in a terrible state.

"What's the matter, darling?" I asked.

"It's all wrong. It's all going wrong." She scribbled on it angrily, close to tears.

"It's not wrong at all. How can it be wrong? It's your drawing and it can be however you want to make it," I said trying to offer some comfort.

"It is wrong. It's stupid. It doesn't look anything like the real thing." She was almost shouting now.

"But that doesn't matter. We're just making our own drawings, they're not wrong or right, they're just our own creations. We're not cameras are we? Who says it has to be like the real thing?"

"The teacher did. She said it was wrong if it didn't look like it was supposed to. She said my drawing wasn't right. I can never get it right." She dropped her head on her arms to hide the tears of frustration. Charley looked up concerned and patted her arm.

For goodness sake – how could a teacher expect a nine year old to make an accurate representation of a real object? I gave Chelsea a cuddle.

"Well, you're not drawing for the teacher now. And you can make your drawing any way you want in this house. There is no right or wrong. Okay?"

She nodded. Wiped her eyes.

"Tell you what; we'll put another activity on our timetable called 'drawing badly'. How about that?" She grinned at me.

The damage that can be done by a chance remark by a teacher can have such impact on lives. Actually, it's made me think that chance remarks aren't necessarily confined to teachers. I'd better be careful what I say.

*

I'm not sure how useful the World Wide Web is going to be. It takes ages and ages to wait for it to dial up. It takes ages for the info we're seeking to load. I don't know how Tammy got her boobs up there so quickly, but as for anything else educational it's still quicker to reach for a text book. We were looking up some bird species the other day. Chelsea went to the computer. I reached for the field guide. I'd found what we wanted before the computer was even online.

But it's great for the CD Roms. The girls are really into them. I can see they learn masses just by exploring and clicking on whatever they want really. Charley keeps telling me about body parts and where our organs are after playing with a programme where she has to put our virtual insides into all the right places on a virtual body. She knows more than I do, it's embarrassing. What a shame all learning cannot be presented like this, the potential is huge, Wish I could think some up and earn us a living.

Home schooling means depending on one income and that is hard. I must write more and see if I can get past the endless rejections and earn more. How many jobs can a girl do in a day? A lot more if she remembers to use her list efficiently.

*

The girls didn't go to mums' today for activities because she wasn't very well. But we did go down and give her lots of love and attention and TLC.

Chelsea made her tea. Charley took the dog out for a walk. I thought; what better education could there be than learning how to care? I filled her coal buckets and brought loads more wood in for her fire. She pretty much depends on her fire for decent warmth, the storage heaters are almost useless. We left her snuggled by it, cat on knee, book to hand, looking a whole lot better than when we arrived.

We got home and made cake together so we could take her some down later. And went to the shop for her.

One of the ladies at the till started to talk to me.

"I hope you don't mind, dear, but I've been telling another lady about you all. She had her little boy with her who was too scared to go to school because of bullying and I was telling her that you were educating yours at home."

(I noticed she said this with some importance and pride – wonders will never cease.)

"And she asked if I could get your number. Well, I said I wasn't sure about that, so she said what if she gave me her number and I could pass it on to you next time you came in and maybe you would be able to ring her 'cause she could do with some advice." She handed me a bit of paper. "She sounded ever so interested in what you're doing."

I was a bit stunned. Nice stunned for a change, not stunned into having to defend myself.

"I think she'd be really interested to talk to you if you felt like giving her a ring."

"All right, I'll do that. Thanks," I said.

"Hope that was okay. I don't want you thinking I talk about all the customers to everyone, it was just that she seemed like she didn't know what to do and all, and I like to help people."

"No, that's fine. I'm glad you did. I'll ring her."

The girls and I came out of the shop glowing. Perhaps we're more supported than we think and not everyone thinks I'm a Christian weirdo after all.

*

Mum's bounced back with her beaming health and her roly-poly, radiant disposition and arrived in our drive just when we were working on electricity at the kitchen table.

"It's such a beautiful day, I'm going into the Wolds and wondered if you wanted to join me?" She invited.

"Oooo. Can we mum?" said two pairs of electric eyes.

"Come on, you can do natural history instead," she persuades, winking at the children, knowing I'll need educational justification. I needed no persuading.

We trundled through the countryside up into the Wolds in her old truck the girls in the back swaying about as if they were in a boat. I wonder if eighty year olds should still be driving sometimes, but the girls think it's great fun especially with her dog panting down their necks.

We drove to our favourite country park and nature reserve; a wonderful oasis of trees and natural habitat within the intensely agricultural one that surrounds it. Agricultural it may be but with the low and lovely November light on it, it looked a picture of burnished gold like an old Gainsborough painting. The stubble fields still left after the harvesting were plains of duskiness and we spotted Lapwing and Curlew and flocks of Finches on the teasel heads round the edges. Some of the fields were being turned under the plough and the big chocolate rolls fold away from the implement with a succulent smell of earth. A trail of gulls followed behind.

We walked round the reserve to the sound of the buzzard overhead, found a few remaining late blackberries still uneaten by the birds and we lingered a while by the stream where the children paddled and found stones, built dams and generally made themselves wet. I reckon there couldn't be a more perfect way to spend their time. Topped off by the hot chocolate and inevitable biscuits mum had stowed away in the back of the car.

When she dropped us off home again we went in to find the books where we had left them, the wires and the pliers and the bits strewn across the table. Charley went straight back to her invention. Chelsea to her reading. Both unsolicited. Both content. It was like they'd never been away. But I know we learnt just as much out of the house as we had in it, just different subjects.

I started supper. My mind was still on our trip.

There must be something uniquely valuable about them learning to be content and to be busy about their own lives of their own volition rather than only ever doing what others tell them to do. If they learn what makes them content and what makes them inspired then surely knowing that about themselves is going to find them a better career than doing loads of boring academic exercises that have no meaning in their lives right now whatsoever. They'd end up like me; teaching, even though I was never happy in a school. How did that happen? Because that's what girls were pushed towards. Either that or nursing or secretarial, neither of which I fancied. And even then it was a half hearted push because the world was still at the stage of believing that it was a bit of a waste of time educating girls when they would be having babies and wasting it. Women's lib hasn't really solved the business of babies. I was just a pawn at the mercy of a big institutional machine.

I'm going to make damn sure that these girls have more control and far more understanding of what makes them tick than I ever did.

Next time it was me receiving the inquisition.

I'd rung the number the shop assistant had given me and invited the woman over. We sat in the living room whilst the youngest were busy outside and Chelsea was doing a creative experiment in the kitchen. I'd been barraged with all the questions I'd been asking all the other Home Educators, about our reasons, our plans, our approach to our children's learning. Answering made me feel like I know what I'm doing and as if I'd been doing it for years.

"We learn most from doing stuff. I think the development of their understanding through practical experience of it is the foundation of true learning," I said, the words almost arriving in my brain as if they'd been stored there all the time but I hadn't noticed. "If they have understanding, then you can easily add the academic skills needed to record or reproduce their knowledge in a more formal way when they're older."

"I absolutely agree," she said. "My son spent so much time in class writing things down in books he had no time to experience it practically or even to ask the teacher about the bits he didn't understand. It seemed more important to just get things copied down rather than understand it."

"I know. I feel sorry for the teachers actually. They have so much pressure to get kids to reach their attainment targets they don't have time to teach properly, as some would like to, let alone explain anything, or encourage questions. And it's questioning that really makes a mind grow."

"True, but I do wonder how I'm going to cope with the incessant chat sometimes," she joked.

I laughed. "Me too. But another home schooling mum gave me a good strategy for time out," I told her about me practising my out-of-bounds sessions. "The other thing is, just because we're Home Educating I think we have to be careful not to feel that we should be with the kids 'educating' them every single minute. After all, the kids in a class only really get a few minutes each day of teacher time, then an awful lot of time filling in really, often distracted by the things around them. And in our situation, one to one, we can get through things much quicker. We'd soon do it to death"

"Yes, I can see that now you've brought it up. I'll try that time out strategy. You sound like you have it all worked out," she said glancing out the window at her son happily playing mud pies with Charley. She didn't seem to mind the muck.

I laughed and she looked back at me. "I may sound like I have but the reality is that you make it up as you go along I think," I said. It was so good to find someone who is more of a beginner than me.

"Mum?" Chelsea stuck her head round the door. "Do you think it would be possible to grate the wax crayon?"

"I don't see why not, darling, try it." She disappeared back into the kitchen.

The woman was looking at me as if we were mental.

"Don't worry, she's making a collage, not baking anything!"

"I'd never have thought of grating wax crayon!" She laughed.

"When you're Home Educating, the possibilities are endless."

We made arrangements to do child swaps and meets and activities as she lives so near. And she was going to come along with us to the next group meet.

The contacts widen. The feeling of being weird becomes a little less.

*

Another drawback to Home Ed The kids are always around to nose into what I'm doing and I have no chance of secrets.

Charley's birthday in two weeks and me and Charles were having a job planning surprises. We can't even have a conversation about it without ears fine tuning to pick up our quietest frequency. In the end we asked mum to step in whilst we nipped into town. It dawned on me that we were also going to have to think of a way to manage our Christmas secrets as that was next.

Mum came to ours so that the girls have more around to occupy them rather than getting into mischief at hers. At least I know they're relatively safe. Charley, ever the experimenter, was striking matches and throwing them into the fire, when I picked them up last time. It looked horrendous, but actually she was quite sensible and safe and children should not be totally excluded from anything the tiniest bit risky or they'll never learn how to keep themselves safe.

However, when she takes risks I want to be there. Our open fire is behind a rigid guard and the matches, pills and sharpest tools are well out of reach.

Not so the oven. We left them in the kitchen baking. My imagination went into overdrive.

"Don't worry, they'll be fine," said Charles as we pulled out of the drive. I wasn't sure if he was trying to convince me or himself.

We walked round town like a pair of teenagers holding hands. It had been that long since we'd had any time to ourselves on our own we didn't want to waste it. Was it worth it, this Home Educating lark, when they could be conveniently tucked away in school? Course it was, we decided; just to see the shine back in their eyes. We indulged a few quick moments shining into each other's eyes over a coffee. But the vision of hot hobs tainted it a bit and we soon made for home.

A wonderful smell of baking greeted us and the three of them were tucked up on the settee in front of Blue Peter. Except mum had her eyes shut.

*

Whenever it's the children's birthdays I start to get all emotional. Chelsea because she was the first born and there's nothing like the magic of that miraculous first new child. Charley because it was a dramatic and traumatic birth that could have ended up with us losing her so it is also miraculous she is here. As her birthday approaches it always brings some of it back. It brings back the reminder that I need to stick to my intuitive feelings.

My intuition at the time was to have a home birth but various people persuaded me that this was unwise, me being an 'older' mum and relatives' faces looking sick with worry over the prospect. Not to mention Charles' expression of sheer panic whenever I mentioned it. As it was he had an even worse scenario on his hands.

I also had the intuitive feeling, that snowy night, that the baby was pushing to be born there and then but everyone had told me these things take time, even though the first one didn't. Ignoring my intuition, and the feeling that she was about to pop out any minute and I should stay put, I threw myself on the back seat of the car between raging, body ripping contractions.

I now know my intuition was right.

It wouldn't have made any difference even if we hadn't got stuck in the snow in the drive for the first few minutes. It wouldn't have made any difference even if Charles had driven faster as per my offensive yelling from the back, he didn't because he'd already passed several cars in the dyke.

It *would* have made a difference if I'd listened to my intuition and had a home birth because the baby would have been delivered properly in the safety and warmth of our own home instead of on the back seat, half way to the hospital, with a flurry of obscenities from me, near tears from Charles and the car slewing across the road as we negotiated the bends, mostly sidewards.

When the baby's head came there was a terrible silence. Was the cord round her neck? I knew this baby needed to be born – at least that was one bit of intuition I listened to. So with the next contraction I pushed and screamed like hell, the baby shot out onto the seat with a wonderful reassuring wail, and I pulled it up inside my clothing until we got to the hospital, Charles still valiantly driving despite the drama coming from the back.

I still remember sobbing when she was taken off me to intensive care suffering only from hypothermia. I still remember standing outside the hospital in the snow with no shoes on. And I don't think Charles will ever forget the terrifying decision whether to stop or to keep driving. Or cleaning the car seat. The next day we all came triumphantly home.

I regret Charley was born in such unwelcoming unpleasant circumstances. I listen to my intuition more now.

I know I would have regretted not paying attention to my intuition telling me that school was not doing right by our kids. I'm glad I listened. And despite the difficulty of nipping out to buy presents Charles felt nothing but gratitude for having our happy children back again.

*

Charley's birthday was wonderful. Even more so because it was on a weekday and would have worked out to be the first she would have had to spend at school. We had the fire on. We relaxed the education for the day. And the rules about sweets, cake and chocolate which is just as well because I needed some.

We had friends and relatives celebrating with us too. And our new home school friend who lives locally. It was lovely.

It was the first time that some of our relatives who live further away had seen the children since they came out of school. I actually think by the way they peered at them with extra interest and by their remarks that they expected the kids to have grown two heads in the meantime. As if they expected them to be no longer normal. There was a sense of examination about the way the aunts and uncles talked to the girls and sneakily looked for pointed ears. Or perhaps that was just me.

My hackles did rise a bit when all Charley's presents seemed to be things educational like pens and pencils and stationery and exercise books and 'how to' text books as if the kid wasn't allowed to play any more. But before I spoiled it all by sulking I gave myself a good talking to about not being over sensitive and remembered that relatives who don't get to see the kids often nearly always end up buying something 'useful'. It wasn't just because we were Home Educating now. Charley, sweet child, received all the presents gratefully, happy to have something to open. Besides, best friends and grandma compensated by giving more exciting offerings.

Charley didn't actually join in the proceedings much. She was too busy following the instructions for the huge Lego model that we'd given her at her request. She was totally absorbed, concentrated fiercely and managing quite expertly to keep her dad's meddling fingers off it. I watched her sneakily whilst laying out the table and pretending to listen to the conversation of the adults. She was completely focussed, interpreting the diagrams, searching for pieces, working out how to put them together. Even chocolate didn't disturb her concentration. And her class teacher had told me she had attention deficit. I think the deficit was with the teaching.

An emotional day. Another milestone passed. We're parents of a nine and six year old now.

Once Charley's birthday was over I could start thinking seriously of Christmas. I was looking forward to all the Christmassy things we were going to do and make. We had a party planned with the Home Ed Group. Charles and I planned to shop in relays. Mum was booked so we could do a bit together.

They had a party coming up at the dance and drama school they belong to as well as the home school party, and my Best Friend's having one too, to mark the new millennium. So the calendar was full along with the usual home school meetings and activities.

Perhaps it was no wonder I had migraine.

When I woke someone was hitting me on the head with a hammer. Or was it a tourniquet round my forehead getting tighter and tighter?

Fearing the usual sight deficit, brain deficit and constant vomiting which accompanies my migraines I called mum, knowing it would be hard to cope with the girls here all day and not too pleasant for them either. Charles had a full shift and would be out all day.

Mum came like an angel and the girls drove off happily with her without a backward glance. She'd promised to make something special with them. Trying not to chuck up at the thought I got gratefully back into bed.

I woke a few hours later feeling a new woman. Hammer thumping gone, sight back to normal, nausea subsided. Thank you Migraleve! House unbelievably quiet. Thank you mum!

Perhaps I just needed a break. I lay a moment revelling in it wondering how long it had been since I could do so. Guilt soon got the better of me and I got up, swayed a bit, and rang mum.

Chelsea answered. "Hi mum, are you better?"

"Yes, thanks, darling, can you put grandma on?"

Charley came on the phone. Her mouth was full. "Hello mummy," she drooled down the phone.

"Hello, darling. You okay? Having a nice time?"

"I made you some mint creams." More sucking noises. Then I heard mum in the background whispering 'you weren't supposed to tell her that'. Rustling noises then mum's voice.

"Hello. How are you feeling?"

"So much better now, thanks. Are you surviving?" I asked.

"Course. We've had a lovely time." I heard a dish crash to the floor in the background and Chelsea say 'you idiot, Charley – good job it didn't break' and Charley's indignant voice 'it wasn't my fault'.

"Sounds like I'd better come and get them. I'll pop down in a few minutes."

"No, there's no need to rush, honestly, it's fine. We're clearing up. Then they can have a bit of telly and lunch, Chelsea's told me there's a history programme you usually watch. So you have a rest and make sure you're better. The girls are fine."

I was torn. A bit of space in an empty house sounded so appealing.

"You know what mum, a quiet house, then a walk on my own to get some fresh air would be absolutely wonderful. Would you mind? Can you cope?"

"Course, silly, take as long as you want. Tell you what, I'll feed them and bring them back later as I have to go up to the shop. What about that?"

It was so tempting, I gave in.

"Thanks, mum. That would be so good."

"Okay. You go rest. I'll see you later."

"See you later." I replaced the phone and lay back a moment. It was bliss. Soon I felt completely refreshed and got my things on to go out and walk.

It was strange walking without them, without their inquiring minds questioning everything, without stopping every second to examine some find, even if it was a just an acorn or a badger toilet. I almost felt odd without it. Almost. It was great to have some thinking time back. That's what I missed the most.

Low sunshine filtered through a gauze of cloud and diffused the glare into a pearly opalescence. The land was tranquil and quiet and the soft wind blew away the last remnants of headache. There was a jewel like shine on the rosehips and brilliant orange hawthorn leaves. The fields stretched away in decorative lines and furrows of cultivated soil. And the sprouts stood in rows of rosettes, tall and becoming, soon to be harvested for Christmas.

The sight of it just what I needed. The peace of it just what I needed. Must pay attention to my own needs as well as the girls' needs if I'm going to be able to Home Educate effectively.

I love being with the girls. I love our Home Education. Love working with them, showing them things, guiding their growing, expanding their world. Love having their spirits freed from school. But in order to continue to do that well I need to think about my own soul too.

As I walked back to the cottage I saw mum's truck come slowly along the distant lane and we arrived back together. Happy people got out of the car. And I was presented with a sticky box of mint creams with thumb prints in and sugary children.

*

"You've got glitter glue on your jumper," said Charles when he got home.

"There's glitter glue on everything," I said.

Was there a ledge in the house without glitter on it? Was there a surface in the place without drying decorations or cards standing up in proud display ready to be sent out? Was there a pair of scissors to be found that hadn't been lost under a pile of coloured paper or sequins or card? And was there any food colouring left after our attempts to make Christmas shortbread which the girls decided would be more appealing if it was multi coloured? No, not one spare space, no food colouring, and no normal creamy shortbread either. Just a heap of odd rainbow coloured shapes.

Charles even found a shiny speck of it on his plate at dinner. "My dinner's sparkling."

"Not everyone's food glitters like ours," I said wiping it off.

"Look at this daddy." Charley held up her latest glittery creation and a cascade of it fell into her dinner. She blew it off and it sprinkled all over Chelsea's dinner. We all thought it was funny but Chelsea wasn't impressed.

"Here, have mine instead," I said halting the tears, and swapped with her. I crunched nobly through the rest of it wondering if I'd have glittery poo.

Even the cat glittered. It looked fantastic on his black fur. I fancied a bit in my hair for the party. When I kissed Charles the speck of it on his cheek was transferred to mine and made the girls laugh.

"You're too old to wear glitter make up mum," said Chelsea. Thanks a lot. Nice to have such valuable advice.

*

The end of the year approached and I felt the need to record on a daily basis what the kids had been doing, ever mindful of the need for some proof of our educational activities to the LA when the time comes. But it was such a boring, time consuming chore it took away the magic that is Home Education.

However, I persevered. I listed what maths we did, what English we did, what science activities and concepts we'd covered, our creative and physical activities, our social events. It looked to be a huge amount. It looked exhausting it was so huge.

But what it didn't show was all the other stuff that we'd done that had taught the kids far more than anything on the record. I may have listed 'worked with money concepts'. But what wasn't listed was the hours of valuable activity they had playing shop. This involved paying and giving change, adding and subtraction, concepts of weight and measurement, reading and writing, talking about percentages, looking at sources and countries of origin on a map, an afternoon making things to sell in the shop and talking about budget, savings and banking. We even talked about health and safety thanks to the input from their dad who is a health and safety officer at work. And finally we made up a story about our shop.

It made all my record keeping look a bit pale and pathetic unless I was going to write all that down as well. Like the teachers, I could spend more time on admin than helping the kids.

I was going to have to rethink in the new year.

*

The girls were so excited in the back of the car on the way to their first Home Ed Christmas party the books were abandoned.

"Are we there yet?"

"Not far now." I was quite excited too. We were meeting at a garden centre where there was a Santa's Grotto, a place for them to have lunch together and a feast of decorations.

The children all sat together round one table and the parents sat at another one. The children behaved impeccably raising many smiles from the groups of old folks also on their Christmas outings. The parents got dirty looks and disdainful glares because of all the giggling they were doing.

I think I enjoyed the walk through the magical wonderland they'd created even more than the kids because I could more readily accept that the reindeer were stuffed and the kids were a bit superior about it. But at least the older children kept the Santa secret alive for the younger ones, unlike at school where Chelsea had her dreams shattered very quickly. Then at the very end there were real reindeer all soft and sad eyed and reeking of animals, a smell that always brings nostalgia having kept a horse for years.

The best bit was the camaraderie and friendship that circled the group in a mutual feeling of care and support. We'd found our community.

We swapped the still sticky, glitter shedding cards with our other home schooled friends and left with a trail of crafty bits dropping in our wake.

The girls sat contentedly all the way home clutching their present and a little Christmas tree sapling ready to plant. The minute we got home we had to go out in the dark and find pots and soil and get them planted. I sniff them occasionally as they take me back to childhood and the smell of pine. Our plastic tree just doesn't smell the same.

I was thinking that the party would mark the end of our first Home Educating 'term'. Time to relax, stop pushing education at the kids every day, and just coast till Christmas.

Actually, I doubt life will be different as education is just so much part of it now.

*

I so rarely got a moment to myself that when I did I revelled in it. Whilst the girls were out for an afternoon walk with Charles in the remaining frost and I sat down to write about not education but the essence of Christmas.

It curled round the cottage as evocative as the smell of wood smoke and cinnamon. The real fire burned with orange flicks and exuded a comforting warmth far exceeding anything a radiator can do. The tinsel on the Christmas trees, (one big plastic one, two tiny real ones), moved occasionally in the inevitable draughts in this old cottage and sparkled magically. The presents underneath were stacked ready.

The oven thermostat ticked as the stew cooked ready for their return. The cupboard was stocked with homemade cake (grandma's) and mince pies (me and the children) and multi coloured shortbread with finger prints in (just the children). The cat sprawled in relaxed warmth on the vacant hearth rug usually taken by restless children. The fire murmured gently, all was peace...

"Is it ready yet?" My reverie was interrupted by the door bursting open with a flurry of cold air and giggles and rosy cheeks and sniffing.

"Not yet," I said closing my notebook.

"Boots off, girls," said Charles keeping his on.

They put their soaking gloves on the hearth, kicked wellies into the kitchen corner as a gesture of putting away, dropped coats on chairs, outmanoeuvred the cat for the best spot in front of the fire.

Peace shattered, but actually it was their happy childish voices which completed the Christmas atmosphere.

*

On Christmas Eve we put on our layers, filled a bag with goodies and went and sang a carol outside mum's cottage door.

"Oh, it's you! I thought it was the cats fighting," she said winking at the girls. She glowed with happiness at seeing us and as brightly as her roaring fire. We jostled for prime position in front of it while mum got her coat on ready to come to ours.

Christmas Day was a jumble of torn wrapping, turkey smell and too much chocolate. The pristine piles of presents were rent and became real objects to be ooohed and aaaahed over. The fire burned brighter than the telly and mum's cheeks even though she was burnished by the sherry. We watched films, figured out how various constructions fitted together and sat on settees nursing groaning tummies. Treasured presents were clasped tired to bed.

Boxing Day brought a sprinkle of snow. There's times when you think it couldn't be more perfect.

New year, new millennium, new term; no school. I almost felt guilty with the joy it brought.

Like naughty children playing truant we celebrated by going out to the pool to work off our Christmas over eating. Charles was able to come too and splashed and played with the girls far better than I do just trawling up and down the lengths. The place was empty. I couldn't help but think of the other children going back to their school routines and their school uniforms and their packed lunches. I appreciate many of them love it. I feel for those who don't.

*

"I think we'd better get back down to some work," I said to the girls. It was the second week in January. I expected moans and groans as that's what used to greet me when they started back at school.

The girls just got out their boxes where they keep all their books, projects, materials and other home school stuff and started rummaging through them as if it was the most natural thing in the world for them to be doing. They were immediately absorbed. It was like I was hardly needed. So I made another plan.

What I want to do is try and help them understand the reason for education, the reason for being educated, for doing all this stuff we do, why they would need mathematical skills, why language and communication skills, how science affects our lives daily and why geographical and historical aspects of our lives are useful to us. How creative thinking helps our world progress. What skills we need to do in order to progress in our understanding of all that. And how with this understanding they will be able to see a purpose to what we do, why education matters.

"Yes mum," they both said resignedly after I was explaining all this. "Can we do our experiment now?"

Obviously I need to shut up and let them get on with it.

*

We'd just got launched into our new 'term' (will I ever get away from that concept – but what else to I call it?) and we got an invitation to another party from a home schooler we hadn't met yet. We added it to the schedule.

We were also back to the question 'not in school today?' every time we went out. I'm becoming a little more used to it but it can still sound like a personal criticism. Sometimes I give an explanation, sometimes when I don't feel so brave I just say 'no' and hope the bluntness will prevent further inquiry. I should have asked for a thicker skin for Christmas.

Inevitably, saying we're Home Educators generally provokes a second question; 'are you a teacher then?' and throws me into another dilemma.

The thing is, if I say I was, then that seems to make it all right, seems to qualify me in people's eyes to be doing this. But it doesn't. It just means that I'm having to de-school myself of classroom practices as well as the children, in order to stop schooling and start really educating. I have to prevent myself from lapsing back into horrible teacherish phrases it's necessary to use in a classroom situation like 'will you stop talking' or 'sit down and do your learning' or 'we're doing this now and we'll do that after'. Because I'm fast learning that none of this works with Home Education. I'm fast learning that actually, the more we talk about a subject the more is learnt. That the children get as much learnt standing up as they do sitting down, as well as walking, in the car, lying on the living room floor, or in the bath. And it's not necessary to stop the kids learning about something they're interested in and motivated to do at the time just because it's not on our timetable till later in the day.

I'm fast learning that I need to rethink the timetable, scrap the school habits, stop being so bloody inflexible and see all the fantastic learning opportunities that are happening right under my nose. Basically get that wretched teacher's hat off.

What the kids need is a caring, interested, encouraging and inspirational adult. No teaching required.

Wish I'd never been a teacher. I'm a mum more than I'm a teacher. I'm more a human being than a teacher. I'm a human being guiding other human beings on their path to becoming more human. Don't need teacher skills to do that.

*

Winter always makes old people older. My roly-poly angel hardly ever looked frail but there was a frailty about her I noticed when I collected the girls having slithered the car down the lane over ice.

"I don't really feel like walking out in this," she said. The wind howled and was penetrating cold. We stood by her fire both girls holding enormous paintings with strange substances on them.

"Well, maybe you shouldn't be, mum, it's treacherous at the moment," I said, stoking the fire.

"Mustn't give up," she said, sinking into her chair whilst the girls sat down again, one on each arm of her chair. She was buried by children and decorated in paint. "It's a bugger this getting old." She grinned up at the girls who were giggling behind their hands at the swear word.

"You're not giving up, you're just being wise. It's a struggle even for us in the cold, isn't it girls?" I checked she had wood and coal handy.

"Yes, I fall down all the time," said Charley.

"That's because you're skating on the ice all the time," said Chelsea laughing.

"Wish I was as young as you," she said putting an arm round each of them. She pulled them off the chair arms and onto her and they dropped their pictures and started wriggling about with glee.

"Except I'd have to do maths again and that would be awful," she laughed, her glasses steaming up as they sat with all their cheeks pressed together.

"You shouldn't be saying that, maths is okay isn't it girls?" I grinned over at them. The girls nodded. Charley took mum's glasses off and wiped them on her painty jumper.

"You'll soon feel more like going out when the weather gives a bit. Spring's not far away and it's supposed to be milder later this week," I said.

"Yes, then we can go on more picnics," said Chelsea tuning into mum's need to be cheered. Charley perched the glasses back on mum's nose and cuddled her tight steaming them up again.

"What we need's a bit of chocolate," mum said mischievously; chocolate her answer to all crises.

"I'll get it," said Charley suddenly helpful. She wriggled free and went into the pantry followed by a hopeful dog. She knew exactly where it was kept. We all sucked on it silently, glad of the excuse for a bit of sweetness on a dull day.

"You've got paint on your glasses," said Charley. Chelsea wiped them with a tissue, after she'd spat on it. They learn a lot from their gran.

We left mum by the fire looking more robust again. It was as if she needed permission to stay in and take it easy a bit. God if you can't take it easy in your eighties when can you?

When the girls had gone to bed I mentioned it to Charles.

"I'm not sure whether she should have the girls really, whether she can cope with it. She seemed so frail and tired when I collected them today," I said.

Charles sipped his beer, thinking.

"I feel a bit bad putting it on her," I went on.

"You're not putting it on her, she offered," Charles reminded me.

"I know but she just seems a bit delicate at the moment."

Charles put his drink down and looked at me.

"Are you sure it's not just you feeling guilty?" he asked.

"No – well – perhaps a little."

"The thing is, she loves having the girls, they brighten her up and you know she wants to help us out."

"Yea, but do you actually think it's right? I wonder sometimes."

Charles licked a drip off the side of the glass and stared into the fire. "Well it would be a shame to take it away from her, I reckon. Insulting almost, if she's enjoying it. It probably makes her feel needed and useful too. Maybe the mornings would be better, when she's fresher. And maybe you should talk to her about it," he said sensibly.

"Mmmm, and perhaps I should talk to the girls and suggest they do more to help when they're there like clearing up. Take the dog out, bring in the coal, stuff like that," I said.

"Yes, and Chelsea is old enough to phone us now anyway, if there's a problem. You should stop worrying. It's just the winter getting her down, that's all I'm sure. She's like this every January – it gets on us all. Look why don't you take her out for one of your special outings tomorrow while I'm off? That always boosts her up."

"Yea, maybe I will."

Charles doesn't often say much. But annoyingly he sometimes has better ideas than me.

*

Mum and I lunched at her favourite garden centre and I brought up the subject of the girls.

"I feel very guilty putting on you, mum, are you sure it's not too much having the girls once a week?" I asked. She immediately stopped staring at the lady in the woolly hat she'd just discussed, loudly, and looked back at me.

"Course not. Whatever gave you that idea?" she said looking far more robust than I felt and about as strong as an iron girder.

"I was worried they might be wearing you out."

Her eyes were twinkling again as she started on the cheesecake dessert. I'd already wolfed mine down, pig that I am.

"I think it's more the other way round, they're always asking for a break and a biscuit," she said, spitting a cheesecake crumb onto the table. She dabbed it with her serviette.

I laughed. "I think it's probably more about the biscuit than the break, knowing the girls."

Mum smiled and looked across to another table. "You see that lady over there? Now she's worn out."

Mum pointed with her fork to some crumpled old dear, whose skin was the colour of the cream tablecloth and who looked about ready to give up on life any minute. Unfortunately her hearing was obviously as good as ever as she turned and stared at mum. Mum carried on eating her cheesecake and I tried not to catch her eye.

"Well, if ever you're not up to them coming you will tell me won't you?"

"Yes, now stop fussing. Shall we have tea or coffee?"

We drove the lovely lanes homeward as the light dropped to pink. It seemed as if her bright disposition had returned and I had been concerned for nothing. I went in with her, made up the fire, tidied a bit whilst she fed her cats.

"Now, you will bring them next time, won't you darling, you need your rest," she said. There's irony.

"Okay, but how about we change to mornings, if that's suits you?"

She's got more energy in the mornings and it would mean she'd get her afternoon sit by the fire.

"Yes, mornings would be better. Now that spring's on its way I have lots to do in the garden in the afternoons," she said. "And I must get the vegetable patch dug over."

So much for the rest in the afternoons. Looking at her she appeared to have more energy than me. I went home and collapsed like an old lady myself.

*

The play centre where the party was held was a hubbub of energy and happiness. The noise reverberated round the apparatus and we could hardly hear ourselves speak. And as we were inducted into another new group of Home Educators, my concerns over it being so rural and quiet where we live and the girls never getting to see anyone were laid to rest.

I met the coordinator of a big group that meets in one of our nearest cities and does activities on a weekly basis. It sounded fantastic. Very well organised with a termly diary of activities, some science, some creative, some social like the party.

The best thing of all; those heretical educational ideas that I'd harboured for so long which would have had me burned at the professional stake should they be aired, had suddenly found a place in a community that welcomes and applauds them. All these years of weird thinking and I feel like I've just found home.

The girls were involved with so many evening activities Charles and I spent nearly every night on the road. But it helped to appease our worries about being accused of isolating the kids and never giving them the chance to mix since being out of school.

Anyway, they loved it, most particularly Chelsea whose life was ruled by dance and drama. What I couldn't figure out was how I got to be mother to a child who's so into performing, when the thought of me having to perform is enough to give me a panic attack. Charley did pottery instead. Next they added horse riding on a Saturday and infiltrated another network.

Whilst I waited for them I sniffed all things horsey and took myself back to the days when riding was part of my life before children came along. I thought about having a go myself. But the sight of the docile old ponies trudging along didn't appeal having been spoilt by having my own horse for years and enjoying the excitement of being tossed about on his manic back like an adrenalin junky on a fairground ride. Terrified though it made me at times, this looked a bit placid in comparison. Anyway, there was always the budget to consider. I had to be content to sit on a soggy hay bale and wait.

"Good ride?" I asked when the horsy smelling girls plopped gratefully down onto the back seat of the car peeling off hairy gloves and scratching sweaty scalps.

"Storm tried to gallop off with me," said Chelsea.

I imagine he's not called Storm for nothing.

"My pony kept putting his head down to eat the grass," said Charley. Such is the way of riding school ponies.

The girls were quiet on the way home, filled up with that peace horses give you. I thought about riding again. Or just doing something else especially for me – like meditation perhaps – help keep me sane. How could I manage to free an evening?

*

I thought I was the only one in the family affected by the winter darkness and Seasonally Affected Disorder but I reckon the girls can be just as bad.

We were all getting on at each other.

I was trying to get Chelsea to clear up her morning's activities where the entire table is strewn with books, felt tips, snipped off bits, odd fibres stuck to the table top, paper and scissors and glue. She was getting on at her sister who was trying to get the papers, scissors and glue off her and cutting shapes right out of the middle of large pieces of fabric instead of being economical as I'd instructed. And Charley was getting on at the cat who refused to 'wear' her creation and was trying to free herself from Charley's grasp.

I knew I had to do something drastic to break the cycle of aggravation – mine included – before I got to the point of snipping off body parts.

"Come on, let's go out for a walk."

This produced massive groans, massive, massive groans. Actually, it looked about as appealing outside as immersing yourself in dirty cold grey washing up water would be. But I knew we needed it and I wasn't about to give up. I fell back on bribery.

"Come on, let's get our gear on. And when we get back we'll have hot chocolate."

The groans diminished a little. I pressed on valiantly, pretending I was really looking forward to it and it was worth the hot chocolate, bundled Charley into coat, hat, scarf, wellies – and teddy – whilst Chelsea got herself ready and I got them out the door before there was any more resistance.

The cold slapped us the minute we stepped out. The damp stuck in our throats and chilled any tiny bit of skin still showing. And it was so grey and manky we could hardly see down the lane.

"Come on, let's head for the trees," I said, trying to cheer everybody on, me included. We could barely make out the trees but I was determined to break the doldrums that winter dumps upon us and set off running which instantly turned into a race and everyone giggling.

"Look, there's a kestrel," said Chelsea dropping back to a walk and pointing to the small bird of prey hovering almost motionless over the fields. Suddenly it dropped fast.

"Wow. Did you see that? Look it's carrying something in its claws."

The bird lifted its prey and swung away until we could no longer see it in the gloom.

It was sheltered and quiet in the trees and we made curly patterns with our breath. We admired the bright running green of the wet tree trunks. We discovered last year's nests and examined the badger trail. We walked out of the trees over the soft settled fields where flocks of curved billed birds lifted up with their wonderful calling.

"Are they curlew, mum?" asked Charley.

"Yes, darling."

"And there's a pheasant," she added.

"Look, mum, quick. A fox," whispered Chelsea suddenly.

We watched the misty shape head for cover.

And that was when I realised the old magic had happened. It worked every time.

We'd all brightened up. Smiles had replaced grumpy faces. Chatter replaced complaining. Singing had replaced bitching. We raced the final few yards to the sea bank to be the first to look over.

And as if our spirits were on a thousand wings a huge flock of wild geese rose up from the shoreline calling excitedly as if they too were thrilled to be free. The girls turned to me in excitement to see such a spectacle, their faces happy and alive. I felt just the same.

We wandered back hand in hand completely transformed, warmed up, chatting about the things we'd seen, about a trip to London, about our new Home Educated friends. When we got back the coats, scarves, hats and wellies, and in the case of Charley muddy wet trousers, were discarded inside the door and we made the hot chocolate. Chelsea stretched out on the settee to read. Charley started creating a new scenario with the Lego. The day was mended and so was the mood.

I can't help thinking of all the school kids trapped in classrooms all day and in front of screens all evening at this time of the year. Then they're taken off to the Doctors for pills to control their hyperactivity and the parents for something for their depression. It seems so ridiculous when there is such a simple antidote.

It was definitely worth it, hot chocolate or not.

*

Mum responded to the TLC and bounced up like the sap that's rising in all the stems. I felt quite ashamed that I didn't spot it sooner and make more effort for her.

The girls helped her tidy the garden, collect up the old stems and search for bulbs coming up after I'd talked to them about giving her some TLC and what it was. She said they're making her lots of cups of tea now when they go, which is lovely but it makes her go for a wee a lot. That made her giggle. I noticed she crosses her legs when she giggles these days.

Whilst they were there I got on with my reading and writing and making notes about their education. Maybe I'd do a book about it one day.

The more I wrote and researched the more I realised we needed a broader objective for education than was catered for in the system.

Yet many parents I talked to didn't seem to have any objectives at all for their children. Like they'd abdicated all responsibility – or interest in some cases.

"What's your objective in your choice of school?" I asked one mum who trails her kid miles each day out of her catchment area to a private school. I might as well have been asking about dead sheep.

"Oh, I haven't really thought about that, I guess," she told me.

I asked one of the Home Educating mums the same question.

"What's your objective in Home Educating your children?" She'd definitely thought about it.

"Well, I think the thing I want to develop in them most of all is confidence. I feel that with that they can do anything. They'll come to understand that they need skills to do things, maybe exams and stuff, and confidence will give them the courage to go for whatever they need to."

Sounded like amazing common sense to me.

I settled on my objectives;

- Development of their individual and personal self, their bodies, their minds, their skills and knowledge, their personalities and interests.
- Development of their intelligence and skills – in all forms not just the academic – through exploration, interaction, practise, experimentation and experiences as broad as possible.
- To gain experience and understanding of the world and their relation to it.

That seems quite mind blowing. How could you fit that into a syllabus or timetable?

*

My best friend and I were sitting drinking posh coffee in our favourite cafe. Just occasionally, far too occasionally, we escape. We leave the children, we leave the mud and the challenges that rural living brings, we leave all responsibilities like behaving like an adult because children are looking and we're trying to set an example, and escape to the city to remember what it used to be like when our lives were our own. It's not that we don't love our children, love being mums, love all that it entails. This just substituted as Annual Leave from it. Inevitably it was the children we talked about. Both our eldest were born on the same date exactly one month apart.

And inevitable we talked about education. But it wasn't Home Education that got chewed over, it was her concern for her child in school and the fact that he is falling by the wayside because of his dyslexia and no one seems bothered. Since he was a really quiet well behaved kid she wasn't even sure they'd noticed, busy as they are with the disruptive ones.

"It's like it's only the bright or the bad ones who get the attention. You'd think it would be the struggling ones who got the help," she said.

"But he is bright," I said.

"Not disruptive bright, though, so he doesn't get noticed."

"Is there anyone who's aware of his dyslexia?" I asked.

"They virtually laughed at me when I mentioned it. It's obviously a school which doesn't 'believe' in dyslexia," she said holding up her inverted commas.

"What about the SEN teacher?"

"He's a total waste of space. Honestly, they have no idea, these people. Took me ages to even get to see him, but he's just complacent. It's like they've just written my son off."

I sympathised. I'd already seen that happen to many kids in a class.

"You know, you've been telling me all these years that teachers are not infallible," she went on, "but I never actually got what you were on about. I just believed that they were professionals and that they know best. But in this case I honestly don't think they do. They can't see what's happening right in front of their noses." She spooned the froth off the coffee. I was half way down mine already. I put it down.

"It's probably not that they can't see it, it's just that they have so many targets to fulfil that they don't have time to see it, or have to make other priorities," I said, trying to sympathise.

We both sipped. The question of Home Education was hanging between us. I'd been so anxious for my parent friends not to feel any pressure or judgement coming from me. We all make the choices we need to. I hoped she knew that. We'd always supported each other in everything we did.

"I wish I could do what you do," she said.

I put my cup down again and looked at her.

"You could. It's not as difficult..."

She cut me off. "I couldn't. I just couldn't. I wouldn't know where to start and what with everything else..."

"What makes you think I know where to start," I laughed.

"Well, at least you've been in a classroom."

"Home Education is so completely different to that. It doesn't really help knowing how schools teach because I was falling back into teacherish ways and that doesn't work with Home Education. Home Education, well the whole of education really if you think about it properly, is much broader than that, I'm beginning to see."

We were quiet again. Then she said, "I'm just not brave enough." We looked at each other over our Latte glasses.

A thought struck me. "Perhaps I wasn't brave enough to leave mine in school," I said.

The choices we make as parents are endlessly challenging. And we thought babies were hard work.

*

The weather lifted and lightened and we got some brilliant spring like days with the sun shining through one or other of the windows all day as it moved round. We watched it throughout the days and did some great stuff on the earth and the sun and night and day and the seasons. Living in such close contact with it made it all the more real for the girls. Their appetite to know almost matched their appetite for chocolate biscuits.

Despite that I got a panic on the other day and thought we should be adhering to all those nicely laid out exercises in the workbooks like they do in schools. Then I looked through them and the term bullshit immediately sprang to mind.

As far as I could see it, children in schools were shut away from real life where science is all around them in the way they live their lives, look after their bodies, feed themselves, use materials and tools, notice the natural world etc. Then they are 'taught' about these things through dull academic practises often in workbooks as far removed from the real experiences as I am from space travel, which switches them off and makes them 'fail' at science. And all the time in the outside world science is so marvellous and fun and exciting to investigate you can't help but absorb it.

Seems arse about face to me.

12

It was almost to the end of February before I noticed the swimming pool was full of kids dive bombing and it was half term again. Time flies when you're enjoying yourself and the girls seemed to be enjoying themselves so much we couldn't keep track of what the days were, except for the evening activities of course.

Chelsea's giggling was back, loud and strong. When I was waiting for her outside the drama club I could hear her laughter over everybody else's.

Charley grabbed her in a cuddle when she appeared. "We could hear you giggling from out here," she said.

"You couldn't!" That set her off again.

"We could, but don't let it stop you," I said.

Half term gave us a break from the evening drives too. Charles and I could slob out like normal people for a change.

"You look really tired tonight," he said.

"Yea, I guess am." I looked at him. "Actually, you do as well."

"Yea, I am too. It's never ending isn't it?" Charley handed him a piece of Lego to fix.

"Do you think it's the Home Educating, or just the parenting?" he said handing it back to her all fixed.

"A bit of both probably."

"I think it's because whenever I get home they're always here. We never get the place to ourselves," he said.

I thought about that a moment. I couldn't believe he just said that.

"But, Charles, they always used to be here when you got home from work because they'd got home from school. It's no different."

"Oh yea!" He grinned and looked a lot less tired once he'd thought that through.

"And what about me? I have them at home all the time. They are with me one hundred percent. Well, almost."

"Yea, I know."

"But why have kids if you don't want to be with them?"

"Yea. I know."

"And I wouldn't want it any other way really."

"Me neither!"

*

I started my meditation club. I thought it might take some of the tiredness away to focus on something else. It took me nearly a month to pluck up courage and join.

I sat among a ring of po-faced people all looking terribly serious and felt terribly frivolous all of a sudden. We were led on a simple meditation to try and focus and visualise the air coming in and out of our nose as we concentrated on our breath. I don't think I've got it right because all I could think about was bogeys.

And the strain of fitting it into our evening schedules was too much. I decided to get the bike out more often with the weather getting better. And rely on my excursions out with my best friend and not talk about education. She was far more concerned than me. Our Home Educating days were going so well I was just worried I was not more worried.

The girls made wonderful crystals at the Home Educators group. It was a session about snow and ice (ironically it's all gone now). The last one we went to was all about the Chinese New Year when they made dragons and Chinese food. They made a huge long dragon and paraded it round the park outside the resources room. The dog walkers stopped and stared and smiled. The dogs raised their hackles and walked stiffly round it.

When the kids have finished their activities they all go outside to play and the parents get to air their Home Education concerns. It all works so brilliantly it's almost unbelievable. I keep waiting for the falling out and the arguing but it doesn't happen. Not even among the parents.

There's no disruption or messing about from the kids because they all want to be there and all do the activity through choice. And outside it continues. Everyone's ready to give support. Everyone looks after one another. Such a different social experience from the school playground. I feel more and more normal. Is this a good thing?

*

"What you up to?" I asked when I walked into mum's living room.

Chelsea was lying on the hearth rug with the dog and cats reading and Charley was on mum's knee when I went to collect them.

"We're telling stories," said mum.

"Yes, and you'll have to wait because we haven't finished making this one up yet," said Charley.

I sat down to listen.

"You can't listen," said Charley.

I got up and went into the kitchen. The table was heaped with dried flowers and seeds and grains from the cupboard. And there were two huge collages drying on the bench.

I started to clear it away, very quietly; I could secretly listen better then.

It was lovely to hear. They did a bit each.

I felt a bit peeved as I'd often suggested making up stories before. Obviously I got it all wrong because I'd had nothing but resistance and here she was reeling off a story like a professional novelist. She was so absorbed she hadn't noticed I'd stopped tidying to listen better. She'd practically taken over the telling of it all now.

So why couldn't she write a story at home?

What an idiot I am. It hit me like a clout round the ears as I watched them interacting; she couldn't do it at home because it involved writing it down. The laborious process of writing completely stunted her creativity. She has this incredible imagination, what a waste if it was only ever expressed through the written word.

In fact, I wonder how much of our children's educational experiences are actually destroyed by their association with print. Because not all kids can handle print – like my best friend's child. And because of that his education is becoming impaired.

I must make sure that the girls' education is not dependent on print even though print is part of it. Actually, when you think about it, with the growing technology our educational system's obsession with the printed word is as outdated as the mouldy yoghourt in the back of mum's fridge.

"Finished, mum." Charley climbed down off grandma and came to get her picture.

I swept the last of the debris off the table and floor. As she lifted her picture half of the bits fell off and littered it again.

"Don't worry about that," said mum coming through. "My lady's coming tomorrow, she'll give it a good clean."

The dog came through and licked up some of the dried peas.

"Charley's got an amazing imagination," said mum.

"I know."

"And have you seen Chelsea's picture?"

"I know it's fantastic."

Chelsea picked it up beaming and kissed mum goodbye.

"I want to be an artist like you," she said to mum.

"I want to be a story teller," said Charley.

"And I want a wee," giggled mum.

We left her to it.

*

"Oooo! What's that?" asked Charley rushing to get a fat letter that had just plopped through the letter box. It said BBC on it.

"It's a schedule for all the schools' programmes," I said. "I thought it would be useful to know what was on so we could catch the best educational programmes."

"Tellytubbies is educational," said Charley.

"That's too young for you," said Chelsea.

"But I like it."

"It's sort of educational, but there are even better ones than Tellytubbies," I said opening the packet.

I'd sent off for the schedule as there are so many valuable history, geography and science programmes on I wanted to make best use of them. But the snag is we could end up watching it all day. Could that be considered an education, I wonder? Not in as much as we need diversity, I suppose.

Home Education is a constant round of decision making. But then I remembered school mornings. They were a constant dilemma of decision making too, as to whether the girls were really ill or not, if they should go to school or not, what I was going to do about it, etc. Nightmare! Yep – with Home Education the decisions are much more positive.

"Look, that one's on now, shall we watch it?" asked Chelsea peering over my shoulder at the huge programme timetable. "It's history. I watched it last time."

We switched on and watched a group of Bronze Age people going about their daily lives in mud huts.

"Can we make a Round House with mud, mum?" asked Charley.

"We've got lots of wooden poles from the trees," said Chelsea.

"It would make a great den," said Charley.

"We could even sleep in it," said Chelsea. The enthusiasm was growing.

"Why not, we could give it a go," I said, glowing with the

motivation my children had to get involved with their history session. "And I think the Home Education group is visiting a site with round houses next time."

We talked about it for ages. Then Charley went and made a mini one in the garden. It was all mud and looked a bit like a mole hill, but I didn't say. I'm looking forward to getting going with the real one. That'll start the neighbours talking.

*

We planned more and more educational outings. Possibilities seeped into my consciousness like flood water. We could visit museums in term times and get to see all the exhibits without crowds. We could blatantly make use of relatives living in cities for visits and educational outings. We planned to dash up to York for the day to the Yorvick museum. I think I was more excited than the girls.

They started a scrap book of their travels – a travel book, we call it. We stuck in all the literature and flyers and postcards we brought back from excursions, sometimes a map or two and when they're really inspired a bit of writing too. The more we go out the more we seemed to learn, the more motivated they were. I loved it.

*

"Smell that!" I said to the girls as we walked round the burgeoning fields. We stopped and tilted our noses up.

"What is it?" asked Charley, sniffing.

"It's the sea," said Chelsea.

"It's not only the sea, it's the earth drying, it's the soil from that plough. It's the smell of spring," I said.

It was beautiful outside. Everything really seemed to be stirring after the coldness. Daffodils bobbed in the wind. The larks were singing. It was as if you could almost feel the sap rising.

The girls' sap was rising with the sunshine too. They didn't even bother going back in the house when we returned.

"Can I make a pond like grandmas, mum?" asked Chelsea.

"Sure, why not."

"Can I make a pond?" asked Charley.

"Well, perhaps one pond is enough and you could work on it together."

"I'll help you dig it," said Charley.

We talked about it and planned it out, chose a spot, marked it out, got the spades out and they started digging. I left them to it.

"What are they busy with?" asked Charles coming home early and finding the construction team busy in the garden, spreading soil over the lawn.

"They're making a pond," I said, putting the kettle on. "It's a great project for them."

"That'll keep them busy. How big is this pond?" he asked looking from the window.

"I think that'll depend on how much digging they want to do," I laughed.

I made us tea and we took it outside, sat peacefully and watched the girls hard at it.

"See," I said, feeling dreamy with the sun. "They're not around us all the time. They're usually too busy. If we just notice and make best use of the quiet moments."

"Mmmmmm," he said turning his face up to the spring sunshine and making use of a quiet moment. "And now it's summer coming they'll be outside more and more."

"Home Education's great isn't it," I said.

"Mmmmm," he said again. And we both sighed contentedly exactly at the same time.

13

The girls made more use of the television timetable than I did, looking for programmes they thought would be educational enough for me to let them watch. I could soon be outwitted. I hadn't noticed but there was a programme about menstruation, puberty and developing bodies on the television timetable. Chelsea noticed though, ever fascinated with the adult world.

"Can we watch it mum?"

"Sure," I said, thinking it would be a good way to broach the subject plus a moment for me to do a bit of note making. Charley busied herself with her toys only half watching. We chatted about it afterwards without squirming or giggling. It is biology after all. It was times like these I felt in control.

When the second programme was shown a week later, I didn't think it would matter them having it on again. Chelsea had looked forward to it. Charley was really more engaged with the toys strewn over the carpet in front of her. And I was only half paying attention again when I suddenly realised that the atmosphere in the room had changed.

I looked up from my notes to see both of them absolutely staring at a very articulate young lad talking about masturbation. Chelsea was riveted. Charley's frown of concentration creased her eyebrows. The toys lay forgotten. And the girls were transfixed by the sight of boys' body parts, not having had brothers and having very little experience of bare boys. The images of the erection were something even I was unprepared for.

The titles rolled. No one moved.

Then, coward that I am, I leapt up and switched it off and started talking hysterically about doing maths before they could ask me any questions. Charles can have the pleasure of that discussion, I thought.

I should pay a lot more attention in the future. I might even rip the timetable up.

*

I think I did overkill at the London museums. I wasn't going to waste any second of it.

We started planning our trip at home. We looked at the England map, where we were on it, where London was, the change in the physical make up of our country and why people ending up living where they do, why cities grow as they do. We've been reading a story lately on how London developed as a city and that tied in nicely. We planned the route, we planned our activities and we talked about London transport in relation to us having to go everywhere by car here. It's two miles to our nearest bus and that doesn't come very often.

Charles' shifts worked so he could came too and we stayed at my brother's house which kept costs down. The only drawback is the contrast in our children's educational pathways but we skirt round that diplomatically.

We went to the Natural History Museum on one day and gawped at all the dinosaurs and bones and stuffed things, most of them far bigger than the children. We recoiled at the insect gallery and travelled up through the earth gallery and shook ourselves about on the earth quake.

Next day we did the Science Museum where Chelsea drooled over the precious stones and Charley fondled the meteorite and I think we pressed every button and pulled every lever in the place. And we ended up in the Launch Pad where there are masses of scientific experiments for the children to get their hands on whilst I gratefully crashed out with the belongings on a bench leaving the girls to rush round and test everything.

The buzz in there was terrific. It was filled with children who are so keen to learn about the things presented to them there's not a still or quiet child in the place and it made me think if schools presented science to children in this way all kids would totally love science instead of being switched off to it as so many are. There would be no need for threats, there would be no truancy. There would be no need for pressure or conflict. No need for teaching even. Because all the kids here were learning because they wanted to learn and because they were finding out that it is actually a pleasure to learn.

I sat and sagged and watched. It was eye opening to see it. It was how learning should really be. Perhaps I'd throw out the science workbooks when I got home.

We virtually crawled out of there on our hands and knees everyone was so tired. It was only the promise of another tube trip that lured them away.

We drove back again that night. It took three hours and the others slept but I was buzzing from seeing the excitement in the girls about their visits. If only we could make all their Home Education like that.

In our dark and quiet kitchen there were flowers on the table and a lovely note from mum who'd been feeding the cat, a bag of cookies and milk in the fridge. Sometimes I think the best part of going away is the coming home again. Not counting the dead bird that the cat's left us on the doormat.

*

The girls were so buzzing from their trip and so inspired it took them all the next morning to do their travel books which was just as well as I was too whacked to do anything else with them.

But I reckon it doesn't matter. It's like they've been 'educated' for the last three days full on, non-stop, even when they weren't at the museums. So I backed off a bit and practised my out-of-bounds session whilst Chelsea sewed up bin liners into outfits inspired from the materials in the science museum and Charley created habitats inspired by the science museum for her little animal collections.

Learning never ends whatever form it takes.

*

I shut the curtains and Charles took his trousers off. We were just getting into bed and having a little chat at the end of the day. It's about the only time we get to confer on things we don't want the eager little ears to hear. And it's about the only thing we have the energy for at this time of night.

"You know you told me that they'd watched that sex education programme on boys and they might want to discuss it?" said Charles, dropping into bed.

"Yea. Why?" I climbed in beside him.

"Well, you were right. Charley did." Charles had that glint in his eye as if there was something funny coming.

I looked at him.

"What did she say about it?"

"It wasn't exactly what she said, it was what she asked."

"Go on, tell me." I snuggled up beside him, head on shoulder, our end of day cuddle.

"Well, I was just in the shower, stark bloody naked, when she burst into the bathroom as per usual and plonked herself down on the toilet. I stayed concealed behind the shower curtain and then she says 'Dad?' as if she's going to ask a question."

I could imagine it. There's no privacy in this house and with only one loo we have to be prepared to share if the children need it while we're in the bath or shower.

"So what happened then?" I raised my head and looked at him. The gleam was still there.

He grinned. "Well, I tried to ignore it and she sat there straining like she does so I sang a tune to try and cover up any plopping noises but she said again between straining, 'Dad?' much louder so I couldn't ignore it really." He giggled again. "So I said 'Yes, what is it?' and she had a few more grunts and then she asked 'Do you have wet dreams?'"

I laughed so bad if I hadn't already been lying down I would have fallen over with it. I put my hand over my mouth to try and keep it quiet.

"I felt utterly and totally exposed I can tell you, despite the shower curtain," he added when we'd got control again.

"Oh my god! I didn't catch that bit on the programme. Whatever did you say?"

"I didn't know what to say, did I. I just felt trapped into it. I had to think quick, so I just said, 'Not now I'm older.'"

We laughed so much my head wouldn't stay still on his chest. I rolled back over to find a tissue to wipe the tears.

"That was quick thinking, I'm glad she asked you, not me. I wouldn't have known what to say if they'd asked me," I said.

"Well, I didn't know what kind of answer to give, it was all I could think of."

We snuggled down again. Then he murmured, "This Home Education is all very well but I think this might be taking it a bit too far."

"I'll pay better attention to what they're watching in future."

"Yea, you shouldn't be so neglectful," he teased.

We fell into our tired comas with smiles on our faces.

Another whole term of Home Education flashed past and we had a legitimate excuse to eat chocolate; it was Easter. But where did that few months go? We had such a happy time Home Educating we didn't notice.

I tried to take a break from thinking about education all the time, took a back seat, slacked off and stopped motivating them to do stuff and what happened? Life was exactly the same.

They were still busy, we still met others, we still went places except we chose the more secluded places that the other hoards of school families were less likely to know about. And we avoided the precinct in town because it was full of young people who didn't seem to know what to do with their time once they were released from the daily toil of school, other than squirt Silly String at the shoppers and drink. They must have started out as bright inquisitive toddlers keen to find out about their world, what happened that switched that motivation off?

Actually I wish sometimes that something would switch my two off too.

They had wanted to dye things this afternoon so the sink was stained, there was wax on nearly everything, the meal was late and we were eating off a little space at the edge of the table as we hadn't had time to clear everything away after such a busy afternoon. Charley had also found a bit of a treasure whilst we were outside earlier which we were keen to dissect later.

"Do we have to eat our food with that bird poo on the table?" complained Chelsea.

"It's not bird poo, it's an owl pellet, and I like it," said Charley indignant about her treasure being called poo.

"Well it looks like poo to me and it's putting me off my dinner," said Chelsea.

I got up and moved it onto the side. But Charley kept her eye on it and gobbled down her dinner faster than if I'd bribed her with a million Smarties.

"Finished. Can I do it now?" She picked up the tweezers.

"No!" we all shouted, trying to eat our dinner without rushing.

"Doh! She's deliberately taking a long time," Charley gestured at her sister with the poised tweezers.

"I'm not," said Chelsea eating her dinner very politely and genteelly, unlike when she's in a hurry to get to her dance classes.

The minute we all finished Charley went into helpful mode – very rare – and whisked our plates away and placed the owl pellet back on the table as if it was pudding. We all gave in, we'd gone off pudding anyway after sight of the object that had been in our eye corner all dinner. Chelsea got up in a huff and stomped off and Charles started the washing up. So Charley and I started the dissection.

But the others soon returned. The owl pellet was so fascinating that we 'oooooed' and 'aaahed' so loud they came to see what the excitement was about. The life and eating habits of the owl were laid out on the table before us.

There were stones and shells, bones and fish scales, bits of shell fish and bits of beetle some of which we actually managed to reconstruct and it was so exciting we were soon all fighting over the tweezers. Chelsea was just as enthralled and she is usually beyond such disgusting aspects of science.

"Look, what's that off?" she asked, holding up a tiny pale triangle.

"Looks like a tiny jaw bone to me," I said.

"I bet it's a mouse's," said Charles drying his hands.

"And look, this looks like a tiny bit of backbone," said Charley. "And look, this is fur."

"Urgh!" said Chelsea. She thought it was her duty. But she didn't want to miss anything.

Pudding was the furthest thing from our minds as we grouped ourselves round the kitchen table totally absorbed.

The more absorbed we became the more I understood that term time or not doesn't seem to matter. All we had to do was to keep this fascination with learning alive whatever the time.

I reckoned that somehow the kids standing around in the town precinct had that fascination destroyed. They had their motivation to look at life and learn about it destroyed. They had their learning so packaged into restrictive subject boundaries and time boundaries, age boundaries and place boundaries, by testing and target getting, by boring academic lessons and by staff who had to care less about the kids and more about the outcomes they were supposed to be achieving. Yet the sad thing is that there are lessons to be learned all the time, everywhere you are, at any age and whatever your ability.

What a loss it would have been if I had said to the girls, 'No, you can't look at this now because it's not term time.' Or told them they were too young, or it wasn't on their timetable for today. How deflated they would have been and how dulled their enthusiasm.

Is that what's happened to all those other kids?

I might get a bit hacked off with endless Home Education sometimes. Or having to eat my dinner in sight of something that looked distinctly like bird poo and wash dishes in a multicoloured sink. But actually I wouldn't swap this excitement for the world.

"I'm going to find another one tomorrow," announced Charley.

I think I might go help her.

*

Spring opened up our home school world. Not only that I could get out on my bike for regular exercise as well as the girls.

When we were not meeting other home schoolers we took mum and went on picnics to Nature Reserves, or historic sites, or sites with rivers or bridges, or hills and valleys, farm parks or garden centres or open farms or market towns. Any destination provoked learning. With outdoor time the girls glowed. Chelsea hadn't had an infection of any sort since she came out of school. It was the longest period of time she'd been well since she turned five. She'd be ten this year. My goodness, double figures!

What I couldn't understand is why the nits still lingered. We'd brought it up with the Home Ed Group but everyone else is clear. We had to keep missing meetings when I found the girls itching again. It was very embarrassing. Despite the fact they say that nits only like clean hair it did make us feel unclean.

"You can pick them up in the swimming pool you know," one mum told me. And both the girls were in regular contact with other school children at their clubs and evening activities. At least Chelsea remained well and had no more impetigo.

"Chelsea hasn't been ill since she came out of school, has she?" asked mum. I was having an hour with her whilst Charles was with the girls at home. We sat in her greenhouse among the geraniums.

"I know, it's great isn't it. It's hard to believe really. But some of the other Home Ed parents have told me that it was the same for their children."

"Why do you think it is?" she asked picking dead leaves off the plant next to her.

"I guess she's just happier, less stressed. They say stress has can affect your immune system."

"And Charley's lost that awful serious frown too, I noticed. She's always giggling."

"She's always giggling with you, mum." I smiled at her. She beamed back.

"We have such fun," she said scratching her head. "I'm not sure about this new shampoo I'm using, it's irritating my scalp I think."

"What make is it?"

"It's a natural one from the health food shop actually. I bought it the other week." She threw the handful of dead leaves down into an empty plant pot.

"Perhaps your head's shocked at the lack of chemicals," I said.

We laughed. She itched away at her scalp with her fingers.

"You look like the girls do when they've got nits," I joked.

Instantly, we both stopped laughing and looked at each other, having the same horrible thought in unison. An image of the girls and mum all sitting together cheek by cheek, heads together over stories flashed into my mind. Then another image of all their nits over the years jumping off their heads onto hers.

"Oh my god," I said.

"You don't think..." she said.

"I hope not."

"Perhaps you'd better check, wouldn't that be funny," and she heaved herself up to go find a comb. She came back with the cat's comb and handed it to me. I looked at it.

"That's all I could find," she said, wiping it on her trousers.

"Here, lean over this," I said sitting her at the table and putting a white sheet of paper under her bowed head. I knew all the tricks. The nits show up on the paper as you fine comb the hair down over it.

The little buggers rained down from her shining, silky, nearly white locks as I combed it through. Big ones. Little ones. Moving ones. It was horrendous.

"Oh, my goodness! I'm infested," she shrieked before bursting into manic giggling.

"I've been wondering why the girls keep getting them since they stopped school. I thought it must be from the clubs and the pool. I'm always having to tell the other parents, it's so embarrassing. And it was you all along."

"I'm sorry darling," said mum, trying to be serious and failing as her smile wrinkles would not comply.

"No, I'm sorry mum. I bet the kids gave them to you from when they were at school and you've had them all this time." I hugged her but couldn't help keeping my head away. We had to laugh.

"Heavens, I feel worse than the dog having fleas. When the dog scratches, I scratch. I was beginning to think I had fleas too." She put her head back and laughed again. I hadn't known a crisis she couldn't find a laugh in.

"Look, I'll nip back and get the Tea-Tree oil and do your hair, okay?"

"Okay, love, let yourself out will you, see you in a tick," and she rushed off to the bathroom still giggling.

*

"What about this one?" called Chelsea.

We were choosing poles for the structure of our mud hut, or round house as it's more educationally known. I got the saw and cut off the tall willow, one of many that lined our garden.

"You'll soon have no trees left," called mum sitting at the garden bench with the tray and snacks overseeing the proceedings. Charles gave us the manpower and helped set the poles.

"They need thinning anyway," I called back. Making the structure was a bit heavy going for the girls so they drifted off. It was a beautiful day and they were as soft and content as the balmy breeze.

Chelsea combed mum's dog with our old nit comb which we no longer seemed to need. Charley was busy making huge quantities of mud for the walls on the dyke side despite me explaining that it will take a while before we get around to needing it. It was the only bit she was interested in really.

We just about got a full circle of poles chosen when we retired to join mum at the table and have a rest. Charley presented us with a tray of brown 'cakes' which Chelsea had decorated with spring flowers. Mum dutifully 'ate' them.

"Is it nearly done yet?" asked Charley looking over at the structure.

"Not yet. We have to weave the other sticks in between the poles next." I explained.

"Then can we put the mud on?" she asked.

"Yes."

We have however made the unanimous decision not to use cow dung in the mixture even though it would have made it more authentic. There are some decisions you have to make even if they fly in the face of education.

Well into the summer term I decided that 'home' education was completely the wrong title. 'Out-and-about' education better described it.

The term 'home' tended to give folks a false impression. It created an image of poor, sad, isolated wretches whose parents kept them trapped in the house all day when in reality the opposite was true. In fact we're out and about so much I thought I ought to timetable some time to be at home practising some of those academic skills we didn't seem to have done much of lately.

Then I decided that winter kept us trapped in enough to make up for it.

We piled our books and activities, lunch and snacks and drinks into the car and headed for the group meet. It was a Bring and Buy sale the children had organised for charity, in the park where the resources room is. I could hardly see over the boxes of stuff out of the rear mirror.

So many families turned up I'd not met most of them.

"You see, not everyone comes every time to every event," the organiser said whilst we unpacked boxes and fiddled about trying to make a variety of junk look appealing. "But when we do something like this everyone tends to come."

Dads were present too lending muscle and erecting trestle tables and generally trying to do what they thought was men's stuff among the women and children. Small boys copied their example even though some of the tables were bigger than them.

The children were busy sorting and organising, pricing and counting change. Some of the older ones gave out home made flyers and cajoled the passers by to attend the sale. The regulars to the park knew about the home school group anyway. None of them said 'why aren't these children in school'. In fact, they looked well impressed. I was too. The kids seemed to have it all in hand. Even counting the money afterwards. They got it wrong at first until they realised it was easier to keep to piles of ten in case they made a mistake and had to do it all again. The parents kept out of it and let them make their own mistakes and put it right. The children didn't want us to interfere – they were keen to learn for themselves. It dawned on me how we often interfere too much.

After the sale was over and we'd tidied everything away most families stayed on for the picnic and a chance to chat and for the kids to play. Everyone was included. No arms folded. No cliques. No one left out. Whatever sex, age, or origin. I suspected that neither the kids nor the parents integrated as easily when school was part of the equation. Put people in a different environment and their behaviour alters. I wondered if kids learnt to be disruptive from the school environment. I'm sure I would have been disruptive if I'd been brave enough, but then, I always was a coward.

We all trouped off the see 'The Tempest' in the afternoon, a production by the theatre company Shakespeare For Kids. It was brilliant. I admit to being a bit of a philistine when it comes to Shakespeare. But just like the kids, I was glued to it. Although my friend and I did say afterwards that it might have been something to do with the gorgeous leather clad young man who was in it.

As I drove home I reflected on the full day. Definitely 'out-and-about' education describes it best. All this education to be had without even putting a step inside school gates.

I filled Charles in on our day when I got back and the girls had gone to bed. Although I left out the leather clad bit. Didn't want him to feel inferior.

*

There were times when I really worried about mum. I was just cleaning out the girls' guinea pigs – how that got to be my job I don't know - when she walked with her roly-poly walk up our driveway.

"Oh, hello, I didn't see you coming, I didn't hear the car," I said giving her a kiss, getting a cuddle in first before the girls came running over to grab her.

"No, I'm not in the car, I'm on foot. I've put the car in the ditch."

"Oh, my god, are you okay? What happened? Where? Are you hurt?" By now we'd all crowded round mum and the girls were cuddling her, Charley still holding her guinea pig. Mum's eyes were twinkling with merriment.

"No, no. I'm not hurt. Stop fussing. It's fine." It was clear she didn't want to alarm anyone. But I was mega alarmed.

"Fine? Fine? You've put the car in the ditch and it's fine? Come and sit down and I'll make you a cup of tea while you tell me about it."

Chelsea took mum's hand and led her to a comfy seat. I noticed mum was shaking a little behind the merry facade. The others stared at her as if she'd forgotten to put her teeth in or something. But she grinned at them as usual.

"Well, I'd just been to the farm shop for some eggs and I was driving home trying to hold them on the seat and must have misjudged the corner and just gently drove into the ditch on the other side of the lane. It was quite funny really. But I'm glad no one was watching, I felt such a fool." She twinkled at the girls again and they smiled back. Charles and I looked at each other trying to decide if she'd had a bump on the head.

"So is the truck on its side, or upside down or what? How did you get out," asked Charles.

"No, it's just a little tilted really. I just opened the door and climbed out. And there was no one about which is just as well as I did look a bit stupid. So I thought it was a nice day I'd just walk round here."

"Oh, mum!" I gave her a big hug. The girls muscled in with hugs too.

"It's alright. I didn't break the eggs," she said brightly. I think it was only me who noticed the brave waver in her voice. We made the tea strong. Her hand was shaking more than usual when she took the cup.

"I think what we need is a bit of chocolate," said Chelsea. Charley put the guinea pig on mum's lap and went to the cupboard and got out the chocolate for special occasions.

She soon settled with the distraction of a guinea pig nibbling her sleeve and a girl on each side of her, so Charles and I went to find the truck. It was about a mile away, just tilted a little in a small dyke as if she'd purposefully driven it in there. It didn't even look damaged.

"I reckon I can drive it out with the four wheel drive on," I said.

I managed it easily. Mum was ever so glad to see the eggs back.

"I'll drive you home," I said.

"You'll do no such thing. I'm perfectly capable. And I'll put the eggs on the floor of the car this time," she joked.

I wanted to take her but it was probably better to let her go herself. It was only a short distance and it was perhaps best she got back in and drove. I gave her a hug. She smelled of guinea pig wee.

"Take the corners slowly," joked Charles.

"Don't be cheeky," she said, the twinkle back and the shakes gone. My heart pounded with emotion as she drove away.

A little hand crept into mine and squeezed it.

"Silly, grandma," said Chelsea. And she smiled up at me intuitively.

*

Our Home Education became more glorious with the summer. But my best friend continued with her worries over her child in school. I could hardly believe the things she told me. It was a constant struggle for her to support him. But what could you do with a child in school who could not easily read?

All school learning was based on print – well mostly. But I could present the girls with learning in so many different ways, practical, experiential, conversational ways. Print was the last approach and sometimes not at all.

Just as well since Charley had as much aversion to print as she did to the washing up, even though she loved books and stories. It would have been a terrible problem for her in school but at home we could just work round her need to learn in other mediums.

I heard this from other home schooling families too. How their children had so-called 'learning difficulties' in school but since being Home Educated and using different approaches these 'difficulties' just disappeared. Apparently Home Ed parents liked to call them 'differences'. Too right! That's all they were. If we educated to these differences there would be no 'difficulties' at all. The Home Educators seemed to be proving that.

I said all this to my best friend trying to give support.

"You know your son is bright, you know he's intelligent. You know he is capable of learning. Don't let them judge him by his ability to read. He's not stupid just because he's dyslexic," I said.

"Yea, but what's the good of me believing that if the teachers don't," she said.

"You've got to keep fighting for support for him. And keep believing in him." I spooned the last dregs of my posh coffee from round the sides of the tall glass. Coming to the city for a tall coffee certainly was a change from drinking out of a chipped mug with stains of dye round the rim.

She did the same. Then she said, "You know, you may be a Home Educator, but I think your approaches would be just as helpful to parents with children in school."

She's sweet. She got me thinking. Maybe something else to write.

*

Her encouragement got me scribbling away early morning again. And I re-read the books by John Holt, especially 'How Children Fail'. His ideas were like a pool of sanity among the muddled and he fuelled my fire. His work should be compulsory reading for teachers.

I researched and wrote till the girls got up. Then all thinking threads became frayed as their needs took priority until I could weave them back together again in the evening when the girls had gone to bed. Sometimes I wrote when I was waiting for them to come out of clubs. Sometimes when they were with mum or Charles. Sometimes the words just floated in my head while we walked or they played and I tried to catch the dropped stitches of ideas by jotting down a word to jog my memory. More often than not my memory was shot with the effort of the day and it took monumental effort to crank up the weave of thought again.

It was hard to keep it going. But I knew if I lived my life just for the kids and did not have my own work it would be too frustrating. Plus I wanted to supplement our meagre income.

Oh the luxury of doing one job exclusive of everything else – every mum's story! I guessed managing to Home Educate was as much about managing your personal time as anything to do with learning. And management was about choices and priorities.

Waiting with the other parents outside the dance school I got a variety of responses to our choice to Home Educate. Some just ignored me – I was obviously too whacky for them to deal with and they wouldn't want polluting. Some were interested and asked me all the usual questions – or perhaps they were just better than me at politeness.

One said "Oh I couldn't do possibly do that because I have to work," suggesting I didn't with the emphasis of the superior on the word 'work'.

I wouldn't have felt the blow of that remark more even if she'd physically knocked me to the floor. For once I was speechless.

Her children came running out. They had top of the range dance wear. Ours was second hand. They had label trainers, ours came from Woolworths. They wore designer clothes. Some of ours were from the charity shop. They went on foreign holidays and booked their kids into holiday clubs. We scrounged free accommodation off relatives and all pitched in. Her kids were whinging at her for something the minute they came out. Mine looked at them strangely.

We could all make choices. But I got very hacked off with the back handed implication, usually from these well off people, that I didn't 'work'.

*

I told mum about it. She was totally over her adventure in the ditch bottom although I still felt decidedly twitchy about her driving. But just then it was me who needed consoling.

"Don't take their attitudes to heart," she said. "What you've chosen to do is adventurous and brave. It rocks their little boats. And, if you think about it, it's challenging what they do and people don't like that."

"I'm not meaning to challenge anyone mum, just do what's right for my kids. I know school's right for many, many families and that's fine by me. I just want to make a different choice but I don't diss them off for the choices they make. Why try to put me down by suggesting they work and I don't?"

"Human nature, sadly," she said. She gave me a hug. "And you work very hard at what you do, put a lot of effort into your family, I know that. Everyone that matters to us knows that too."

"Thanks, mum," I said cuddling her back, although I wasn't quite as confident about the last bit, but she knew when I needed reassuring. Making controversial choices can make you feel vulnerable, make you feel alone sometimes.

"What we need is a nice cup of tea and a bit of chocolate. Good job the girls aren't here I've only got a little bit left." She twinkled at me and trotted off into the pantry.

Sometimes it was me who needed the mothering as well as the kids and she came up trumps every time.

As I cycled out of her yard feeling much encouraged I noticed the truck still had long trails of weeds hanging off the front bumper.

We packed the car, we said goodbye to the cat and the guinea pigs who mum was in charge of feeding and we locked the door. We were making use of another fantastic advantage of Home Education; going away in term time. This kind of doubled as a holiday but it was really just Home Educating in a different venue.

Thanks to our kind and tolerant relatives we could go and stay in places we could no way afford and get to see new things. The snag was it made it difficult for the ones who had kids in school. It could be a bit tricky when we were going off to the Sea Life Centre whilst others had their uniform on were grabbing packed lunches and going to school. I quietly suggested to the girls that they didn't go on too much about their exciting day whilst there was a school child in the house getting ready for a very different type of education. They had empathy; they knew what it was like.

It was even worse when the household we were staying in was stressing and desperate about the latest batch of tests.

"How did yours do in the tests?" our host asked me as we were in the kitchen together making a meal whilst the men managed the total mayhem that was the living room full of kids.

"We don't do any," I told her. She looked at me, carrot poised, as if I'd grown that extra head again.

"But they have to do tests, how do you know how they're doing?"

"They don't have to do tests for me to know," I said. "I just know my children. Tests aren't relevant to what we do. We just learn day by day and I know how they're progressing by the things they do and talk about. And we don't have to prove results or scores to anyone or compete with anyone. So it's not really important."

"Oh, I think it's terribly important. I wouldn't want them not to do tests." She chopped the carrot so aggressively I felt quite pathetic gently peeling potatoes. Perhaps potato peeling wasn't as stressful as chopping carrots.

"Why? How does testing help them learn?" I said keeping my eyes on the peelings.

"Well, they have to learn how to do it for a start." Chop. Chop. Chop.

"Learn how to do a test you mean? Doing a test is only one small part of an education and besides there are so many different tangibles involved, how do you know exactly what you're testing? Do the same test on different days under different settings and you'd have different results. So what does that tell us? And who's it all for anyway? It doesn't really help the learner."

Silence. She chucked the carrots into the pan as if they'd personally offended her then changed the subject after a sneaky look at me to see if I had three heads. I should have kept my mouth shut. It was outside the Home Education community that I could feel most alone.

*

Mum managed the feeding routine beautifully. But two days after we got back there was a terrible tragedy. Something ate the girls' guinea pigs. One of them anyway. The other little body was lying stiff and trapped under the corner of the run.

We'd put them out of their secure cage in the run in the garden like we do on nice days when we're around, putting them in again when we go out.

But we were running late to get to the group meet and we forgot to put them in before we left. We got back and found one missing, one corpse. I felt wretched.

It was hard to tell what had happened. There was very little sign. No mark on the poor dead one. No sign of how the other had escaped. Could it be foxes? I doubted it in broad daylight. I had more of a suspicion about the little terrier who liked to visit our garden from his home across the fields. It was a fierce little thing often chasing our cats.

I decided to keep these thoughts to myself to minimise the girls' grief letting them think the other had escaped. I picked up the poor little body and stroked his smooth fur.

"We'll return him to nature and bury him," I told the girls, giving them practical things to do.

"What about the other one?" asked Chelsea wiping her eyes.

"Well, I expect he's having a wonderful time out in the countryside," I said maybe a bit too joyfully, hoping for no more questions. Sometimes you just don't want enquiring minds.

Charley found a box and put the little body in it with some of its bedding. Together they dug a hole placed it in and Chelsea planted flowers on top. We talked about the natural cycles of life and death, how all the dead things in the world propagate new things, how it's the way of the world and yes – even people too. They listened attentively whilst I spouted off all this educational stuff. Then Charley said,

"Can we have another guinea pig?"

"Oh, Charley!" Chelsea admonished, knowing intuitively that it wasn't proper to ask that question right now yet clearly hoping for the same.

Sometimes their pragmatism is shocking. I guess they get it from their mother.

*

I watched the girls cycle down the summer lane way ahead of us. I could not be more convinced that our Home Educating lifestyle was completely right for them.

We'd covered some basic skills during the morning with the

promise of a picnic later. It didn't take long to get through what would take hours in a class situation. Charles got our bikes ready and we packed everything in a back pack and set off for the marsh.

The weather was absolutely perfect, still, warm, sunny. There were plenty of bad weather days in England for indoor stuff, I justified, as if I needed to. They sped ahead whilst Charles and I pedalled slowly along behind savouring the blue view and the lark song.

"Come on you two," Chelsea called, looking back over her shoulder. Charley was nearly to the marsh bank already.

Once there, Charles and I laid out the rug and opened our picnic thinking they'd be ravenous. But they were far too busy finding things to be bothered with food. Chelsea collected shells and treasures from the tide line. Charley hung over the creeks and searched for crabs. Charles and I dropped down and basked a bit.

"Don't you want some food," called Charles.

"I've caught a crab," Charley called back.

"You can't put that in a sandwich," he called again. Charley of course had the right answer ready.

"Some people do."

"Not with the shell still on," he said, needing to have the last word.

"Don't eat all the crisps dad," said Chelsea, plopping down beside us and scattering sea shells, crab cases and mermaid's purses onto her plate.

"Careful," I said and picked bits out the sandwich box.

Charley ran over with a crab in her grasp, pincers clawing the air.

"Look at the size of this one," she said.

"Urgh, keep that away from me," said Chelsea getting to her knees. I wasn't terribly fond of them myself.

"Better put it back in the creek, I think," I said after we'd all examined it.

"Come on, I'll come with you," said Charles.

"You take it, I want my picnic," said Charley and held it out to him, pincers first. He recoiled.

"Put it down first, then I can get hold of it," he said. Charley dropped it deliberately near her sister and Chelsea leapt up again.

"You did that on purpose," she shrieked.

"I didn't!" Charley got hold of it again. "Don't fuss. Alright, I'll take it." She grabbed it again, made off for the creek and we all breathed easier.

She let it go and came back to sink her grubby hand among the sandwiches.

"Mine tastes of dead fish," she said sniffing her fingers disconcertingly.

I went off the sandwiches and opened the biscuits.

As the afternoon wore on we watched the tide far out across the marsh begin its long journey in, pushing huge flocks of wading birds off their feeding grounds on the sands. They lifted and turned, the light catching their wings and reflecting in a magical moving display. The tide pushed nearer as we watched the birds, filling up the little pools and creeks and creating places for the girls to splash and paddle, until along with the bird calls there was the sound of laughter and shrieking happiness. We were reluctant to pack up and leave especially with the trudge back again with the bikes and Charles and I were soon in front.

"My legs hurt," called Charley.

"Soon be home," Charles cajoled.

"How much longer?" asked Chelsea knowing the answer full well.

"Not long."

"Wait for us!"

We waited. I changed the subject to distract them from their tiredness.

"So, are you still thinking about more guinea pigs then?" I asked, pedalling forward again.

Charley surged ahead suddenly. "Can we have some then?"

I hated caged animals, but I knew the girls got so much from them.

"Well, if you promise to look after them more than you did the last two." Charles raised his eyebrows at me the minute I said that. We both knew that wasn't going to happen.

"I will, mum, honest," said Chelsea.

"And we've still got all the stuff so we might as well put it to good use," said Charley, with her ever ready reasoning. How did these kids learn the power of logical argument?

"And they're very educational," said Chelsea knowing exactly how to press my buttons.

Charles grinned at me. He likes it when I'm outmanoeuvred.

"I want a ginger one, what colour do you want Charley?" asked Chelsea cycling ahead with her sister.

"I want a multi coloured one," Charley replied, pedalling harder to ride by her.

"You can't get multi coloured ones," said Chelsea.

"Yes, you can..."

We were home in no time.

*

I could hardly tell whether I was asleep or awake. I was only aware of pain. Followed by nausea. Followed by the distinct impression I'd be better off dead. Such was the onslaught of migraine. I got up carefully, not thinking vomiting and staggered down for the pills.

Will I ever be free of this migraine I've suffered all my life?

"You okay mum, you got migraine?" asked Chelsea reading the signs.

"Yes darling, I'll feel better when I've had some Migraleve.

Luckily Charles was at home. "Go back up to bed, I'll see to things down here."

I went gratefully. Least I got a day in bed. What some people would do for a day in bed! What a thought; did I have to have a migraine to get a break? Perhaps I should have a day in bed before it got this bad. Perhaps if I did I wouldn't get migraine in the first place.

"I would think Home Educating is enough to give anyone a migraine," said one of the mums while we were standing waiting at the dance school. The day after I still felt a bit groggy.

"It's not Home Educating. I've always suffered from them."

She looked at me in surprise. "I'd never have known, you seem such a calm person. I suppose you'd have to be doing what you do."

I smiled at her – I was trying to appear normal.

"To be honest, I think I'm calmer now the girls are at home than I was when they were in school and I had to witness them being so unhappy all the time."

"That's amazing," she said. "The very thought of having the kids round me all day frightens me to death."

"They're no trouble really. When we're not working together they just seem to be busy doing something."

"So, are you breaking up for the summer like the schools do? God, it's nearly the long holiday and I dread it every year. Six weeks of hell."

Sometimes I wonder why people have kids.

We were breaking up for the summer but for the girls it was just the same. For us it meant that Charles and I could stop planning educational things, stop motivating the kids to be busy, stop recording all the things they do, stop feeling life had to be educational all the time, and just drift a bit. Trouble was, I was beginning to find this very hard. As if Home Educating was in my bones.

But perhaps it was, because Home Educating was just extended parenting and as a parent I wanted to show my kids the wonderful world. It was all part of loving them and caring for them and I reckoned it was the best thing anyone could ever do.

The new guinea pigs produced a flurry of caring and responsibility in the girls. I knew this would wane but I wasn't bothered. The experience of caring for them even if just a bit was well worth it, it taught them so much.

I watched them hold and caress the little furry animals with a look of rapture on their faces and I could see exactly how much worth. Because it put me in mind of that wonderful holding time we had when our babies were small and their heads tucked under our chin and we needed nothing else in the world. I wouldn't have denied the girls that feeling for anything.

The summer flashed by and somehow it got to be late September again and time to be thinking about work mode. Charles of course had no break from his schedule. His alarm went off at five forty five as usual and he got up and wandered over to the window to draw back the curtains on a late summer dawn.

"Oh, heck!"

I was instantly alert.

"What?"

"The guinea pigs are still out in the run on the grass, we must have forgotten to put them in again."

"Shit!" I threw back the covers.

"Don't worry, no need to get up. I can still see them moving, and they're chomping the grass quite happily.

"How the hell did we forget again?" I said flopping back down on my pillow.

"Well, it's the girls' responsibility really. Why do we always have to remember?"

"Because we're the grown ups. And we're supposed to remember to remind them. They learn by our responsible example."

"Let's hope they don't learn memory loss then," said Charles grinning and made for the bathroom.

I waited in bed till he came out again, thinking. September always seemed such a poignant time. Chelsea was born in September and we now had a child of ten – how did that happen? It was the time when the schools started back and all the streets went quiet and something sad settled in my soul.

But this year it was different. Ours were not. For the first time after the summer there was no 'going back'. I curled up my toes with that same excitement we'd felt when we first started Home Educating almost a year ago.

I could hardly believe we'd done almost a full year without school. I'd never have thought, when we first started out, that we would get to the stage when we'd been Home Educating for a whole year. Aside from still feeling both a beginner and an old hand what else did I feel about it now?

I loved it.

I loved every minute. I loved it that ours were not entrenched in a school schedule, in learning boundaries, in school restrictions. I loved our learning life that took our children out into the world and taught them so much. I loved their health and their happiness and their curls of laughter circling through the cottage infecting everyone. I loved their motivation and their eagerness to learn, their fascination and their curiosity. I loved our explorations and investigations and experiments, the diversity of their learning days. I loved watching them grow and achieve, develop and mature. I never ever once throughout the whole of the year doubted that we'd done the right thing, or regretted the decision.

"Come on sleepy head," said Charles coming in with a cup of tea.

"I wasn't sleeping I was thinking," I said sitting up.

"The guinea pigs are safely caged again," he said.

"Aw, thanks, see you later. Have a good day."

"You too." He kissed me goodbye and I picked up my pad and pen and started writing.

*

I looked at our new schedule. We had lots of exciting things scheduled for this 'term'. We were planning a trip to new museums which meant an overnight stay. Our Home Ed group had drawn up an autumn schedule and had wall climbing, field trips and orienteering on it among other less glamorous events, and socials at indoor play centres with climbing apparatus for when the weather got bad. We'd found a sports centre that for a reduced rate would hire us courts and agreed to put out tumbling mats, forms, extra racquets, balls and bats free of charge.

I'd drawn up another list. A table; but not a *timed* table, of things to cover each week just to make sure no subjects were overlooked. It looked reassuring, as if I knew what I was doing. It made me feel better in my head, and gave a focus for the children. Was it essential for their education? Probably not, they just seemed to be getting educated anyway because when we got back down to some more academic activities, I was expecting a drop in their abilities since we haven't practised any formal maths or writing all summer, and what did I find? Mysteriously they'd got better at it.

Teachers were always going on about how children 'fell behind' over the long summer holiday. It wasn't like that at all. Despite not doing any they still seemed to have improved. I assumed the reason was that whilst they were doing other things, they were still developing skills and knowledge, their brains and bodies were still stimulated and improving and that progress overflowed into all things. That was so exciting, and proof perhaps that we didn't need to sit kids down and drill academic stuff into them all the blinking time.

Just as well, we'd got so much other stuff planned, they were not going to be doing that much.

*

"Oh my god!" I just opened the post.

"What?" asked Charles, looking over my shoulder at the letter I was reading.

"The Local Authority have finally decided they want to visit us and see how our Home Education is going."

"Well, they can't be desperate, they've taken a year to get round to it. Your letter probably frightened them off." He grinned.

"I'd forgotten all about it really."

"Probably just as well. You're not worried are you?"

"No, but you hear some awful stories."

I'd heard many. Parents who had been bullied by inspectors known to be thoroughly disapproving of Home Ed Visits where the families had been made to feel like shit on the bottom of the LA shoe. Children furtively tested and Inspectors who had intimidated children and parents alike with their results-orientated mind set.

So I wasn't exactly relishing it. But I wasn't going to let it affect me, was I? I had complete faith in what I was doing, didn't I?

I scrambled about looking for notes about what we'd done, digging out anything of the children's that looked a bit 'workish', amalgamating the mass of art work and science projects and models, wishing I'd kept much more detailed records whilst we were having fun over our education. Even the fun bit was making me feel guilty.

I spent the next few days turned into that awful 'teacher' person making the kids write about every single thing they did which ended up with them in tears and me wondering what the hell had come over me.

Every single day since the children had been out of school I believed they had been learning. Every single activity they had done I was convinced had contributed to the development of their minds and bodies – the whole of their minds, the whole of their education. When I looked back they had made enormous developmental progress since this time last year. Why was I suddenly trashing all that just in a stupid attempt to try and prove it to someone else like schools had to?

I forgot; I wasn't schooling – I was educating for real. I needed to calm down.

Next day I talked to the girls.

"Next week, we've got someone coming to visit you and talk about what you've been learning at home."

"That's nice," said Chelsea, not really listening because she was concentrating on fractions.

"You'll have a chance to show them all the incredible things you've been doing and talk to them about the places we've visited."

"I'm going to tell them about the Science Museum and show them my scrap book," said Charley.

"Shall we make them some biscuits?" asked Chelsea.

"Yes, that's good idea," I said. It wasn't bribery...it's what we do for all the visitors.

I talked about our forthcoming visit to my new Home Ed best friend when they came over. I told her some of the horror stories I'd heard whilst the children built dens in the garden.

"But they're not all like that," she said. "Our visit was quite inspiring really. Me and the inspector just sat and talked about all the things we did together with the children, we showed them all their bits and pieces, and the inspector could see how stimulated and busy learning the children are and we had a lovely afternoon. It was nice for me to have someone to talk to about education. And it was quite nice for the children to have someone interested in their work other than the relatives who don't really know what to say."

"Yea, I suppose. I was a bit anxious not having a very formal and structured approach that many of the authorities like to see," I said.

"It's just about seeing all of what the children do as educational and describing it in those terms. Look at them now. You could say they were playing dens. But you could also list the educational experiences they're gaining like; exploring materials, gaining scientific understanding of their surroundings, making observations and analysis, problem solving, construction, articulation, creating ideas, coordination skills, reasoning skills, communication, overcoming challenges the materials set them, all the thinking required. It's endless really," and she laughed.

"Yea, I see what you mean." She got me laughing too.

"Everybody always tries to structure everything into their neat little tick boxes and it totally devalues the real learning experience. The kids will never forget this afternoon. They won't realise how much they've learnt. They don't need to be writing about it to make it valuable."

I'll scrub that activity off my list then. Anyway, I could totally see how right she was. Confidence restored, we topped off the afternoon with supper at our place. And when they'd gone I scribbled a few things down to tell the LA when they visited before I crashed out in bed.

*

Another migraine brought me to consciousness. That sick feeling and pain enough to make me vomit. I got up, determined not to, and stared fixedly at the news on the telly to distract myself.

An hour later I was no worse surprisingly. It was also surprising that I hadn't had one for ages – perhaps thinking differently about not having to have a migraine to get a day of respite has made an impact. Perhaps I needed a day of respite today so it didn't turn into a real stinker.

Sleepyheads appeared.

"You alright, mummy?" asked Chelsea, knowing it was odd for me to be sitting there in front of the TV with my dressing gown on.

"Just a bit of migraine I think."

"Are you going to be sick? Do you want a bucket?" asked Charley, knowing the routine. It made me smile.

"No. I'm feeling better all ready. But I reckon I'm not up to much today. Do you think you can find things to be busy with?"

"Don't worry mum, we'll be fine. Do you want a cup of tea?" asked Chelsea. Charley glanced at the telly.

"That would be lovely, darling."

They went off into the kitchen all important with helping.

They found things to do all day and I got better and better, no vomiting, headache eased. Eyes returned to something like normal vision instead of me having to work out what I was looking at. We stared at lots of schools programmes together. They made me 'Get Well' cards which made me feel a fraud. And they scrubbed potatoes to bake for dinner and grated cheese.

I tried not to notice the sticking plaster on one knuckle.

They were stars. And do I think they missed out because I didn't have much input that day? Not at all. They learnt about responsibility more than anything. Even the guinea pigs were attended to.

Perhaps I should have a day like this more often then perhaps I wouldn't have migraine at all.

I ignored the time and carried on reading. I knew it couldn't be that late because it was hardly light yet outside. The girls were still asleep and the book was too interesting to put down. It was about using the power of thought to heal oneself and I was glued to it. If you could change your health by the way you thought about it that would be amazing?

I lay there before the girls stirred thinking about mum; she had an incredible capacity to enjoy the world around her, maintain a positive outlook, take pleasure in her own company. She was in her eighties and had no pain anywhere, was rarely stiff or achy in her joints, hardly ever got ill and giggled her way through most things. I felt I would be old before her, stiff as I was with hours of horseback riding through my youth and crippled sometimes with migraine. My book said migraine was about holding onto criticism. Did I do that? Was I too critical of everything, self included?

My mum had no worries about what other people were thinking of her and the way she lived her life and was not self critical. She gave an impression of life as bountiful and to be enjoyed. She was kind and good, loving and caring.

If I could instil in the girls her kind of positivity it would be the best kind of gift to bestow, never mind education. And if I could take all criticism out of life I would gladly do so. Criticism has no place really, not even in education.

Next time I saw her I brought the subject up.

"My mother used to always worry so much about what everybody thought," she said collecting seeds from a dried plant head and putting them in a brown paper bag. "It seemed a terrible waste of energy to me. I couldn't wait to get away from it."

I knew she and her mum hadn't exactly been close.

She looked out of the kitchen window at a Wren in the hedge. "I must have been an awful disappointment to her," she said wistfully. Then she twinkled at me. "Not like you though!"

I smiled back. "I get worn down with people's attitude to Home Education sometimes. Does it bother you; us Home Educating?"

"Of course not. I think it's marvellous. I worried at first but look how the girls are doing. And they're so happy. You want to take no notice of what others think. People are so afraid of anything different and they never question. They can behave like sheep. I didn't care what anyone thought when your dad and I lived together before the war, but it was so frowned upon then," she said. "But we did it anyway," she added with an extra twinkle.

She obviously didn't care too much what anyone thought right now either because there was a mouse sitting on the cooker.

"Mum, there's a mouse sitting on the cooker."

"Oh, I know, he does that sometimes." It didn't bother her at all.

*

We spread out lots of books we'd been using over the kitchen table, with folders of worksheets and drawings and diagrams etc, laid out the many text books we used on the dresser, and covered most of the living room floor with various models and artwork and constructions and experiments. It looked an enormous amount all collated together.

"I didn't realise you'd done so much," I said to the girls.

"You see, you work us too hard," said Chelsea grinning at me.

"Yea, you work us too hard," repeated Charley. I grinned at them both.

"I don't think so!"

"What time's she coming?" asked Chelsea.

"Any time soon, if she doesn't get lost," I said.

Chelsea rearranged the biscuits. Charley licked a finger and, pressed it down on spilt crumbs then sucked it.

"When can I have a biscuit?" she said.

"Let's just get on with what we're doing, we don't want our education interrupted, do we?" I said, hoping I sounded normal. I think I was about as normal as a pig in corsets.

I did feel distinctly twitchy. My educational ammunition was primed and I was determined to give a very 'normal' impression of our Home Educating days rather than the usual ones with Charley hanging upside down in a tree or covered in mud and Chelsea buried under a mountain of textiles and craft materials. People just got the wrong impression, jumped to the wrong conclusions. I was obviously not as good as mum about not bothering what people thought. But this was our first inspection and these people could actually take us to court.

There was not really anything normal about the way we sat and worked in silence, but it did give a good workish impression. Not that the education inspector saw that because as soon as the car came into the drive the girls abandoned it and were at the door.

A small tidy woman with a briefcase to help her look important greeted them with smiles, put them at ease and they started talking and from then on I hardly had a chance to. They answered all her questions about what they did, whether they liked it, what they liked best. There was one dodgy moment when Charley answered that question with "playing" when I was hoping for something more educationally impressive. But the lady didn't mind and said playing was important so Charley got the Lego out. Chelsea took over telling her all about the books she'd read and how she loved reading, and they swapped titles. A second dodgy moment arose when Charley butted in with "I hate reading" but was answered with "yes, but you like playing don't you and you'll probably like it one day" as if that was perfectly okay.

"I love stories, though," added Charley. "Me and grandma make them up all the time." Good recovery, I thought.

Then she asked the girls about seeing friends and clubs and dancing and couldn't get another word in whilst the girls told her all about that and their new Home Educating friends.

I was really disappointed not to be able to have an educational argument.

"Well, I can see they are very happy, and obviously getting a lot out of their Home Education," she said. "So I should continue as you are, I'm very satisfied with your provision. And I shouldn't worry about having to justify their educational experiences with writing all the time, they're obviously learning and they're both content and healthy. It's good to see."

I could have kissed the woman. Instead, the minute she was out the drive I snatched the girls up and kissed them instead. They were totally confused, wondering what all the stress was about.

"Let's go for a bike ride to the shops for sweets to celebrate," I said.

"But what are we celebrating, mum?" asked Chelsea.

"What beautiful clever children you are and how proud I am of you both," I said feeling like a very drunk Cheshire cat. But they weren't passing up an opportunity for sweets.

We left the mess on the table and pedalled out into the autumn afternoon. I don't think my feet touched the pedals; I think I flew.

It wasn't that I'd ever doubted over the last year that we were doing the right thing. It was just absolutely wonderful to have it endorsed by someone else.

We were doing okay. We were proper Home Educators now. We had the official seal of approval. I reckoned I deserved sweets too.

*

"You see, all that worrying for nothing," mum said as we sat in the tea shop. It was a particularly small teashop and I was trying to talk quietly.

"I know, I don't think I was really worried about what we were doing. I just didn't want anyone to come into the house and make the girls feel small or disapprove of it in front of them. I know some families have had that."

"Pardon? I wish you'd speak up."

I repeated it.

"Maybe those other families were doing something that needed disapproval," said mum loudly and twinkling that smile at me.

I sensed a few heads switch on to listen to what she was saying. I laughed and changed the subject.

"Mum, I thought you said you were buying an expensive hearing aid. Has the man been for a fitting yet?"

"Oh, yes, I've done all that. It came the other day."

"So aren't you going to wear it then?"

"Why, do you think I'm deaf or something?"

"No, it was you who said you miss out on conversations sometimes."

"I don't need to wear it when it's just me and you. And I don't fancy walking about with it in my ear and everyone thinking I'm elderly."

"I thought you didn't worry about what others think," I laughed.

"That's different. Anyway I'm saving it till I'm old."

*

I decided after our 'royal' visit to continue noting down what we did each day because I so easily forgot. And one small ten minute session could lead to so much.

We had been sitting together on the settee talking about a book on deserts Charley had picked from the library and I realised we had brought in so many subjects in just in that one lesson. There was natural history (wildlife, area, habitat), geography (peoples, customs, places, climate, environments), maths (time passing, temperatures, distances), science and evolution and just about everything else. This then led onto doing some Aboriginal artwork and the use of dots in British art history.

Just from one book. I realised how integral all subjects were and how disjointed they all became when divided up into subjects in schools. I bet half the kids in schools didn't understand at all why they were doing half the stuff they did. I'm sure I didn't either.

Relevance must surely be one of the keys to successful learning. The lack of it probably why many school kids were unmotivated and consequently less successful than they might be.

*

Every now and then I remembered I was supposed to be having a life as well as Home Educating. It got neglected most of the time. Especially at the time of the autumn when dance shows and exams took over. I had to do something about it.

I opted for a Yoga class in the local community centre. I had high hopes it would help relieve some of my stiffness, especially since that book said flexible body meant flexible mind. I was aware I was about as flexible as a steel bed frame and I daren't ask the girls if I had a flexible mind.

I read the pamphlet carefully. It looked manageable and there was to be a short relaxation at the end, plus breathing exercises. That must surely do me good. As long as I made a huge effort not to think about bogeys all the time I was sniffing in and out. And keep my mind off Home Education.

"Not in school today then," a new receptionist at the swimming pool asked us as I paid for our three swims.

"No, we're Home Educating." I didn't feel so sensitive about it now we had the Royal Seal of Approval from the LA. It had upped my confidence that much I was in danger of becoming smug. But it was so nice to feel less like we were doing something we shouldn't be.

"You lucky girls," she smiled at them. "Enjoy your swim."

"Thank you," I said and we made for the changing rooms.

"She was nice, mum," said Chelsea.

"Yea, it makes a nice change to have someone with a more open minded attitude doesn't it?"

"What's an open minded attitude?"

"Well, one where people are ready to accept new things, or others doing it different yet still accept them as they are."

"Like the lady who came the other day to talk about our school work?"

"Yes, a bit like her."

"I liked her," said Charley dragging all her tops off in one tug and stuffing them in her bag and then all bottoms off in one go and stuffing them on top.

I was aware of two older ladies getting dried, listening to this conversation. I was also aware of their massive wrinkly thighs.

"You're like that too," said Chelsea, folding hers up. "I love you, mum."

Aw! Perhaps I didn't have an inflexible mind after all.

"I love you more," said Charley. The two ladies smiled warmly at the girls. I was glad that the thighs were clothed before Charley had time to comment. And relieved that for once her observant eye hadn't noticed.

We dropped into the caressing water and floated apart. I cleaved through the water happily while the girls played feeling so blessed to have had this opportunity to watch my children blossom. I didn't know how other parents coped with missing it. Home Educating seemed just perfect sometimes.

The girls were ready for their snacks in the car on the way home while I sagged in front of the steering wheel gagging for coffee.

"Did you see that lady's massive thighs?" said Chelsea, grinning cheekily, hand over mouth.

"Yea, I thought her tights were going to rip," said Charley. And they both started laughing until the chlorine dripped from their eyes.

"Oh! You two! Everyone's different," I said trying to be serious and not join in the giggling.

"Yea, but I'm glad yours aren't like that," said Charley.

"You'd love me just the same though, wouldn't you?" I said grinning at her then in the rear view mirror.

She was sucking on her drink and thinking hard. I wished I hadn't asked.

"I would," said Chelsea always taking a hint. Charley picked up her magazine.

"Charley?" Chelsea nudged her and stared at her hard.

"What?" Charley said crossly.

"You'd love mum even if she had fat legs, wouldn't you?"

"Course," said Charley, not getting it, her long wet hair dripping on her arms. "She'd be just like grandma then."

I think that was meant as a compliment.

*

Sometimes I wondered how the kids could continue to love me when I got in such a foul mood. Most of our home school days were wonderful. Some I just lost the plot.

"Right. Mega tidying up, I think."

The table looked like there'd been an explosion. It was submerged with the fallout from our day which had gone from activity to activity without a moment in between to put any of it away. Craft materials, sticky things, pens, crayons, paints, textiles, string, various forms of glue, experiments with food stuffs, bits of wire and batteries, cooking oil and ink, strange unidentifiable substances, and endless papers.

We'd had a great morning being busy. But there was a not so great mess as a result.

They girls had already given me about fifty reasons why not to tidy up, they must be running out of them surely. Sometimes I regretted their developing discussion skills.

"But I wanted to do this craft kit," said Charley pulling out yet another box from the cupboard where we stuff everything away. We'd had to contrive a lot more storage space since we'd been Home Educating. But the stuff mountain still outgrew it.

"There's no room to do it," I said. "Tidy some of this away before you start anything new."

"I can do it here," said Charley, always good at problem solving and settling on a space on the settee I'd earmarked for myself once I'd brewed something restorative.

"And I'll be using most of this stuff again," said Chelsea from a little corner of the table. She was standing up next to it – there was no room to even sit on a chair.

"Look, we just need to clear some of this before we get anything else out," I tried to insist, feeling a bit worn.

"Doh!" Chelsea complained, but tossed her creation down and began to put some of it away. Charley ignored me and took the lid off the box.

I was getting desperate for a bit of order, only a little bit, but it seemed to be slipping away from me along with somewhere to sit down and have a nice cup of tea. So I went over and took the box off her.

"Tidy this lot first, then you can do another activity." And I threw it back in the cupboard. It fell out and spilled on the floor.

"Look what you've done now," she said angrily.

She sat there and stared at me from under the same intense brows I'm reputed to have. I tried not to notice.

"She's not helping, why should I do it all?" complained Chelsea, stopping her tidying and folding her arms defiantly.

"Come on, both of you, get on with it." I put my hands on hips as stubbornly as them.

Charley glared at me. I glared back this time. Chelsea glared at Charley. The cat got up and walked away from what was obviously a glaring atmosphere.

I distinctly felt my own sense of reasoning slipping away from me like curled smoke. I think it was coming from my ears.

We'd reached a shoot out and my patience tank was on empty.

"You either tidy this lot up or you can go to your rooms." I hated this kind of approach. It wasn't me. It wasn't how I parented. It wasn't what they were used to. But I was too tired just then to think up something different.

Charley burst into tears. Chelsea, whose desire to get her sister into trouble now melted into sympathy because she hated to see her upset, went across and put her arm round her to comfort her.

"Come on, Charley, we'll both go upstairs." And she took her little sister gently by the arm, shot an accusational look in my direction, and off they went stomping up the staircase. But I saw the confused hurt in her eyes too.

I could feel a bubble rising. It wasn't wind, it was a build up of something else; frustration and irritation and most of all guilt that I'd upset them.

I was tired of having to be on top form all the time, tired of having to set a good example, fed up of being a good parent, a good Home

Educator, a good family manager, a good bloody clean-upper. And I felt like a tantrum too. I was damned if I was going to do the clearing up on my own.

I lost it.

I marched over to the table and with one hard scoop of my arm swept the entire heap of stuff; books, crayons, materials etc onto the floor before I'd noticed that there was a glass jar, painted on one of their group sessions and holding all their pens, among the debris. The whole lot hit the floor with a satisfying and shocking crash and smashing of glass. I stood still and looked at it. It looked even more shocking than I'd intended. It shocked me right out of my mood and back into something more reasonable. I might be tired, but that wasn't their fault.

The house went deathly still. The murmuring from upstairs stopped. I could feel the strain of them listening. Even the cat returned to see what was what and gave me a disdainful swish of the tail. The atmosphere hung like the cobwebs; trembling through the house with tension.

A minute or two went by. No sound.

There was a massive jumbled heap on the floor. I stood there looking at it. But at least the table was empty. In another rush of devilment I pulled out a chair and tipped all that stuff on the floor too. I was enjoying it now. I put the kettle on and made a cup of tea – very quietly, still listening for sounds of movement upstairs, and sat on my empty chair at a clear table waiting and drinking my tea.

I felt completely different; my mood had lifted and I started to see the funny side or perhaps hysteria was setting in. The bubble of irritation turned into the need to laugh. But that would spoil the impact so I tried to hold it together. See what would happen, whether it would make the girls more cooperative.

I heard no voices but little creaks as they moved on what must be tiptoes across floorboards above. Then I heard whispering on the landing. Then very controlled and careful footfalls as they crept down.

I was bursting to laugh and let out the tension but wanted to see their reaction. I picked up the mug again and hid behind the steam keeping my eyes on the strong and comforting tea. Even that suddenly looked hilarious.

Two very contrite little faces appeared at the door. Still silent. Out of my eye corner I saw them look at the heap on the floor. Then at the empty table. Then at me, although I wasn't going to catch their eyes – I might give into hysterical giggling if I did. I kept sipping.

They stood very close together. Perhaps they were hoping that like that they could protect themselves from this wicked mother. I couldn't bear the suspense any longer I had to say something.

"Well, I did ask you to clear the table." I sipped again, not looking, trying my damndest to keep my voice from wobbling and any smile from twitching at my mouth corners. If they saw any twitching they mistook it for anger.

Very quietly, without speaking, they came in unison over to the heap on the floor and started to clear it up and put things away. Their faces were deadly serious. This was obviously bad; mum doesn't usually behave like this. When they got to the broken glass they hesitated, expecting me to tell them to leave it in case they cut themselves, but I ignored it. They were old enough to clear it up sensibly I decided.

Chelsea got the dustpan and brush out. Charley carefully picked up the bigger bits of glass. Very, very quietly they sorted it all out. Collected the pens and books, put away all the materials, cleared the messy stuff, tidied the settee, even plumped up the cushions. It never looked so good. I kept sipping and kept control of my burning desire to crack out giggling by burning my throat instead.

Then very, very quietly they went back upstairs. The tension flowed round the spacious tidy room and away. The cat returned to his favourite position on the settee. Peace descended, flowing back into its rightful place in our house and in our Home Education. Calm settled. Nice!

Perhaps I should have my own tantrum more often. Perhaps I should just get out more. I couldn't leave them any longer.

I got up and went to call up the stairs.

"Shall we go out for a cycle while the sun's shining?"

Two grateful pairs of feet clattered noisily back down the stairs. The relief in their faces made me feel very guilty. Mum was back to normal. I had to crack jokes all the way to justify my silly giggling.

*

"Well, it's a relief to hear all that," said my Home Ed best friend laughing when I told her on the phone about my awful tantrum.

"Why?" I asked, laughing with her although I wasn't sure why.

"Because the other day it happened to me too. I think I was just tired, not to mention premenstrual and I ended up shouting at the kids because they wouldn't come off the computer games..."

"Oh, it's not just mine then?" I butted in.

"No, they're on far too much and I was becoming worn down with the constant arguments over it. So I just lost it I'm afraid. It must have been bad because my youngest went and hid," she laughed again, probably with the emotion. I knew how it was.

"I'm glad to hear it's not just me. What happened?"

"We soon made friends again and I apologised for shouting and said that it was because I was tired. They have it easy most of the time."

"God, you feel so guilty," I said.

"I know, but we're only human and Home Educating isn't easy however much we love doing it and love being with the kids. It's good that they get to see that adults have moods and needs too and they have to learn to work round them. Just as we do. Kids in school probably have to work round the teachers."

"Yea, you're right, and it shouldn't be all one way otherwise the children will end up thinking it's alright for them to go on receiving care and attention but never bother to give any."

"That's right. I talked about it later with them and my youngest said 'Mum, you were scary' so I said back to him 'Well, you're scary too when you have a tantrum' and we had a good laugh over it."

Talking to her and hearing that was a relief.

"It got me to thinking that I should really take more time out before I get to that stage," I said.

"Yes, me too, but it's so difficult with the children always here. I've been thinking of doing an evening class when their dad's here."

"Oh yea? Me too. I'm thinking of Yoga. What you got in mind?"

"Well I reckoned it had to be something to really lighten me up. Promise you won't laugh?"

"What? Not flower arranging?" I said laughing already.

She laughed even louder. "Belly dancing! You promised you wouldn't laugh!"

"Sorry, I can't help it. It's just the last thing I expected."

"I thought it would be fun and I've already got the belly for it. Stop me thinking about the children and education all the time. Pity you're not nearer, you could come too."

"I guess it's times like this I'm glad I'm miles away from everywhere," I said, setting us off again.

Nothing like a good friend to share the bad bits with.

*

Mum thought my tantrum was hysterically funny.

"But you never even had tantrums when you were a little girl," she said her wrinkles crinkling into a full face smile.

"Well, it looks like I'm going to make up for it now!"

Then it struck me. I could not remember her ever getting in an awful mood with me. My two would never now be able to say the same about me.

"I still feel awful." I said to Charles when we talked about it. "Mum, never got in a mood with me. Did the girls say anything to you about it?"

"Yes, they said you were an awful ogre and they were terrified of you and wanted to go back to school!"

"Sod off and stop trying to wind me up," I said throwing the tea towel at him. He just smirked all satisfied that I'd got it wrong instead of him.

"Sorry for my mood the other day," I said to the girls.

"You smashed my jar," said Charley accusingly. Nothing like kids for making you feel better.

"I'm sorry darling," I gave her a hug.

"But I can make another one," she added trying to make me feel better in her own way.

"It doesn't matter mum, we all get in a strop," said Chelsea with the same comforting voice I'd often used for her.

"Dad got in a strop the other day. He said 'shit'," said Charley.

Charles' smirk didn't look quite so squeaky clean. Nothing like kids for making you feel better.

Autumn was like one big run of events from Chelsea's birthday, then mine, Halloween, bonfire night and Charley's birthday just before Christmas. The calendar looked all party.

"What do you want to do on your birthday this year, darling?" I asked Charley as we sat round the table for dinner among the usual Home Ed debris. "Do you want a party?"

"No. Not really," she said. Big relief. "I want to go ice skating," she added. Relief shattered.

"Ice skating? I'm not sure there's anywhere round here we can go," I said thinking, why can't my kids pick something easy for once?

"Ted goes near where they live," Chelsea said helpfully. Terrific – that's miles away.

"I've always wanted to go skating," said Charley making me feel guilty for not being enthusiastic.

"But you do, you go roller blading every week," said Charles.

"It's not the same. Ice skating's bigger and faster."

"Can we mum, can we? I've always wanted to go too," Chelsea chipped in.

I supposed I could give the rink a ring, get a group booking for her birthday to keep costs down.

"Shall I tell you a secret?" I said trying to heap spaghetti on my fork.

"What?" Chelsea looked up.

"What?" Charley looked up sucking hard on a spaghetti strand.

"I've always wanted to ice skate too." They whooped.

"So can we? I'd much rather do that than have a party. The others could come too. And we could have chips after." She'd got it all worked out.

"Can we mum?" Chelsea sensed I was coming round to the idea.

"I'll make some enquiries."

They gabbed about it excitedly all the way through dinner. Charles kept very quiet, head down.

*

The Yoga teacher flexed her ultra mobile joints and beamed at us all sweetly. Her svelte and Lycra clad body made the rest of us look like stiff lumpy sacks of potatoes. We listened intently to her instructions not to strain and only do what our bodies told us we were capable of. Then we leapt around like a load of teenagers on Ecstasy to warm our bodies up. And when we did some postures I found I wasn't nearly as stiff as I thought. Maybe a more floppy bag of lentils instead of spuds.

Finally we lay down on our cosy blankets to meditate. My body felt all soft and used as if I'd had a good massage and I was determined to keep it up every week and try and practise in between.

The two most important things to practise are not snoring like the other women in meditation. And clenching my buttocks really hard so that during postures no one hears me fart.

*

I thought all we did in maths was played. But when I wrote it down on my record list it looked quite different.

We had both sets of weighing scales out, the calibrated metric pair and an old balancing pair with weights in pounds and ounces too. We weighed everything in sight, from the kitchen cupboard, from the bedroom and even the guinea pigs although that wasn't accurate because one weed and the other kept scrabbling off. Chelsea knows all about units of measurement easily now and filled in two pages of workbook weight calculations and Charley understands that even though some things are smaller than others they can weigh more. It was magic to see the dawning of understanding on their faces.

I tried the joke about which weighs the most a kilogram of gold or a kilogram of feathers but Chelsea got it straight away and so did Charley when we tried the same thing with ten grams of cotton wool and ten grams of lentils.

"Which weighs the same dad, a kilogram of gold or a kilogram of feathers?" Charley asked Charles at dinner. She said flaunting her new knowledge.

"Oh, I'm too tired to think of that now," he said craftily, playing for thinking time. He looked at me for help. I wasn't giving anything away.

"Oh go on, which? It's easy." said Chelsea.

"Well, I'm not very good in metric I still work in pounds and ounces," he said, still stalling.

They were giggling away to themselves and looking at me across the table.

"What's the joke?" he said, not getting it.

"They're both the same, silly," they both chimed in. He still looked confused.

"Pound of feathers, pound of lead?" I said winking at him.

"Oh, I get it! You two are getting too clever for me."

"Perhaps you should play with the scales too, dad, then you'd get to know kilograms just like us," said Chelsea.

So they obviously think of their education as play too. When I think of what their learning used to be like and their burdened little faces I know that Home Ed just rocks.

*

I stood looking at the witch and wondered if I felt brave enough to go and talk to her. She looked very intimidating. Straggly black hair, pointy hat, hefty black eyeliner and black lipstick. It was no wonder no one was talking to her. But she looked a bit lonely so I decided to brave it and I didn't want to appear discriminative.

"Your costume's very convincing," I said smiling. "I feel very inadequate being a pumpkin."

She laughed. "Yea, but a witch isn't very original for Halloween, is it?"

She turned out to be a terribly sweet lady and not a witch at all. We spent most of the Home Educators' Halloween-come-bonfire party together. The group coordinator had laid on a wonderful event and decorated her house beyond recognition to host it – well the kids had. You could hardly move for cobwebs. She came over to chat, puffing with happiness.

"I can't believe it. Last year, when the group started we had five families. I think there's five times that many here today."

"It's because you do it so well," I said smiling at her.

"I think next year we'll have to find another venue," she said, not really seeming to mind.

"Yes, your house looks absolutely wrecked," said the witch.

"It's not really, it's just the decorations and the children had such a great time doing it they went a bit overboard," she laughed. "Anyway, they're mostly running about in the garden where it's darker and more spooky."

Out of the door I could see lots of strange beings flashing about with torches and shrieking with laughter. With all the costumes it was difficult to tell who was who.

"What's Charley come as, I haven't seen her yet? It's hard to tell them apart," she asked.

"She's a black cat and Chelsea's a firework, she's been fabric painting her outfit all week."

A vampire rushed in.

"Mum, can we eat now, dad says the barbecued fingers are done."

While we ate various body parts I told the sweet witch woman about the awful tantrum I'd had.

"I shouldn't worry," she said. "All parents lose it sometimes. I bet parents of school kids lose it most of the time when they're trying to get homework done."

"Yes, homework was a nightmare, it just messes up your family evenings," I said.

"Seems crazy to me for little kids to be doing home work, as if the school day wasn't enough. I was so glad when mine came out of school." A fourteen year old Goth with rigid black makeup that looked scary enough to frighten crows sauntered up and asked sweetly, "Mum, can Beth sleep over tonight?"

"Okay, we can take her back tomorrow when we go out," the witch answered.

"Cool." The Goth disappeared again. And the witch continued what she was saying.

"Falling out is just a natural part of family life whether you're Home Educating or not. Besides, there's a saying among Home Educators about bad days. Have you heard it?"

"No," I answered.

"One bad day Home Educating, is far better than a bad day at school!"

I laughed. Definitely true. I learned something new about Home Ed every single day.

*

"Mum, look at the state of you, have you seen yourself," admonished Chelsea when I got back from my bike ride.

"What?"

"Look in the mirror," said Charles grinning and pointing to my back. I turned and looked, there was a brown stream dripping off the back of my jacket.

"I thought my bum felt wet." The girls giggled.

As the roads got wetter with the season, the lanes got muckier and consequently so did I as I whizzed out on my bike for mental and physical exercise. Mountain bikes are all very flash but even with mud guards they don't stop a continual stream of liquid mud splattering up into the air from the back wheel and down onto me.

It flicked up onto my jacket and the back of my head and if I went fast enough sprinkled my face as well. I looked like a spotty teenager.

"Perhaps if you go even faster you'll be able to get it to miss you all together," suggested Charles.

"Funny!"

"Don't laugh at her," said Charley giving me a hug of consolation. I bent down to kiss my little ally. She pushed me away.

"Urgh! You've got mud on your lips."

I went to change and clean up. I didn't mind the mud. I wanted to write down the memory of what I'd just seen. The sun sliding down into violet shoulders, the strips of opalescent mist drifting along the dyke sides, the tree skeletons filtering the building sunset and the welcoming glow of the cottage lights as I pedalled homewards to warm and happy hearts.

*

I finally realised a childhood dream. For the first time in my life I got the chance to ice skate.

I'd always wanted to ice skate as a kid. But I grew up in the days when parents didn't pay for their kids to do things when there were streets to play in, doorbells to ring and run away, and swings in littered concrete playgrounds. At least it was usually only litter, not syringes and broken beer bottles.

Chelsea was dreaming about the sparkly outfits the ice skaters wear. Charley was dreaming about the speed. I was just thinking how many layers I could get on to keep me warm and pad my bottom.

We met the Home Ed group at the rink and everyone congratulated Charley on her birthday but she wasn't interested in her haste to get her skates on.

The girls took to it immediately. It was okay for them, they'd been blading regularly all their young years. I hadn't been on skates since I was roped into being the back end of a pantomime horse at a roller disco fancy dress party in the eighties. And then I was just towed. Somehow we couldn't get the horse's four legs synchronised enough to both skate so the arse end just rolled along behind as if it had mobility difficulties.

I was prepared for mobility difficulties just as much today.

I don't know what I was expecting but god it was slippery. Nothing like roller skates at all. It was like someone else had control of my feet. If I could just get control of the trembling – I like to think it was excitement – I knew I'd stand a much better chance of sliding round the rink in the image of my childhood fantasies instead of clinging to the side like someone drowning.

"You okay mum?" asked Charley whizzing by too fast to wait for an answer.

"Look at meeeeeeee," called Chelsea, sweeping past in her coordinated outfit hand in hand with another girl and skating in perfect unison. I wasn't taking my eyes off my feet.

When a little six year old came up and offered to take my hand to help pride got the better of me. I let go. And I actually skated. I went round the rink once, twice, three times. I actually overtook someone even though it was a mum walking her little tot round on foot I still overtook. And I actually stayed upright.

I don't care it wasn't all sparkly leotards and fancy spins. It didn't matter that it was as about as graceful as a cow giving birth. I did it. I was skating. It was magic.

My Home Ed best friend was working her way tentatively round too so I slithered in beside her and we continued together. It may not be Torvill and Dean but it was one step better than all those parents standing round the side with cold noses and faint hearts.

Driving home after the chips party my legs were so wobbly I could hardly keep my foot on the accelerator. I looked at the girls in the back all rosy cheeks and shining eyes. Particularly Charley clutching her presents and her '7 Today' cards.

"Enjoy your skating then?" I asked.

"Yea. It was brill," said Chelsea.

"You looked ever so funny trying to skate," said Charley.

I wasn't having my bubble burst.

"Well, I've never done it before."

"I think you did really well," said Chelsea.

"Did you see Sam's dad. He was brilliant," said Charley.

Bully for Sam's dad I thought deflating a little.

"But he shouts at Sam all the time, I don't like him. You're much nicer than him," said Charley perhaps realising what she'd implied. It was quiet a moment.

"Thanks for taking me mum, it's the best birthday ever," she murmured dreamily.

Aw!

"Yea, thanks mum," said Chelsea. "Shall I make you a cup of tea when we get home?"

"That would be lovely," I said knowing full well they'd be asleep by then. But it's the thought that counts. And obviously they really did think more of me than Sam's dad despite his skating prowess.

Christmas stole up on me while I wasn't looking. I think it must have been while I was star struck by my skating and Yoga achievements.

It was funny being the learner again. It made me think more carefully about how I enabled the girls to learn and how important it was to stick closely to what each individual needs. Perhaps it would be good for all teachers to return to the learning side of the fence every now and then. It might them more empathetic. They wouldn't be so smug about accusing people of being stupid for not being able to do stuff.

Meanwhile, I was having trouble keeping Christmas secrets. It was my own fault because I'd been encouraging the children to be inquisitive about everything as a basis for learning.

"What's the postman brought, mum?" asked Chelsea as I was trying to be furtive about a parcel. She was spread out across the floor making jewellery.

"Nothing, darling, just some stuff I ordered."

"What stuff?"

"Nothing." I shoved it in a drawer.

Next time I got back from shopping; "What's in that bag?" asked Charley in the middle of cutting out lots and lots of triangles.

"Nothing, just some bits and pieces from the supermarket."

"Why is it in an Argos bag then?" Clever little madam. Next time I think I'll fool them by putting the secret shopping inside an Asda bag.

Next time; "What's in that Asda bag, mum?"

"Nothing special, just routine shopping," I said running up the stairs.

"Why are you taking it up to your bedroom then?" The children were too inquisitive for their own surprises. That was probably what made them so bright. The desire to find things out and it wasn't just restricted to Christmas secrets. They were just fascinated by the whole world around them and wanted to know about everything.

I used to think that curiosity was something children would grow out of as they got older. But when I saw mine learning, when I saw Charley's eagerness to know, find out, experiment and Chelsea's keenness to create and learn and read about everything, I just thought about all those crushed little curiosities in school having to learn what everyone else wants them to know which doesn't interest them, and by parents who only ever seem to say 'leave that alone', 'put that down', stop asking questions'.

Yet it was all of those questions that gave adults the opportunity to teach the children so much.

I was determined to educate my children to question. What if Isaac Newton hadn't questioned why the apple fell down? What a loss that would be.

As far as I was concerned they could question all they liked. Even if I did have to fob off their questions about the Christmas secrets.

*

I came out of the village hall after my Yoga session completely spaced out. My legs were wobbly and it was as much as I could do to get in the car and drive it. I wasn't sure whether this was because my muscles were so well flexed they'd about fallen apart. Or because I'd meditated myself onto another planet. But at least I didn't disgrace myself by snoring or passing wind. And it was definitely doing me good.

I had a little practise at home. But I wasn't confident enough to display my contortions in front of others and tried to slink off into the study whilst the others were working with Charles in the living room.

"What's mum doing in there, dad?" I heard a little voice ask. I could hear the breathing as the little face was squashed to the door. So much for them working.

"She's relaxing," he said. "But she won't be able to if you keep trying to look through that little crack."

"Why doesn't she relax in here?"

"Because she wants to relax in there where she can concentrate."

"But why does she need to concentrate if she's relaxing?"

Listening to that through the door I was about as relaxed as I would be watching Psycho. I'd have to try and do it while they were out. That way I only have the cat looking at me strangely.

*

As soon as we got to mums for one of the girls' sessions they headed for the fire. The open fire was as welcoming as hugging arms or a loving heart.

"Can we light ours when we get back?" the girls always asked afterwards. I would find it very hard to live in a house that didn't have an open fire. It is the soul of a room. No need for the light of the telly. As we had central heating we only lit ours on special occasions. It wasn't the same.

But mum didn't have a fireguard and I worried about the children. Particularly Charley whose desire to experiment could outweigh her common sense.

"Don't sit too close, darling, in case of sparks," I said as Charley moved the dog to stretch out herself on the hearth rug. She moved about half an inch. The dog stood looking dismal.

"Yes, the new logs do spark something awful," said mum. "I saw a tiny spiral of smoke coming from the cat the other day and there was a terrible smell of burning wool."

Charley moved back rapidly and looked at mum alarmed.

"Don't worry. I've put coal on today and that doesn't spark," said mum.

"But was the cat okay?" asked Chelsea, stroking his large ginger ears.

"He was fine. He just leapt up, shook himself and looked accusingly at me," she laughed.

"Be sensible round the fire then girls, won't you?" I added.

"When I was little, all we ever had was fires in the house for warmth. I even had one in my bedroom. But no one ever seemed to get burned. We just knew how to behave with fires. It's like the sea and the weather and the other natural elements. It has to be respected," said mum.

The girls sat up close to her.

"Tell us some more stories about when you were little?" asked Chelsea, both of them cuddling in.

And with that simple question another history lesson started. A lesson where the girls hung on every word. I left them with her and went home to practise my Mountain posture and meditate away any worries about kids getting burned. And afterwards I'd lay our fire ready to light when they got back.

*

"I can't believe it's Christmas already, it's come so quickly," said Chelsea as she painted her salt dough stars gold. Time was obviously going quickly for them. I loved the thought that it was because they were so fulfilled.

"Yea, when it was at school it took ages and ages and we were always having to go in the hall and sing," said Charley painting the same gold paint on her fingernails.

"That's because we were always having to practise carols. It was so dull," said Chelsea. She had finished the row of little stars and now started painting the hearts metallic red.

"What's carols?" asked Charley moving onto the sequins and sticking one on each wet nail.

"They're Christmas songs."

"But we only ever sung boring ones. I like the Muppets' Christmas song best."

"You're a muppet," I sad kissing the top of her head, the only bit that wasn't sticky, and removing the sequins from reach. "Better get tidied up, it's your Christmas ride this afternoon."

"Cool!"

It was hard and frosty underfoot. And very, very cold. The ponies' breath wisped away from their open nostrils as the girls and the other riders walked slowly down the lane. The ponies were decorated with tinsel round their necks and in their tails and bells on their harness. Most were led by other children walking and they carried tubs for collecting in. They were going carol singing on horse back. I hoped Charley didn't think this was going to be boring.

I had to sit and wait but it was too cold in the car. I walked round the stables where there was at least some warmth from the remaining animals and heaps of straw. Everywhere was quiet as I looked out from the shelter of one empty stable. The paddocks, the land all around, the trees, the birds; all silent. Except for a sudden trill of the robin and a flash of red. The sky turned slowly pink as I waited. I did a lot of waiting. I'd been reading a book about women writers and the struggle to marry the desire to write with the demands of family and home. Try being a Home Educator, I thought. And modernity might change women's work but it could do nothing about their struggle with maternal instincts.

Yet despite the frustrations I wouldn't have had it any other way. The writing will always wait. Growing children will not. You don't get a second chance at that.

A clip clop and singing voices alerted me to their return. And puffing ponies and frozen children came back into view.

"We sang the Muppet song," called Charley excitedly making her pony jump and completely forgetting the rule to ride quietly.

Their legs and feet were so cold they could hardly dismount. I know that feeling well.

"Good ride?" I asked as I helped Charley slide to the ground on stiff legs.

"Brilliant. We went and sang outside three houses and a farm. We raised lots of money," said Chelsea.

"And we got some sweets and a lollipop," said Charley. "But I'm so cold."

"You'll soon warm up when you get moving," I said.

"Can we have the fire on when we get home?" asked Chelsea.

"We sure will; it's nearly Christmas!"

They stretched out on the floor in front of it when we got back like contented cats. The discontented cat had to sit on a chair.

*

"It's snowing! Look mum, it's snowing."

I knew that as I'd already been outside to bundle extra hay into the guinea pigs' cage and fetch the wood and coal for later.

It was so exciting even I wanted to go out and play in it. We got out the battered old drum lid that the girls used to slide down the dyke on and they played out for ages. Then we went down to mums' to see she was okay, fill up her fuel buckets, and run about in the acres of untouched snow that lies in the fields round her cottage. She is as snug as a bug in a rug waiting for Christmas.

Back at ours the house soon reeked of drying gloves, hats and wellies. A day or two later and that was replaced by the reek of cooking turkey, plum pudding and since Charles sawed up a few logs for us the occasional whiff of burning carpet.

The snow lasted right up to New Year's Eve. After tea I had an idea.

"What better way to celebrate the passing of the old year than a walk in the moonlight," I suggested.

"What? Walk? Now?"

"In the dark?"

Charles didn't have anything to add to this opposition, he was just hoping the girls would manage to get him out of it, I could tell by his face.

"It's not dark. Look. It's a full moon. It's brilliant. And with the snow on the ground it makes it almost as light as day. It'll be brilliant."

No one else seemed to be thinking it was brilliant.

"I'm scared," said Charley. By the look on Charles' face she'd just voiced what he was feeling.

"But it's not scary. It's exciting. We might see the fox. Just think, it'll be our last adventure of the year." I worked hard to raise some enthusiasm.

They looked at the roaring fire. They looked at me. They clearly thought me mad. But I kept at it.

"Come on. It'll be such fun. I bet no one else will be having such a great adventure on New Year's Eve as you."

I glared towards Charles daring him to say anything about other people being more sensible and staying by their fires. Then I got the coats out. Charles knew I was serious and there was no dissuading me so he helped bundle the girls up in attempts to get it over with as quick as possible.

It was magic outside. The moonlight cast strong black shadows on the white night world and laid the rest of it out in moonshine brilliance. The ground was crisp and slidy so we skated in the wheel ruts and crunched across the icy bits.

The girls held out hands tightly.

"Let's walk really quietly now and we might see some wildlife," I encouraged.

But they were really too excited and besides, we wanted to talk about the magic of the night. It was absolutely still, silent; Silent Night exactly. Then suddenly a pheasant rattled up squawking nearly giving us all a heart attack. The little hands in mine jumped and I jumped and they jumped again. Then peace settled once more. It was so still and quiet we could hear our cold raspy breathing.

"Isn't it magic?" I said, making breath patterns as I spoke. Shouldn't have asked.

"Are we going back now?"

The church bells started to ring across the fields.

"Happy New Year," I said to the girls.

"Happy New Year," they said back, cuddling.

Charles and I shared a kiss over the tops of bobble hats.

"Well, we've ended the year with an experience you've never had before," I said, swinging our arms as we walked along.

"Yes. But can we go back now?"

22

"Look at this girls, it's the new list of activities from the Home Educators' group for this coming year," I said, printing off the email. We sat round the table and looked at it.

"Oooh, the Butterfly Park. I want to go there," said Chelsea.

"What's w-e-t-land?" asked Charley.

"It's a bit like the marsh here really, loads of water. But they have hundreds of the migrating swans there for us to see."

"Look, they've got ice skating, cool!" said Chelsea.

"Yes, everyone enjoyed it so much on Charley's birthday the group is going to go regularly now. And there's also a visit to a climbing wall, look, in February."

"What's a climbing wall?"

"It's a wall with little bits sticking out for holding onto and you learn to climb properly with ropes."

"I can climb properly. I can get to the top of the tree and I don't have a rope," said Charley.

Yes, and frighten the living daylights out of me too.

"This is different," I said.

"How?"

"It's safer!"

"What else is there mum?" asked Chelsea.

"Well, in between there are activities at the resources centre. Here's one. I pointed and Chelsea looked.

"What's In it arts and crafts?"

"No, that's Inuit; people who live in the snowy places and build igloos," I explained.

"Oh yea," Chelsea laughed at her mistake. It's taken her ages to regain the courage to laugh over mistakes again.

"Am I an Init person? I built an igloo and was in it," asked

Charley.

"No darling, In-u-it, these are people who live in snowy places all the time, it's always snowy where they live. Like the North Pole."

"How do they grow their crops then?"

"They don't grow things, they eat fish and hunt for seals and whales. And often eat it raw."

"Urgh! That's disgusting." said Chelsea.

"You ate a beetle and that was raw," said Charley.

"That was when I was little and didn't know," said Chelsea glaring at her.

"The Inuit people don't have anything else to eat, they have to eat fish," I said. "When we go to the library this afternoon we'll look for some books on Inuit people. Right now though, we'll see what's on our list and get on with some work here."

We'd made new lists for this new start. We made them together and talked about what we needed to have on them, like the science, English and maths. Not that we really needed them but it made us look like we were doing 'proper' education rather than just having a great time with our learning.

In my mind, there shouldn't have to be a difference.

*

My best friend and I settled ourselves down with our posh coffees and prepared for a good chat. We hadn't managed to get together for ages and ages. She worked at home too on the farm and trying to get time off made us both feel like truants. But we got over it.

Her struggle to get help for her child in school remained as worrying as ever. My worry was that we were enjoying our education too much. I listened while she sounded off.

"I hate it," she said. Hate is rarely a word she used, I could tell she was angry. "No one seems to be able to offer any help. They've shoved him in with a group of children who are slow learners supposedly to get extra support but the others are so disruptive they hardly ever have a proper lesson. How is that supposed to help?" Was that smoke coming from her lips or is it just cold in here?

"Have you said that to them?"

"Course I have. But even that's worrying as they've got me down as the proverbial fussy mother who is too maternally blinded to accept her son is thick. They behave like there's nothing to be done and it's not worth teaching these kids. Even he said yesterday when I woke him for school there was no point in him going in because the teachers aren't bothering with this group until they're quiet so they don't bother being quiet and they do nothing."

"It sounds awful." I sympathised but knew that wasn't much help. "I'm sure Charley would be in the same position as I'm convinced she's dyslexic."

"Well, if I hadn't read 'The Gift Of Dyslexia' by Ron Davies I wouldn't have a leg to stand on. I think every teacher should be made to read it. You just cannot accept that these intelligent children can be so written off just because they can't read. How staff can disregard children's difficulties as if they don't matter is beyond me. For god's sake, what the hell are they paid to do?"

She raged some more. It took a whole second coffee. I felt doubly relieved we were Home Educating especially as Chelsea would soon be going to secondary school. Her son was in his first year there. He'd about coped with his difficulties at primary but now there seemed little chance.

"What are you going to do?"

"Dunno! Maybe I'll just have to leave it a while. I daren't keep on going in I'm afraid the teachers will make it worse for him. I just find it so hard to believe that no one seems to know how to help my child learn. And even worse they don't appear to care."

I was secretly wondering why parents think that teachers are such god like creatures they know everything. I know they don't.

"They don't teach the teachers how to cope that's why," I said.

"What the hell do they teach the teachers then?"

"Not a lot. Most of them are just graduates; know their subject, know nothing about enabling others to know it," I said.

"I'm worried sick about it. I just don't know what to do for the best. I feel like the more I go in the worse it makes it for him. But if I don't keep fighting for him he's going to spend the rest of his school years in a group that's basically been written off by staff while they concentrate on the grammar stream who make the school look good. What's so sickening is that all the publicity for the school focuses on those kids, the ones who play the game and tick the right boxes. But the others who don't fit conveniently fall off the radar and are made into failures and no one says anything about them."

She was seething with upset again. I didn't know the answer. I'd seen it happen so much in school even before the children got to this stage. Thank god it wasn't my kids. The only comfort I could give was more cake.

*

"Not in school today?" We were at the plant centre with mum. She was always buying plants whatever the season and despite the fact that her garden is so overgrown you get your face lanced every time you go through the gate. The girls will be riding home in a jungle.

They were becoming quite adept at gauging people and answering for themselves.

"No. We're Home Educated," said Charley so sweetly I could have swept her up with a big kiss and cuddle but thought I'd better restrain myself.

After the silly laugh from the assistant and glance at me for confirmation as if a seven year old wouldn't know what they were talking about, she said, "Oh, don't you go to school then?"

"No," said Charley.

"Oh. Don't you like school then?" pressed the assistant.

"No," said Chelsea offering no more than that. She'd accurately gauged the kind of reception we were going to get if we tried to explain and wasn't having her little sister put down any way.

This shut the assistant up. We moved on through the till. Mum stored the jungle in the car and the girls climbed in excited to be buried in it. They were learning a lot about plants and plant families, seasons, growing their own vegetables just from going to a plant centre, not to mention how to deal with people who are a bit obnoxious. Like with all events in our lives there was always something to learn.

I was a bit stewed up though.

Of all the questions we got asked I found the 'Why don't they go to school?' question the most difficult. That was because the simple answer was 'They don't like it' yet it never seemed enough for people, despite the fact that it was the consequence of not liking it that created the problems. It caused them unhappiness, subsequently illness, stress, and as a result of all those things they were not learning. They weren't having their strengths strengthened or their weaknesses overcome. They weren't having their potential realised because they never had a chance to find out what that potential was, schools being so busy with government targets.

Now I knew there was a line of thought that maintained that children needed to be exposed to things in order to get used to them. And that worked for some people. But not all the time and not all the things and not for all people. I had been exposed to crowds all my life but I still hated crowds and frankly I didn't think that was ever going to change. And some children also hate crowds and noise and hubbub which pretty much described all the classrooms I'd ever been in. And I don't see why they should have to get used to that in their learning environment, if they preferred a different one. They also should not have to 'get used to' humiliation, bullying, shame, being made to feel a failure, not achieving or being picked on, which was often also part of a school climate, just in order to become educated. There was no way any adult would accept that as part of their life if it occurred in the workplace. Why should kids have to suffer things they didn't like just because they were small?

So the fact that my kids didn't go to school because they didn't like it was a good enough reason for me. It qualified. For not liking it impacted on their education. And we can't afford to get education wrong.

Of course I accepted children change. And we continued to offer them the chance to try again.

We'd ask; "Would you like to go back into school and see what it's like now you're older?"

We still got the kind of look you might give someone who'd lost their mind. Our kids don't go to school because they don't like it. And they have a right to have that feeling respected. But I remain guarded as to whom I tell that to.

We unloaded the plants at mums when we got back.

"Can we plant that tree with you when we come next week," Charley asked mum, struggling down the garden with her face in a tree.

"Course my pet, it'll be okay as it is for now in its pot. We'll have to dig a big hole."

"I'm good at digging holes," said Charley. Charley didn't dig holes she dug mantraps.

"And can I plant the rose?" asked Chelsea, untangling her long hair from thorny strands.

"We'll do them all together," said mum.

"Wish I got help in the garden at home," I teased the girls.

"You don't give us chocolate biscuits afterwards," giggled Chelsea, her quick wit always ready to make us laugh.

"Shush. You weren't supposed to tell her that," twinkled mum. Just as well the girls are good at gauging people and when it's time for appropriate honesty and when isn't.

*

I once met a really brilliant maths teacher. He was so enthusiastic, so inspiring, he had me gagging to do maths when I usually find it as appealing as a smear test. Unfortunately that was the only time I'd been inspired by maths and sadly for the girls I found it hard to think up inspirational ways to present it.

I wasn't too bad at inspirational English, inspirational science – didn't even have to try with that as our world is inspirational and science is our world – we can find inspirational geography and history that relates directly to our world, and are inspired by our creative activities all the time. Maths I failed miserably. I often resorted to workbooks.

Luckily, one look in a maths workbook was so excruciatingly dull I immediately thought; I must be able to present this in more relevant ways, so I managed to be a little bit inspirational. Some dullness they just had to put up with.

Sometimes I gladly used a maths programme to start us off. But there was a huge drawback to having the telly on in the day, even if it was educational. Watching the telly created a soporific effect that lasted long after we'd pressed the off switch. Not to mention the fact that the girls would always try to convince me there was something even more educational to watch following. I decided that despite the good bits it would just be easier to have one rule – keep it off in the day.

Charles looked like he'd had his favourite toy confiscated when I told him the plan.

"I think it'll just be easier to have one rule; no telly during the day, than to have arguments to keep it on or crank them up again afterwards," I told him.

"Yea, I know what you mean, once it's on they always want to keep it on and it's hard work to get it off sometimes," he agreed.

"And the other thing is that sometimes they're busy doing other things anyway, I don't think they need to stop to watch 'Number Crunching' or whatever it's called."

"Mmmmm. Does seem daft to stop them if they're busy just to change topics. Seems too much like school!" He grinned.

"Course, it will mean that you can't have it on in the day either," I smiled my very best winning smile at him and his grin disappeared.

He thought about that a moment. "Well, I'll just have to slip upstairs and watch it then they won't know." He grinned.

"What? You think they won't work that one out?"

"Well, let's see how it goes."

I knew how it was going to go. They were not going to be conned by that.

23

"Mum," yelled Charley. "Dad's watching telly in the day." She raced down from her bedroom where she'd been collecting another handful of little creatures to copy in Fimo.

"You said no telly in the day," said Chelsea, looking up from making complicated Fimo beads.

"I said no telly in the day for you," I corrected.

"That's not fair," said Charley. "How come he gets to watch it when we don't?"

"You get to watch it at tea time when you've finished your activities for the day and on Saturday. Your dad will be working on Saturday so he's watching it on his day off today instead."

"That's not fair," said Charley.

"What's not fair about that?" I asked. I wondered if I was going to have the energy to continue this battle.

She ignored that and tried another argument. "If I get this finished quickly, can I watch it then?" Who taught my kids never to stop at the first hurdle? Me I think.

"No!" I was tired. Actually, I wanted to slump in front of the telly myself.

"Doh!" She threw the Fimo down and sulked. I tried distraction.

"We've got our visit to the Climbing Wall tomorrow," I said brightly.

"I don't want to go, I want to watch the telly," said Charley, arms still folded.

"That's a shame because I think you'll be really good at it," I said picking up a piece of Fimo and moulding it into a pig's ear. She took the pig's ear off me and stuck it on the pig she was making.

"What do you think we should wear?" asked Chelsea ever fashion conscious. She laid her row of beads onto the tray for baking.

"Not a stupid dress," said Charley.

"I know that," said Chelsea crossly. "Anyway dresses aren't stupid."

"Yes, they are."

"No they're not, just because you don't like them doesn't make them stupid."

Oh well, at least I got the subject off the television. But Chelsea made a better job of the distraction than me.

"Is your pig ready because I want to put it in the oven?" she asked. And they both thought that was so funny they forgot the argument with laughing.

*

"That's exactly why we don't have a telly," said one dad from the group whilst the kids ran around outside playing, after doing technical things with ropes and harnesses. Charley had been straight up the top of the climbing wall and touched the roof which set a bit of a precedent for the other children who were a lot older than her.

"I don't blame you," I said. "It'd be a lot easier if we didn't have one. We wouldn't have arguments then." I didn't add that I didn't think I could cope without it. I needed to crash in front of it when the girls were in bed after a manic Home Educating day.

"It's the advertising to the kids that's the worst," he said. "No wonder that there's so much competition over who has what with class mates."

"Mmmm, I'm not sorry to see the back of that," I agreed, remembering the awful party bags debacle.

"Why don't you get rid of it then?" he asked.

I squirmed. I wasn't sure I was up to it. Besides, there was a lot of good stuff on there too. And Charles would find it hard – well we all would. Not that we were couch potatoes or anything, but it was great for a bit of relief sometimes. Besides, it was so much part of our world's culture I wasn't sure that banning it all together was the right thing, even educationally. I tried to think of an intelligent answer that wasn't just laziness talking.

"Well, sometimes I think it's good to have these things and make the kids be selective," I said. God, I sounded contrite, especially since I'd rather just be a slob and let them watch it sometimes when I needed a break.

"Well, what with telly and all these computer games, I just felt they were in front of a screen too much. It's like easy childminding," he said. "Can you believe kids are in school all day and in front of telly all night?"

I think there might have been a slight second when I thought that sounded rather blissful.

*

The telly rule was completely broken when we all got a terrible virus. There was nothing for it but to give in a bit.

It was the first major bug the girls had had for ages. But the joy of it was I didn't have the hard decision as to whether they were well enough to go to school or not. Besides, 'teacher' was ill too and hadn't the energy for anything.

I managed to make it a bit educational and compromised the telly rule by saying we'd watch schools programmes and documentaries all day. But in the afternoon we ended up watching an old war film which prompted lots of questions and the girls learning far more than if they'd watched a documentary anyway. The film made the war rather glamorous which was far from the truth they'd heard from mum's tales so we discussed how producers bend the truth just for a bit of television.

"A bit like they did with the adverts for Gymnast Barbie, mummy, who couldn't do anything like she did on the telly when I got her," said Charley.

"Exactly darling," I snuffled. You even get to learn stuff when you're ill with Home Educating. Even from the telly. Even from fiction on the telly. Does this mean I should relax the telly rule then I wonder?

*

Whilst we were convalescing and as a distraction from the telly I decided to do some cooking with Charley whilst Chelsea read. I must have been mad.

"Look will you keep your hands out of it darling, and mix it properly with a spoon," I said. She removed her hands and wiped them down the front of her jumper. Then her nose.

"Not like that," I said a bit crossly and tossed her the cloth and she wiped her clean hands on it.

"Right, time to add a little water," I said.

"Can I do it?" she asked. I had visions of running slime and irreparable pastry. My patience was the first to go when feeling off colour. I kept telling myself, 'one bad day Home Educating is better than a bad day at school'.

"No, because you don't know how much to put in and if we put too much in we'll spoil it." Course, I could have just given her a jug with the right amount in but my head was still a bit befuddled from the virus. So I tried to make up for my snappiness.

"Tell, you what, you mix it in." I turned away to put the jug down on the side away from her grasp and turned back to find her hands in it again right up to the grubby wrists and she squeezed goo up between each finger.

I dragged her hands out of it and over to the sink and we washed them again. By now she was silent and as cross as me.

I felt a right bitch. So I gave her the cutter to cut shapes out. But by then she was totally fed up with me bossing her around and not being able to get her hands in it and I thought to myself what the hell was I doing?

I hated baking. She hated being told to keep her hands off all the time. We were both beginning to hate each other. It was a classic example of me trying to accomplish an outcome of making something proper like pastry and totally ruining her outcome of trying to explore the material with her hands. Once she'd got her own investigations done only then would we be able to pursue something more structured. It was exactly the same for all subjects; the kids needed a good play around to discover all they could before putting them into a more structured context. I knew that!

"Tell you what darling, why don't you have this bit," I cut the pastry in half. "And you can make whatever you like with it whilst I finish making the pies with the rest."

"Okay," she looked totally happy now. Took me five minutes to finish the pies. She was busy for half an hour and I got a sit down on the settee to finish nursing my cold.

"Can I make something now mum?" asked Chelsea, closing her book and going over to the table to look. "You don't have to help. I know what to do."

'Keep out of it' was written between her words.

"Okay, darling."

Chelsea got out some more ingredients and made some scones. Charley copied her and made some scones for her Gymnast Barbie. I stayed on the settee.

"These are scrumptious," I said later, feeling better for my rest and butter dribbling down my chin. Chelsea smiled happily. We weren't allowed to eat Barbie's 'scones' which was just as well as they'd turned a funny colour. And judging by the sick makingly perfect figure of Gymnast Barbie she didn't eat them either. But we seemed to have a much better afternoon once I kept out of it.

Sometimes I learned lessons the hard way with Home Educating.

24

The kids and I were just getting ready for a spring walk to see what we could find for natural science when the phone rang. Chelsea answered it. Then handed it to me.

"He's asking for you mum, I think it's grandma's gardener," she whispered.

Old Len went down to mum's once a week to help with the heavy stuff. He was the same age as her so I wasn't sure who was doing the 'heavy stuff' but they managed it all together between them.

He sounded very agitated. "Your mum's on the floor, me duck, she's been there all night. I can't get her up," he said.

"I'm on my way." I dumped the phone and raced off, thanking the universe that it was Charles' day off.

Len opened the door. "She was shouting for help when I arrived but I didn't want to move her in case she's injured," he explained as if I was going to blame him for anything.

Mum was lying on her back on the cold quarry tiles in her living room, the fire out. She had pulled a cushion under her head and had a rug over her. She was attempting a smile as if she'd just decided to have a lie down.

"I'm ever so sorry to bother you, darling," she said to me. "But I can't seem to get up." Only then was there a glisten of something bleak in her eyes.

"Oh, mum, don't be silly. Are you hurt? Are you hurting anywhere? How long have you been here? Why can't you get up?" Poor mum had been lying on the floor all night and now she was getting a grilling.

"It's my shoulder. It's such a pain that whenever I rolled over and tried to push myself up with my arms I just couldn't. It happened last night, I couldn't even reach the phone so I thought I'd just snooze here till someone came. The dog thinks it's all a bit strange, but he's kept me warm."

"Sod the dog, mum. Are you hurt anywhere else? Shall I call an ambulance?"

"No, no, please don't. It's just my shoulder. And the worst thing is I want a wee. And my trousers are wet." She covered her face with her hands.

I knelt beside her. "Look, don't worry, it doesn't matter. Just take a minute while we work out what's best." I took her hand. It was freezing.

"I just so want to get up," she said. I didn't know what to do for the best, but could see the desperation in her eyes and knew that dignity was more important to her than anything else.

"Well, if nothing else is hurting perhaps I can help you sit up, then we can assess things better. Shall we try that?"

She nodded. "I feel so bloody useless," she cried. I eased behind her good shoulder and gently helped her sit up. Then wrapped my arms round her and hugged her whilst she got her breath back. She gasped and flinched when her shoulder was touched. And now she looked grey.

"Are you sure we shouldn't call an ambulance?" I asked.

"Yea, let's call an ambulance, duck," said Len.

"Don't you bloody dare," she said. "Just help me up now," she said recovering a bit.

"Well, let's get you into this chair." I pulled her easy chair up behind us.

"No, I want to stand up, I want to go to the bathroom." She was adamant.

My roly poly angel suddenly seemed so heavy in her immobility but between us, and minding her shoulder, Len and I got her to her feet where she swayed and gasped as we held onto her.

"Thank goodness for that. I was beginning to think I'd never be upright again." She went white. "Help me to the bathroom." Len made a sensitive exit whilst I attended her, helped her change and manoeuvred her back to her chair where she collapsed gratefully.

I gave her a moment and went into the kitchen to make some tea and phoned Charles.

"Is she alright? I've been so worried."

"I'm not sure. She's too exhausted for me to tell. Christ, she's been on that cold floor all night. I'll give her a few moments to rest, then see what's what. She's obviously done something to her shoulder."

"God, she must have been freezing."

"Well, luckily she's got enough fat and layers to keep her warm and the dog and cats lay close to her all night too."

"Poor woman."

"She suddenly looks her age Charles. It makes you realise how old she is and I never noticed before. Look I'll have to stay, keep the girls busy..."

"Don't worry about them. We'll be fine. I'll give you a ring in an hour to see what's happening."

"Okay, speak later."

When I went back to mum her eyes were closed and she looked grey. For one awful moment I thought...then I saw the cat rising and falling gently on her tummy as she breathed. I put her tea beside her then slipped out again leaving her to rest and made Len a cuppa. He'd had a bit of a shock too.

"I should call the doctor out, mate," he said slurping his tea.

"Do you think? They're always so reluctant to come unless you're at death's door."

"Make the buggers earn their money. She's not fit to sit in the surgery. Look at her, she's exhausted. On the floor all bloody night, poor soul."

"I know. I feel terrible. Thank God you came this morning."

"Not your fault, mate. Give the Doc a ring. She needs checking over even if she doesn't want it," he said winking. He was a bit shaky though. I was half thinking it would be him needing the ambulance.

When I went back to mum her eyes were open and she was smiling. But as soon as she reached for her cup she groaned in pain.

"I've called the doctor, mum. He's on his way," I told her.

"Oh, you shouldn't. I'll be fine. Just make me another cup of tea, this is cold. I don't want to be a trouble though." She looked at me and knew I wasn't convinced. She tried to smile, but her eyes were wet. I hugged her again and made a fresh brew and some toast. When I handed it to her the effort of holding it in her good hand was almost too much. The greyness in her face and lack of twinkle I knew wasn't just fine.

"I don't want to be a trouble," she said to the Doctor.

"No trouble," he said examining her shoulder gently. I could see mum was struggling with the pain. "Yes, you need to go to casualty and get this x-rayed, I think it's dislocated."

Mum looked surprised and perhaps a little bit brighter that it was something important and she wasn't just being a trouble.

At the hospital I stayed with mum except for the bit where they snapped the shoulder back. She appeared in a wheel chair all strapped up, a sick basin on her chest.

"She's feeling a bit faint, but she'll be fine now. Perhaps a cuppa before you go. Here are the painkillers." And the nurse bustled off leaving mum shocked and shaken with me not far behind in feeling the same.

Mum looked far less fine than when I first found her on the floor.

"Just take me home," was all she said with a voice far smaller than her. I knew that was what she needed.

By the time I'd settled her back at home mum looked totally all in. I felt she probably just wanted to be on her own a bit and properly rest.

"Look mum, the phone's here, and some lunch." I'd set up a table right beside her. "I'll just pop home for an hour and sort things there, then be straight back, okay? Don't go anywhere." I tried to raise a smile.

"Yes, you go darling, thanks for everything, I'll see you tomorrow." She was trying to get her brave face back on. She didn't fool me.

"Mum, I'll be back within an hour, or a little longer to give you time for a rest. Then we'll have to sort out how you're going to manage with one arm."

"I'll be fine honest." She wasn't even convincing herself, let alone me.

"So you think you'll be able to get your knickers off and your nightie on with your arm in a sling do you?"

At last a twinkle of a smile. "Oh, I hadn't thought about that!"

"Well, I'll be back later and we'll think it all out together." I hugged her, carefully, and kissed her soft, pale skin. I suddenly felt close to tears myself. I also suddenly felt the need for a hug myself from Charles and the girls.

*

I stayed the night at mum's. The girls and Charles came down in the morning to see her and her bright beam was back.

They were very impressed with the sling and we had a quick anatomy lesson, ever education conscious. Then I sent the two of them out to walk the dog whilst Charles and I made mum a proper bed up downstairs. The social services came and arranged extra help. I'd go down every morning and evening. The girls could help. Caring is as much of an education as academics. Caring makes good citizens in a way that academics can't and what this world needs is good citizens. It has brought home to me how quickly things can be different. Life is precious. This puts a new slant on education. On what is really important – that's the question we need to be asking.

I was angry with Charles. He'd used the excuse of mum's fall to get the telly back on. But it was my concern for mum, guilt over spending time with her instead of the girls and the disrupted education that made me get that out of perspective.

"We needed the distraction, the girls were just as upset as you, you know," he said. "You're not the only one who cared." Now he was angry. I realised he was right. It had been quite a shock for all of us.

When I phoned my Home Ed Best Friend who actually has her mum living with her, she helped me get it back in proportion.

"The thing is, a bit of extra telly whilst you had this crisis isn't going to harm. And just because it's back on now, doesn't mean it's always going to be." She was the calmest, most reassuring person I knew. And she had three boys at home full time and been Home Educating longer than us, she should know.

"Yea, I suppose."

"And you don't have to keep the kids stimulated every single second of every single day, you know. Let's face it, it wouldn't be like that in school. There'd be masses of wasted time."

"I know. I suppose I just felt so guilty for spending lots of time with mum instead of getting on with their education."

"Life is their education, don't forget. That's what you meant it to be."

"Yea, you're right, I just forgot in the crisis, I guess."

"How is she doing now anyway?"

"She's back to normal now, with only one wing!" We laughed. I felt better.

The girls came with me to mums and I didn't bat an eyelid as they sat watching the telly all together whilst I sorted laundry and went out to take the dog for a walk and get a bit of fresh air. When I got back all I could hear were three sets of giggling. Mum looked a whole lot less ancient. What better therapy could there be than that?

*

"It's a good job you didn't break your humerus," said Chelsea as she helped mum fasten her seat belt. She was heaps better and we were taking her with us on one of our trips to the Farm Park to see the new lambs and other animals.

"Or your radius," piped up Charley from the back.

"What's your humerus and radius?" asked mum winking at me.

"It's the names of your bones in your arm. Fancy not knowing that," said Charley lording it over us with her new knowledge.

"How do you know it?" I asked, wondering not for the first time how they know all this stuff I hadn't taught them.

"It's on our Human Body CDRom."

"Oh!" They obviously knew a lot I didn't even know they knew. Did it matter? I wondered how many other seven and ten year olds knew what their bones were called.

"So, where's the femur?" I called as we drove.

"In the leg," answered Chelsea.

"I thought that was a little fluffy animal," twinkled mum.

"No, that's a lemur," shrilled the girls excitedly. We all joined in the joke. It was infectious.

"And what's the hip called?" I asked.

"The hip," said Chelsea, making us all laugh again.

"Oh, stop it, you'll make me want a wee," said mum. She was back to normal.

*

"Is your mum's arm okay again, now?" asked my Home Ed best friend when we next got together. It was the first time the girls and I had ventured further afield for one of our outings since mum's fall. But she was out of her sling and back to her usual antics now. She was up a ladder when I went down the other day.

"Yea, it's fine now, thanks. And she's driving again. It made me realise how limited it would be if she couldn't drive. Us too for that matter, considering where we live."

We walked round the Butterfly Farm talking. It had taken us an hour to get to the venue but was well worth it. The girls were enthralled by the exhibits. Their faces full of awe over the large blue butterflies in the hot houses. Awe is not something I ever saw in their faces when at school. In fact, did I ever see awe in school children's faces? When did awe go out of fashion? I supposed school kids didn't get out much. Ours got this kind of stimulation every week. Awe was part of their life.

We stared in awe at the ant colony marching large pieces of leaf across a line of string to another camp. It reminded me of the girls lugging stuff about when they're making dens.

"And how's it going with the telly rule, now?" she asked.

"It's about restored now too. Especially since it's better outside, they're not so bothered about telly. But it's so much better when we don't have it on; they motivate themselves to do things. If they've watched it they're all floppy and disinterested in everything, even stuff I know they'll enjoy."

"Yea, I know what you're getting at. It's almost as if you have to push them into something to help them achieve it, yet once achieved they clearly feel so fulfilled. Our trouble is the computer games not the telly. There are so many of them now."

"We're lucky. Our Internet is so slow it doesn't make games worthwhile."

She grinned at me. "There are advantages to living so far out then?" I nodded laughing. I was thinking I'd try and keep them off the games as long as possible. Make it easy on myself for once.

Another dad had joined us and contributed to the conversation.

"I don't have any problem. I just say no games or television until we've finished what's on the timetable for the day," he said. "After all, that's what it would be like in school."

It would, but if we wanted it to be like school we might as well send them, I thought. But I asked, "And does that happen?"

"Oh yes. I make it happen." My skin crawled a little when he said that.

"You stick to quite a structured style then?"

"Yes, well you have to, otherwise they wouldn't learn anything." I looked across at the children running from exhibit to exhibit all fired up and learning like crazy.

"Do you consider this sort of thing educational then?" I asked.

"Perhaps a bit. But it's not proper education really. I think they learn best when they're sitting down concentrating." He looked over to his son who was chatting happily to Chelsea and called to him.

"Pay attention, Tom, I'll be asking you questions later and you'll be writing about it." Tom's happiness vanished. I wondered if dad's words were for Tom or to impress us. It didn't impress me.

My Home Ed best friend and I looked at one another. Perhaps we weren't having the right approach after all. But she raised her eyebrows.

"Well, mine won't be writing anything. I think they take from these experiences far more than could ever be written down. How can you write down how their maturity grows, or their articulation, how their brain is storing the knowledge and making connections, their pleasure in learning. Those are the important things surely."

I waited for his reply. But he walked off and called his son over to him and gave him a good talking to. I noticed that when we all sat together for our picnic he sat separately. He obviously didn't want any of this far out thinking to rub off on them.

I had known my Home Ed best friend for a year now. She looked like she took a very laid back approach to her children's learning. But actually I hadn't yet come across a more well educated, intelligent, articulate, and caring bunch of kids. Funny that.

I chewed it over later. There always seemed to be this dilemma between an autonomous or structured approach to educating out of school. But surely they weren't exclusive of one another. It was the kids' needs that were important and we did what worked best for them. We'd had an autonomous day apart from structuring their safety of course. Tomorrow we'd write a little in their travel books to practise those skills. They'd moan at first but these scrap books of their outings were becoming quite treasured, they loved looking back in them. We'd soon have to start new ones they were so full.

It all benefitted them whatever we did. And all the kids I met all seemed to be learning whatever approach the parents took. Made me wonder why we needed all this institutional stuff in school.

But one bit of structure I'd be sticking to however autonomous the rest of their education; no telly in the day.

25

"Look mum, we found some!" Charley rushed into the kitchen with a jam jar full of tadpoles. Charles had taken the girls off into the Wolds to a place he used to go to as a boy to see if there were any about.

"Oh fantastic," I said closing my notebook. "Where did you find them?"

"In a wheel track. There wasn't any in the pond," said Chelsea coming in with her jam jar full too.

"Goodness, will there be room in our little pond do you think?"

"I'm not putting mine in the pond, I'm having them in my bedroom," said Charley staring adoringly into the jar.

Charles came in buried under a heap of coats and wellies, pond nets and basket of picnic remains. He dropped them all in the corner of the kitchen in a big heap. Then he collapsed in a big heap on the settee. I bet he'll be ready to go back to work tomorrow for a rest.

"You can't keep them in your bedroom, they wouldn't survive," he said.

"Oh, please!"

"No, it wouldn't be fair on the tadpoles. Besides you wouldn't want a jar full of dead ones, would you?" he added. Knowing Charley, I thought he was taking a big risk saying that, I could imagine she'd be fascinated by a jar full of dead tadpoles.

"Can we go put them in the pond now?" asked Chelsea.

"Sure, off you go," I said and got up to start the meal. The girls raced outside.

"God, I'm whacked," said Charles. "They never stop asking questions."

"That's what we want, that's what keeps their minds alive; all the questioning," I said switching the oven on and looking to see what vegetables we had in the cupboard.

"I'm not sure I'm going to be able to keep alive long enough to survive it." He pulled his shoes off and stretched his legs out. Funny how when he's out at work and I'm working with the girls I get the dinner. And when he's at home with the girls doing what I do all day whilst I try and write I still get the dinner.

Charley came rushing in again.

"Come and look, dad."

"In a minute, I'm just having a cup of tea."

She ran off out again. I could see them kneeling by the little pond staring in. I looked back at Charles.

"You don't regret it though, do you?" I asked, making us a cuppa each.

"Regret what?" he said only half listening.

"Home Educating."

"Course not. It would just be nice to be able to switch off from all this learning sometimes, they're at it all the time."

"That's what we want," I said again, grinning.

He laughed. "Yea, I know." He sighed. "But it would be nice if they had an off switch."

"Perhaps it's more about us just switching off from them instead."

"How do you mean?"

"Well, maybe we should try and switch off a bit at weekends, explain to them that weekends we're all going to do our own things and they have to do their own things without involving us, because we have stuff to get on with too. And just sometimes make them postpone what they want to do if they need our help. Ignore them a bit more than we do, after all they get plenty of our attention."

"Do you think that'll work? I'd feel guilty."

"Perhaps we should try. They understand when I have my 'time out' in the day and they just do stuff on their own. Perhaps we have to try and get them to do that at a weekend?"

"Yea, but they have riding and dancing at the weekends," he said.

"Well, apart from those things. When we're not taking them places, we'll just do our own thing. It's worth a try. But we have to stick to it – and try hard and not give in," I said.

"Dad, dad, come and see," yelled Charley from the doorway.

Charles looked at me half smirking. "Okay, coming," he said giving in. "Well, we haven't started yet have we?" And he was dragged out.

I wasn't sure how possible this plan was going to be.

*

The business of weekends off was going to be tricky at show time. Ever since she was four Chelsea had been involved in performances several times a year which meant weekends were geared to rehearsals. But it couldn't be any other way. There was something in her that just needed to perform. I sometimes wondered if performance would be her future rather than arts or textiles. Problem was; it always involved weekends. Perhaps we could have our ignoring sessions on other days.

Performance didn't really count as education among some of the relatives. And they still found our learning life rather strange even after doing it over eighteen months, having the royal seal of approval and still no second head.

They rarely mentioned education, rarely asked how it was going, how we were getting on, or even attempted to understand better. It was almost taboo. Probably because they didn't know what to say because they couldn't talk about Results or Grades or Reports or Happy Face Stickers or any of the normal things normal school kids got.

What could we talk about? Mud Pies? Creating collage or an outfit Chelsea made? A sagging model of a robot so big we had to ban it to the garage? We mentioned a five metre swimming certificate and a medal from a dance exam but it wasn't maths and English. We did plenty of maths and English but the sad thing was still no one asked.

People used to ask 'How are you getting on at school?' But no one asked the girls how they were getting on with their Home Education.

I tried sometimes to encourage a dialogue.

"Show our visitor your picture, darling," I said. I couldn't bring myself to ask her to show the workbook or the maths we did it was too dull so perhaps I didn't help the situation. Chelsea proudly held it up. The visitor didn't know what to say. It wasn't a SATs Result was it?

"Why don't you demonstrate your experiment?" I suggested next time. Charley got out her experiment of trailing wires and batteries. Our visitor looked at it; he clearly thought it looked a mess.

"What is it?" was the best he could come up with.

"It's an alarm for the door. When the door opens the buzzer goes off, see." Charley demonstrated and it buzzed.

"She even made the switch herself too," I added hoping this might get Charley some reaction. But no. It got the same response as if she'd shown him a used tea bag - indifference.

"I made one of those electric games," said Chelsea, joining in. "Look, you have to get the hoop all the way along the wavy wire without touching the sides or the buzzer goes off."

"Oh, yea, I've seen these before." He looked a bit more like he was interested.

"It's part of the National Curriculum syllabus," I said. Suddenly he looked impressed now he knew it was 'proper' work. I had an overwhelming desire to spit.

Then Charley took him a book over.

"Will you read me a story?" she asked.

"Read you a story? You're old enough to read it yourself," he replied. Charley looked crestfallen while he opened the book and pointed to a word and said, "Look. What does this say?" She looked utterly wretched. And I was incensed. Lioness protecting her cubs didn't describe it.

I marched across the room, took the book from him and snapped it shut. He actually flinched.

"Look, she wants you to read her a story not give her a test. Shall I pick a book off the shelf and see if you can read it?" I snapped. He looked like I'd slapped him.

"Oh, oh," he retracted. "I see, give it here then and I'll read it."I knew I'd been over the top but what was the matter with people.

"Not if you're going to make it into an exam." I knew I'd spoiled the moment, but frustration got the better of me. I bet he didn't walk into any other household and test the kids' reading. I felt like asking him right there in front of the girls how to spell onomatopoeia, except I couldn't spell it myself without looking it up.

I wondered when it would be that people accepted and maybe even approved of what we were trying to do.

*

The Sunday before the next performance we had to ourselves. No rehearsals. No other classes. No visitors. So we could ignore the kids. Even better, the sun was shining.

I got up before anyone else was awake, dragged some clothes on, snatched a cereal bar and made for my bike before anyone else got up. Except I didn't quite make it...

"Can I come?" A little pyjama-ed body topped by a sleepy face caught me at the back door.

"Not this time, darling." I give her a kiss.

"Why not?"

I wavered. Then I remembered the plan.

"Well, I think I need to go at my own pace and have a really good workout. See this bottom. It's getting bigger by the minute." I grinned at her. She grinned back.

"Can I watch the telly then?"

Oh sod it! I had a quick mental battle but sometimes you just had to give in. I applied the weekend rule; ignore the kids.

"Go on then. Just for a bit." She went off happily. My bike ride was a bit tainted with guilt but a few miles on the beautiful morning and I forgot it.

As soon as I got back in the door, "Mum, can we go for a picnic?"

So much for weekends off.

*

The 'weekends off' plan went out the window at show time.

All we could do while we waited on rehearsal was either sit in the foyer at the theatre or go to Asda as it was the only place open. I was more familiar with the inside of Asda than I was with the life lines on the palm of my hand. Sometimes I sat in the car and read or wrote. Sometimes Charles went. Sometimes we just did the travel back and forth and clocked up forty miles a day. Then it was the performance and we all got dressed up ready for a night at the theatre.

You can tell you're getting middle aged when you start becoming throaty at children's performances. Mum just openly cried.

Charley stared at her with big concerned eyes. Mum twinkled back but daren't speak. I developed a strange cough. And Charles went all gooey.

Chelsea pulled it off like an old pro and I was left wondering as always where she got it from as I'd rather be in the back of a cupboard than on a stage. And I also wondered how much her Home Educating had contributed to the personality that made her the performer she is. The longer she'd been out the more performance had grown within her life. The more her creativity was restored.

*

The tadpoles had become frogs in the time it's took us to get the weekend rule working. But at last it did, but only when we remembered what we were doing. I kept thinking; shall we go for a picnic? Shall we get the bikes out? Perhaps we could make some scones for tea? Then I remembered.

One weekend long after the shows were done we managed to keep at our independent activities for the whole time. It was as uncomfortable as hell so I wasn't sure it was worth it.

26

Mum was having a panic button. This sent her into a panic.

"But what if I set it off accidentally?" she said fingering the age defining pendant round her neck.

"It doesn't matter," I said. "Better to have the odd false alarm than you lying on the floor all night like before."

"Oh, I was alright really. It was just not getting to the toilet that was the worry. The dog thought it was lovely having a warm body to curl up with all night," she giggled.

"Can I press it?" asked Charley.

"No, darling."

"Why not?"

"Because what happens is it rings a call centre then they ring me to go and see if your grandma's alright."

"You'll be able to press it when you want a cup of tea," giggled Chelsea.

"It's not a waitress service, you know." I tried to make light of it. Mum wasn't fooled.

"I think I'm more worried about falling down now than I was before I had it," she said.

"I'm sure you'll get used to it," I said. I could see that slightly cantankerous look in her eye as if she was thinking she wasn't planning on getting used to it. She lifted it over her head and hung it on the mantelpiece next to her chair.

"I'll put it on later," she said.

"You need it with you all the time."

"But I'm sitting down now, aren't I and you're all here." She put her arm round each of the girls perched on the chair arms.

"But you might forget." I tried to persist with this battle I knew I was losing.

"I won't forget. What do you think I am, ancient?" The three of them giggled together.

"You're an Ancient Briton, we've been reading all about them," said Chelsea which set them off again. I felt outnumbered.

As mum stood at the window of the cottage and waved us off I had a vision of the pendant still hanging on the mantelpiece where she left it.

*

Every time the phone rang I thought it was going to be the alarm centre. It never was.

The girls scrambled to answer it as a distraction from the work they were supposed to be doing. It must seem to the callers that there's always a fight going on in our house.

"It's for you, mum," said Charley having won the battle this time. I suppose they hoped that one day it will be for them. It was my best friend.

"Sorry about the background noise. It was quiet two minutes before," I said.

"It sounds like our house on a school morning," she said. "It's a manic panic. It's worse now they're at different schools. I shall be so glad when our youngest catches up with her brother."

"I'd hate it," I said thinking how serene our Home Ed mornings are as we settle down to our day's activities. Not counting the phone fights.

"The evenings are even worse. The kids come home in a foul mood demanding food and then it's just a nightmare of homework. When are kids supposed to play or have a life?"

"It sounds awful. Do you have to do the homework even in Primary then?" I realised how out of touch with school life I'd become and the life of thousands of families going through the same every day whilst we were having a nice family time.

"Oh, yes, they get really snotty with the kids if they don't get it done. Despite the fact that some like mine have so far to travel there's hardly any evening left to do it after supper. They don't take that attitude to my face, of course. But I've been in so many times about the dyslexia I worry I'll make it worse if I start on about the homework. Do you know he brings stuff home every night to write up because he couldn't write it down fast enough in lessons? But the crazy thing is his notes are so scribbled we can't make head nor tail of them. It's a nightmare."

"What are you going to do?"

"I'll just have to go back in to see if they'll give me the text books so we can go over the lessons at home."

"So, he'll be at school all day, then have to repeat it all again in the evening?" I was gobsmacked at what she was telling me.

"Well, some of it anyway. I don't know what else to do. I can't just let it go. He won't have the stuff written that he needs to get the grades."

"God, it's crazy. I so feel for him. For you both. There should be some other way." I couldn't help thinking of the blissful learning life we had in comparison.

"I'm damned if I'm going to write him off like they have. I refuse to believe he's just too thick to read, like they try and make out."

"He's not thick. No way. Don't for one minute entertain that idea." I remembered him as a little boy growing up with our kids, the bright, adventurous, inquisitive little kid like ours were. It fired me up to think of what was happening to him now. "Just always keep in mind what he was before school. Thick and stupid he was not. Remember what other complicated skills he's mastered, that aren't reading. He can drive a tractor for god's sake. How can anyone say he's thick? How can teachers make judgements about kids based on that one small skill? How dare they? If you look at the whole child, the whole of his achievements to date, anyone can see how intelligent he is. The system is so blinkered. Remember, it's the system, not your child." It went a bit silent and I felt guilty for ranting.

"Sorry, sorry, I was ranting there and it was your turn," I added quickly.

"No, no, it's fine. I'm just relieved to hear that. Thank you so much. I get so drawn into the system I think it must be me that's thick, as well as him, and I'm too biased to see it..."

I interrupted. "No way. Don't even think it for a minute. Don't forget, I've worked in a classroom. I've seen kids like him and I know the system completely fails these children. I have taught bright intelligent kids who for some reason just can't grasp reading – not in the timescale they're supposed to anyway. It's the over prescriptive system that's wrong. Not the kids. God, it makes me weep with anguish to think of it."

"Well, it's not all of them. The youngest manages okay."

"I know, it's okay for those who take to reading easily. But what about those who don't? There should be some alternative. Kids are all different. Why should we try and make them all fit the same pigeon holes and then make out they're stupid when they don't. It's like trying to fit everyone in the same size knickers."

We both burst out laughing and the tension was relieved.

"Aw, thanks. And thanks for listening," she said.

"Listening? I think I might have been ranting. Wish there was something I could do."

"You help just by reminding me what I'm supposed to be thinking when I get drowned in school attitudes."

"Yea, well, just remember it's not you, it's them who've got it wrong. They are supposed to be providing an education suitable for your child – that's what it says we Home Educators are supposed to do and they come down on us like a ton of bricks if we don't. I don't know how come the schools get away with failing to provide the same."

"I know. It's mad. Anyway, better go now. Thanks again, speak soon."

"Bye!" We rang off.

"What's that about knickers?" asked Chelsea.

"We all need different sizes," I said.

"Just like we all need a different education."

"Absolutely!"

They know that even if nothing else.

*

Summer spread our education out round the cottage. The sunshine shone across the land as if it would give it kisses of honey and we took our activities outdoors almost every day. The girls spread rugs out and the door was constantly open. Our learning was interrupted with observations instead of phone calls.

"Mum, I can hear a cuckoo!"

"I think cuckoos are mean taking other birds' nests," said Charley.

"Well, you could say we take other species homes when we clear ground to build our houses," I said.

I could almost hear them chewing that over, trying to think of an answer.

"Yea, but we don't chuck their babies on the floor!"

Sometimes I interrupted it to make them aware.

"What's that bird singing up there girls, look?" I asked.

"A lark. A lark is the only bird that sings on the wing," said Charley proudly.

"Well done, you remembered."

We looked up the all creepy crawlies and larva we came across and watched ants nesting. We interrupted education for more education, for our quest for knowledge and understanding. Chelsea hated anything creepy. Butterflies and flowers were her thing. She'd got some chemistry going instead and made perfume while Charley counted the legs on things.

"What are those pigeons doing mum?" The pair of them knew exactly what the pigeons were doing and giggled behind tanned fingers.

"Making love," I said setting them giggling again.

"Like you and dad," said Charley cheekily.

"Yes, exactly like me and dad, except we take a lot longer and enjoy it more!" That shut them up. They looked at each other and sniggered some more.

In the evenings there were pulses of thrush and blackbird as sweet as any symphony and the girls played outside late not even bothering with the television. Best of all I didn't even have to call them in early to bed to get up for school the next morning. We could be as flexible as we liked as I knew that their learning did not really need clock watching, it was just part of everyday life.

*

"Goodness, are you actually going to use all those library books, darling?"

"Course, you know I do mum." Chelsea had the full twelve she was allowed nearly every week. She read so much I sometimes had to remind her to do other things. She read non-fiction as well as teen novels. Women's Lib was her latest historical focus.

Charley mostly brought non-fiction for us to look at together. And wasn't going to be out done by her sister on numbers. I picked up topics they wouldn't just for broader interest.

"I shall have to get a shopping trolley for us to carry them all in," I said.

"You can't do that mum, you'll look like an old lady," said

Chelsea.

That was nice. She obviously didn't think I was an old lady yet already despite sometimes feeling like one.

"You're going to be very busy," said the library assistant. Most of the ladies in there knew us by this time and didn't have to ask the dreaded question. Instead they smiled at the girls and were always happy to help. Except for one. I think she was the supervisor as she was as miserable as sin and seemed to be able to wipe the smile off the faces of the other assistants when she was around.

We'd made a poster to put up in the library about Home Education, offering help and contact to other families in the area. This was an attempt to try and make a big enough group nearer to home and lessen the miles on the road. I collared one of the smiley assistants and asked her to display it.

Despite me thinking they now understood what we were about she looked all awkward and went red when she read it.

"I'll have to ask the supervisor about putting it up first," she said. Back to the feeling we were doing something criminal. By the look on her face anyone would think I'd asked her to put up an advert for prostitution.

"Leave it with me, dear," she said tucking it underneath the counter out of sight and continuing to check out our mammoth pile of books.

Somehow I didn't think it would be up on the notice board when we next went.

Once home the girls were so keen to look at the books they'd brought I never planned anything for a library afternoon. Chelsea was immediately absorbed into reading and Charley and I plonked down on the settee in the shade as it was so hot outside. We had random books on Henry the Eighth, Deserts, Shakespeare, cloud formations and the sea. I used to worry that this was a bit of a hotch potch of learning but they put it all together with their marvellous self organising brain. I knew this from the questions.

"Henry the eighth was before queen Victoria wasn't he mum," asked Chelsea looking up from a Horrible History book.

"Yes darling," I said.

"And the Romans were before both of them?"

"Long before."

"Look at this mum," said Charley opening a book to create pop up farm with separate animals. "Could we make one?"

"I'm sure we could."

Chelsea came over to look. "That's cool!"

"We're going to make one," said Charley.

"Can I make one?" asked Chelsea.

"Course. You could make something different from a farm though, if you wanted. It could be anything, a shop perhaps," I suggested.

"I could make a fashion show one," said Chelsea.

The books were abandoned and the card and pens and scissors came out. We spent the whole of the afternoon drawing and painting and sticking, discussing technicalities and farming and fashion, and both of them concentrated on it for hours and produced beautiful pop-up books. They were completely chuffed. What better thing to learn than how to create within yourself a sense of satisfaction.

I had a sudden flashback to one of Charley's early school reports; 'Lacks concentration'. Like hell she does.

27

It was nearly midnight. I was just getting into that state of half sleep where thinking is fuzzed with bizarre things happening to my reality but giving in to it. My head was nestled on Charles' shoulder, body relaxed, and the phone rang. His shoulder whacked my cheekbone as we both jumped.

"Oh, no," he groaned. He'd had a spate of call-outs to work lately and it got a bit gruelling with early starts as well. I groped about over him to reach the phone. But it wasn't work. It was the alarm centre. Mum's alarm button had gone off. My reality became stark cold in an instant.

"Want me to go," Charles muttered from somewhere beneath the covers.

"No, no. You stay there. I'll phone you. Try to get some sleep." I fell out of bed and groped for some clothes.

"No chance, not until I know what's wrong."

"I can't believe she's fallen again." I hopped round the bedroom trying to get my jeans on.

"Let me know straight away, won't you?"

"Sure." I dragged on a fleece and raced off with my nightshirt hanging down my back and my wellies on bare feet.

Please, please, let her be alright. I was there in five minutes, just narrowly missed a fox and a heart attack as an owl swooped across the windscreen, white and ghostly.

I unlocked the door. The house was in darkness.

"Mum, mum?" I called. No answer.

I ran through the downstairs and surprised the dog who was as efficient at guarding the place as our guinea pigs. Still no answer but no body on the floor either – a good sign surely.

I kicked my wellies off and dashed upstairs. There was a gentle light coming from under her bedroom door. But I couldn't hear any sound because my heart was banging louder than Phil Collins on the drums.

"Mum?" I gently eased the door open almost too wimpish to look. She was snuggled down in bed on her side, covers up to her chin and her glasses right on the end of her nose, concentrating so hard on her book she hardly even noticed me. Then her face broke into a wonderful smile as I stepped into the room.

"Oh, hello darling," she said with such joy to see me, just like when I call round unexpectedly for a cup of tea.

"Are you okay?" I asked.

"Yes, fine. Just reading my book. You?" Then I saw it dawn on her that it was a rather odd time for a social visit. "What are you doing here? I thought you'd be in bed by now?"

"The alarm centre called me. You must have pressed your button."

"I didn't," she said very indignantly. "Look, it's there. I never touched it." It was hanging on her bedside light.

"Perhaps you caught it accidentally when you undressed," I said. "No matter. As long as you are alright."

"I'm fine, thanks for coming." Then she caught sight of my nightshirt hanging over my bottom and realised this might have been a tad inconvenient.

"Were you in bed?"

"Only just." I made light of it. But her face went all serious and upset.

"Oh I'm so sorry. What a nuisance this is going to be."

"Don't worry about it. It's okay. Really." I took her shaky hand and tried to put the smile back. "No worries, honestly. It's great you're okay. That's what matters. I'll leave you to your book and get back before Charles phones." I bent down and kissed her. It reminded me of tucking the children in. How roles reverse. But her smile didn't reappear.

"Stupid thing," she said crossly. "I won't touch it till morning. And I'll be ever so careful."

"Just make sure you put it on." I smiled reassuringly. I wasn't convinced that would happen. "Night mum!"

"Goodnight, sleep tight." I could see her plotting. My mind was on overdrive too and I was as stirred up as the owl disturbed from his night's hunting and watching me with his evil eye from the fence post. I hoped this wasn't going to be a precedent.

*

Back at the library misery guts hadn't put my poster up. I screwed up the courage to climb up past her bigotry with a brave effort.

"I wonder if you've had time to put my poster up?" I asked knowing full well it wasn't there.

"What poster?" She looked grumpy as hell.

"I left a poster with one of the other assistants with information about a local Home Education group for other families to see," I said. I smiled politely and hoped I was giving the girls a good example of social interaction. I suspected they might have guessed there was something seething underneath. Sometimes Home Educating split my personality.

"I don't know anything about a poster." She officiously moved books about and avoided looking at me as if that other side of my personality was showing and it had copious facial hair. I spotted the lady I gave it to.

"I handed it to that lady there," I said pointing. She looked, then shouted like a teacher would at an unruly pupil picking their nose.

"Moira. Moira? You know anything about this lady's poster?"

Moira looked as unhappy as a pupil actually caught picking their nose, in front of their classmates too for added misery.

"Yes, I showed it to you last week. I think you said you'd look at it later." Good old Moira.

"Well I don't remember seeing any poster." More officious shuffling of papers this time. Moira looked so extremely uncomfortable I hadn't the heart to continue.

"Okay, don't worry if you've mislaid it," I looked at the supervisor when I said that with an ever so slight emphasis on 'you'. "I'll bring another in next week when I come."

I turned away, winked at Moira who went very red and whispered something rude under my breath.

Once we got outside Charley asked, "Why is she a mean cow, mummy? And why did you wink at that lady?"

Perhaps I hadn't whispered under my breath after all. We had a lesson in social niceties on the way home.

*

The paper farm book was such a success that we opted to run the next group session on how to make them and adapted the idea to other topics. This meant we had to make several more prototypes that would appeal to the wide range of children who went to the group. So we made a paper jungle book, a paper shop book, a paper football pitch book and a paper ocean all with added pull out accessories. There'd been some mega creative thinking behind these projects not to mention mega blisters from all the cutting out.

The idea storming was tremendous, I loved it, especially watching the girls solve all the constructional problems and working out how to keep everything in reasonable perspective. Their thinking, design, inventive and manipulative skills, plus all the problem solving, exercised their little brains faster than a book of long division.

It dawned on me that it was exactly those kinds of challenges that kids needed to keep their thinking active and their brains exercised. And if their brains were exercised they would be able to apply themselves to academic activity when required.

In fact, it is thinking that this world needs. Creative and analytical thinking. For it is creative thinking that makes the world evolve, that makes our race evolve, that solves the problems of cures or inventions or makes discoveries, by thinking beyond the norm. The norm makes the world stand still. Creative thinking advances it. I actually cannot think of anything better that the children could be doing educationally than thinking through creative challenges in whatever form.

And one day all this creative thinking might be able to find a salve for blisters.

*

It was just as well we decided not to have more children. In our tiny cottage where every creak and grunt was heard it was almost impossible to create one.

We used to manage it when the kids were little and went to bed early. And when they got older and went to school we could slink upstairs in the daytime and make as much noise as we liked.

These days it was virtually impossible.

I was already tucked up when Charles climbed into bed beside me, nestled up and slipped a hand underneath my tee shirt.

"They're both asleep early," he said with heavily loaded innuendo.

"Mmmm, you sure?"

"Dead sure. I checked." The hand is roving.

"Mmmm, tempting. What if they wake up?" I turned towards him.

"You know they never wake up once they've crashed." He tried to drag the tee shirt off. The hand was hard to ignore.

"What if they hear us?" I asked in between mouthfuls of snogging.

"I've latched the bedroom doors."

"Didn't that wake them?" All doors creak in this house.

"No. I'm sure. I listened for ages."

We were fully engrossed by then. The tee shirt was off and he heaved over my side.

"Sure?" I asked almost past caring.

"Sure," he said with his mouth full and we both gave in.

But not quite completely as there was always that little tiny fear that we'd be discovered. What's that saying about self fulfilling prophecy?

As the climax of the activities approached like a tidal wave my alarm sensor went off with the slow creaking open of our bedroom door.

"Charles," I whispered manically and heaved him off me as unceremoniously as a sack of potatoes. It's amazing how much strength you have when you're panicked.

He groaned his way in anguish over to his side of the bed and curled up round his erection. And I tried to act as normal as you can with senses heightened and sweat all over.

"Mummy, I had a bad dream," said a tearful bod standing next to my bed in the dark as I yanked the bedclothes back round me.

"Did you darling?" I made sympathising noises, adopted the foetal position as I would for sleep and hoped she'd go away. When I peeped I could see Teddy tightly clutched under her chin. She wiped her nose on his head as she does in times of crisis. And carried on standing there...waiting.

After a minute; "What's up with daddy, he made a funny noise?"

"He had a bad dream too," I said. I kept my eyes shut in the hope it would be dismissive enough to work.

After a few more agonising seconds; "Mummy?"

I peeped. She had her best wretched look on.

"Yes?" I tried to sound ultra sleepy. I think frustrated better described it.

"Can I have a cuddle to take my bad dream away?"

I sighed. "Come on then." I lifted the covers and she slipped in beside me and curled up with her back to me in the warm cocoon of my arms folded round her.

Then her voice added brightly, but with the tone of admonishment I'd use when they did something disgusting in public . "Oh, mummy, you forgot to put your nightie on."

*

"Hey! Why does it have to be a man? Let's give it boobs!" Chelsea shrieked, getting well into the activity of helping to build the scarecrow for the allotment. The other kids thought this was hilarious and extended the laughter with imaginative variations on the theme.

We'd joined the group for the final meeting before the long summer break. They had a great allotment under way with lots of vegetables growing and decided a scarecrow would add a certain horticultural professionalism. Each family had brought something crafty to contribute to the making of it.

Two bubble wrap boobs were fashioned and stuffed up the tee shirt it was wearing. Someone produced some lipstick and got to work on the face. She also added big rosy cheeks and long painted lashes.

"She needs long hair."

"Here." The group coordinator produced some raffia and long tresses were made.

"What about earrings?" someone else suggested.

"Use these." Someone offered two shiny CDs and hey presto she had dangly earrings to scare the bravest old crow. More children gathered round to see what the shrieking and fun was about.

"She needs hips and a big bum," shouted one boy with a mother who had the same.

"And a handbag."

"She's not Tinky Winky off Teletubbies!"

"How about a hat with flowers on?"

"That's the tartiest looking scarecrow I've ever seen," laughed the coordinator. "I don't know what all those neatly dressed retired gentlemen at the allotment are going to think of it!"

"They'll just be jealous," I said.

"It can mate with the other scarecrows," shouted one boy. A group of them ran off no doubt to giggle about that concept further.

That finished we got on with the BBQ and summer party. I hardly got to see the girls for the rest of the afternoon. All the kids just played together, or sat around in little batches talking. Everyone brought something to contribute to the food but the kids were so engrossed with their fun half of it remained uneaten. The adults had the tough job of eating most of it.

It was great to be able to talk to others about our Home Educating life. When I was with them I got an injection of feeling that everyone is the same as me and that I wasn't some weirdo with peeling skin. That it's completely normal to educate your children without school, to have a learning family life rather than a school life which segregates it. It was only when all the other children appear on the streets again in late July that I remembered that life could be so entirely different. Our life goes on just the same with our children always in it. And it feels completely right.

28

The summer hung with the scent of abundant roses and we had strawberry taste on our tongues. I sat in the garden and talked to mum whilst the girls made scones indoors. I was told to keep out. My role would be the washing up. Charles had been dispatched to the shop to buy the cream.

The girls had set up a pretty table outside for a summer cream tea for grandma like she said she used to have. Mostly it was Chelsea who got the finer points of hosting it. Charley was more concerned with arranging a cluster of little animals to join us.

"Mum, where's your pendant?"

"Oh, that bloody thing. I hate it. Anyway I don't need it this afternoon, I'm with you, aren't I?" She sparkled at me. I couldn't be bothered to spoil the afternoon by saying anything.

"Besides, it makes me feel old," she added. I was about to say 'But you are old' when I thought how stupid that would be. Hope I don't feel old when I'm old. Perhaps it's just a culture of ageism that ages us anyway.

"What a perfect afternoon." She kind of sighed out blissfully, looking round the garden. The girls came running out.

"They're in the oven," said Charley.

"Ten minutes," Chelsea said sitting down next to grandma.

"Tell me a story of when you were little, grandma?" asked Charley. She climbed onto her knee.

"Well, Sundays were awfully boring. You're so lucky. I had to wear my best things and go to church and we had the vicar for tea. And I had to keep my gloves and hat on all the time even when it was hot like this."

"What else?"

"I had to sit with my cousin and behave nicely because you

weren't allowed to play on a Sunday?"

"Why not?" asked Chelsea.

"It was the Sabbath, a religious day. You had to sit and think about God and stuff. My mum was very old fashioned, not like yours." She beamed at me.

"I would hate that," said Charley.

"I hated it too. I wanted to climb trees like you do but I wasn't allowed. My cousin was a horrible boy too."

"Why?"

"He just was. He was spiteful. But maybe that was because I scratched his face!" Mum giggled mischievously. The girls shared it and giggled behind their hands. I tried to look disapproving as a parent should but couldn't really be bothered.

"Oh grandma," said Charley laughing with her at the naughtiness.

"Are those scones done yet?"

They raced off in their shorts and tee shirts, strawberry stains and grubby knees from the pick-your-own farm we'd been to earlier. No shoes on never mind hat and gloves.

"How different it is," said mum. She seemed wistful and sentimental. You must get to a point in life when you realise there's more behind you than in front. Perhaps she was nostalgic and missing it. I squeezed her hand. She twinkled a smile at me and squeezed my hand back.

"Good job too," she added. "They were such a lot of boring old farts in those days!"

*

I switched on the telly at breakfast.

"No telly in the day, you said," Chelsea reminded me.

"I'm just looking at the forecast. Thunderstorms. Great! Just what we need for the group picnic."

"Don't worry, it might not happen," said Charles looking at the forecast over my shoulder. He's always much more laid back about everything than me. Sometimes he's so laid back it's hard to tell if he's upright.

With all the favourite places teeming with school children in the holidays the group made the long journey over to our house for a get together. This is fine in good weather, but our cottage is like the Tardis in reverse; it looks bigger on the outside than it is indoors. If we have to have everyone inside it could be Sardines.

The girls had organised a 'Gallery' in the garage and everyone was been told to bring something they'd created or invented to exhibit. They swept the grunge and dead leaves off the floor, pinned up their own exhibits and arranged a table for models. Indoors Charles and I pushed all the furniture and the big kitchen table we work at back to the walls to make more floor space. And I even excelled myself and did some edible baking for once. And the morning stayed dry.

It was still dry as everyone arrived. Some had never been before and there were exclamations about 'out in the wilds' and 'back of beyond' and some poor city folks wouldn't let their kids take their shoes off and run on the grass because of germs. But mostly everyone loved the place and relaxed and went up trees and down dykes and explored the meadow and the Hut construction and had a fab time. Even the parents. Then relaxed in the garden and chomped their way through their picnics so were sadly too full to manage my flapjacks. But I suppose they did look a bit like bricks.

Mum popped in to meet everyone. I am always proud to show off my lovely mum.

And the weather only gave up being dry and summery towards the end when there was an almighty clap and rain drummed down like a waterfall.

"Can we stay out in it mum?" asked Charley, already pretty well soaked. She wouldn't normally ask but other children were being called in. Except my Home Ed best friend's boys who were out there too.

"Sure, don't get wet." I grinned at her. Chelsea joined them but she had her umbrella. Charley had started an exodus.

"Can I go out, mum?" asked another kid. Then another. And so on, until there was a whole crowd of screaming children running around in the rain with no shoes on. This left me inside with the parents all staring from the windows. If I hadn't been the host I would have joined in with the kids outside.

"Hasn't it been a great day," I said to the girls as we waved the last of the soggy families off into the reappearing sunshine.

"Yea, did you see Ted's model?" said Chelsea.

"It was great, wasn't it," I said picking up the remains of soggy pictures left behind in the garden.

"And Em's drawing of her guinea pig."

"Talking of guinea pigs, you'd better go and bring them in, they'll be soaked."

They were soaked. But seemed happy and squeaked crossly when we put them back in the cage.

Indoors the floor was streaked with mud. I had to break the habit of a lifetime and mop it over whilst Charles and the girls finished up outside. I took some leftovers outside to them while it dried and we found a dry place to sit finish nibbles.

"Nick told me he wasn't supposed to take his shoes off, isn't that weird," said Charley, crunching flapjack while holding a sausage roll.

"That's funny because when we go to his house we're not allowed to keep them on!" said Chelsea. She still sat under her umbrella even though the sun was shining.

"That's what I hated most about school," said Charley.

"What?"

"Having to wear shoes."

She climbed onto my lap, nestled down into me with that

contented sigh kids do best. And I rested my lips on her hair and breathed in that magic scent of child.

*

As soon as the school children go back parents walk about town with the step lighter than it's been for ages. And some look at my two as if they were contaminating their space. It used to make me angry. Now I love it – love the freedom in our education.

"Not started back yet then?" asked the girl beeping our shopping at the supermarket checkout.

"No we don't go to school," said Charley.

"Oh! Don't yer!" said the till girl winking at me and smiling patronisingly.

"No we're Home Educated," said Chelsea helping her sister out.

The patronising smile vanished. She'd been caught out; Home Education didn't have a bar code.

"What's that when it's at 'ome then?" she asked.

The girls looked up at me. They didn't get the question.

"It means what they say; they don't go to school. They do all their learning at home," I explained. I hastily stuffed shopping in the bags. Then smiled at her as patronisingly as she had the girls.

"Oo-er, I didn't know you could do that. Is it legal?" she asked as she slid the cat food across the scanner.

"Yes, quite a few families Home Educate now."

"Oo-er!" she said again looking at the girls to see if you could tell. Then she added, "I wish I could've done that, I 'ated school. And I was useless. Couldn't wait to get out. I learned meself more after I left school than I did in it."

"Yes, a lot of people say that." I lifted the heavy bag into the trolley. Chelsea picked up the bag of cat biscuits and Charley clung tightly to the crisps.

"My youngest, he 'ates school an all," she said. She didn't look old enough to have a youngest or an oldest or even a baby never mind children of school age. But it was hard to tell under the crust of make up.

"Oh, dear, that's a shame."

"But I couldn't learn 'im at 'ome. I don't know nuffink!"

I wanted to say 'you know enough to hold down this job which is more than many'. But I wanted to get out of there even more so I smiled and we pushed the trolley away from the till.

"Bye girls. 'Ave a good Home Education," she called after us with genuine good humour. The other bored shoppers in the queues all looked towards us too in case they were missing something. They were; their children!

*

Two years Home Educating! Where did they go? We were having such a nice time we didn't notice it.

But for my best friend it's gruelling all the way.

"Whatever's the matter?" I asked. She sounded so upset over the phone.

"I've just come from that bloody school and that bloody bitch of an assistant head. Can you believe? She's the head's wife. How can that be good? She should never have got the job. She has about as much understanding of children as I have of space technology. And you know what she's just said to me? 'There's no such thing as dyslexia'. I so could not believe it, I couldn't even speak."

"I'm stunned. I can't believe it, either. After all the coverage there is now about it."

"It's true. She said there's no such thing and if my son's not picking up what he needs in lessons then he's not paying attention."

My breath kind of squeaked out. "My god, what on earth did you say?"

"I said whether he's paying attention or not it's not going to help because he cannot read the stuff on the board and he can't copy it down quickly enough because he keeps losing where he's up to and they don't give him enough time. So I asked her to send the text books home and you know what she said?" I could almost sense anger spit coming down the line.

"She said they don't give the lower streams text books because there's no point, they don't read them anyway, and there's not enough to buy for everyone so the A stream get them."

I think I kind of grunted. "Bloody hell!"

"It's true. And when I pressed her to tell me which books they used and I'd buy my own copies she said I was making too much fuss over it. Too much fuss? For Christ's sake I only want to help him learn – which they should be doing." She couldn't speak for a moment. I heard her swallowing her upset and trying to keep from crying.

"Did you get a reference for the book? Maybe I've got a copy," I said, I so wanted to help.

"I got it from the form teacher in the end. I feel so upset. She looked down her snotty nose at me as if I was shit."

"Aw! I'm so sorry. What you going to do now."

"I'll get the books and I'll go over the lessons like I said I would, despite what the bitch says. If I can just get the syllabus."

"You could get it online. You've got a better connection than us haven't you? I'm thinking we'll have to switch to broadband soon as this dial up's a right pain and we're using the computer more and more. The Net's amazing, isn't it? It's all on there, have a look. Soon we won't have need of teachers!" I joked.

She didn't brighten. "I don't know what else to do. The only other school is the Grammar and it's no good him going there."

"Well, if it's any consolation my other friend's having just as much trouble as her daughter's so bright they're just hot housing her through the academic subjects and won't let her do what she wants to do. Her mum thinks it's too much, she never gets time for her outside interests as she's got too much homework and she says the school are just using her to bump their position up the league tables."

"I reckon that's all the bloody schools care about; the league tables."

"Hmmm – well you know what I think!" I managed to get her laughing again.

I came off the phone mighty glad that we don't have that hassle. Especially as Chelsea would be coming up to doing the eleven plus. Several of her friends are getting stressed about it and putting that stress onto her.

"Mum, what's the Eleven Plus?" she asked me the other day while we were catching up on the entries in their travel books. We'd had another trip to London to record and to Isaac Newton's house where we'd had a great day doing experiments.

It's a kind of exam, darling, and whether you pass or not determines which school you go to next."

"Don't you get to choose schools then?" She stopped sticking in and looked at me.

"No, not really."

"That doesn't sound fair." She carried on arranging her book page. "Will I do the Eleven Plus?"

"We hadn't thought you would. Not unless you felt you wanted to. We don't think it's valuable to your education really and you seem to be learning a lot without doing it."

"That's not what Jen at drama said." She looked a bit awkward.

"Why, what's Jen said?" I asked feeling alarm building.

"She said if I didn't do the Eleven Plus I'd be stupid and not learn anything or get anywhere in life." She looked at me to see what the reaction would be.

Calm yourself before you answer, I thought, before steam comes out your ears which is always a giveaway.

"Wow. Did she indeed. And what does she know about it, she's only eleven isn't she? Now, let's think about this. You've already said some of the girls at drama group don't seem to know as much as you even though they go to school, haven't you? And you do seem to be learning an awful lot, don't you?" I smiled at her. She nodded, smiling back, looking a bit smug and a lot easier.

"And me and your dad are quite happy with what you're learning without the Eleven Plus or school. Now I suspect that Jen's mum and dad probably want her to do really well at school and they've told her things that will make her work hard like 'do well in the Eleven Plus or you won't be clever' because that's what some parents think and that's what Jen's said to you. But the real truth is that doing the Eleven Plus doesn't make any difference to whether you're clever or not. Lots of folks don't know that."

She ginned and went back to the sticking and writing bits down.

"The thing is darling, if you want to go to school or do the Eleven Plus like the other children that's absolutely fine. We can arrange that. You let us know if you'd like to go try school again, won't you?"

"I don't. Jen hates it actually, she's always saying she does and wished she could be Home Educated like me." She looked happily at me.

"Well there you are then."

"Next time anyone says anything like that I'll just tell them I'm learning more out of school than I did in it. I never seemed to do as much as we do at home and it wasn't nearly as much fun."

"And perhaps you could tell them there are lots of different ways to get educated too."

"Yea, I will. Look, do you like my London page?" She held up her book as if the conversation didn't matter any more. She just needed the right things to say.

"I love it!" I said. And I love Home Educating these brilliant kids.

29

I walked across the open stubble fields to mum's. There was a beautiful muted lustre about the still ranks of stalks left from the harvest that perfectly described the peace of autumn after the succulence of summer. It was chill enough to need a coat but balmy enough not to worry that winter was too close for comfort. The curlews called and the berries shone with brilliance.

Mum was in the greenhouse squatting down in the corner trying to catch a rat.

"Blasted thing! It's gone now, look, there's a brick missing there, where it sneaks in and eats my plants."

"Let's get it sealed up then. You don't want rats in, mum."

"Oh, I don't mind really. Besides, it gives the dog something to do." She struggled to her feet. "Tea?"

"Mmmm, please. Tell you what; I'll make you one!" We settled down for a little natter. Her alarm pendant was nowhere to be seen."

"Oh that thing. Makes me feel worried wearing it. All the fuss and bother it creates. I was better off without it," she said. I had been down twice more to false alarms.

"But isn't it worth it, in case you fall again?"

"I'm not going to fall again. It was the dog tripped me up. How often have I fallen over? Anyway, if I was to fall it's more likely to be out walking and it's no good for that is it?"

She was distracted a moment by more scrabbling under a plant pot. Then carried on.

"I don't think it's doing me any good at all. I'm forever worrying about setting it off and am being so stiff and careful I'm more likely to trip than before I had it. Wish I'd never got it. Who's it for anyway?" She looked directly at me as if I should be guilty for something.

"What do you mean?"

"Well, is it for my peace of mind or everyone else's because I have peace of mind without the damn button." Again there was that slightly accusational stare.

"I just didn't want you lying hurt again, like before," I said.

"It didn't matter. I knew if I waited someone would come." She paused, listening. Then went on. "You know, I never once worried about lying hurt before I had this thing now I think about it all the time. I was definitely better off before." She got up, picked up a brush and swept spilled earth and dried leaves across the greenhouse floor making clouds of gritty dust. She must be agitated. She's not usually prone to sweeping up.

She'd started me thinking. Was she right? Who was the button for? Who was most fussed about it? Had I pushed her into something she didn't want just for my own peace of mind?

"Well, if you feel like that mum," I said slowly, "maybe you shouldn't wear it. Perhaps you should just go on as you were before."

She looked at me with the glee of a school kid let out early, then tossed the brush down leaving the little pile of sweepings where they were and sat down again.

"I was fine before," she said enthusiastically. "One fall and everybody panics."

She was right again. Everybody was panicking – everybody except her! Besides, we speak every day. I could always ring to check she was back from her walk and then to say goodnight or something. I suggested it.

"What, you mean I have a curfew!" She tilted her head back, giggling. "Okay darling, if it makes you feel better," she said, twinkling at me again. I laughed. I'd been outmanoeuvred.

"Don't look so worried. I'm fine. Honest." She got up from the table, scuffed the pile of silt, giggled, and came round to give me a hug.

"I must go," I said. I got up, went through the kitchen and tripped over the rag rug.

"Perhaps you should have an alarm button on," she said and dissolved into more giggles before rushing off to the loo making popping noises.

*

I was sure I was becoming more flexible at yoga. My body could flex into places it never knew existed.

I just wished it was as easy to control my mind. Instead of concentrating on clenching and unclenching each muscle as we were supposed to be doing, I was thinking about tomorrow's dinner, next week's education, and our forthcoming trip to see the Lion King on stage with the London Home Educators. So it seemed to be stuck in the same old ruts.

At least I can clench enough not to fart. Unlike my mum!

*

The group session with the pop out books was a great success. All the kids were inspired to make one whether they were sixteen or six. The variations on the theme were inspirational. Kids have such brilliant ideas – if they can get away from their parents controlling their ideas all the time. Sometimes I think kids could educate themselves all on their own. After all, they see what adults do and they want to do the same whether this is reading, driving, working, earning or using the mobile and they want to be part of it. Why would they not want to become educated? Only when education is so dull it has no appeal.

It certainly wasn't dull during this group session. And the variety of subjects involved to invent, design and produce the books was beyond imagination. Who needs subjects to be bound? Who needs time boundaries and age boundaries and curriculum boundaries? Kids don't.

Trouble was my kids were becoming too good at making everything they wanted to do 'educational' like mum did, just so I didn't suggest more boring approaches. Goes to show how boring my ideas can be. We were about to have an indoor day. Charley was ahead of me already.

"Mum? You know it's reading on our list this morning?"

"Ye-es?" Why do I sense being outwitted?

"Well, I thought I'd do mine on that English CD Rom.

I immediately wanted to resist and make reading 'proper' as in sitting tidily and reading a book. Then I thought; she's reading on the CD Rom isn't she, she's enjoying it, she's learning. I stepped back and got out of the way.

"Okay, darling, go on then."

We'd got maths on our list next. Chelsea had a workbook out. She still likes to keep a parallel with her school mates. Charley had a different approach.

"Mu-um? You know it's maths on the list next?"

"Ye-es?"

"We-ll, I thought I'd get my Lego out and make a chart."

I had to admire her ingenuity.

The afternoon's list had crafts. Charley as usual wanted to do something that would create the most mess. She had foot painting in mind. I didn't worry too much, I've seen foot artists manipulating the brush with their toes. She can give that a go if she wishes. It'll keep her occupied whilst I help Chelsea with some more complicated sewing.

Out of my eye corner I saw Charley get out a massive piece of card, bigger than her, which were old advertising posters Charles brought home from work, then she sat down, took her socks off, and painted the bottom of her foot. Despite the desire to hover I tried not to interfere until I was suddenly conscious it had gone quiet.

"What's wrong?" I asked. She was frowning.

"I can't get to my card without walking over the carpet." Foot painting meant walking paint about with her feet. I laughed and got up to carry her across to her card.

"You could have crawled on your hands and knees," said Chelsea looking up from the heap of fabric in front of her.

"Oh, yea!" Charley used all the paint then crawled back for more. I spread some newspaper then moved the paints nearer. She was obviously too busy to bother with the obvious.

"Do you want a go?" she asked Chelsea, catching her watching.

"No way, it's disgusting. Besides, I'm making a skirt."

That sounded a bit ambitious. Was I up to that? Charley sorted I went to help – or was that interfere?

"Wow, is that the fabric you're using? Where's your drawing?"

"What drawing?" Chelsea asked as she wielded scissors big enough to head fish with.

"You need to draw it first, see how it's going to work out."

"I'm not going to draw it; I'm going to make it."

"All the designers sketch their designs out first."

"No they don't."

"I think they do darling." I should have kept out of it.

"No, mum, they don't. I've just been reading Versace's autobiography and he was a top designer and he couldn't draw. All he used to do was drape the cloth round his models and work from there." She draped the fabric round herself. I felt past may sell by date.

*

Our next group meeting was at the recycling centre. It was like an Aladdin's Cave. A warehouse heaped with every imaginable load of junk that's been kept for reuse. A small group fee and we can take what we like. This was where Charley restocked her paint hoard with tubs and tubs of little test pots whilst Chelsea headed for the textiles.

"Just one bagful each," I called, hoping for once it would work. We had enough of these materials to do art work for a lifetime.

There was everything from massive cardboard tubes to treasure chests of buttons, bags of shredded paper to plastic cones which made me sense another robot coming on. There are balls of wool and braids, magazines and foil trays. Even I started drooling myself when I spotted some off cuts of beautiful water colour paper. We were more over laden than when we went to the library.

"It's all very well," laughed one dad. "But where do you put it all?"

"Yea, that's the trouble. Our house already seems to be bursting at the seams. It's not only the materials it's all the artwork they do too. Our walls are covered with pictures of footprints at the moment." I looked at my two struggling to get bottle tops and cotton reels in already bursting bags. Charley had found the wall paper paste – that meant more paper mache.

"It's brilliant though, isn't it?" I added. "To think all this stuff would otherwise be thrown away, yet in their hands it becomes something creative."

"It might still be thrown away," he whispered, grinning furtively as his son grabbed a handful of plastic cups and stuffed them in his bag. "If we Home Educate much longer we'll have to move to a bigger house."

I knew the feeling; Chelsea had found a mountain of glittery card just right for Christmas.

*

Home Educating seemed so right and normal I forgot there was another world everyone else inhabited. At the clubs the Christmas present one-upmanship had started.

"I'm getting skiing Barbie for Christmas," I heard one kid say whilst I was waiting to collect the girls.

"I'm getting Princess Barbie," said another.

Who's getting Braindead Barbie? I wondered.

"I'm getting a Lego Starship. It has a zillion pieces and costs nearly £100," said one boy trying to outdoor the Barbie mania.

"I'm getting a telly for my bedroom," topped the next voice.

"I'm getting my own computer." It was never ending.

I was glad the girls were out of all that. Besides, our one income wouldn't stretch to that kind of competition. But although budget was a constant worry, the girls didn't seem to hanker for much. Give them a bag of buttons from Restore and you'd think you'd spent a million pounds on them. Perhaps it was because they didn't have to maintain that materialistic image some communities create. Sometimes I wonder if it's the schools which are breeding grounds for consumerism, probably in cahoots with big commercial companies – they certainly were with the vending machines. But I still worried I was depriving the girls.

Chelsea's laughter which resounded about the foyer where I waited didn't sound deprived. Gratitude swelled my heart so fiercely I feared it must be showing.

When they appeared among the throng I grabbed them both and kissed them.

"What's that for?" asked Chelsea, still giggling and only half pushing me away.

"Er, because you like buttons," I said grinning mysteriously. They looked at each other and raised their eyebrows in a sufferance parents usually endure.

"She's getting as funny as grandma," said Charley. Chelsea erupted into giggling again.

I sure hoped so!

30

With it being our third year of kids at home full time around Christmas you'd think we'd have engineered a plan for secrets. We decided we'd try honesty and appeal to their mature natures now that they were eleven and eight.

"Your dad and I are just going upstairs for a while and it's important you don't disturb us. Have you got things to do?"

"What for?" There was a little twinkle in Chelsea's eye as she asked which reminded me distinctly of mum.

"It's a secret," I said smiling.

"A Christmas secret?" asked Charley also grinning now and knowing exactly what we were up to.

"Maybe," said their dad. He tried to be mysterious but the girls are too clever for him. "So you won't disturb us, will you?"

"Maybe!" returned Chelsea copying him and Charley smirked.

We went upstairs and de-hid all their presents from our various drawers.

"Do you think they'll disturb us?" said Charles, cutting paper on the slant and wrestling to find the end of the sticky tape.

"I don't think so, but look, we'll turn back the bedcovers then if they come up whilst we're wrapping we'll throw the duvet over everything." You have to be inventive when you're a Home Educator.

"Do you remember doing this when they were at school," I said.

"Yea, life was easy then," he said grinning and spitting sticky tape from between his teeth.

"What? You think tears and illness every day were easy?" We laughed. I wrapped. He stuck. If he was in charge of the wrapping all the presents would look like parcels of fish and chips.

"No, it was awful. I can't believe we've done this as long as we have. It just seems so ordinary now. You should hear the others at work going on about homework and packed lunches and stuff. Not to mention Christmas concert practises. They're complaining the kids aren't getting on with their learning" He stuck my finger to the parcel.

I extricated it and reached for some ribbon.

"I can imagine. Do they say anything about ours then?"

"Only how they can see why we do it." He put his massive thumb on the delicate bow I created, squishing it. I tied his thumb down.

"Not enough for them to have a go though!" I laughed. Then the stairs creaked. Charles leapt off the bed, smacked his head on the sloping ceiling but still managed to toss the duvet over the presents as I stuffed the paper under the bed. We sat there and listened. Sniggering was coming from the landing.

"Go away," Charles called.

"We're not coming in, we're only going to our rooms." The giggling got fainter. We exchanged looks. Charles sneaked a peek through a crack in the old planked door.

"What they doing?" I whispered.

"They've gone into their bedrooms but their doors are open."

"Let's carry on. I don't think they'll come in. They wouldn't want to spoil their Christmas surprises. Besides, I think Chelsea's becoming aware of other things that go on in bedrooms!"

Charles raised his eyebrows in glee. "In that case, perhaps we should make good use of it."

"What? You think you could enjoy sex with giggling going on at the bedroom door and creaking floorboards?" We laughed like naughty kids but continued wrapping.

"What you laughing at?" came from right outside the door. We bundled the duvet back over everything once more.

"Never you mind. Go back downstairs," I shouted. I crept over and peeped to see if there was any peeping coming from the other side the crack. None.

"Come on, let's get it done before they come up again." The rest were wrapped in haste and I fear my parcels looked like fish and chips too.

*

Charley looked shocked and uncomfortable. Her face was full of both thunder and distress and very red. Her eyes looked like they were going to fill up any minute. She turned her head away and would not look at Charles or me either.

Chelsea just folded her arms across her chest, adopted her most disdainful position and stated emphatically "If anyone asks; you are not my dad."

Charles couldn't help it. All the staff were told to dress up for the Christmas market for charity but the girls weren't impressed. And Charley absolutely hated anyone dressed up in costume. I got a bit of a shock myself seeing this large rotund red fellow with two cushions up his jacket and his face adorned with a mass of flowing white stuff. It's very off-putting seeing someone who you are as familiar with as your own body parts taking on another persona. He was sweating so much the bits of his face you could see were authentically shining as Santa's does in all the pictures. It did the trick. A good crowd had gathered at the store and money was being thrown continually in the charity bucket.

"God, I keep losing my trousers," he said grabbing a handful of red bottom and hoisting it up. I couldn't help laughing.

"I knew you'd laugh," he said.

"Sorry, I'm not laughing at you, it's just your trousers." I tried to help. But grappling with Santa's trousers seemed even funnier. Obviously everyone else thought so too as two more pounds went in the bucket. It's not every day people see Santa being groped.

"Do you have to behave like that?" demanded Chelsea, standing holding Charley's hand a little bit distant whilst we tried to control our hysteria. She still wouldn't look at him.

"Have a sweetie," said Charles holding out the bucket to her.

"No!"

"It's only a bit of fun," I said.

"You look stupid."

I didn't care, I was in the Christmas spirit. I had a quick snog with Santa and left him to his collecting.

"We'll go look round the Christmas Market. See you later."

"Okay. See you later girls." They ignored him and pulled me away. But Chelsea called back over her shoulder.

"Save us some sweeties, dad."

We bought a few Christmas presents and then had to get some new wellies for Chelsea. Charley just got the hand-me-downs but she was still at the stage where anything of Chelsea's was revered. Wellies had taken on a new persona of their own in the shops. They were more pictorial than the efforts we see in the Tate Modern and a hell of a price. I refused to be ripped off, plus the fact we had tight budgets. But Chelsea ogled the bright ones wistfully.

"I'm sorry darling, these will have to do. The others are just too expensive," I said picking up the plain green ones, the cheapest we could find. I felt a bit wretched about this. In order to Home Educate, time isn't the only thing we sacrifice and all I ever seem to say is 'we can't afford it'. But she's so intuitive she must have picked up on it.

"It doesn't matter mum. I'll paint my own with the paints we got from the recycling centre."

I was so grateful for her magnitude I cuddled her up. "What a brilliant idea! And I bet they'll be better than any in the shops."

"Yea, and no one else will have any the same," she said looking at a girl wearing some we'd just seen in Woolworths.

"Can I paint mine too?" asked Charley.

"Sure. We'll have a wellie painting session. We could even paint your dad's," I said winking at them. They really liked that idea.

When we went back later Charles looked his normal self again. He opened his arms to Charley and she leapt into them with clear relief. Chelsea lobbed her arms round his waist.

"Is that better now?" he asked carrying Charley to the car. She inspected him slightly doubtfully. Chelsea smiled happily up at him holding the free hand.

"You did look daft, dad," she giggled.

"Did you remember the sweets?" asked Charley.

He put her down and produced a packet from his pocket. Finally Charley grinned at him too. It was definitely better now.

*

"Mum! You can't go out like that," Chelsea said as I tied tinsel on my shoes ready for a Christmas party.

"Why not? It's Christmas isn't it." I looked at her in feigned indignation. She'd got that suffering look on again.

"Doh! What do you look like?" She was getting to be a right Tweenager.

"I think you look nice," said Charley clasping my leg in a cuddle from the carpet where she was building a structure with our logs.

"Well at least put some lipstick on," said Chelsea still trying to make something out of me. She rummaged in a make up bag so extensive it would be the envy of Julian Clary. "How about this?" She produced something nearly black.

"Black?" I shrieked. "It's Christmas, not Halloween."

"It's not black, it's plum."

"I'll have some," said Charley hopefully. She was ignored. I sneaked a look in the bag of sticky powdery tubs and jars and pencils. It staggered me how she loved it so, I wasn't into it at all. But I humoured her and found a jar of lovely sparkly glittery gluey stuff with sequin stars in.

"Ooo, this is nice." I opened the pot and smeared some across my chest. It made grubby stains as if I hadn't washed for a week. "Oh!" I looked in the mirror, disappointed.

"Oh, mum, not like that." Chelsea took over and I had the sense our mother and daughter roles were reversing. She wiped it about and the smudges disappeared leaving a myriad of glistening sparkles. Then she added the sequins.

"Can I have some?" asked Charley again, thinking her sister had softened her attitude.

"No!" was the emphatic retort.

"Can I have some then?" asked Charles.

"NO!" they both shrieked together. And gave us their parents-are-prats look.

We finished getting ready.

"So do we look alright now?" I asked.

"Yes." They smile united. But I couldn't help a last word.

"You know it's not how you look, it's what's inside that counts."

"Yes, we know!"

They know too much, my kids.

*

"Mum, what's wrong with her? Why is she making that noise?" asked Charley as we had our last swim before the schools break for Christmas. There was a group of children and young adults from a special school with their carers in the pool who were making loud noises.

"Don't point darling, it's rude. She's just finding swimming difficult. It scares her."

We worked round the splashing and uncoordinated swimming.

"She looks different to other people," said Charley. Chelsea was looking embarrassed by her sister.

"Shhh, Charley," she said.

"She is different. We're all different," I said.

Chelsea butted in. "It's not how people look it's what's inside that counts."

Where had I heard that before? Perhaps she understood that despite the bag of make up. And we were all pared down in the pool. Couldn't pretend to be anything other than our naked selves. Didn't have any extra trappings other than who we were.

Not quite though as Chelsea spotted. "Mum, you've still got sparkles on your chest."

*

Christmas continued sparkly all the way through.

The best thing about it was the painted wellies. They were works of art fit for exhibiting in The Tate themselves, with swirls and colours and rainbows. If I'd bought the coloured ones we never would have had such creativity. Being on a tight budget certainly makes you think creatively so maybe I shouldn't worry after all. Charley painted gold stars on hers. But she painted straight over the mud so the stars had a brown tinge.

Charles and I used the 'holiday' from education to ignore the children and just live life. But it didn't work. We didn't want it to really. We were a family, we were a team. Life and education were as indistinguishable from one another as our family and love. I suspected it always would be.

31

Every time all the other kids went back to school I felt a sense of celebration that ours were not. Despite the fact it was hard sometimes.

Back at the library as we got back into a routine of mammoth book piles again our poster was up. It lasted two weeks before it disappeared again. I couldn't be bothered to fight about it. Home Education was obviously something the miserable cow in there had a problem with. I wasn't going to make it my problem. But it was a shame because there were always flurries of inquiries every time a new term started.

The problems that drove families to Home Educate were repeated over and over; bullying, child unhappy, ill or school phobic, apparent learning difficulties, attitudes of teachers, parents unhappy about the increasing focus on testing, worry about poor schools. Funnily enough many of these 'problems' disappeared once out of school. You'd think the government would twig they'd got a problem with schools, which is why they'd now got a problem monitoring all the Home Educators. Instead of making it difficult for parents to Home Educate, they'd be better off asking why so many feel the need to do so.

I sat upstairs reading and practising being 'out of bounds'. I came across a wonderful sentence that said some people go through life and some people *grow* through life. I couldn't think of a better way to describe the difference between school children and Home Educating children's learning lives. And even better; it was the parents who got to see the growing.

I went downstairs to see how my two were growing and there was earth all over the kitchen table.

"What you up to Charley?"

"I'm making a wormery," she said filling a tall glass jar with soil.

"And what you doing Chelsea?"

"I'm planting these apple seeds to see if they'll grow." She picked the pips out of her apple core and pushed them in her pot full of soil.

"I need some worms," said Charley. I looked out the window at Charles who was fiddling with the lawn mower wishing on an early spring.

"Your dad's out there, get him to help you find some." She yanked on her half painted wellies and went out. Chelsea finished her planting.

"I'm going on the computer now mum."

"Okay, what you going to do?"

"That maths CD Rom. Will you help me? I can't do it very well."

"Sure. Get it booted up and I'll come."

I spent some ten minutes trying to excavate the kitchen table when I heard crying coming from the study.

"Whatever's the matter, darling." I gave her a hug.

"It's not fair. Charley can do this and it's for older kids than her but I can't," she sobbed.

"Show me what you're doing." I looked at the screen.

"I can't get past this bit."

"Why don't you just try the cursor on something and see what happens?"

"I might get it wrong."

"But it doesn't matter. When you get things wrong you know how to get it right after."

She wiped her hand over her eyes. "You think I should?" she said tentatively.

"Yea, that's how Charley does it. She just tries any old thing till she gets it right. She's not bothered if it's wrong."

She pressed Enter. It was wrong. "No, it's this one," she said getting it right next time.

"That's it. Carry on. Which of these decimals is the same as two tenths?"

"I think it's that one."

"Try it then."

She did. As I sat with her she got braver and braver. She got beyond that old feeling of shame she had, left over from school, for getting things wrong. She'd been made to stand up in front of the whole class for missing the L out of play. That was when she was seven. She still cried about it when she told me at nine. Charley had not been in school long enough to endure that kind of shame. Thank god. The concept of wrong has no judgement attached for her.

"You can get it wrong as many times as you need to in order to get it right, you know," I said to Chelsea. "It really doesn't matter. What matters is you keep going till you find the right one. Give it a go."

She was pressing buttons like a typist and racing through it now.

"Call me if you need any more help." I returned to the soil. It had worms too now. Charley was watching them wriggle about on the table. I glanced at the book she was using to help her make her wormery and read up how to look after worms, as if guinea pigs weren't enough. Half an hour later I heard 'whoopie' come from the study.

I went through. "How's it going," I asked, peering over her shoulder.

"I've gone up two levels. I'm ahead now." She was beaming right across her face.

"Amazing what you can achieve by getting it wrong, isn't it?"

We giggled together as if we were doing something clandestine.

*

Mum was much better without her panic button. It was only me that panicked when there was no answer to the curfew call. But I was beginning to understand she wasn't going to keep to times, she'd no need to, the night and day and the seasons were the way time was described for her.

I'd rushed down the other morning. It was pouring with rain and she wasn't answering the phone.

"She can't be out with the dog in this, surely," I said to Charles.

"Nip down and see, I don't have to go for half an hour," he said pulling his tie into place.

Mum's house was empty. No mum. No dog. No answering call. No sign of life in the garden either. As I went out of the gate mum came staggering up the muddy track with her boots and her outdoor gear on. Her hood framed her damp and smiling face, wet dripped off the edges and a rain drop decorated the end of her nose.

"What a morning," she gasped cheerily as if it was a brilliant sunny day. She wiped the drip on the back of her gardening glove.

"You haven't been gardening, have you?" I asked slipping my arm in hers as she negotiated the slippery pathway. I wouldn't have put it past her.

"No, these gloves were all I could find this morning. Phew, let's get in and get warm. What you up to?" We went through the gate getting showered in drips from the overgrowth.

"I just came to see if you were okay."

"Why, what's the time?" She took her soaking coat off and shook it spraying us all with a fresh shower.

"Half eleven."

"Goodness! I thought it was only about ten o'clock. No wonder I'm whacked. I must have been out longer than I thought."

"You sit down, I'll make the coffee." I went into the kitchen. There was a disconcerting scrabbling from the skirting board.

"If I sit down, I'll not want to get up again." She went into the living room and made up her fire.

"Sounds like a good plan to me." I laughed.

In fifteen minutes her fire was going and her neighbours turned up. They'd brought her a piece of cake to try. They often swapped recipes. But since they were rather particular I wondered if mums' offerings went straight to the birds. The bits with the hairs in anyway.

I left them laughing together and went back to the girls. She was surrounded by love and created happiness whomever she was with.

*

I must have been mad agreeing to visit The Wetlands Centre on a freezing day late February that promised to be spring like but felt more like an arctic winter. I had so many layers on I could hardly move my arms let alone lift binoculars to my eyeballs. Not sure if my frozen fingers could focus them when they got there either.

Most of the group turned out too, as hardy – or foolhardy – as me for the sake of Home Education. Thinking longingly of the coffee shop we trundled into the posh looking hide to a groan from all the ardent Twitchers already in there. Their faces dropped before they could get their expressions hidden again behind their massive magnifying extensions. They all looked as if they were trying to outdo each other with equipment. I hardly dare get our plastic binoculars out.

Thankfully our lot ceased their excited gabbling as they saw the hundreds of swans gathered just outside the hide on the water.

"Mum, mum, look."

"Shush, darling, you have to be really quiet or we'll frighten them." This is repeated throughout the other parents. Then the warden comes in to give us a 'Talk'.

I'm not sure who switched off first; me or the children. There is nothing more boring than someone so in love with their own self importance they can expertly kill any interest about the subject in everyone else.

I thought the children did really well to have listened enough to be able to ask questions. I wasn't listening. I was thinking that this person was everything that was wrong for kids about some teachers; patronisingly thinking you're the only one who knows stuff, abusing a position of power, expecting respect without earning it, thinking it is enough to know and everyone should revere that, forcing info on others without giving them choice, attempting to keep kids down. He irritated me so intensely I glazed over. Then I caught my Home Ed best friend staring at me. She winked, crossed her eyes and raised them to the ceiling. My irritation was overtaken with the bubbling desire to laugh. Mercifully he finished at that point and we all escaped for the hot chocolate.

The girls really enjoyed it though because they spent all the next morning on recording it in their travel books. They had pictures and pamphlets to stick in with a collection of feathers. Wrote up a little report. Drew pictures of swans and printed off others from the computer. They were so absorbed so, encouraging them to work independently of me, I thought I'd try and write alongside. Succeeding was difficult.

"Mummy?"

"Mmmm?"

"How do you spell Bewick?" Chelsea chewed her pen. Her lips were turning inky blue.

"Look. It's there in the bird book in front of you."

Silence for two minutes.

"Mummy?"

"Mmmmm?"

"I don't know what else to write." Charley was stroking her face with a feather thoughtfully. We read it through together and she set off again.

"Mummy?"

"Mmmmm?"

"What we doing after this?"

"Let's decide later." I didn't look up trying to catch my curls of thought that evaporated like steam.

Another minute or two's industry.

"Mum? Can we do art next I want to do a chalk picture of a swan?" said Charley.

"Okay."

"I want to do a collage swan with some of these feathers," said Chelsea.

"Oh, that sounds lovely." I was still trying to concentrate.

"I want to do chalk on grey paper, a big one," said Charley spreading her arms wide and bashing her sister.

"Mum, Charley hit me."

"I didn't mean to."

"Look, just finish what you're doing by yourselves if you can while I finish what I'm doing." I tried to focus on my work.

Next there's a whisper. "You could say sorry!"

"Sorry," Charley whispered back.

I glared at them. And battled on bravely trying to get to the end of at least one coherent paragraph despite the mounting frustration. Two more minutes passed. The phone rang. Chelsea got to it first.

"It's for you mum." How did I know it would be? It was some woman trying to sell me double glazing. It wasn't her day.

"For Christ's sake," I said very heatedly down the phone, "I don't give a shit about double glazing and you're disturbing my work with my children." I banged it down.

The children looked a bit worried. Two minutes later.

"Mummy?"

My patience store just emptied. "Can't you two just go one minute without saying 'mummy'?" I spat out longing sometimes for a proper job.

Chelsea looked at me red faced. "I was only going to say I love you." She gave me her best hurt expression.

"And I do too," added Charley trying to get suitable indignation in her voice.

My heart melted like chocolate in their hands. I closed my file.

What could I do except soften and smile and give them both a kiss. There'd be time enough when they were older for all the proper work in the world.

*

"Tell you what," said Charles when I told him of my frustrations. "I'll do their work with them this morning. What's on their timetable?"

"Writing," I said. He visibly cringed. I went on encouragingly, "I thought they could maybe write a letter to your sister with all their news. You could sit and do one too, she'd love to hear from you. And you're always saying you will since you don't email because your typing's too slow." I'd caught him out there. His face looked so pained I thought he must be going to lay an egg.

"You know I hate writing letters."

"Yea, and I hate wormeries and Wetland centres and climbing walls. Your turn I think." I called out to the girls. "Hey, girls, your dad's going to do some writing with you this morning. You can all do your letters." They looked quite chuffed. Charles looked like if he could throw daggers I'd be dead.

But he said bravely, "Come on, we'll sit together and see who can get the most done."

I slipped away thinking he might regret saying that once he sees how their writing has come on. I went to my desk. I'll soon need an entire drawer just to keep my rejections in. The amount of rejections is only surpassed by the amount of Home Ed stuff we have. When I nipped back ten minutes later for a book he'd just about got the address done.

"Don't forget to tell her how well the girls are doing," I said trying to help.

"Look mum, dad's only just done the first bit and I'm half way down the page," said Chelsea giggling.

"That's because I've been helping Charley," he said indignation squeezing his voice.

"No you haven't. You asked me what the date was," said Charley always on the side of justice.

I grinned at them and escaped again. Ten minutes later I saw them all out on the grass playing football.

As I went through he left them outside in the spring sunshine and came in to get a drink.

"So how did the letter writing go?" I asked, joining him in the kitchen.

"It didn't."

"What do you mean? Didn't they do it?"

"Yea, they did it. It was just I couldn't."

"Why not?" I put the glasses of juice on a tray.

"I couldn't think what to say. You know I hate letter writing," he said looking so miserable I had to give him a hug. Funny how you live with people for years yet still find new things out about them.

"Okay, well I'll do the writing stuff in the future. You do the practical. It's swimming when you're next off."

He looked marginally better, for a swimmer who doesn't like water on his head. I suspect he's extremely grateful he's the one with the proper job!

32

Spring picked up and Home Ed rocked with expanding possibilities as we returned to learning more out and about than in.

We revisited all our favourite haunts; the nature reserves, the castles, the outdoor museum the less commercial places only we knew about but were rich in things to observe and talk about.

I was thinking out-of-school education would describe it better than Home Education. The word 'home' suggested being shut away from the outside world (bit like school), whereas we were that much in the outside world with people we had to plan to stay in and get something academic done sometimes.

It still surprised me that despite time spent on all these other experiences, the girls could return to the academic exercises and do them okay without having sat and practised them endlessly like they do in classrooms. I began to suspect that sitting writing in classrooms was about convenience for the adults rather than the education of the children.

The Saturday before Mother's Day I didn't wait for the curfew call from mum but decided to go down to hers with the girls. We had cards and gifts still hot from home manufacture to hide beside her bed for her to find when we were not there. We also wanted to invite her to the slap up dinner Charles was cooking in honour of the next day.

Her trees were full of bird song and swelling with buds. I was sure I could even smell the grass growing. Her favourite season; fast becoming mine.

"You go through and find her girls," I instructed. "You can keep her busy whilst I sneak these beside her bed."

The girls went towards the living room whispering as I sneaked to the bedroom. I quickly deposited the parcels and cards then went to find them. They stood rigid by the open living room door as if they dare not enter.

Across the living room in her upright chair sat mum. Her head was back, mouth open, her eyes were closed. There was a slight frown on her grey face. And I knew the minute I set eyes on her that although her body remained, the spirit that we knew and loved so dearly had disappeared.

None of us moved. We just stared. There was no fire, no welcome, no life in that room, we all knew. Dread hung heavy.

"Oh dear, oh dear," I heard some strange quiet voice saying that I thought was mine but it could have been someone else acting the part. "I think she's left us, girls."

I called her name gently, just going through the motions really. I walked over to her slowly, mechanically, not wanting to make what I suspected into a certainty. I touched her cheek. Nothing. No movement, no warmth, no smile. She stayed still and stony and grey as I knew she would.

"What do you mean, mummy?" asked Chelsea her voice climbing in alarm. There was something in her voice that told me she knew too. Mum's cheek and hands were cold. Dead cold.

"I think she's died, darling," I said slowly. "I think she's gone." How on earth did you say such things?

I didn't know what should happen next. I didn't know what to do. I only know I heard the girls crying as they disappeared out into her garden, maybe they thought they might find her there. I just sat looking at the grey shell that was my mum, knowing I would never see my roly poly angel smile any more. I didn't know what to do I just knew I had to hold it together for the girls.

I know I phoned the surgery. I know I phoned Charles' work. I know I went and sat out in the garden with the girls, arms round each other, Chelsea crying, Charley absolutely silent, I know we were waiting for someone, anyone, to come. I know I did all this. I know that I felt none of it.

"I'm s-sorry mummy," Chelsea wept. "You can c-cry if you want to, you don't have to not to j-just for us," she sobbed. Charley just held onto me, stiff faced and frozen despite the spring sunshine. The dog looked like something had died in him too.

*

Charles arrived white faced, red eyed and quiet and cuddled us all. Then I thought he'd better take the girls home. Mum just sat there grey and cold, course she did.

"Perhaps you'd like to say goodbye before you go, this will be the last time you will see her," I said to the girls in as gentle voice as I could. But death is not really gentle. Chelsea gave her a quick brave kiss. Charley didn't want to go anywhere near this horrible dead body that wasn't her gran. I didn't blame her; I didn't either. It was all wrong, but then Charley had known that all along because she had peeped in the window and seen her and had guessed the awful truth before the rest of us.

When they left so did the remains of the life and the warmth from the house. And I was left with this lifeless form of my mum who had a slight look of irritation on her face about not being able to get on with her day. She had her gardening trousers on.

When her doctor came he lifted her eyelid, searched for a pulse and then callously announced, "Yes, she is dead, well I suppose you want to know what to do now."

Callous bastard. You could tell I wasn't myself or I would have groined him.

I phoned her nearest and dearest neighbours. He broke down on the phone.

"But she can't have, she can't have," he sobbed. "We've not long left her; we'd all been chatting and laughing together."

What a way to go. Perhaps she proverbially died laughing. Mum still sat there, grey and unmoving. Not laughing now.

I made a few more calls then couldn't bear it there any more so I phoned Charles.

"I don't want to leave her on her own," I said. "But the undertaker won't be here for a while yet."

"I'll come. You come home," he said. We swapped vigils.

"You don't have to be brave for us, mummy," said Chelsea again, as we sat on the settee together talking and cuddling. But I couldn't cry. Brave didn't come into it, numb was the word.

The girls asked endless questions and I answered with as much sensitivity and honesty that I could. Bloody hell, even death is educational. I resorted to television for a distraction to stop me staring weirdly into space and freaking the girls. The day was surreal. A surreal veil of unreality. I still didn't know what to do other than sit and stare into the space between me and the screen.

*

Later that evening when we'd made endless phone calls, after we'd eaten – or not eaten – our meal that I went through the motions of making, I felt it coming on me. At first it was a feeling of something coming up. Was I going to be sick? Then a tightening of bands around my head and neck. Then a bubbling monster of a thing, thumping up through my torso, fighting to get out. It was the crying coming. It was overtaking me like a tsunami.

"Just going upstairs for a bit," I managed to get out before making for the bedroom leaving sight of those bleak little faces. I sobbed until I thought I would be sick, until the duvet cover was soaked, until my chest hurt and my throat raged, until I knew it would still make no difference and I had to stop.

Charles came up at one point and sat and stroked my back but I was too concerned for the girls and sent him down again. As the fever of crying abated and the cold bleak reality of how to face life without her took over the shaking started. I had to cope. I had to keep going. I had to get up off the soaking bed and open the window and get some fresh air.

I leaned out into the evening, it was soft and cooling on my wretched swollen face. The smell of spring wafted through what little bit of my senses weren't blocked with the inflammation of crying. The breeze was soft and the sun sank into a spring sunset of hope. How cruel that she should survive the battering of winter only to die now. Her favourite season. I leaned out further to dry the fresh wet on my face. And as I did so a blackbird, her favourite song bird, began to sing. It shrilled the most rich and soothing and luscious song I have ever heard a bird sing, bringing balm and comfort in exactly the way she always did. Surely not just a coincidence?

*

"Happy Mother's Day mummy," said the girls coming into the bedroom the next morning with their cards and chocolates. We went through the ritual of it. What else could we do? After all, their mum was still alive – or supposed to be.

"Happy Mother's Day," said my brother ringing me from abroad where I'd been trying to reach him. "I've tried ringing mum, but there's no answer. I guess she is with you."

I'd run over in my mind what I would say, but what could I say but blurt it all out to him. What a wretched shitty thing to tell him on his great family adventure of a lifetime. He had to ring off before he could get himself together enough to speak and ring me back.

*

Mum would have seen the funny side. But I was hard pressed to find one as I had to have her decrepit old cat put down after we discovered he was riddled with cancer, have the old dog put down as his epileptic fits were soon going to kill him anyway, bury the guinea pig who'd died the same day just before Chelsea could tell her troubles to him as she'd gone to do, and deal with the endless decisions we had to make as the result of my mum leaving her remains to medical science. The kindest of men told me in the most softest and sympathetic voice of all that actually her body could be rejected if it wasn't suitable. How funny is that – she would have laughed. The ultimate rejection of all; my manuscripts have nothing on that.

But as she wasn't rejected – hooray she made the grade – there were subsequent phone calls about which bits would be left and what would we want doing with them. He seemed far too sweet a bloke for me to tell him to shove them up his arse. It wasn't the time.

And through all this I tried to keep some normality for the girls who didn't even have school to go to, with the help of friends, the swimming pool, the Home Ed group and the video player. And love and warmth even in the coldness of death. Breaking up doesn't describe it.

*

Friends and relatives supported us. They looked after the girls sometimes when we had grim things to do, and made life a bit normal by taking them to play centres and all the usual stuff. I wanted them not to feel guilty for having a nice time.

"I feel I shouldn't be enjoying myself," said Chelsea through another bout of crying.

"Why not darling? You know grandma would have wanted you to."

"I know." She cried afresh. Charley looked bleakly at her sister.

"Grandma would have said 'what we need is a cup of tea and a bit of chocolate,'" she said offering comfort in the best way she knew how and getting the Kit-Kats out. She was so right I could have howled. And I began to feel almost hysterical telling people about what happens to body parts when you leave your body to science.

"A grand gesture to make," someone said.

Not so grand though for the people who are left behind. I tried very hard not to allow any mental images to creep into my mind. And tried to explain to the girls without going into any gory details.

"By examining grandma, they will learn how to help other people who are ill," I said.

"Even in death she thought of others," said Chelsea. "She was like that." It was rich insightful comments like that which cracked me the most.

"The world will be a less full place without her in it," said a friend. No one's ever said anything nicer.

*

My brother and I stood in the field outside her house and held each other and cried. Then we started the practicalities. The practicalities rescued us from the unbelievable awfulness.

"No body, so there's no funeral?"

"But perhaps people will want something," he said.

"Sod 'em," I said. I didn't care what 'people' wanted. It was what she was that mattered. He was absolutely silent in the face of my grief and shock. And I wasn't the only one who didn't know what to do.

"How about we make a little card, like they send round in funeral services, to explain and to give something to remember her by," he suggested.

"What do you mean?" I felt my hackles rising at anything remotely religious as my mum was fairly anti religious although the kindest, most caring and charitable person you could have in your life. Far nicer than many a church going Christian I've met.

"Well, perhaps a photo or something, just to let folks know what's happened and why there's no funeral or flowers or anything and what her wishes are, were." He choked.

I wasn't sure, then I remembered something.

"You know, immediately after we found her, Chelsea went home and wrote a poem about her. It was really something. Perhaps we could use that. And that lovely photo I took of her last year among the may flowers."

We both stared into the fire with that to cling onto. Her fire. In her cold lifeless house. It brought no warmth. So we carried on with the practicalities.

33

For the first time ever I perhaps would have been grateful if the girls had been in school so they didn't have to witness the wretched, cheerless grief. Or perhaps not. It was wonderful that they were around to fill up the days with their laughter and lightness. And of course the education.

They knew I would not let them get away with no education and we were all pleased to get back focussed on our untimed table of activities after this wretched gaping hole in our ship of life sunk us for a while.

Our check lists were our lifesaver. We looked at the subjects we had to cover and just got on with it. The girls were as keen as me. It was normal life again. It was how the past two and a half years had been and to kids two years is a lifetime. We moved on through it on remote control and we were really grateful. Home Education was there waiting for us, restoring our life to some of what it had been before. Just as long as we didn't think to hard about what was missing from it.

*

Visiting mum's house was extremely painful but it was old and isolated and a perfect target for crime and wildlife to invade. It was also stuffed to bursting with ideal rat nesting material she had collected over the decades as older folks are prone to do, which needed sorting and removing. It had to be faced.

Every time I opened another cupboard I found some more paraphernalia of the ages; magazines, vintage clothes, blankets, textiles for sewing, newspapers, food tins so out of date I reckon we could donate them to a museum. Clearing the old place was like living history to the girls.

"Look at this mum," called Chelsea as she found mum's ration book from the war years. History lesson followed.

"What's this?" Charley found an old stone hot water bottle stored in the pantry. Explanations followed about materials that were used and how they changed lives.

"Wow! Look at these gloves." Chelsea unearthed a pair of long, white, elbow length gloves so we discussed the style of the times.

"What's this for?" asked Charley holding up an old suspender. Lots of giggling followed the explanation.

"Urgh! What are these?" Chelsea had opened a dusty rusty tin but innocent looking tin. In it she found two yellowed disgusting objects; my dad's old teeth. Mum was prone to storing unlikely keep sakes. He died twenty years earlier but his clothes still hung in the closet. The sleeves were chewed and there was mouse poo in the pockets.

Sometimes the girls didn't come with me. Gratefully they weren't with me when I noticed the urn.

I was wondering what that ugly plastic pot was that was sitting on top of her drawers. It was such a gross object I was really surprised that she'd even have it in her house as she only liked objects that were naturally beautiful, creative or useful. This plastic tub looked like a big version of something you'd get free at McDonalds. The grim truth woke me with a nightmare in the night.

"Oh my god! I've got to get it out of the house." I shrieked, reaching to put the light on.

"What? What's the matter?" Charles groped his way up from sleep and tried to understand what the crisis was. "You're having a bad dream," he mumbled. "Go back to sleep."

"It's not. It's not a dream. It's my dad. He's still in the house," I gabbled the words out between crying. Charles pulled me over for a cuddle like he always did when I had bad dreams.

"It's only a dream. Wake up. It's okay."

"I'm not dreaming," I said shaking him off and sitting up. "It's my dad. He's on top of mum's drawers in the bedroom. He must have been there all the time." I sobbed.

"What the hell are you talking about?"said Charles, really alarmed and wide awake by then.

"Yesterday. I found this horrid old plastic tub on my mum's drawers. I didn't know what it was, but I've just realised. It must be my dad's ashes."

"Are you sure?" Charles said looking a bit white even through the warm flush of sleep.

"It must be. I must go. Don't you see? He's been there with her all the time. And now he's on his own. And he wants to get out of the house and be with her and he can't." I'm not generally prone to funny turns but I seemed to be having the most awful illusion. I blubbered into the sheet, unable to stop.

"Oh, dear. Come here." Charles pulled me close to him and wrapped the duvet round me making comforting noises.

The illusion became more bizarre. "He's never been alone in the house. He needs to be with her." I sobbed. I knew there was no 'her' and no 'him' either but the feeling was so intense I was desperate.

"Look. We'll sort it tomorrow okay?" Charles was desperate to get back to sleep ready for work in the morning. I was as ready for sleep as the electric chair and worried about my dad until there was a lightness of dawn showing behind the curtains, then I couldn't wait any longer. I'd do it and be back before Charles went to work.

I made the journey alone. The morning was grey and there was a screaming gale force wind, drying the land and filling my nostrils and eyes with blowing silt. There was that awful smell in mum's house of empty damp decay. I took the stairs two at a time, grabbed the urn from the top of the drawers where it had been for twenty years and ran out again, over to the field to the place we'd designated as special to her, where we were to erect a memorial stone. I wrestled with the top of the urn but couldn't get it off. Then I dropped it. The top buckled off and some of the ashes spilled out. And as I picked it up, trying to make a ceremonial and respectful scattering over the flowers and tree we'd planted in her memory, all that happened was that the gale blew the ashes all over me. I screamed down the wind as I was covered in my dad's ashes and collapsed in an undignified sobbing heap, crushing the daffodils and desperately brushing the macabre covering off my clothing.

*

The girls knew none of this. I still had Home Education to get back on track.

"What's on the agenda today then, girls?"

"Can we go swimming. We haven't been for ages. Not since the schools went back after Easter and the pool will be nice and empty again now," Charley asked hoping to distract me from anything dull on the agenda with reasoning.

"Great idea, get your things ready. We'll go this afternoon when we've got our other stuff done."

"Oooooh!" They can't fool me that easy.

We picked up other Home Ed children on the way. The swimming pool was lovely and quiet and as I slipped through the water it massaged some of the recent tensions away. Beyond the pool windows the sky was blue and cherry trees pink. It reminded me of mum. I surged up and down keeping my head above water so I could watch the kids. I'm like the old ladies trying to keep their perms dry. The sight of old ladies reminded me of mum and made me want to cry. But then, everything did. It could be tears or pool water on my face, even I wasn't sure.

Charley did her underwater swimming until we were all thinking she'd drowned act. How she managed to stay down so long is beyond me. I tried holding my breath at the same time and it had me gasping. She surfaced and heaved her little body out and lay flat on the side, one hand trailing in the water. I noticed the life guard climbed down and walked over to her. I swam across as he squatted down beside her.

"Are you okay?" he asked.

She sat up embarrassed and nodded.

"The thing is, if you keep doing that, we're going to think you're drowning," he said. Charley made no response. She didn't really see that as a problem. I smiled at him. He didn't smile back. She went redder.

"Come on darling, let's go to the shallow end for a bit and have a rest." She rolled back into the water and swam along beside me until we caught up with the others.

"What did he want?" asked Chelsea who always stuck up for her sister despite calling her a cow occasionally.

"He was just seeing she was okay," I said.

"Don't know what he did that for," said Charley, still uncomfortable about it all.

"Well, you can hold your breath so long under water, he gets worried. I get worried sometimes. And if you got too exhausted you wouldn't be able to get yourself out of the pool," I explained.

"I'm not that stupid."

"Yea, we know that. But he doesn't." I grinned at them.

"Come on, let's go up the slide," said Chelsea always good at getting her sister out of a tight corner. "Who's going to ask the guard to open it?"

"You do it," said her friend.

"I'm not going to, you go," said Chelsea.

"No you!"

"No you!"

"Oh I'll go," said Charley who was younger than the lot of them and braver too.

They bombed down the slide whilst I did a few more lengths. Exercise is always an antidote to a multitude of ills, grief among them. And with swimming no one could tell if I was crying or not.

34

Education is all very well but there are no classes to help you with bereavement. No classes to help you with real issues like how do you get through life when there's suddenly a sodding great hole in it full of black sludge that you fall into when you least expect it. Nothing to help you deal with other people's grief either which gets dropped on you under the guise of empathy.

We had lots of conversations about evolution to help the girls deal with the starkness of life passing and what happens next. It was the season of renewal. At least that helped. We talked about the never ending cycles of life and death through flowers and trees, night and day. We talked about the energy and spirit of someone and the legacy that is left behind not only in our genes, but in our minds through our ideas and attitudes. We talked about mum's incredible capacity for happiness and her giggling and we got the chocolate out a lot.

It was almost like the grief had to get worse before it got better. And every day the girls had to face me and my plastic smile as we went through our Home Education routine, just like anyone has to go through life's routine, and they were terrific. When I heard their laughter ringing through the house once more I knew that we would survive.

Our summer schedule with the group kept us so busy, plus dance and drama classes, shows and riding, trips away to visit other places and other people, it helped fill our lives with the prospect of a future without mum. I had to keep myself in check when we were out in town as I still had the burning desire to go and chat to old ladies.

While all this was going on Charles and I had the monumental decision about her house. Decisions about its contents, both large and small, inanimate or living. We talked about the possibility of us living there and thereby having more space, whether I could bear it, whether we want to give up our lovely cottage with its memories of small beings and happy childhood days but which felt increasingly small as the girls grew and our educational accessories became increasingly plentiful.

Mum's house had more rooms, more space, an incredible natural surround. But it also had no heating, dodgy electrics, windows so beyond draughty the curtains billow in the East wind, penetrating sea damp and wild life in the roof space.

But then, we are used to a challenge; we Home Educate.

*

Over the summer whilst we thought about it we managed two houses. The summer also marked the time Chelsea would be changing to big school if she were in the system.

"You know Jane, from dance club?" she said as we were driving along in the car. Just us three.

"Mmmm."

"She's getting her new school uniform today."

"Is she? Is she pleased about that?"

"I think so. New clothes are always nice."

"Do you think you'd like a uniform," I asked as I negotiated a tractor.

"Well, I soon got fed up with it at Primary school."

"Mmmm. I suppose it's alright for a bit. I guess Jane will get fed up with it eventually."

Charley joined in. "I hated my uniform, especially having to wear shoes all the time."

"And Jane's mum says that since she's starting 'big' school she's going to buy her a new mobile phone," Chelsea added.

There's bribery for you, I thought, over taking another tractor. But I could hear a little bit of envy in Chelsea's voice.

"Do you ever think about going back to school?" I asked.

"Not really."

My heart started to thump as I put the next question. "You know, you could always go and try out your next school if you wanted, as Jane's going. See if you like it any better than the last one. Or if you miss it."

"I don't miss it mum. And anyway, my older mates at drama club who go to that school are always moaning about the homework and stuff. They think I'm really lucky getting home schooled and not getting home work."

"You do get homework. You just do it in the day," I laughed. She laughed too. I passed the third and final tractor, I hoped. Then said, "But you can always change your mind, any time. It's okay with us."

"But I won't, mum!"

She looked at me through the mirror, then out of the window. I drove on wondering what it would be like with them back in school.

*

The next morning Charley dropped a bombshell that had me stewed up worse than grief. She was busy playing schools with her dolls and animals in a den she'd created in the garden. Then she got tired of that and came and lay down next to me as I weeded.

"I think I might like to try school," she said, staring dreamily at the sky.

I jerked so suddenly I pulled up a whole plant as something clamped my heart and gave me a massive electric shock. That's what it felt like anyway. Outwardly I was a master of playing it cool.

"Oh, do you darling?" I said about as cool as a pig on a barbecue. I felt like I was wearing electric fencing. My thinking had fits. Out of the two of them I would never have suspected it was her who wanted to go to school.

"But you never liked it much when you were there and you don't like sitting still for long. Do you think it would suit you?"

"Yes, I could give it a try, anyway." She was thinking hard, her imagination racing. I wasn't sure it was on the right track. But I said,

"Okay. If that's what you want. I'll make some enquiries." I straightened up hoping the sick feeling would go away.

She ran off to tell the toys. I noticed she had shoes on.

*

"I can't believe it," said Charles when I told him after supper, eventually getting some time alone to discuss it, whilst the girls were upstairs getting into bed.

"You can't believe it? How do you think I've felt all day? I've been in a trance – not a nice one either."

We dropped on the settee together.

"But she'd hate it," he said, scratching his head like he always did when thinking.

"I know, I know. But she wants to try."

"I can't believe it," he said again like an old record.

"What I feel so utterly wretched about is the fact that all the effort I put in to make their education so rich and interesting and fun, all the things we do together with the others, counts for nothing. It's not enough for her."

"Oh, come on, it's not like that. She's just inquisitive – you know what she's like, into everything. She wants to try it out. And she doesn't have a comparison really. She ought to try it, see an alternative, I suppose."

"Well, I don't know. I really don't. And now I think; whatever we could provide it is perhaps not enough and it certainly hasn't been much fun over the past months since mum died."

"Well, there's a good enough reason for that," Charles said

sharply. "And don't diss off all the good stuff you've done just because Charley fancies a change. It doesn't devalue the education we've provided. School didn't provide enough either if you remember." Charles could always be objective when I was having an emotional crisis. We were silent a moment. I picked at the cushion. He did some more scratching.

"On the other hand," he said. "If they want to go back to school at least you'll get your time back."

"Yea. But school? I mean, she can't sit still for two minutes she's always so busy and determined and investigating stuff. She'd be absolutely bored mental in school."

"Yea, I'm sure she would."

"I feel like an utter failure. I feel that despite my best effort I could never make it interesting enough and I think I'm totally stupid for thinking that I could."

"That's rubbish. Don't lose faith. She's had such a stimulating time, look how she's developed. She's just inquisitive about school, that's all. Probably her friends have been talking about it and it's good she wants to push her boundaries. Says a lot for her character."

"Yes, but Chelsea was talking about it too because all her friends are getting their new stuff for their new school. I mean, in a way I can imagine her in school, but not Charley."

"Look, I'm sure it's just a little blip, especially since losing your mum. Things change. It's rocked their world too you know. It hasn't been the same since then."

"I know, I know. But we do need to think about it. I'll make some inquiries. It's funny, you just go on expecting life to stay exactly the same then wham, everything changes and you don't know where you are any more." I tried swallowing the lump that seemed to have been in my throat for ages.

Charles moved over to me and we hugged. I stared tear blind over his shoulder.

"Mummy, come and tuck me in," yelled a voice from upstairs.

Charles covered my hand with his large warm one and squeezed it in comfort. "Look, give her a day or two to think about it."

"Well, I suppose it's the right time to start with the beginning of a new school year coming."

"Mummy, mummy," yelled Charley much louder this time.

Charles grinned. "Just think, all day every day without kids!" I have to admit, there was a minute glimmer then the memory of her dumbed down, school day face wiped the shine away. I trudged up the stairs, it seemed hard work; even my legs felt as if they were grieving.

"You were ages coming," said Charley glaring at me from under those intense brows. "I can't sleep. You and dad were making too much noise."

I sat down on the edge of the bed and put an arm round her.

"I was just talking to dad about you going to school."

"Going to school?" her face flushed with alarm. Her eyes widened in what looked like horror.

"Yes, you said this morning that you'd like to go to school again."

"No I didn't. I don't want to go to school. I hate school. I want to learn at home like we always do." The mega shocks were at my heart again. I stared at her, speechless. She mistook it for admonishment.

"You don't want me to go to school, do you mum?" Teddy was stuffed up to her mouth and there was a bleak look of shock in her eyes.

"I just thought you wanted to." I felt totally confused.

"Course not, I love being Home Educated. School was so boring," she told me as if I was a complete idiot for thinking any different.

"Oh!"

She tossed herself down for sleep with teddy as a pillow and I tucked her in with trembling hands.

"Night mum."

"Night darling." I switched off the light. That way if my emotional breakdown was showing in my face she wouldn't see it.

"Love you mum."

"Love you too." I headed for the door before I cracked up. But I didn't make it. She sat upright again.

"Mum?"

"Yes?"

"You wouldn't send me to school, would you?" Her mouth wobbled as she spoke.

"No darling, never. Not unless you want to. And one day you might want to. Lots of kids love going to school."

"Course I won't," she said in a tone that indicated I was stupid for suggesting it.

She flopped down on Ted, pulled the covers over her shoulders and dismissed me and my idiot ideas for the night.

It was as much as I could do to get back down the stairs to Charles' arms before going to pieces.

*

It made me think.

In one small time span everything can easily change and never be the same again and it was easy to get complacent, take things for granted. Mum never took things for granted. She saw the beauty in so much. But she was gone. One minute she was here with her bounteous approach, with her full, active, contented life right up to the second before she died. The next minute that had ended.

It had shaken the bedrock of our lives, making us realise it wasn't bedrock after all, it was shifting sand on which our lives were built, yet we had got complacent.

Perhaps we'd almost got complacent about our Home Educating too. About the joy it brought us. About the privilege we felt at being able to watch our children grow and develop with happiness and health. We had got complacent about the blessings we had that many do not. And we should never take anything for granted.

For despite the time and the energy, the struggles and the worries, the daily toil sometimes and the time that was not my own, I knew that I wouldn't want it any other way.

It looks like the girls didn't either. I wouldn't be taking that for granted again.

35

Time raced on towards autumn and thankfully some of life began to flood back in and fill up the black hole. The terrible times of needing so much just to speak to her or see her smile became a little less frequent. We began to have things to celebrate again; we had completed, (or is that survived?) three years of Home Education, we were the parents of twelve and soon-to-be-nine year olds. We had finally made the decision to move to mum's house.

Selling our 'character' cottage was an education in itself.

"Mum, there's a strange man coming up the drive," said Charley coming in covered in mud as usual.

"He's come to look at the house," I said. He was about six foot six and I knew it was not going to be him. My head brushed our bedroom ceiling and that was with my shoes off and I'm only five foot six and a half.

The next bloke was a builder who stared at our beautiful little cottage and talked about raising the roof, knocking out walls, building an extension. But I managed not to say 'Why don't you just go and buy another bloody house?'

The third lady, who knew all about quirky cottages from her sister, fell in love with it and put me into a right panic that she might buy it. It was all very unnerving. Whilst all that was going on the sorting at mum's continued along with the history lessons.

"Look, mum, look at this," said Chelsea. She handed me an aged piece of paper. It was an old school report from the 1920s. It must be mum's.

"Goodness, what a find," I said, putting down the books I was sorting.

"And look. She won a prize." Chelsea showed me a book plate inscribed with her name and the fact it was awarded in honour of her achievements at Sunday school.

"What is Sunday school?" asked Charley.

We sat on the settee and talked about the child who would walk across the fields to school each morning and on a Sunday to the church, with her hat and gloves on trying not to get dirty when she'd rather be out playing in the countryside. What a world away from our Home Education where getting dirty seemed to be compulsory.

We found a long sharp hat pin set with amethyst at the end and a pair of large white men's cotton gloves.

"Fancy a man wearing gloves," said Chelsea laughing, obviously thinking of her dad's huge grubby paws digging the garden.

"Well, they'd be dressed up for dinner in a suit with tails and a stiff white collar."

"What's tails?" asked Charley. "Like on a cat, you mean?"

More discussion. We found the collars and the neck studs later. I made a mental note to point out all this stuff next time we went to visit the V&A museum.

We found mum's portfolio of art work and old newspaper articles about her exhibitions. And we talked ages about her and her life and times as we let the physicality of her go and just kept the treasured memories.

*

We were at the kitchen table working when Chelsea brought up the subject of 'big' school again.

"Mum? You know Jane who went to that new school?"

"Yea, how's she getting on?"

"Well, at drama club last night she said she doesn't like it any more. She gets loads and loads of homework every night."

"Every night?" exclaimed Charley looking up from the English we were working on. "I think that's wrong. The teachers should do the work their selves."

I made a mental note about a grammar lesson.

Chelsea went on, "And someone's stolen her new phone."

"Oh, dear, that's awful," I said. I pointed Charley back to her place in her book.

"But her mum's going to buy her a new one."

"Can I have a mobile phone?" asked Charley.

"You don't need one. You're at home all the time," I said grinning at her. "Anyway, how are you going to afford it," I added putting the responsibility of paying for it on her shoulders and off mine.

They went quiet again thinking about that and not concentrated on their work.

"Jane said she wished she could be home schooled like me," said Chelsea. I smiled, trying not to look smug or take anything for granted.

"I think all children should be home schooled," said Charley.

"It wouldn't work for every family and lots of children are happy in school," I said.

We worked for a few more minutes in silence, but I wasn't hoodwinked into thinking they were focussed.

"Well, I'm glad we're Home Educated," said Chelsea. "Aren't you Charley?"

Charley thought about it a moment whilst I squeezed breaths out silently. If she didn't answer soon I'd faint for lack of oxygen.

"Yea, it's definitely not worth a mobile phone. And we get to go swimming and out with friends and to cool places to learn. And to play all the time."

Nice! If that's how she views her education; playing all the time, without noticing the terrific amounts of learning going on, what could be better than that?

*

Our cottage was sold and moving to mum's became a reality. So our Home Educating took place around the final push to clear it, get central heating in before we moved, and try and eradicate some of mum's wild companions. There was a mass of renovation to be done but that had to wait till the following spring. Thankfully, everything I found daunting about the place the girls found fascinating and showed it off to their friends.

"Come and look at this," said Chelsea enticing her friends as if she was offering the most exclusive play centre. They all rushed round to look at the coal house and the little building in the garden only just big enough to stand up in. Most of the kids didn't want to put their heads in the spidery place.

"What is it?" the boys asked.

"It's the 'Old Bog' grandma used to call it. The toilet!"

"That's so cool." They all fell about giggling and pushing each other to peer in the tiny doorway.

"And, guess what?" Charley added for extra impact. "It used to be a double seater!"

"No way!" The laughing rang round the garden and into the kitchen where I was listening.

"You've got to see this next, in here." They opened the larder door onto a little room lined with shelves.

"Cool, what is it?"

"It's the pantry. But look, look here, this is the best bit." Charley pointed with glee to some tiny black droppings on the pantry shelves. "Mouse poo!" Suitable exclamations of horror follow.

"Urgh. That's disgusting." But obviously very, very funny.

"Wait till you see in the living room." They all rushed into the living room and stared at the ceiling where there was a small mysterious hole with ragged edges. "Look, a mouse has been eating the ceiling."

I couldn't help but laugh. I'd probably throw a wobbly otherwise and panic about what we were letting ourselves in for. They all rushed outside to go up the trees and into the wood, and down the dykes and through the fields. I hoped they'd still be fascinated by the time we moved in.

*

I was right to panic. Trying to sleep on our first night in mum's house was a bit like a rerun of the Hitchcock thriller The Birds. What the heck had I let us all in for?

"Mummy. It's happening again," yelled Charley from across the landing.

It sounded like a herd of bison were running through the sloping roof above our heads. I got up wearily, for the third time, off the floor where we'd chucked our mattress as there'd been no time to erect the bed in the turmoil of the day we'd just had.

"Don't worry about it darling," I comforted Charley. "It's just a little bird looking for a place to shelter for the winter. I wouldn't want to be out on a night like this, would you?" The wind rumbled down the chimney breast.

"But listen mum, it sounds more like a pterodactyl than a little bird," said Charley making me laugh. I was sure that it wasn't just a little bird but I wasn't going to alarm her even more. Her little anxious face peeped out from the duvet. I banged on the ceiling and the scuttling went quiet.

"I don't like it, I can't get to sleep."

"I know, it's all a bit strange, but it's nothing to worry about. Look, why doesn't teddy put his hands over your ears." I giggled and arranged teddy's arms each side her head. She giggled too.

"And if you hear it again just knock on the ceiling like I did and tell the little bird to go back to bed," I added, smiling down at her.

Her eyes smiled back. But they looked wide awake. I knew it was a big step coming here. For all of us. I bent over her and gave her a big kiss on her forehead.

"Night, darling."

"Night, mum."

"What's going on," called Chelsea from the other side of the partition wall.

"I can't sleep because a little bird is keeping me awake," Charley called back.

"I've got one over here too," said Chelsea. Oh god, they're everywhere. I just hoped the girls didn't remember that birds aren't usually active at night, but mice were. And rats. Sometimes all this knowledge wasn't a blessing.

"Well, we'll sort them out tomorrow, don't worry. Let's try and get some sleep because we've had such a busy day lugging furniture about and we're all very tired."

"Will we put the top of the staircase back tomorrow?" asked Charley. We'd had to dismantle part of it to get the furniture up. It was a special take away staircase with a turn at the top specially designed by my dad to fit the space and replace the ladder that was there when they first came.

"Yes, probably, but forget it now and go to sleep."

"I like it better without, it's much more fun climbing up."

"We could have a ladder," suggested Charley. Sometimes I think life is going backwards.

"Goodnight girls," I said loudly. All I wanted to do was to get my shivering body back under my own covers again.

"Night mum."

"Goodnight mum."

"Love you, mum." Duplicate.

"Love you too."

I scampered back across the freezing landing and fell into bed. Charles pulled me over to his side for a warm cuddle. "What's up with those two?"

"Oh, they can't sleep. It's all so strange. It wouldn't be so bad if it wasn't for all this galloping noise through the roof. I've told them it's birds. But it isn't, I'm damn sure it's rats. Mega rats. Mega rats with clogs on!" The galloping about stopped and the munching started.

"We'll ring the pest control chap tomorrow," he said. It went quiet above our heads, then scratching started again.

"God, do you think we've done the right thing coming here?" I looked up at the ceiling in the moonlight, it had black mouldy patches and was as warped as a seascape and looking like it might collapse any minute. There was a draught past my nose end like a mini gale, black mould all around the curtainless windows, and enough sea salt in the bricks to make them the consistency of putty. I was so grateful we'd got the girls rooms sorted and decorated before we'd moved in.

"Course we have. It's a beautiful place and in a beautiful location. Just look at that." Charles looked towards the little window where the moonlight was illuminating the land beyond and laying a silver shine upon the strip of distant sea. With that view in sight I tried to go back to sleep before the munching started up again.

*

Everything was different in the morning. The doubt had gone, replaced by excitement. The sea was blue and pearly. The winter robin was singing. The worst was over; the sorting, the move, the first unnerving night. All done. I even felt excited.

So what if our life was still in boxes and the roof over our heads was alive with problems. We were on another new adventure. We could move on from the crush of grief, start our new learning life.

Now which of the hundred boxes has the craft materials in? Christmas was coming.

Charley sat at mum's table in mum's old kitchen getting through glitter glue faster than chocolate. Chelsea sat opposite creating an intricate bead purse from a diagram in a book. This looked to me more horrendous than knitting as it was crafted by adding beads to one string. The skills she needed to accomplish it were staggering, the most difficult of all; understanding the instructions. She'd end up better at Flat Packs than her dad.

"So how's he going to get rid of the things in the roof?" asked Charley as the glitter glue dripped onto her legs. The pest control man had negotiated the half staircase really nimbly as we still hadn't got it back up again yet.

I was truly hoping that this subject wasn't going to come up. But Charley as ever wants to know everything about everything. Chelsea was wiser, she was beginning to realise that some details were better left unknown.

Charles looked at me, hoping I would answer. As usual he was leaving the tricky explanations to me.

"He's going to put something down that the little things won't like and we're hoping they'll go away," I said. It was as near the truth as I could possibly make it without actually telling he was going to poison them.

Charley caught me out though. "Animals? You mean it's not birds?"

Damn! I had to think fast.

"Well, it's not only birds I think is it? We've seen mice droppings so there might be mice as well."

Chelsea looked at me knowingly. I tried to look innocent, as innocent as I could with the thought of corpses scattered throughout the roof. I hated it. But it was obviously a wildlife adventure playground up there and the breeding rate didn't bear thinking about.

We heard the pest control officer clambering down what was left of the staircase. Charley rushed to see him.

"Did you see anything?" she asked. The man looked at me and I tried to give a sort of furtive head shake in negative.

"No, I didn't. But I think it'll go quiet up there soon," he said tactfully. I smiled gratefully and ushered him out the door.

*

We were fine and busy with our new adventure and Home Ed business right up till Christmas day then the smell of the turkey reminded me so much of mum grief was like a slap from a cold wet rag. I could hardly swallow anything let alone turkey. We pressed on bravely with friends rescuing us from living with it in her house. But it was all around us really, in her artwork about the house, in her garden, in her kitchen and living room where images of her peeped out at us from every corner and just had to be got through with talking and cuddling and accepting that was just how it was but it would pass. We would soon make it our house.

It was Chelsea who brought up the truth that had to be faced. "It doesn't feel like Christmas without grandma," she said. The remark covered us like a black shroud.

"No, I know. But we will make new Christmases and a new life and we'll feel different soon," I said, fighting to keep wobbles out my voice.

We went through the motions. We kept as cheerful as we could. We just got through it.

*

A few weeks later the smell set in.

"There's a horrible smell coming from my bedroom," said Charley.

"You'd better check for vagrant socks," I joked.

"Oh, mum. It's not that."

"My room smells disgusting too," said Chelsea. I was beginning to have awful suspicions but I just made light of it.

"It's probably still the remains of the paint and new carpet smell," I said.

"What the hell's that awful smell? I don't remember it smelling like this before we moved in," said Charles just as we were dropping off to sleep. I looked at him accusingly. "It's not me!" he added indignantly.

I laughed. "I know. But I do have a nasty feeling about it."

"What?" He turned over to look at me.

"Well, think about it. The pest man put poison down didn't he? Now it's all quiet up there. I guess it's rotting rats."

I would be extremely glad when the January gales set in and provided a good cleansing draught.

36

We only unpacked the materials and books we needed and made ourselves a little oasis by the fire to work as renovations began. The efforts of the central heating were eradicated by the icy draughts from all the old windows and doors we hoped to replace. And the fact that builders just left all the doors open.

We got out a lot, went to many group activities and other people's houses and other visits, just to get away from it. Focussing on education when there was banging and drilling and the sound of our house being knocked down round our ears was like trying to make the girls eat cabbage when there was sweets on offer. The swimming pool, library and the chip shop took on a whole new appeal. Lunch at home usually had brick dust in it.

At the end of each day when the loud men, radio noise and swearing dropped back into silence the girls and I went to look at the day's destruction. There seemed to be more destruction than construction but there was still a lot to learn.

The builders had probably never been questioned so rigorously before. I tried to roll with it. It was all learning after all. The girls found a whole lot of new materials to experiment with and lots of new topics to discuss, especially the language.

Thankfully spring came warm and early and rescued us from being trapped indoors with the sounds of knocking and sawing and dirt cascading down.

"Look, what's that on the bird table?" said Charles. Mum's garden was so full of a variety of birds it was an ornithology lesson right there on the bird table.

"It's a chaffinch," said Charley, identifying it as easily as she would a Mars bar.

"You sure?" said Charles. He looked at me. Neither of us were that sure how to handle a nine year old who seemed to know more than us.

"Sure," she said, carrying on making patterns in the brick dust on the table. I got the bird book out. It was a chaffinch.

A little later Charles called, "Look Charley, what's this one?" as he caught a glimpse of a bigger bird slipping out of the garden into the field.

"It's a pheasant," said Charley.

"It wasn't a pheasant," said Charles sure of himself this time. "It wasn't a strong enough colour."

"It was a female," said Charley, sighing and trying hard to tolerate his ignorance.

All this knowledge. All this stuff she knew. It would be so nice to be able to be able to channel it into something tangible, I thought, forever in mind of making our education look good. Especially for the next inspection.

"You know such a lot about birds, Charley, wouldn't it be a great idea to do a project," I said, dreaming of all the lovely writing and drawing and bookish type of learning that would take place.

"But I don't want to do a project," she said.

"Why not? You could draw the birds and write how to identify them. It would be fun?" Who am I trying to kid?

"But why would I want to do a project?" she asked.

Why indeed. She liked being out in the field learning. She was happy with what she knew. She had no need to prove it to anyone else unlike her mother. Home Educating three years and I still kept falling into the trap of trying to make it look all schoolish, because if I was honest that was all the project idea was about. Getting her to regurgitate what she knew for the sake of showing it to someone else. Like they do in schools. Kids in schools spend a small amount of time learning something new. Then an awful lot of time writing it down to show what they've learnt to someone else. Do mine need to do that?

No!

Now what was that just flew over?

"A kestrel," Charley told me. I left it at that.

*

"I cannot imagine anything more boring than doing a project," laughed my Home Ed best friend when I told her how my great plan to 'produce' something had been thwarted. "I hated doing them when I was a kid and I certainly wouldn't be able to get my boys to do one. They'd quite rightly ask me what was the point."

"I know, I just thought it would be so nice to have some tangible proof sometimes that the girls were actually achieving things." We laughed over the shared dreams. A great tonic for the Home Ed anxieties.

"I know what you mean though," she added commiserating. "But the thing is, the children are learning so much by doing, writing about it isn't really going to teach them anything new and it can actually harm the valuable learning that is going on by making them dread it."

"Yea. I know that really. I just lose sight of it sometimes. Especially at the moment when there is so much chaos at home I wonder how much proper Home Ed is going on."

"Proper Home Ed?" she shrieked. "You have lost sight of it! Course you're doing proper education. Everything is educational; they don't have to be writing for things to be educational, do they?" I felt admonished. She went on. "The problem comes when you start to compare what you do to the education children do in schools where they produce lots of stuff which is often just to keep the children busy. It's not teaching them anything new. If we look at the way our children are learning all the time by the things they are doing and the experiences we are providing for them, I think we'll find that they're actually far ahead in much of their understanding than school children."

Our children were hanging precariously over the pond at that precise moment intently studying the sexual antics of the frogs.

"I know. It seems that the children in school are kept so busy doing all this stuff to meet targets they fail to see what's under their noses most of the time," I said. Charley had a frog under her nose just then. It had a second frog clinging to its back oblivious to the fact it was being observed by a gang of fascinated kids. She put it back in the pond gently.

"Some of the parents aren't much better either. They never explain anything to their kids. If it's not in Asda they don't know what it is!" The children heard us laughing and came to be part of the joke.

"But how do we know?" I asked her.

"Know what?" asked Charley climbing on my knee. The garden chair creaked worryingly. I wondered how big she would be before she got out of this habit.

"Know things. Know what a blackbird is or an oak tree or a potato."

"You've told us," said Chelsea.

"But how do we know?" I smiled at them.

"You looked it up," said one of the boys.

"Off the internet," said the eldest.

"Anyway, why?" asked Charley.

"We were just wondering how much you learn by writing up what you know."

"Nothing. I hate writing. It's so boring," said her middle boy lying on his back and looking at the sky.

"I learn by doing it, by seeing it," said the eldest boy.

"That's right," said his mum. "We were thinking that's probably the biggest difference between learning at home or in school. You learn more by doing. They learn more by studying and writing. But they also spend a lot of time justifying what they do to others. When we get caught up in trying to justify what we do we lose the real educational value."

"Come on," he said, getting up. "All they ever talk about is education they're so boring. Let's go!" They all got up and went back to the ponds. Their dad brought the pond dipping nets out for them, then joined us.

"We were just talking about justifying our education to others," she said to him.

"Oh, that old thorn," he laughed. "Nothing like a bit of justification to spoil a good Home Educating day."

"What's your take on it then, on your role as a Home Educating parent?" I asked.

"Probably to keep out of the way! The kids are going to learn anyway, despite us, and I think we often spoil that learning process by interfering all the time. Besides, whatever we do, their genes will out!" He left us with that to chew over and went to join the children by the ponds and help them identify their finds.

"He's like Charles," I said watching them. "Annoyingly right much of the time!"

"Well, if he's right, you don't have to worry so much about it, do you!"

I didn't. The kids were proving that, having great fun engrossed in the mating habit of the frogs. I must remember to have faith.

*

I seemed to need to keep faith with a lot of things. Faith that the children were still growing and learning as they had for the past three years despite disruptions. Faith that when the builders had knocked the house about enough they would be able to put it back together again. Faith that our Home Educating life would eventually get back to normal and we would be whole and healed.

I got through my second Mother's Day as an orphan but it was a nice respite from decisions about how much of the ceiling should come down, what we should do about the rotten floor, should we have opening windows and how should they open, and which toilet should we choose? Who gives a toss about toilets, they were all the same weren't they? Apparently not. We had quite a lot of lessons in B&Q. And even Asda's cafe suddenly looked appealing compared to scrambled eggs with grit.

The girls realised how valuable it was having the builders as a distraction from concentrating on working.

"I can't concentrate with all this noise," said Chelsea looking up from her book.

"I can't either," said Charley. I wasn't even aware she was concentrating.

"They're not making too much noise today though, are they?" I said hopefully.

"It's not their noise, it's the radio," said Chelsea.

"I thought you liked music?"

"Not this stuff," she said as another dreary oldie rang out from Radio Drivel.

"Perhaps we could ask them to turn it down," I said glancing through the door to see where they were.

Charley got up from the settee where we were working.

"I'll turn it down," she said with that determination in her voice that would make her dad quail.

The builders were out in the garden nowhere near the radio and as usual nowhere near getting on with the work either. Two stood smoking, the third was emerging from the farm buildings doing up his flies. Another need for me to 'have a word'. The music from the next room went quiet and Charley returned looking pleased with herself.

"See if they notice," she grinned at Chelsea. Chelsea grinned back;

guilty allies.

Over the next few days there was a game going on between the builders turning the music up and one of the girls sneaking out and turning it down. The builders didn't seem to work out what was happening.

*

"Mum, shall we make the builders some biscuits today?"

"Well, I was planning to go on with what we started yesterday."

"Aw, let's!"

"Go on then." Sometimes I just had to give in and go with the flow and console myself there's much to be learnt through cooking. Today we made shortbread. Or it could be called grit bread, or rubble biscuits. Flapjack was the best to make as is always comes out looking the colour of brick dust anyway and mine's often the same consistency.

"Who's taking the tea out to them?"

"My turn," said Chelsea.

"You did it yesterday," said Charley.

"Perhaps I should have a turn," I said. They looked at me funny. On the other hand, non of the builders were the types you could fancy. I handed the tray to Charley.

"You carry, Chelsea can do the doors."

"Okay!" I watched the tea, sugar and biscuits with a sprinkling of brick dust go out the door. Then I opened a nice airtight packet of Hobnobs for myself. There had to be some compensation for the stress of it all.

Something else for me to have faith in; the house being finished before I completely cracked up with the stress of trying to Home Educate in a building site.

37

"Oi! You! Get down from there." A man's voice thundered through my few quiet moments trying to pretend I was usefully writing something.

"It's all right. I'm quite safe. I climb up here all the time," I heard Charley shout back. P.E. has taken on a new dimension; the scaffolding.

I ran out into the garden and looked up. Hanging on the highest bar was Charley whilst Chelsea was making camp on a lower level. Not only is Charley hanging at the highest point, she's hanging upside down by her legs. I swallowed my resident lump back down again and yelled up to her.

"Darling, can you come down please." I sounded remarkably calm for someone with a throat constriction. She righted herself and did a fireman's slide down an angled pole.

"You too, Chelsea." Chelsea tidied up her belongings and joined us.

"It ain't safe for her to play up there," said the builder puffing fag ash all over himself. You couldn't tell it apart from the plaster dust.

"I know. I'll explain," I said hastily.

He turned to Charley. "It ain't safe up there, duckie. It's not a playground, yer know."

She gave him her absolute best glower, then turned to me. "It's alright if I climb up things, isn't it mum?"

I led her away quickly. "Not while they're trying to work," I said.

"Does that mean I can climb on it when they're not around?" she asked brightly.

"Let's talk about it later, now where's the paints?" I said walking swiftly inside and hoping he didn't hear.

My plan had been to contain us in one room to work, with the stuff we needed, and move from room to room around the builders. That didn't work when the windows were going in and they tackled every room at the same time.

I gave up and we went out. Friends were very tolerant and we got lots of invitations. But inevitably we had to go home and face whatever was waiting. There was either another hole in a wall, another wall missing, wires hanging and the electric off as the electrician replaced all the chewed wires which turned out to be all of it, and plaster tramped absolutely everywhere. It even got in the bed.

Once when we got home there was a massive hole in the wall big enough to drive a mini bus through and a brand new view of the garden that shouldn't be there.

"It just fell out," said the builder not even looking guilty. "Must have been a big opening at one time."

I looked through it into the garden-come-building site and tried to see the positive side. I felt that positive I wanted to toss myself down in the brick dust and howl.

"Ooooh! It's so cool. Can we keep it like this mum?" said Charley stepping in and out.

"No darling, we can't live with a huge hole, can we?" I turned to the builder. "I guess it must have been where the barn doors once were and this opened into the crew yard."

"What? We're living in a barn?" said Chelsea dramatically, stepping disdainfully over the heap of rubble that is our house.

"That's really cool," said Charley again, sitting in the gap admiring the view of old bricks, rotten wood and mouldy plaster that was heaped up where the flower bed once was.

"It will be more than cool, it'll be freezing if we don't get it sealed up quick, when are the new French doors coming?" I asked the builder.

"Not sure yet," he said taking his cap off and scratching what was left of his hair and avoiding my eye. He had a tide mark of dust round his face like clown's make up. "But don't worry, we'll board it up till then."

I didn't feel reassured. As always with builders 'till then' got pushed further and further beyond my grasp.

A warm soft not-so-little-any-more but comforting hand found its way into mine. "Shall I make you a cup of tea mum?" asked Chelsea. If I looked at her I certainly would cry.

"That would be lovely darling," I said.

"And I'll get those Hobnobs out that we save especially for us and not the builders," said Charley in their earshot. At least with laughing so much you can pretend it's what's responsible for the wet on your cheeks.

Later, when Chelsea was at dance classes and Charley out of earshot hanging off the scaffolding once the builders had gone for the day, I had a good cry on Charles.

"It won't go on forever," he soothed, stroking my hair like he does the girls. I noticed he kept examining it for debris.

"It feels like it," I sobbed, thinking it was easy for him to say, out at work every day.

"Well, you've got another London trip coming up again soon, so you'll get away from it then, and maybe you need a day out with your friend. You haven't been out for ages have you?"

He made things sound lighter. I'd been so busy trying to keep Home Ed on track, running errands when the builders ran out of materials, making endless decisions about trivia like basins and window catches, I felt absolutely drained.

We looked at the calendar and fixed dates. Then finished off the rather crunchy Hobnobs. Even they had brick dust in now. As we watched Charley swing expertly down from the scaffolding Charles picked something gritty from between his teeth.

When he came back from collecting Chelsea he had a fresh new sealed packet of biscuits in his hand.

"God, it sounds horrendous," said my best friend. We were sitting in her garden. It was absolute bliss. There were no builders, no rubble, no noise and no film of muck on my tea.

"It is," I said. "We're sleeping on Chelsea's bedroom floor at the moment whilst the girl's double up. There's a colossal hole in the studio wall. Our bedroom ceiling has all but collapsed and we found rat city in the roof space. The fireplace has fallen off the living room wall and there's soot all over the living room. And the kitchen windows are wrong and are having to be remade. Thank god it's a warm summer. And why are you laughing?" I asked also bursting into giggles at the sight of her.

"Aw! I'm sorry, I don't know. It sounds the worst sort of nightmare."

"What? And you think that's funny!"

"You'll see the funny side of it one day. When it's all done." She picked a fly out of her tea.

"I'm going to die before it's done!" If I get a fly in my clean tea it'll be the last straw.

"Don't say that! And I hope you're writing about it. When we did our house we lived in the outbuildings. It must be hell for you living in it and trying to Home Educate as well. How are the girls finding it?"

"They find it fascinating. Besides, it's a great distraction when I'm trying to get them to concentrate."

"I don't know how you manage to work at all."

"We do a lot outside. Chelsea is making a table with left over wood at the moment..."

"CDT. That's what my youngest does in school!" she laughed.

"...And Charley is making a mosaic with left over pottery and some of mum's chipped plates. Well, nearly all mum's plates were chipped so she's got plenty to go at. Actually, I think they're learning so much with all this going on, certainly about living creatively through chaos. Everything has to be coped with, and what better skills for life than coping."

"Probably better skills than my kids are learning at the moment," she said.

"How's it going?" I asked.

"Well, my eldest is learning in disruptive chaos worse than yours. I go over stuff with him at home when I can. The school's got me down as interfering and close ranks when I go in when all I want to do is help. But they're only interested in bright kids. You know what the peripatetic teacher said to me?"

"What?"

"He said 'you want to get your son out of that class'. What an admission. Now our youngest is getting daily tummy aches and I think that's to do with the school too."

"I'm sorry. You must feel so worried." It sounded worse than what I was going through. At least I was sure my kids were happy even round the demolition. We listened to the bird song. It made a great change from hammering.

"Actually, I've just thought of a funny side," I said changing the subject and looking to cheer her up.

"What's that?" Her smile returned again.

"Well, you know how quiet it is at our house, never anyone about being at the end of the lane?"

"Yea?"

"I was just getting dressed yesterday and had hardly anything on and walked over to the window to look at the sea and someone walked along the footpath gawping in. They must have got an eyeful!"

"See. There is a funny side after all!" We laughed our troubles away.

*

I reckoned I was a fairly patient soul. I rarely got cross with the kids, give or take the odd tantrum. But one thing sure to put me in a dreadful mood was cleaning up. When everything was normal I did the bare minimum, enough to keep me reasonably sane. But cleaning up through building work was like trying to hold the tide back. There was grit in the bottom of all the cups and dishes so if I forgot to give them a good wipe I got a sludgy residue with my tea like before tea bags were invented. Grit crunched beneath my shoes and cut our feet. It was in the bed, in the shower tray and somehow even in my knickers. Dinner has film on it before we could get it in our mouths and mashed potatoes had the same crunch as when eating on the beach.

As if all the building muck wasn't bad enough there was the wildlife. They'd had free reign in the house for a while and were obviously reluctant to be evicted.

"Mum, there's s slug in the pantry!" said Chelsea.

"How on earth did that get in there? Put it out will you darling?"

"I'm not touching it!"

"You don't need to touch it, just collect it in something."

She used my tea towel, the one I just happened to have washed.

"Mum, there's a dead mouse on the carpet."

"Oh goodness, throw it out will you?"

"Give it to the cat," suggested Charley.

"It was probably the cat who left it there," said Chelsea. "Dad, we need you," she yelled.

Charles bravely shook the mat out; I noticed he didn't want to touch it either.

Next; "Mum, there's a blackbird in the kitchen."

We captured it in a towel and studied it for a few minutes until I was anxious it would die of fright. It was so light and delicate we could not imagine it surviving so I let it go into the shrubs and away, scolding us for its inconvenience. They were obviously more resilient than we thought. Next moment it was bashing hell out of a snail on a slab of concrete.

And one summery afternoon lying on my back in the garden in relaxed gratitude that the builders weren't about I had this niggling sensation I was being stared at. I thought everyone else was inside out of the sun. I raised my head to look round and stared the fox straight in the face. He was poised, absolutely still, wondering what to do about me, foxy little eyes staring, long pointy nose sniffing my smell. I kept absolutely still, also staring, feeling as vulnerable as Jemima Puddleduck and wondering if he was looking for something to take back to the cubs. He decided I wouldn't do and slunk off noiselessly through the garden leaving a slightly musty scent behind him. I didn't feel quite so relaxed after that.

Mum's garden was truly amazing. Despite the building scars the roses unfurled round the scaffolding. The bush of stripy roses bloomed magnificently outside the hole in the wall. The barn wall was covered in Golden Showers. And we had huge peachy pale petals nodding outside our bedroom window. They were so exquisite even the builders noticed.

"Aren't they stunning," said the one with the huge tattoo of a rose on his bum, cupping his grimy hand round a satiny bloom. It was like a vision of beauty and the beast.

"Indeed they are," I said losing my nose in one and getting an insect up it for my trouble.

The girls collected the petals to make perfume and potpourri. I collected bouquets of them to stand upon whichever table we worked round just to have something clean and free from brick dust.

38

Patient for the most part I may be but there were times it was thinner than the membrane they were dry lining the walls with. Thinner than even I realised.

Charley and I finished our experiment and she made for the door to investigate the latest round of scraping noises coming from the builders. I wanted her to record it, not necessarily for education's sake but to give me something tangible to put in her folder, so I called her back.

"Hey, hang on, we'll just finish by recording what we've found out today."

"But I have finished," she said.

"Yea, but I want us to record it so we won't forget what we've achieved."

"But I won't forget."

"Okay, but I'd still like you to record it. All scientists record their findings."

"But I don't need to, I'll remember. And I want to go out now." She drew patterns in the dust with her bare big toe.

I could feel my patience eroding away as clearly as the salt air was eroding our bricks. I wanted to shout 'just write the bloody stuff down will you' but I tried something else first. Chelsea looked up from her work sensing eruption.

"Come on, it won't take a minute, and you need something down on paper to show all the good things you learn." I was trying to be persuasive, but we both knew the argument was thin.

"I don't. I know what I've learned. And I want to do something else." She said it with such emphasis it made me feel totally unreasonable for asking any more of her. But my patience just ran out. My voice rose. I think I was becoming hysterical.

"Look, Charley, if you can't get on with your work and do what I ask there's no way we can Home Educate, you'll have to go back to school."

The second the words were out the horror of what I said reflected back at me from her face. She gave me a look of utter betrayal. She slammed the paper down, she snatched up a pen, yanked a chair out and plonked on it, breathing heavily. She didn't look at me. Chelsea got her head down and quickly finished.

Feeling completely ashamed I attempted to return to the helpful caring mode I usually try to operate in.

"Look, this is how..."

"I can do it," she snapped at me angrily. And dismissively. I slunk away more hang-dog than the fox and with a million times more shame.

She did it in five minutes, chucked the pen down and went out. Had she learnt anything? No. Had it gained either of us anything? No. Had I ruined what was otherwise a nice day? Yes.

I slunk off up the plaster splattered staircase to hide for a bit. There must have been an atmosphere – even the builders were getting on busily like naughty children. From the upstairs window I caught sight of her on the swing talking to her sister. They both looked serious. They both looked like they were making a pact against their evil mother.

*

Charles as always issued hugs and comforting words. We sat in the garden that evening monitoring them on the scaffolding and surveying the day's wreckage.

"Look, don't beat yourself up about it. You lost your rag, that's all. Teachers do it all the time."

"I know that, but to use school as a threat. I can't believe I said that! There are good things that go on in schools, I want the girls to know that, I should never ever use it as a threat."

"I know," he said gently. "But don't worry, the other side of it is it's also partly true that if they don't work at home, Home Educating can't continue and they will have to work at school."

"I suppose, but it's up to me to find approaches to make Home Education work better, not just threaten them when it doesn't."

"Ideally, yes, but you're only human. And it is a bit stressful trying to work here at the moment."

"A bit?" I virtually shrieked. The girls turned to look.

"Okay, a lot stressful," he said grinning and defending himself from the piece of plaster board I threw at him.

"I should say so. And on the subject of stress, the new bath's leaking!"

*

Charley grabbed my neck and pulled me down in a tight clasping cuddle as I leaned over the bed to kiss her goodnight. She held me down and whispered in my ear.

"I'm sorry I didn't do my work without arguing today." She clung very tightly. Perhaps she didn't want me to see her face. My throat swelled to the size of a snake's with an antelope down it.

"I'm sorry too darling, that I got cross and threatened you with school. It was wrong to do that," I squeezed out.

"It's okay," she said. I managed to ease my neck into less of a strangle hold and rested my cheek next to hers.

"The thing is, some schools are great and thousands of children enjoy going. You might one day."

She pushed me up hands still clasped behind my neck and looked at me to see if I was teasing or anything.

"I like being Home Educated," she said staring into my soul very intently.

"And I like having you to Home Educate," I said smiling. "But we will need to work together so we can continue."

"I know. I will. Honest." Her little face shone with good intention.

"Goodnight darling." I kissed her hot and sun sweet cheeks.

"Goodnight, mum." She arranged Ted on her pillow and dropped her golden head down upon him.

As I closed the bedroom door that wonderful feeling of restored love and happiness descended as softly as a summer dusk.

*

I had to wait while my best friend stopped laughing. It was her reaction to my shameful story. I told her everything.

"Oh, that's so funny," she said. I could imagine her wiping her cheeks down the other end the phone. "Here's you threatening your kids with going to school whilst the majority of the kids in my son's group are threatened regularly with being expelled from school!"

Nothing like a change of perspective to make you feel a bit better about your faults.

*

It was hard to tell which was worse; having the builders around all the time bashing and hammering and swearing and caterwauling in time to Radio Drivel. Or not having them on site and not getting on when there seemed to be such a long way to go. But at least over the summer I could ease off trying to Home Educate around total mayhem. I declared 'Breaking up' day. It was a change from breaking down.

"Can I make another table for my new room mum?" asked Chelsea straight away and demolishing my image of a bit more time for me.

So while the builders weren't around she provided the noise of sawing, hammering and the occasional 'Oh shit!' It was a bit gruelling to complete but if I ever doubted her staying skills I wouldn't any more. She even painted it. And Charley used the opportunity to hammer lots of collected nails into bits of wood she found lying around and paint her toenails with emulsion.

I tried to re-establish my 'out of bounds' session during the break from Home Ed I bought myself a beautiful basket from a charity shop to store my books and writing in so I could carry it from room to room round the disruption, or into the garden and work out there sometimes. It made me feel I was actually achieving something.

Then I noticed a change. Instead of bashing and knocking and ripping out, there seemed to be more of a building up. Instead of naked brick and ripped down ceilings there was smooth peachy plaster like silk to the touch. Instead of sledge hammering, those skilful hands were piecing things back together and proper rooms with walls and windows were appearing. The only drawback was the all pervasive smell of substances.

"Mum, this stink is making me feel sick."

"I should go outside then."

"What's that brown stuff they're painting on the beams and why is the builder wearing a mask.

"It's woodworm killer. Keep out of there, the fumes are toxic."

Charley walked around with a mask on like Michael Jackson.

"What is that awful smell?" asked Charles when he got home.

"Which one? Take your pick."

All our dinners tasted of something like paint stripper. But I suppose it was a marginally better smell than decaying rats.

"Shall we take our tea down the marsh?" suggested Chelsea holding her nose.

"Brilliant idea," I said. "Get the things out. What time's the tide?"

Charles checked the tide table and the girls went into the pantry to get the basket. It was great having a pantry. I could throw all sorts of rubbish in there and shut the door on it. They came out with a multitude of snacks and no basket. Whilst I got salad and drinks together Charles made what he calls sandwiches; I call them doorstops. They're made for man's hands.

"I can't get my mouth round that," complained Charley. I glared at Charles to restrain him from making a clever comment about the size of her mouth and he grinned.

"Where's the basket?" he asked instead, looking innocent. Charley went off again and came back with no basket but with one of mum's old rugs.

"Shall we take this?"

"No it smells of dog," said Chelsea finally packing the basket.

"It'll do to sit on though," I said. Picnic and accessories finally assembled we walked across the field to the sea bank and the incoming tide. Chelsea spread the smelly rug and was the first to sit on it. Charley was the first to stuff a man-sized sandwich down then kicked her wellies off and sat on the edge of a small creek watching it fill with water. I was just content to sniff the lovely substance-free sea smell.

"Can we paddle?" called Charley.

"Wait for me," said Chelsea also kicking her wellies off.

They waded about in the incoming gushes of shallow water.

"Mind you don't slip," called Charles as parents inevitably do.

"It wouldn't matter really," I murmured, feeling relaxation ooze round tense and tattered muscles as softly as the water oozed round the girl's ankles. With perfect timing Chelsea slipped down, soaked herself and scrambled up giggling. She looked at me gauging my reaction.

"Well, you might as well jump in now," I laughed with her.

"Can we?"

"Why not?" I said.

"In our clothes?"

"Yea, go on. You might as well. It's so lovely and warm."

They looked at each other grinning.

"You first," said Chelsea, even though she was already soaked.

"No you."

"Let's do it together." Holding hands and screaming with laughter and happiness they splashed about as the water got deeper until they were swimming. It looked so delicious I was tempted to join in. Silly adult inhibitions kept me on dry land. That and having to walk back across the field in soaking knickers.

Some neighbours also enjoying the summer evening walked round to see what the noise was and their dog joined the girls in the water. The happy screaming quadrupled.

"Look at that," exclaimed one of them. "They're having real proper fun like we used to."

"Better than the telly any day," said the other.

We stood watching them until two tired wet muddy urchins emerged from the water with one spindly wet dog.

They wrapped the smelly dog blanket round them both like a cloak and walked hand in hand back through the evening field. Charles and I straggled behind with all the other stuff plus two pairs of wellies, the only dry items the girls had. A barn owl sat on the fence posts wishing we'd hurry up and leave his hunting ground to him.

When we got back it wasn't the smell of substances that hit me. It was the perfume of the roses and the honeysuckle. The scent heavy orange blossom. And the musty taste of harvest on the tongue. Plus the smell of two salty children getting showered ready for bed.

*

I was in heaven. I had a toilet outside my bedroom door. I never had a toilet within easy reach of my bedroom in the whole of my life before. Where I grew up in our house in London my little box bedroom was right at the top of the house and toilet was at the bottom with three flights of stairs in between.

When my folks first bought this old house the toilet was in the garden. When they got an indoor one installed it was downstairs and my room was up. At our other cottage the bathroom was downstairs, right through the house and at the back; about as far away from my bedroom as possible.

So a toilet outside my bedroom door was the height of luxury for me. In fact we had two toilets. We thought we were royalty. I didn't care if it hadn't got a door on it; I intended to wake up regularly throughout the night just to use it.

39

"Remind me who my daughter is," said Charles as Chelsea got ready for her thirteenth birthday. She looked about sixteen by the time she'd finished getting ready for her friends to come.

Thirteen! Can we cope with a Home Educating teenager?

We managed to string some balloons among the remains of the plastering and wet cement and make a bit of a party, mostly in the garden. The building site filled with other teenagers and those that weren't practised hard. And just to make the day really special the builders didn't turn up so we could enjoy it without seeing grimy underpants straining out the top of loose jeans and eat a meal without brick dust in it. And listen to decent music although the teens' idea of decent differs greatly from mine.

That over it was back down to Home Ed as the others go back to school.

"Do you realise we've been doing this for four years now?" I said to Charles.

"Can't believe it really."

"And I have a feeling we'll be doing it for a few years more yet," I said.

He looked at me and smiled.

"I can't see it any other way now," he said, happily sighing.

"Me neither!" Home Educating was our life and I couldn't see it changing.

What we wanted changing more than anything educational was the state of house. It was almost a year since the disruption started and we were all ready to have a proper house back instead of a shifting state of construction. But rooms were actually beginning to look finished. I could begin to imagine a life without builders' bums.

One thing that was definitely changing was the smell of

substances. We had paint stench rather than the treatments or the filler or the plaster.

"You've got paint in your hair, dad," giggled Chelsea. He wiped it out with his hand and ended up smearing more on.

"There's paint on my favourite tee-shirt," said Charley, standing picking dried paint off her fingernails.

"How did that get there? You had your old one on when you were helping?"

"I changed it, then I forgot and leant against the wall."

"So where's the painty tee-shirt now?" I asked looking down at her from the top of the step ladder.

"On my bedroom floor."

"What? On your new bedroom carpet?" I shrieked so neurotically the ladder wobbled.

"Just a sec." She disappeared and then came running back. "Mum, there's paint on my new carpet."

I would have screamed but I was saving my energy to get the house finished. Every moment not working with the girls we were painting. And the painting forced us to give the girls some healthy neglect when we weren't doing our learning. But as with everything in our lives it involved them too.

"What we doing this weekend?"

"Painting."

"Can we help?"

"Okay, if you're careful."

Studious painting followed.

"No! Don't paint that bit. You don't paint the door handle otherwise how would we get the door open?" said Charles.

"Oh!" said Charley looking disappointed.

"Mum!" yelled Chelsea sounding alarmed. "I've just kicked the paint over and it's running down through the cracks in the floorboards." Terrific!

Next day; "Who painted the cat's tail?"

Charley was very, very quiet. Charles smirked so I didn't tell him about the turquoise smear on his cheek.

I decided to give Chelsea free reign with doing something creative with an old door tucked in one corner. She painted sun flowers all over it in bright colours. I loved it.

"It reminds me of grandma," she said as we stood admiring it.

"Why?" I asked.

"Don't you remember? She painted the sunflower on the bonnet of her car to hide the rusty bit. And I thought it would go nicely with her painting on the other door," she said. I had forgotten about the car. Mum was gently fading from my senses but there were little memories of her throughout the house.

She had painted a panoramic masterpiece on the toilet door next to where Chelsea was working which we'd carefully kept as it was. I looked at Chelsea. Not only did she have mum's warm brown eyes and capacity for giggling, but it looked like she had her creative talent too.

"Do you miss her?" she asked me suddenly. She'd caught me staring.

"Sometimes. Do you?"

"Not really. I think she's all around me here," she said.

"Yes, she is really isn't she?" I kissed her paint streaked cheek. She was thirteen going on twenty.

"Mum, you've got yellow on your lips now," Chelsea laughed.

"I want to do a flower," said Charley. She picked up a small brush.

"It's finished now, you can't," said Chelsea.

"Doh!" Charley went away crossly and I tried to think of somewhere for her to paint.

I was too late; when I went upstairs there was a little dolphin on the new bedroom wall. Then a message 'I love you' underneath as if in afterthought she realised it would soften the crime.

*

Charles and I did the Locomotion round the studio space. Then on through the living room. Then the kitchen. Then the new light filled conservatory. The girls stood in the doorways worrying their parents may have lost their minds.

"It's finished, it's finished," I whooped, arms above my head. "Ye-es! Ye-es!" Footballers had nothing on my chanting. I tried to drag the girls into it but they were having none of this immature behaviour.

"What, you mean they're not coming back?" asked Chelsea.

"No more builders?" asked Charley.

"No! No more banging and bashing!" I whooped.

"No more awful singing!" said Chelsea.

"No more swearing," added Charley.

The broken window frames, old plaster boards and rubble heaps had gone. The skip had gone. The tattooed, chain smoking men had gone. The house was ours again except for a few dog ends in the garden.

"Let's make a cake," said Chelsea.

We could make cake without grit in it. We could work in any room we wanted without boots tramping through. We could clean up and it would stay like that. We could actually work in separate rooms and have a bit of private space. The only distraction will be the song of the robin. The rooms radiated silence and glowed with newly applied colour. All spidery and rat infested corners were excavated and renewed. No mould anywhere. The garden, even in the throes of winter dying, looked like it could be a garden again. There were glistening French doors where the hole had been. And we could at last unpack the remains of the boxes.

I was going to be ultra fit. The rooms seemed so spacious and empty I had to take paces across them rather than just turn round and fall over plaster board. The girls could work in different rooms so I was running between them like a dog between two people playing catch. It was worth every stride for the space and privacy.

Chelsea shouted me to the studio just when the experiments in the kitchen were getting exciting. She held up a beautiful bag she'd made. Her eye for colour and texture could make me feel inadequate.

"I made it for Jane for Christmas," she said.

"That's lovely darling. Let me get a photo of it for your folder." She was building up quite a pictorial portfolio of her achievements and activities. Whilst I had the camera out I went back and photographed Charley trying to make an electromagnet. She might not be going to do the recording but I had my methods. I also had my own folder to remind me of all the educational processes going on that no one knew about, only us. When I looked back through it, it reminded me of the wonderful education the girls were getting. Over the last year some of that had been buried under broken bricks and broken hearts. I really felt we were on our way to healing.

*

Christmas was much better than the grim affair of the year before with still a sense of celebration about being whole again, in more ways than one. We had a huge house-warming come New Year's Eve party straight after. Friends came and admired the house, sat round the open fire, and the children went to explore outside despite the cold. To them it was like a mega adventure playground. The parents weren't quite so sure.

"Doesn't it bother you not having any neighbours?"

I have got neighbours," I said pointing to another cottage across the green winter wheat field.

"No one to complain about the noise," said one dad enviously, as he watched the kids yelling and laughing and generally doing the kind of thing that annoys neighbours, as kids do.

"How far are you from the shops?"

"About three miles from the village one and ten from a supermarket."

"I couldn't do without the shops."

"I'd rather have no shops if it meant no neighbours, especially with the kids at home all day," said the dad again.

"Will you still Home Educate now they're older?" asked a parent of one of Chelsea's new dance club friends who had joined us for the first time. Funny how people asked this as if our principles about what we want for the girls have changed now they're older. We still want them to be happy, to be healthy and to learn and be interested in learning.

"Sure, why not?"

"Well, Charley will soon be old enough for second school too, won't she?"

"Yea, but it makes no difference. Their learning develops all the time. I don't see a need to change at the moment. We'll just take each stage as it comes, as we've always done." I smiled and hoped she understood. Our approach was hard for some parents to understand, needing as they did school guarantees. But that hardly bothered me these days. And there are no guarantees anywhere.

"I wouldn't want my two at home all day," she laughed.

"You just get into a different way of being," I said.

"Not sure I want to!" She laughed.

Sometimes I forgot others didn't enjoy being with their kids as much as we did. But then, perhaps Home Educating made them different kinds of kids.

*

Charley's first writing task as we settled into our new Home Ed routine in the new year, in our new builder free house, was writing down all the swear words she knew.

"How do you spell bloody?" she asked.

"That's not a swear word," said Chelsea, working alongside her.

"It is when dad uses it," said Charley.

"What are you doing darling?" I asked, looking at the neglected English book beside her.

"I'm making a swear jar. Everyone swears too much in this house. You have to put money in the jar every time you do from now on."

"I don't swear!" I said.

"Yes, you do!" they both said with shocking emphasis.

"Do I?"

"Yes!"

"Well, not much anyway and only when provoked."

"How do you spell bugger?"

"You should have made it when the builders were here you would have got rich then," laughed Chelsea.

"Anyway, what's happening to the money?" I asked after I'd spelt bugger.

"I'm going to buy more Lego."

"I see," I laughed. "It's more of a money making ploy than about stopping us swearing!" It was rather worried to think we swore so much she felt she could make a good income from it.

"It's not!" She glared at me in indignation. "You do swear, and dad's worse. It's got to stop." I felt admonished. I wished I'd got my own back earlier and said something about the dolphin now!

"How do you spell cobblers?"

"I don't say cobblers!" I insisted.

"No but dad does," said Chelsea.

"And he says bollocks!" added Charley.

I tried very hard not to laugh. I'd get Charles about that later. I hoped she didn't ask me how to spell the F word but I doubted she would, we never used it, not in front of them anyway.

When I looked later fuck was there along with all the others. It was worth fifty pence where damn was only worth ten. I thought she was undercharging.

*

Chelsea's new task for the new year was to make herself another timetable. She wanted to keep on track with her mates. Partly because all anyone ever asked her now she was older was about GCSEs.

"But I don't get what all the fuss about GCSEs is anyway," she said. I guessed it was very likely that none of the kids at school did either, they were just another boring thing adults were making them do without true understanding why.

We talked about building skills that they might one day need in adult life when they want to work or study further and how they will need to prove those skills to someone else.

"That's all GCSEs are really," I told her. "They show that you've reached a certain standard of education and you are given a certificate to prove you have which you can then show to employers or universities."

"Shall I do GCSEs?" she asked.

"It's up to you. We haven't thought that far ahead yet. But we could start looking at them and the coursework and then you'll have something to focus on."

She decided she wanted to. She was a bit younger than the norm but I was happy to go with it, she'd certainly got the brain.

When I looked at the GCSE Art syllabus it looked about as mind numbing as going to the supermarket. I decided she'd be better off continuing her creative skills in her own way even though I kept a sneaky eye on the topics in the syllabi.

I sensed Chelsea was getting ready for something more challenging and directed so I looked at some other courses online.

"Look at this." I showed her a brochure from the Open College of the Arts and the textile course in particular.

"What is it?"

"Well, it's a textile course. You have a tutor assigned to you and a course book which sets out little projects to accomplish which you can work through at your own pace. Then the tutor gives you some feedback. I thought it might be something you could focus your artwork on."

"Will other children be doing it?" she asked looking interested.

"Not children of your age. They'll be doing their school work. It's mostly for older students. Those who've finished school and are going onto university."

"So it's for older people?"

"In a way. But I think you're so good at textiles you could make a good job of this Level One module. See how you get on with it. I think you'd enjoy it."

Her eyes were bright as she was reading the brochure. "It leads to a degree. I'm only thirteen. Do you think they would let me do it?"

"I could ring the tutor and find out. If you'd like me to. I just thought you might need someone more than me to inspire you..."

"You do inspire me mum..." she looked honestly into my eyes. My heart swelled. "But...it does look good."

"You'd need to do your basic subjects as well. But this might be something more interesting along side."

"I think I'd like to." She beamed at me and looked so proud of herself I was nearly welling up. I think she grew an inch and she was already catching me up. Bloody hell, where did my little girl go?

Ooops! That was ten pence worth!

40

"Who's that shifting about?" said Charles cocking an ear to the ceiling and the bedrooms above just as we'd collapsed on the new sofa for a bit of telly before bed. It was our special bit of time together. Clean sofa. Clean house. No unnerving scrabbling. Magic! Trouble is we were usually too knackered to do anything exciting with it.

"Sounds like Charley, perhaps she's just getting a book and she'll get back in bed" I said. The stairs creaked even though she was creeping and she came into the living room very quietly. She sat down in front of the telly, notebook and pen in hand, without saying anything to us and started writing.

Charles caught my eye and mouthed 'What's she doing?' I shrugged and looked back at her.

"You okay darling?" I asked. She normally goes out like she's drugged at the end of the day. Not surprising really considering she uses the energy of fifty puppies.

"Yes. Except I couldn't sleep because I want to write a book. How do you spell fairy?"

I had trouble believing this. She had as much fondness for writing as I do mammograms and it was just as painful trying to squeeze any out of her.

"It's not the best time to write just now darling. You're tired and your dad and I are too tired to help you right now and we'd just like to relax and watch this programme which will probably distract you..."

"Yes, I know. But how do you spell fairy?"

I looked at Charles. I looked at the telly. I looked back at her pen poised. I gave in.

"F-a-i-r-y!" She scribbled it down and carried on writing. I was too tired to get involved and I couldn't believe she'd keep it up long.

"How do you spell imaginary?"

I stared at the programme. I sensed I was beginning to lose the plot in more ways than one. I thought of all the times I'd wanted her to write and she'd argued. All the effort I'd made to choose my moment when she wasn't tired or hungry, when there were no distractions and conditions were the absolute best for her to be able to concentrate. All the input I had in giving her inspiration and encouragement and all she could produce was a few lines. And here she was tired, distracted by telly and two hacked off parents who were being as unhelpful as possible and she was writing a book? I had to wonder where I'd got it so wrong.

I spelt imaginary then attempted to pick up the plot again.

"Decided?" she asked two minutes after murder had been committed and just at the moment the main suspect said something important.

"Mum?"

"What?" My exasperation was showing – at least I hoped it was.

"Mum's trying to watch this programme," said Charles.

"You spell decided then."

He spelled it out. I concentrated but the plot was beyond me now. It was the dilemma that got to me most. Should I encourage her to do something I've been anxious to get her to do for years? Or should I maintain that it is my time now and not Home Educating time and thus waste the opportunity? I glanced across at her scribbling, staring at the telly, scribbling again. She looked as endearing as ever.

By eleven she'd written two whole pages the most she'd ever written in her entire life in one sitting. Charles and I had completely failed to understand the motive for the murder and we decided to go to bed. He nodded his head towards the bedrooms. I shrugged towards Charley.

"We're off to bed now sweetie, I think you should too," he said.

"Okay," she said brightly. "I'll do this again tomorrow." And she closed the notebook, clasped it to her as if it was a real treasure, and nipped off up the stairs ahead of us. "Come tuck me in again, mum," she called.

By the time I'd done my teeth and got changed she was nearly asleep with the notebook tucked beside her pillow, tangled in her golden curls.

"Night darling." I bent and kissed her.

"Night mum... Thanks for helping."

All my irritation melted away.

She continued her story writing first thing. And all the while we ate lunch. In the car on the way to our group meeting. While she was watching her favourite programmes. All through supper. And when I tucked her in again that night she announced, "I'm going to be a book writer when I grow up."

"That's wonderful," I said snuggling the duvet tight round her. She looked up at me.

"What are you going to be mum?" She giggled realising what she'd just said.

"I want to be a writer too."

As I closed the bedroom door on her sleepy form I had a sudden premonition; one day I might actually be something other than a Home Educator. Inconceivable!

*

We moved into the modern age. We got broadband! And a new computer. I daren't invest in one before for fear of it being ruined in the renovations nightmare. I lost count of the number of times we shunted it round the rooms and excavated it from brick dust.

Now we could actually use the computer like normal people. There were so many excellent educational sites we couldn't use before because it was just too slow, I could see we'd be spending increasing amounts of time on line. The Home Ed group network took on a whole new extension of support and gossip. And I'd be able to keep one step ahead of the kids' and what they know more easily!

The potential for children's learning online was mind blowing. Made me wonder what we need schools for as all information is there. Other than mass child minding that is.

*

The lady at the OCA was very encouraging.

"The only thing that may be of concern is the motivation especially with students who are young," she said after I'd told her we were interested and all about Chelsea.

"I can't see that being a problem," I said. "She is already motivated to work because it's part of our daily Home Education routine. And she seems very keen on her textile work I think it would just inspire her more."

"Yes. I've come across home schooled children before and see that they are generally very motivated young people. Although your daughter will be the youngest that we've ever taken on. But after you've seen the course pack you have thirty days to change your mind."

"I can't see that there would be anything to change. She seems already excited about doing it already."

"Well, I'll look forward to seeing some of her work then," she said.

I related the conversation to Chelsea and a new shine of doing something important stayed attached to her throughout the day. Even the relatives couldn't tarnish it.

"So when are they starting their GCSEs then?" Same old question.

"They're only thirteen and ten," I reminded her.

"Yes, but the kids in school will soon be starting at this age."

"Yea, and they have to go over and over it because they're too young to get half of it," I said. "Besides, we don't necessarily do what they do in schools. That's why we Home Educate."

She looked at me. I think she was examining me for that alien head again. And there was me thinking we'd got beyond that now.

"But they never get anywhere in life without GCSEs," she said.

"Yea, that's what we're all conditioned to believe." I walked away from the argument before I increased my swear jar debt.

I reckoned it was that kind of conditioning which made parents so desperate for their kids to own all the right bits of paper they forgot to pay attention to the cost of getting them.

However, we went up a notch or ten in everyone's eyes since we were doing a 'proper' educational course. Chelsea told everyone enthusiastically about her textile work. I tried to be on hand to dilute any narrow mindedness.

Some didn't know what to say. Some raised their eyes in amazement. Some just didn't believe that she could do degree level work when she hadn't even taken her GCSEs.

"It's just more appropriate to what she's doing at the moment," I explained.

"But when is she going to do her GCSEs?"

They were like BBC repeats.

But somehow, the structured Textile course moved our Home Education into a more sophisticated framework. We were entering a different phase.

*

My best friend's life revolved around GCSE coursework too. Stories like hers made me so glad we were doing it differently. She virtually Home Educated her son in the evenings whilst he was at school in the day just to help him understand, up his grades, and get out of such a disruptive group.

"But I still cannot believe that the school are happy to let a whole group of kids struggle while they concentrate all their energies on the kids who achieve good grades," she said. We licked cake off our fingers. It had been some time since we'd been able to have one of our restorative jaunts out and we were going for the full monty. I had 'Death by chocolate' and she had chocolate cheesecake. We'd need another coffee to swill it down it was that sickly.

"Oh, I can," I said. "You see, the kids with the good grades are the ones that make the school look good." I was going for full cynicism now she was more used to it.

"But surely not all the teachers are only interested in that, surely there are some that care about the kids?"

"Course there are. But look at the constraints on them. They're all terrified of OFSTED. They'll all be getting pressure to make the kids achieve grades and don't forget that's what most parents want and many of them are not that bothered about the method. As long as the bits of paper are forthcoming. And in the end, that's where all the focus has to go."

"But what about the rest of the kids, the ones who have other talents?" she asked.

"Other talents aren't important really. Not within the system."

"Well, I don't know what to do any more," she said. I'd never heard her so defeated. All of her fight seemed to have gone. We swapped cakes. I gave her my bigger bit.

"You just have to do what you've always done. You have to stay on his side. That's the best thing you can do. Make sure he knows it's the system, not him, that's failing."

We were silent and concentrating on licking last bits off for a while. Then she looked at me.

"I never believed what you told me, you know, about the system being there for the good of the school and the league tables and the government and not for the individual. But I can see exactly what you meant."

I sighed. "You're not the only who's disappointed. I know I'm an old cynic, but I really wanted to believe things had changed since I was in the classroom. And perhaps they have a bit. But they still haven't changed enough to work for the less able. To work well in the less affluent areas like ours where there's such a high proportion of kids who are disruptive and don't value education and are not supported by their parents. If the kids aren't backed up by parental values then it makes it harder for the teachers. What can they do? They have so many kids who don't want to be there, who can be as disruptive as they like because no one can do anything about it. The teachers and the kids who really want to be there are just stuck with it."

"Yea, that's exactly what's happening at his school. And I can only see it getting worse."

"It's alright for the ministers up in Westminster with their kids in select schools. I'd like to see what grades they got if they learnt in the climate ours do. I'd like to see what decisions they make about policies then."

"But in poorer communities, how will it ever change?"

"I don't know. It's a downward spiral. And the trouble is the good teachers move on all the time so there's no continuity."

"I know. My youngest has had three different teachers for maths this term. Her tummy aches are getting worse and the doctor says it's tummy migraines brought on by anxiety. It's so disappointing. I had such high hopes."

"What makes me sick is the way the government comes down so hard on Home Educators even though we are enabling failing children to succeed out of school. The government is also getting twitchy about how many of us are doing it now. There are thousands and thousands; increasing all the time. But they never seem to ask themselves why that is. Why parents actually put themselves through the challenge and enormous sacrifice of Home Educating. They just don't get the fact that parents must be fairly desperate; why would that be? And another question they need to ask why are so many teachers leaving the profession too?"

"Absolutely."

"But can you imagine what it's like teaching kids who don't want to be there, delivering a prescriptive syllabus that's totally inappropriate for half of them, with the Inspectorate breathing down your neck. I would hate it. As I'm sure many of our teachers are beginning too. It's all so bloody sad." We had to change the subject before we depressed ourselves.

The really depressing thing is that education is so wonderful. But how many school kids knew that. I sure hope mine did, for now and forever.

When I got back I went straight to find the girls. Chelsea was making jewellery. Charley was lying outside making up stories with a friend. They were alive and intent. And happy. As they should be as children.

It was conversations like the one I'd just had that made me remember how very, very different it had once been.

41

Sophisticated phase our learning may be entering but it didn't take long for our tidy house to dissolve into the more normal Home Ed chaos that we usually worked in. There were books, materials, tools, science apparatus, craft work, models and papers strewn all over. I loved the busyness of it. Trouble was; we had more space to strew the mess through.

With visitors due I could fill the swear jar just trying to get the kids to help me tidy up. We stacked all the books on the side, stuffed all the craft and science materials back in the cupboard and tied it up with string so it wouldn't burst open again, and put the best pictures up on the pantry door which is now our official gallery.

The girls behaved extremely well; made articulate and intelligent conversation like I'd taught them to then disappeared to their bedrooms. I took on the cooking for the day to try and avoid having to make small talk but one of the guests followed me into the kitchen to make conversation. They were the kind of visitors who didn't like to mention education so the subject hung between us like a bad smell.

As I peeled vegetables I realised she had gone quiet. I hadn't been listening so it might be that she needed an answer to something. I looked to see if she was expecting an intelligent contribution but she was staring intently out the window. No, not out the window; at the jar on the window sill and even more closely at the list of words written on the bit of paper on the jar on the window sill. We'd forgotten to put the swear jar away.

I had a hot flush as she turned and rummaged in her handbag, got her glasses out and put them on. She picked up the jar and examined it. I felt our kudos plummet again. As if it wasn't bad enough our girls didn't go to school; we also let them write rude words. I could imagine what she'd be thinking.

I was wrong. She took her glasses off and squealed with laughter.

"Oh! I wondered what it was. It's a swear jar." She had to break off for giggling. Then she turned back to her handbag.

"Well I think I'd better have a pound's worth for all the bad language we were using in the car coming over when we got stuck behind that tractor."

She dropped a pound in and took it off into the living room to make her husband pay up too.

I shouldn't be so judgemental. I suddenly liked her immensely.

*

The wildlife was still keeping me awake, but thankfully most of it was outside.

Late spring was announced by a very loud cuckoo far too early in the morning. In fact if he'd kept it up I might have been tempted to borrow Charley's catapult. Doves strutted about on the roof above my head purring and cooing loudly from some horrendous dawn-like hour. At night randy foxes barked their blood curdling bark.

In all other aspects the season was spectacular and we got restored opportunity to enjoy the natural world on our doorstep. Last year with the builders wondering about and debris being thrown into the garden from on high our learning opportunities outside had been restricted. Like summer coming, we could blossom again. Our Home Ed days resumed the familiar uninterrupted peace and happiness with which they'd started out all that time ago in our old cottage. Not counting phone calls that is; one day I'd get an answer machine.

The especially-loud-for-the-hard-of-hearing phone bell mum had installed shattered the silence and interrupted my attempts to show the girls how to make an acid indicator out of red cabbage. What we seemed to be doing most of was splashing red stain down clean clothing.

"We could use this for dyeing," said Chelsea collecting the red water.

"And painting," said Charley dribbling pictures with it on my new white dishcloth.

"We will, but we'll do this experiment first, and write it down..." Groan. Phone goes.

"I'll get it," they both said simultaneously and nearly sent the carefully collected cabbage water flying in their fight to get to it first. Chelsea got it; Charley went and got on the stool where Chelsea had been sitting just to get her own back.

"It's for you," said Chelsea handing the phone to me. I'd never have guessed.

"Hello?"

"Oh, hi there, I got your name out of the Home Educators' contact book as I wanted to talk to someone about Home Education," said a woman's voice at the other end.

I often got these calls now. The same ones that I had made almost five years ago. Now it was me giving the support to other beginners.

The girls were wise to phone calls; knew it was an opportunity to sidle off and get on with something else. I didn't mind too much. We could be flexible and it was a beautiful day anyway. They drifted outside while I talked to her, trying very hard to remember what it was like when we'd started and how scary it all was. I kept any really radical ideas to myself, answered her terrified questions and reassured her with how Home Educating had been a delight and a pleasure from the moment we started. And a decision we never ever regretted.

Telling her that made me realise something; how that pleasure had perhaps become tarnished by the turmoil of the last couple of years.

Time to polish it up again.

I called the girls back in and we made our acid indicator then used the remaining water for dyeing.

"Can I put this tee-shirt in?" asked Charley holding up the one with paint stains on.

"Good idea," I said.

"I'm going to dye this old sheet then sew something," said Chelsea. "What you going to dye mum?"

"I'm going to dye this white cloth bag, it's got so grubby now."

We submerged our items in the rich purply water and watched them soak up the colour.

"I hope my tee-shirt won't always smell of old cabbage like this does," said Charley. I had my doubts.

The phone clanged again. Charley fought off her sister and picked it up first with wet purple hands.

"It's for you, mum."

It was my best friend. The girls knew I'd be even longer this time and went back to their outdoor activities. I guess there'd be as many distractions in a classroom, just different ones.

"Hiya, how's it going? Is this a good time?" she asked.

"Yea, go on, how's things your end?" I watched Charley climb up the tree and Chelsea swing happily underneath. Calm and contentment oozed from them like sunshine.

"Fine. I just wanted to tell you something." She sounded excited.

"What?" She immediately sucked my attention back from the hankering to be outside with the girls.

"Well," she took a deep breath. "I'm going to keep the youngest off school for the rest of the year and Home Educate until her tummy settles down and she matures a bit and copes with it all a bit better."

I couldn't help but gasp. "Oh, my god! Are you really? Wow! That's so brave, how come? I didn't think it was really what you wanted."

"I know. And I'm terrified. But I'm not going to carry on with her like she is and have her take all these drugs the doctor's recommending when I know in my heart it's stress from school causing it."

"My goodness, that's amazing. Are you sure? Er...It's not just because of me is it?" I panicked it was my influence making her do something that perhaps wasn't right for her.

"No, it's not just because of you. Although, it's perhaps because of you I feel we could give her this bit of flexibility. I see how happy and bright your kids are and it's given me confidence to make this change. I think when she's matured a bit, or had a longer break, she'll feel better. And anyway, we've got all the books from using with my son. And there's no point in her being at school and me doing the work at home with her as well, like he did."

"Absolutely," I said. "That's so exciting. I'm so pleased for you. And if there's anything at all I can do to help, then please ask."

"Well, you can bring yours over to play then she'll have company and know Home Educating is not weird."

I laughed. "It's not weird. How dare you!"

She laughed too. "Yea, I know, only teasing. You know what I mean."

"Well, I'm really proud of you! I know it's such a major step for you, such a brave decision. And I'm sure it will work out okay."

"She's been a different child since I told her. More like her old self. Seeing her looking better helps take away the panic I feel. But I keep telling myself, it's only for a little while."

"Mmmm." I couldn't help the tease. "That's what we said at the beginning. Five years later we're still at it!"

*

I told my Home Ed best friend about it next time we went over sporting our purply things that still smelt faintly of old cabbage. I'm glad I didn't have to actually wear mine. It was unnerving the way her dogs sniffed us out.

"I'm sure it'll help the child to have a break from school. I know Home Educators who have done that, just home schooled for a short while to give a problem a chance to rectify itself with time," she said.

"Yea, I know. I think it's great. Even with the worry she feels about it, I know she feels huge relief to see her daughter looking better."

"We know all about that, don't we?" she laughed. "I remember when we first started when ours was five, how wretched he was. Look at him now." A tall intelligent looking teenager sat in earnest conversation with Chelsea on the river bank whilst the younger ones paddled and continued to pond dip as we'd been doing all morning. They caught us watching and waved cheekily.

The sun shone down on the children and the shallow water sparkled. It looked a perfect place for kids to be on a perfect afternoon. She and I sat a little away from them with a scattering of equipment, towels, food and bags all round us.

"We ought to put those poor creatures they've caught back in the stream, they'll be getting too warm in the inspection tray now," she said. The sun was making us both relaxed and reluctant to move after our busy morning.

"Mmmm, they love looking at them though, don't they?" Charley was squatting down next to the tray now emptying another net full. She said something too quiet for us to hear and the others all rushed over.

There was something utterly right about watching a group of kids absorbed in discovering and learning and exploring their world. They seemed so totally relaxed about it when they were so stressed out by learning before. I hoped it would stay that way whatever they strive to achieve in later life.

"I wonder where they'll all end up?" I said, as we watched them.

"Yes, I do sometimes," she said. "I feel our Home Ed days are changing a little now, as they get older."

"That's funny, I've been thinking that too. I look toward the future more than I did at the beginning." I said. I leant back on my elbow and sucked a grass stem.

"Yea, me too. I was telling mine about university the other day. The eldest sounded fascinated by the opportunity to do science in labs and that sort of thing. It's almost a shame they have to wait until they're so much older to do it. They're interested now."

"I know. I think all kids probably would be, it's just they seem to have to jump through certain hoops before they're allowed the interesting stuff. Chelsea's really keen to start this textile course in September. Who knows where that will lead, although somehow, I see her going forward with her performing too. Her teacher says she's really outstanding."

"The thing is, with the wide range of experiences Home Educating gives them they're more likely to end up knowing what they like which is so important. So many young people are absolutely passionless about what they do. It's so sad," she said. She called out to her eldest son to start to put the creatures back. Groans of disappointment followed.

"Whatever they do, I'm sure they'll be motivated," she continued, getting up. "I really can't see them ending up with no qualifications, on the streets, without work and unmotivated, as one horrible man told us would happen when we started. The irony is that his son has now dropped out and they're having to go up the school regularly because he's playing truant. I'd like to remind him of his offensive remarks but he has enough on his plate."

We laughed as we packed up the equipment and the picnic and collected the soggy clothes from beside the water. We'd shared such a lot together, our two families. We'd supported each other through Home Educating crisis, personal crises, child crises, and masses and masses of very pleasurable Home Ed days.

"Do you ever think about when our Home Education days will be finished?" I asked stuffing wet towels in bags and retrieving Charley's abandoned shoes.

"Not really, it's just unimaginable. Like trying to imagine your kids as adults out in the world doing their own thing. I mean, you don't ever think about your family life with small kids ending do you, and Home Education is just how our family lives every day really."

"Yea, that's exactly how I feel too."

We trundled all the gear back to the cars with the kids dragging much of it behind them and squeezed everything back in along with the damp but happy children.

"What were you two talking about?" asked Chelsea always intrigued by adult conversations. "You kept looking our way?"

"I bet it was education," said the eldest boy. "They're always talking about education, it's so boring."

"You think that's boring, you should try school," giggled Chelsea.

"You must be joking!" he said.

*

I never did get the smell of cabbage out of my bag. The girl's were luckier; with all the wearing and washing and blowing dry in summer breezes we didn't notice it on theirs. My bag retained its smell so long the cat thought it was worth using for personal purposes and peed in it. But autumn had come by then and I was ready for a new one.

It had been five years since we'd started on this adventure. I'd never have imagined that we would be Home Educating that long. I also could not imagine that we would ever not be Home Educating.

Or imagine what my life would be like when the girls were so grown up they weren't of educating age.

I doubted it would ever happen that learning would not be some part of their life. That's how we lived our life, through learning and discovering, exploring and most of all enjoying. They now truly understood that learning was there to be enjoyed, and education was there to make your life all the more enjoyable. Always.

"Wow! Look at the sky! Come on outside, you two." I could see a magnificent sunset building through our west facing kitchen window. It had a sense of closure that autumn does so well. An arm round each waist I steered them outside to see it.

"Chase us?" called Chelsea breaking away, Charley following. They ran ahead and got through the back gate first.

As I ran after them I had a flash back to five years ago when they were so small and full of fun and it hadn't really changed even though they were taller. We'd got through some really grotty, grieving, gruesome bits. But there was always joy; joy having the kids around, watching them grow, watching them learn, watching them laugh.

"Come on mum, push us," they called climbing on the swinging tyre together.

"I'll get you two," called Charles appearing through the front door to do the pushing. They shrieked in delight. Watching them made me almost want to weep with happiness. The squealing got louder the higher he pushed.

I didn't doubt they'd been happy. The giggling said it all. When I thought back to their school face days it was very different. I knew they wouldn't have been so fulfilled, so motivated, so engaged if they'd remained in school. And perhaps even have learnt so much.

Charles came over and put his arm round me, panting. Chelsea stood on top of the tyre swinging, tall and confident. Charley hung upside down underneath, her pale ringlets swishing the dusky leaves.

"Look at us." Chelsea called out. We stood and watched as the sky raged into oranges and pinks for a big finale behind them.

Charles squeezed me.

"What a sight," he said.

"Did you mean them, or the sunset?" I teased. I knew what he meant really. The sight of all of it filled us up with gratitude. We watched them against the fiery backdrop.

"Do you think they're still happy Home Educating?" I asked.

"Are you blind?" he said grinning. "Happier than I was during my school days." We watched as the swinging slowly stilled and the bats came out.

"I wonder what they'll think when they're older and look back. I wonder if they'll think; 'that was a funny kind of education'!" I said.

"Mmm! Maybe." Charles grinned. I squeezed him.

"Well, if they do, I hope they say it fondly!" I said.

We laughed and turned to walk arm in arm back inside and the girls came running to join us.

End

21073039R00181

Printed in Great Britain
by Amazon

After graduating with [a degree in]
Political Science, **Eva** [worked in]
journalism and as an a[dvertising copywriter.]
She began writing historical romances because
it combined her love of a happy ending with her
passion for history. She lives in Christchurch,
New Zealand, but spends her days immersed in
the world of late Victorian England. Eva loves
hearing from readers and can be reached via her
website, evashepherd.com, and her Facebook page
at Facebook.com/evashepherdromancewriter.

Also by Eva Shepherd

Those Roguish Rosemonts miniseries

A Dance to Save the Debutante
Tempting the Sensible Lady Violet
Falling for the Forbidden Duke

Rebellious Young Ladies miniseries

Lady Amelia's Scandalous Secret
Miss Fairfax's Notorious Duke
Miss Georgina's Marriage Dilemma
Lady Beaumont's Daring Proposition

Rakes, Rebels and Rogues miniseries

A Wager to Win the Debutante

Discover more at millsandboon.co.uk.

A WIDOW TO DEFY THE DUKE

Eva Shepherd

MILLS & BOON

All rights reserved including the right of reproduction in whole or in part in any form. This edition is published by arrangement with Harlequin Enterprises ULC.

This is a work of fiction. Names, characters, places, locations and incidents are purely fictional and bear no relationship to any real life individuals, living or dead, or to any actual places, business establishments, locations, events or incidents. Any resemblance is entirely coincidental.

This book is sold subject to the condition that it shall not, by way of trade or otherwise, be lent, resold, hired out or otherwise circulated without the prior consent of the publisher in any form of binding or cover other than that in which it is published and without a similar condition including this condition being imposed on the subsequent purchaser.

® and TM are trademarks owned and used by the trademark owner and/or its licensee. Trademarks marked with ® are registered with the United Kingdom Patent Office and/or the Office for Harmonisation in the Internal Market and in other countries.

First published in Great Britain 2025
by Mills & Boon, an imprint of HarperCollins*Publishers* Ltd,
1 London Bridge Street, London, SE1 9GF

www.harpercollins.co.uk

HarperCollins*Publishers*, Macken House, 39/40 Mayor Street Upper, Dublin 1, D01 C9W8, Ireland

A Widow to Defy the Duke © 2025 Eva Shepherd

ISBN: 978-0-263-34511-7

03/25

MIX
Paper | Supporting
responsible forestry
FSC™ C007454

This book contains FSC™ certified paper and other controlled sources to ensure responsible forest management.

For more information visit www.harpercollins.co.uk/green.

Printed and Bound in the UK using 100% Renewable Electricity at CPI Group (UK) Ltd, Croydon, CR0 4YY

To my editor, Bryony, whose excellent advice
made this book so much better.

And to Hayley B—
thanks for my wonderful new website.

Prologue

Hampshire, England—1891

There was no point crying. Tears would not change Lady Adelaide Wentworth's fate. That had been sealed from the day she was born. She was a girl, therefore she had only one purpose: to make a good marriage. And there was no better marriage, at least from her mother's point of view, than one to the Duke of Hartfield. It mattered not that she was barely eighteen years old and the man she was to wed was well into his forties. Nor did it matter that he had daughters who were older than Lady Adelaide. It was also deemed irrelevant that they had nothing in common and rumours painted him as a dissolute womaniser.

He was wealthy. He was a duke. Therefore, he was the perfect husband in every way.

With her head held high and her eyes dry, she walked up the aisle of the church near her family's Hampstead estate, on the arm of her uncle, while the church organist joyfully played the wedding march. She would not focus on the life this marriage was condemning her to, but on all the good it would do for her family.

She drew in a shuddering breath. It was time to put aside all dreams of love and face reality. A marriage full of happiness and affection and mutual respect was not for her, but her happiness would be found in saving her sister from a similar fate and her brother and mother from a life of penury.

She caught the eye of her siblings, looking over their shoulders at her from the front pew, and forced herself to smile. They must never know the extent of the sacrifice she was making for them.

Since her father's death her family had barely been able to make ends meet. Her brother had inherited the earldom, but little else. The estate was saddled with seemingly insurmountable debts and her mother had deteriorated from a woman who'd thought she was financially secure to one who fretted constantly over money and her family's future.

When Lady Adelaide reached eighteen, every last penny had been scraped together and a great deal more borrowed to provide the necessary gowns and accessories, so she could be presented to Queen Victoria and have a proper coming out Season. But her mother had made it clear there would be no second Season. If she did not find a suitable husband by the end of that first

Season, all hope would be lost. The family would have gone further into debt, with no means of paying it off.

So, with as much resilience as she could muster, she had endured the humiliation of a Season where her one attribute, her renowned beauty, had been placed on display so she could be sold off to the highest bidder.

Like a good debutante, she had flirted, she had shone and she had flattered at every social occasion. And she had succeeded. It wasn't long before several offers of marriage were made. As the Duke was the richest and most illustrious of all the men vying for her hand, his offer was accepted immediately before the Season had barely begun and before any more money had been squandered.

Her mother had been ecstatic and had ignored all Adelaide's pleas to have a full Season, so maybe, just maybe, she could meet a man who had the necessary fortune, but was one she could also love, or, if not love, then at least respect. Those pleas had fallen on deaf ears and Adelaide eventually gave up all hope of being rescued from her fate.

She reached the altar and her husband-to-be smiled at her, a smile that reminded her of a fox who had just stolen the plumpest chicken from the henhouse.

She struggled to maintain her smile while fighting off the urge to recoil.

It could be worse, Adelaide reassured herself. Lord Grimswald had also offered for her hand, an offer her mother had been tempted to accept. Such a marriage would have stretched Adelaide's fortitude to breaking point.

The man was known to be cruel to his servants and would undoubtedly be cruel to his wife as well. But it wasn't those rumours that had made her mother reluctant to accept his offer. It was that he was also rumoured to be mean with his money and that would never do.

Adelaide swallowed down all lingering resentment she still harboured towards her mother and reminded herself that fear of poverty had made her desperate, desperate enough to consider sacrificing her eldest daughter to a man such as Grimswald to save the family.

But there were no such rumours about the Duke. Despite keeping innumerable mistresses she had heard no whispers about further mistreatment of his last wife. In an attempt at consolation, her mother had also informed Adelaide that once she had provided him with the much-needed heir, she would probably see little of the Duke, the implication being that he would return to his mistresses.

And the Duke had done exactly what they'd hoped for. He had promised to support her mother, provide her sister Felicity with a substantial marriage settlement so she could have her own Season when the time came and had already extended substantial loans at no interest to her brother to save the estate from its debtors. It was this generosity she would try to focus on.

'Adelaide Wentworth, repeat after me,' she heard the vicar say, breaking her out of her reverie.

Dutifully, she repeated her vows, promising to obey, love and cherish the Duke until death did them part.

Had she just committed a sin?

She did not love him, nor could she ever imagine cherishing a man who had effectively bought a wife, one young enough to give him his wished-for son and heir. But she did love her sister and her brother and this sacrifice would be worth it if it brought them financial security and happiness. So perhaps it *was* a marriage based on love, just not between husband and wife.

When it came to promising to obey, she knew she'd had no choice but to do exactly that. Despite once wishing she could make her own choices and live her own life, she had done what was required of her. She had obeyed her mother by agreeing to this marriage. Now she would have to do what every other young woman of her class was forced to do, obey the husband who all but owned her.

'I now pronounce you man and wife,' the vicar continued with a smile. 'You may kiss the bride.'

Her husband leant down and lightly pecked her lips. Her first kiss. She resisted the temptation to wipe her mouth.

It was done. She was now the Duchess of Hartfield.

On her husband's arm she walked back down the aisle, trying to think only of all that this marriage would achieve for her family. Felicity would have an enjoyable Season, where she would dance and flirt with whomever she wanted and eventually marry for love, not duty. Her brother's estate would be saved. Her mother would be secure and never have to fret about money ever again.

Her gaze swept over the guests, who were all smiling back at her as if this really was a happy occasion and they were witnessing two people in love tying the knot.

Her smile faltered as she locked eyes with a man sitting in the back pew, or should she say, sprawled in the back pew. One foot balanced on his thigh, his arm stretched along the backrest, he gave every appearance of a man relaxing at his club, not of one in a house of worship.

And unlike the other guests, he was not smiling. His full lips were curled into a dismissive smirk as he looked her up and down with an expression bordering on derision. Such insolence should cause offence, but it wasn't his audacity that had sparked an unexpected reaction deep within her.

Her progress down the aisle faltered slightly. Who on earth was that man? Why was he looking at her like that? And why, oh, why was her heart suddenly thumping hard and fast in her chest?

She closed her eyes briefly to bring her heartbeat and rapid breathing under control. It was ridiculous. All day she had kept her emotions in check. She had pushed down the turmoil threatening to erupt inside her and kept her fears at bay. She would not succumb now.

It must be the stress of the day finally affecting her. It had to be. She didn't know this man and had never been the sort of flighty young woman who could have her head turned simply because a man was exceedingly handsome.

She dared another look. But by God, he *was* handsome. Slightly long, tousled black hair framed a strong face and his olive skin gave him an exotic, sensual quality she was incapable of ignoring.

The smirk died. His dark brown eyes held her gaze and a surge of hope and expectation welled up inside her.

This is the man who will save me.

Adelaide turned quickly to look straight ahead, shocked at the absurdity of that notion. Harbouring fantasies of a dashing knight in shining armour saving her from her fate was even more pointless than tears.

She had surely learnt that lesson by now. Throughout the Season she had secretly hoped that a man would come into her life, one she could love and who would love her in return. Then the offers of marriage came in and none was from such a man. Yet she had still clung on to a deep wish that, somehow, someone would rescue her.

It had been ridiculous at the time and was even more ridiculous now. It was over. She was already married and no one would save her, least of all this contemptuous stranger.

Cheerful church bells rang out as her husband led her out through the church's arched doorway. Rose petals were tossed into the air, showering the couple, and they were instantly surrounded by guests, shaking the Duke's hand and kissing her on the cheek. She smiled at each of them, thanked them for their good wishes and tried not to cringe as she agreed again and again that this was indeed the happiest of occasions.

All the while, from the corner of her eye, she could see the dark stranger, standing apart from the crowd, leaning against an oak tree and watching the jubilant guests, still with that look of derision.

He moved towards her and she swallowed a gasp of horror. Was he actually going to take her hand and whisk her away? She knew it was absurd, but with each step he took towards her the tempo of her heartbeat increased, until she was sure it must be heard above the pealing bells and chattering guests.

'Isaac, my boy,' the Duke said as the other man reached them, opening up his arms so he could wrap them around the stranger. 'I'm so pleased you could come.'

Isaac? This was Isaac Radcliff? The Duke's notorious illegitimate son? Her husband had invited his illegitimate son to their wedding? The child he had fathered with one of his mistresses? Unbelievable. Did her new husband have no shame?

'Allow me to introduce you to my gorgeous young bride,' the Duke continued, his arm still around his son's shoulder, as if there was nothing improper about this whatsoever. 'Adelaide, may I present Isaac Radcliff? Isaac, the new Duchess of Hartfield.'

Her heart still pounding to a furious rhythm, Adelaide managed a small curtsy and a stifled, 'How do you do, Mr Radcliff?'

He took her hand and bowed over it, and she was grateful for her white glove that was keeping her naked skin from his, but that did not stop the warmth of his hand from seeping into hers and sending small shock waves up her arm.

'Please, call me Isaac,' he said, his deep voice mocking. 'That is surely acceptable as you are now almost my stepmother.'

Adelaide bristled at the underlying insult. He was born before the Duke had married his first wife, so he must be at least twenty-one, about three years older than herself. But her husband seemed to think calling her his stepmother was a jolly jest and, laughing heartily, slapped his son on the back.

'So how are Henny and Prissy taking to having a new stepmother?'

The Duke continued to laugh, but there was nothing funny about that question either. Lady Henrietta and Lady Hampton had made it very clear they were not happy with their father marrying a woman almost the same age as themselves.

The contemptuous look made it obvious the illegitimate son was as equally opposed to the marriage, but Adelaide was not about to be the butt of anyone's jokes or the subject of such disrespect.

'I am now the Duchess of Hartfield and I expect everyone to treat me as such, including my so-called stepchildren,' she said, holding Isaac Radcliff's gaze as steadfastly as she could manage.

'Isn't she a delight?' the Duke said, glancing benevolently at her, while the son's eyebrows rose slightly and a smile curled the edges of his lips. In surprise? In approval? In contempt? Whatever his opinion, she would not let it matter to her.

'A delight, indeed,' he responded, his gaze sweeping up and down her body. Damn it all, once again she had that inappropriate reaction. The same one she'd had when he'd glared at her in the church. Tingles raced up and down her spine, her pulses quickened and the flush of heat enveloping her could not be explained by the mild weather.

She lifted her head higher, fought to ignore her

body's irrational behaviour and stared back, to let him know she was not to be trifled with.

'Well, my boy, I want to hear all about what's been happening in the world of the theatre since I was last in attendance.'

The son thankfully turned his attention back to his father, allowing Adelaide to take in a few slow, deep breaths in an attempt to regain her equanimity.

'Yes, you've been noticeably absent of late. Presumably you've had other distractions keeping you busy.' He once again looked at Adelaide, his mouth lifting in a rueful smile.

Adelaide kept her face impassive, as if ignorant as to what they were discussing, but like everyone else in society, she knew about the Duke's penchant for actresses. Isaac Radcliff's mother had been an actress and a reputed beauty. If the Duke had not been frequenting the theatres lately, that suggested he did not have another mistress at present. As his wife, Adelaide should be pleased about that, but she remained unaffected. How could she possibly care if the man she felt nothing for spent time with other women?

'You can tell me all the news once we get the formalities over at the wedding breakfast,' the Duke said, wrapping his arm around Adelaide's waist.

She was tempted to pull away from her husband, but the tightening of Isaac's lips as his gaze dropped to the encircling arm filled her with indignation.

How dare you judge me? How dare you disapprove of me? You know nothing about me! she wanted to shout at him.

Instead, she moved closer to her new husband and smiled up at him in a manner expected of an obedient new wife, trying to prove to herself, and hopefully to Isaac Radcliff, that she cared nothing of what he thought of her, even if her frayed nerves were telling her otherwise.

'I'm afraid I won't be attending the wedding breakfast,' he responded. 'I just wanted to watch you marry again and meet the new Duchess.'

The Duke released his arm from her waist and leant over towards his son. 'No doubt you've got some beauty of your own waiting for you back in London,' he whispered, but not so quietly that Adelaide could not hear. 'You really are a chip off the old block,' he added with approval as if being a womaniser was an admirable trait.

In response the son at least had the decency to look slightly uncomfortable.

'You haven't told me yet whether my new bride is all you expected,' the Duke added, smiling possessively at Adelaide.

'Yes, she is exactly what I expected,' Isaac said ambiguously. 'Goodbye, Father. Goodbye, Duchess.' He made a small bow, wandered off and was absorbed by the milling crowd.

Adelaide and her husband were immediately surrounded by the wedding guests and she kept that happy smile plastered on her face while fighting off the emotions swirling within her.

How could she have thought, even for one fanciful moment, that such a man had come to rescue her? He was undoubtedly the most arrogant, judgemental pig she had ever met and she could only hope she never had the misfortune of meeting him again, if for no other reason than, despite his despicable character, the feelings he evoked in her were far too unsettling.

Chapter One

London—six years later

No one, least of all Isaac, had expected him to be summoned to the reading of his father's will, so the looks of bewilderment that greeted him from the assembled family when he entered the lawyer's office came as no surprise.

Once they had recovered from the shock, Lady Henrietta and Lady Hampton sent him the expected sneers, while their husbands discreetly nodded their more polite greetings. Just as she had at the funeral, the Duchess of Hartfield barely acknowledged him, a slight tilt of her head being all she was prepared to offer the bastard son

Only the new Duke of Hartfield seemed pleased to see him. The five-year-old boy, seated at his mother's feet, looked up from playing with his toy soldiers and sent Isaac a welcoming smile and a small wave. His friendliness was probably because he was the only one in the room who did not know that Isaac was the errant son. Isaac returned the wave and the smile and took a seat at the back of the room.

While the lawyer continued to shuffle papers, Isaac's gaze strayed to the Duchess. They had barely acknowledged each other at his father's funeral. He had been more grief-stricken than expected, but had no idea how the Duke's sudden death had affected her. The heavy black lace veil that hid her face throughout the service made it impossible to tell how she was reacting to becoming a widow at such a young age.

Had she grieved for his father, or had she been thinking of the life she could live now that she was an independent woman and the mother of a young boy who was about to come into possession of several large estates, a substantial country mansion, town houses, and heaven knew what else?

Her face was now unveiled and, with her nose firmly in the air, she looked just as conceited as she had at her wedding and no less alluring. She had been a beauty on the day she wed and it was hard to believe but the intervening six years had only increased that beauty. She had matured from a pretty eighteen-year-old into a captivating woman of twenty-four and she certainly looked stunning in black widow weeds.

Unlike on her wedding day, today her chestnut-brown hair was not ornately styled, but pulled back into a simple bun at the nape of her neck, exposing the creamy skin of her neck to his view. She was also unadorned with jewellery, but certainly did not need any augmentation to increase her attractiveness.

One thing had not changed, though. She still possessed that superior demeanour he had seen on the day she became a duchess. Her head was raised, her back ramrod straight, and he suspected that her small nod of greeting would be the beginning and end of any exchange between them.

He looked towards his two half-sisters, also dressed in black and dabbing their eyes with black lace handkerchiefs. No doubt the Duchess's superior demeanour and haughty attitude stood her in good stead when it came to dealing with those shrews.

They had tried to make Isaac's life a living hell during the odd occasions he'd been invited to Hartfield Hall as a child and he doubted they had easily accepted their father's young wife.

The sisters were seated on large leather couches beside their respective husbands. Isaac had expected marriage to temper their unpleasant dispositions, but at the funeral they had been just as venomous as ever.

Lady Henrietta had somehow bagged herself the second son of an earl, a lieutenant colonel, who was today decked out in his scarlet dress uniform. He was trained to command battalions of fighting men, but Isaac had no doubt as to who gave the orders in that household. Lady Hampton had made a slightly better marriage and somehow captured an earl and a diplomat, one who presumably had to use all his diplomatic skills when dealing with that harridan.

The lawyer coughed to draw their attention. Seated behind an expansive rosewood desk, large enough to create a barrier between himself and his clients, he exuded the expected air of authority. His gravitas was intensified by the framed certificates on the walls, the stacks of serious-looking legal documents on his desk and the bookshelves containing rows of imposing leather-bound volumes.

The dim light from the gas lamps and the closed dark blue velvet curtains blocking out the bright sunny day were presumably there to give an extra air of solemnity to the reading of the will. The assembled group were certainly taking it seriously, although Isaac suspected his presence was a sign that this was not going to be an entirely sombre event and his irreverent father was about to play one last joke on his family.

The lawyer placed a pair of pince-nez glasses on the end of his nose and sent the assembled group a somewhat embarrassed look. This got Isaac's full attention. What was in the will that would cause an unflappable lawyer to look uncomfortable? Were more illegitimate children about to be revealed, a harem of mistresses who had been granted an annuity, a hidden life no one knew about?

Isaac wouldn't put anything past his father.

'I'm pleased the entire family has been able to join us today,' the lawyer said, glancing in Isaac's direction as if to include the outsider. 'The will is straightforward, with most of the late Duke's estate being left to his heir and generous provisions being made for the children from both his marriages. The Duchess of Hartfield has been bequeathed the Dowager's Cottage on the Kent estate, along with a town house in London and a substantial yearly income, which she will receive for the rest of her life, or until she marries again.'

So far, so expected. But that did not explain Isaac's presence. Presumably he, too, had been left something, maybe a small annuity or a keepsake or two. It would not be out of character for his father to do so. He had always been generous and supported Isaac's mother until she had passed away when Isaac was seventeen. Although that might have been as much for the Duke's benefit as his mother's. It meant his father's frequent visits could take place in a luxurious Kensington flat and his mistress was always dressed in the latest fashions so never looked out of place on the arm of a duke.

He had also sent Isaac to a prestigious private school, much to the delight of his mother who had mistakenly thought it would turn her son into a gentleman. Isaac had hated the school from the day he'd arrived, along with the self-important aristocrats he'd been forced to mix with, much preferring the honest, accepting company of theatre people. But he'd endured those miserable school years for his mother's sake. He had received an education and for that he was grateful, but it had also instilled in him a deep and abiding dislike of bullies, which many of the privileged classes seemed to be. Including his two half-sisters.

'As you said, that all seems straightforward,' Henrietta said impatiently, as the lawyer continued to stare down at the papers in front of him. 'So what has he left Lady Hampton and myself?'

The lawyer looked up, shuffled the papers again, then shifted in his leather seat and pushed his glasses further up his nose. 'It is a straightforward will, but I'm afraid there is a problem.'

'A problem? What sort of problem?' Henrietta said in her most officious tone, making it clear to the lawyer she would tolerate no nonsense from a mere tradesman.

'As instructed, after your father's death I went through the papers he kept in his office. They were in somewhat of a state of disorder.' He gave a weak smile. Only Isaac smiled back. A state of disarray was a polite way of describing it—the chaotic study was indicative of everything else in his father's life.

'It took me quite some time to put them into any sort of order.' The lawyer once again looked pained, but if he was expecting any sympathy for the ordeal he would have been disappointed.

'And?' Henrietta said.

'And I discovered an unexpected document which, while not changing the nature of the will, does call into question who exactly is the new Duke of Hartfield.'

The lawyer cleared his throat while the sisters scowled at him and waited for his explanation.

Even from this distance, Isaac could see the lawyer's shoulders tense.

'It appears the late Duke of Hartfield married Miss Annie Radcliff on May the sixteenth, 1869.'

Silence filled the air, as if the very room, along with everyone present, was holding its breath.

'That's ridiculous,' Henrietta finally spat out, saying the very words Isaac was thinking.

This was the reason for Isaac's presence. It was a joke. Any minute now the lawyer would surely slap his thigh, give a raucous laugh and tell them it was all just one last prank he'd been instructed to play on the family by the old Duke.

'I believe you'll find Father married our mother in 1870, the same year in which I was born,' Henrietta continued in a condescending voice as if the lawyer was slightly dim-witted and needed things explained to him in simple terms. 'He could not have married Mother if he was already married. His marriage to that actress must have been illegal, or it was annulled or it's a forgery, or something.'

Henrietta looked at her sister. Priscilla nodded vigorously as if that was all that was required to make this go away.

'The marriage was legal,' the lawyer said firmly, giving no sign that he was joking. 'I have searched extensively in legal records for any documentation to show that it was annulled or that he divorced Miss Radcliff, but none exists.' The lawyer drew in a deep breath. 'I'm afraid that means his marriage to your mother, Lady Henrietta and Lady Hampton, was illegal.'

'No,' the two sisters squawked out together, the black handkerchiefs quickly covering both mouths.

'This can't be true,' Henrietta continued, lowering her handkerchief and twisting it into a tight knot. 'Our father would never do such a thing.'

'And of course that means the son of the late Duke's first marriage, Isaac Radcliff, is now the new Duke of Hartfield,' the lawyer rushed on.

'No,' the two sisters cried out again.

'That cannot be right,' Henrietta screeched. 'It's a travesty, an act against nature, that he…' she pointed a long, black-gloved finger at Isaac '…would be a duke. A bastard cannot be a titled man.'

Isaac flicked a quick look at young Joshua, who was now sitting on his mother's lap, sucking his thumb and watching the badly behaved adults with avid curiosity.

'Be careful whom you refer to in that manner, Henny, as it will soon be what people are calling you,' he said, enjoying being able to turn the tables on his half-sister, even if he was still certain this had to be some sort of gag concocted by his father.

He looked over at the Duchess to gauge her reaction to this bizarre news, which affected her as much as it did the spiteful sisters. She was now cuddling her son, but nothing else about her demeanour had changed.

'But Henny is right,' he said, turning his attention back to the lawyer. 'Surely the marriage certificate you found cannot be valid. If it was, he would never have been able to marry Henny and Prissy's mother.'

The two sisters nodded vigorously, their attention so fixed on the disturbing news they did not react in their usual manner to the nicknames he had used since their childhood to irritate them.

'And my mother never mentioned any such wedding to me, which I'm sure she would have done if she'd thought she was the rightful Duchess,' Isaac added.

The nodding increased and the sisters' focus was now firmly on the lawyer, who had suddenly been cast in the role of their saviour.

'We can only speculate on what happened, but it changes nothing.' The lawyer sent the Duchess a polite smile. 'Your marriage was, however, legal, Your Grace, as you were married after the Duke's first wife had passed away, along with the woman whom he'd then married…' his voice lowered '…bigamously.'

Henrietta and Priscilla gasped at this affront.

'But my son is not the Duke of Hartfield?' the Duchess asked, cutting through Henrietta's and Priscilla's
howls of protest.

'No, I'm afraid not. He is now the late Duke's second son.'

Isaac waited for that superior demeanour to collapse, for her to show some emotion, maybe even
throw insults in his direction the way Henrietta had.
She merely kissed the top of her son's head and smiled
at the unexpectedly demoted little boy.

That was curious.

'But the Duke made ample provision for his children,' the lawyer continued, still addressing the Duchess. 'Your son will receive a generous annual annuity,
along with yourself, as I have already mentioned.'

She nodded as if that was all that needed to be said.

'And what of us?' Henrietta asked. 'You said he
made generous allowances for his children. What will
Lady Hampton and I inherit?'

The lawyer looked down at his papers and dots of
perspiration appeared on his brow. 'I'm afraid he only
made legal provision for his legitimate children. Isaac
and Joshua.'

The looks of horror that crossed the two sisters'
faces were priceless. If Isaac was a more compassion-
ate man, and if he did not remember all their attempts
to belittle and humiliate him over the years because
of his illegitimate status, he might feel sorry for them.

Instead, he braced himself for the expected hysterical outburst. As did Henrietta's and Priscilla's husbands, who had both placed restraining hands on their wives' arms.

'You won't get away with this,' Henrietta shrieked, shaking off her husband's arm, and turning in her seat to face Isaac. 'We will challenge it in court.'

She stood up, still glaring at him. Priscilla followed suit, as did the two embarrassed husbands. 'No court in the land would allow the bastard son of an actress to become a duke. The mere thought of it is an abomination. Your mother was little more than a—'

'I'd watch what you say next,' Isaac said, standing up and glaring back at his half-sister. He would tolerate a lot from her, but not disparagement of his mother. She'd been a kind, loving woman and a successful actress who had never needed the financial support of the Duke, but for reasons of her own had seemingly been in love with the old cad and had graciously accepted the gifts he'd bestowed on her.

Henrietta's husband once again placed his hand on his wife's arm. 'I believe we should leave it at that for now, my dear,' he said. 'Nothing is to be gained by trading insults.'

'Indeed,' Priscilla's husband added, looking somewhat out of his depth beside his angry wife, despite his reputation as an accomplished diplomat who had successfully negotiated treaties between warring factions.

'This will not be the last you hear of this,' Henrietta hissed as her husband attempted to lead her from the room. She turned to face the Duchess. 'And I assume you will be joining us in challenging this absurdity, Adelaide?'

'I have been well provided for,' the Duchess said, taking the tin soldier her son was handing her as if completely detached from the entire proceedings.

'But your son will be a nobody, a mere second son, while that…that…' She looked at Isaac and he waited to see which choice insult she selected from her large repertoire to describe him. 'That bastard will be the Duke.'

'Now, see here, Lady Henrietta,' Priscilla's husband said, looking at Henrietta's husband, who had turned as scarlet as his uniform at the insult to all second sons.

'I'm sorry, my dear,' Henrietta said to her husband, not looking the slightest bit sorry. 'I just mean Adelaide only married Father because she thought she was going to be the mother of the next Duke, not the mother of a second son.'

The Duchess's spine stiffened almost imperceptibly, while her lips pursed slightly, but she made no reply.

Henrietta huffed out her exasperation at this lack of outrage from her father's widow. 'Well, some people might be happy to sit back and let everything that is rightfully theirs be taken away from them, but I for one am not prepared to just accept this without a fight.'

Isaac did not doubt it for a moment. 'I suppose I will soon be seeing you in court, then, Henny,' he said with a smile he knew would further inflame her wrath.

'You will and I will see you in hell before I will ever let you become the Duke of Hartfield.'

With that the sisters stormed out of the office, followed by their husbands, and Isaac sank back down onto his chair, thoroughly amused by the situation.

'Pick up your soldiers, Joshua,' the Duchess said gently to her son. 'It is time we were going.'

The little boy slid down from his mother's lap and began gathering up the red-and-blue-uniformed armies and piling them into a box.

'And what of you, Your Grace?' Isaac asked. 'Will you be taking me to court as well?'

'I'm sure Mr Standish has done his due diligence and everything is in order,' she said calmly, looking at the lawyer, who sent her a nod of thanks.

She turned back to face Isaac. 'It must be heartening to discover that your father loved your mother so much he went against everything that would have been expected of him and made her his wife.'

'Knowing my father as I did, if this marriage did take place it must have happened when he was well and truly in his cups and the next day he'd have had no recollection of doing so. We all know what he was like, impulsive, disorganised, and he often forgot what he'd done when he was three sheets to the wind. He was far from a perfect man, but I don't believe he would have deliberately deceived Henrietta and Priscilla's mother, or his two daughters.'

'But your mother must have known she married him.'

He shrugged. 'As I already said, if she did, she never said anything to me. They both must have been rather young at the time. Perhaps she didn't understand the law. Perhaps she thought it was all a bit of a lark or some play acting that meant nothing—certainly nothing official, anyway.'

'Anyway, it appears you are now the new Duke of Hartfield and I wish you well.'

With that she took her son's hand and left the room, as if these entire proceedings had been beneath her.

For a moment he remained staring at the closed door. She really was the most intriguing woman he had ever met. Would anything ever upset that perfectly composed demeanour? But for now, he had more important things to consider than the Duchess of Hartfield's unruffled feathers.

He turned to the lawyer, who was gathering the files together in a pile and tying them into a bundle.

'Are you absolutely certain the marriage certificate is genuine?'

The lawyer looked up at him. 'Yes, Your Grace.'

He recoiled at the ridiculous honorific. 'But they

must have been so young when they married. Are you sure they were of legal age?'

'Your father was twenty-one. He could marry without the consent of his parents. So their marriage was definitely legal and binding.'

'Well, I most certainly do not want to be a duke, so how do I go about handing over the title to little Joshua?'

The lawyer frowned. 'I'm afraid that is not possible. Should you die without leaving an heir then Lord Joshua will inherit the title, but you are now the Duke of Hartfield and will be so until you pass away.'

'So I have to kick the bucket to be free of this?'

'Yes, Your Grace.'

'Please don't call me that.'

'It is your title and I believe you're going to have to get used to it.'

Isaac exhaled loudly. He doubted that was ever going to happen. He did not want to become a member of a class he had despised since he had been subjected to their taunts and insults in the school playground. He was more than happy to remain a theatre manager and spend his days with people he liked and admired.

He grimaced at the thought of giving up his life in London for a life on the land, overseeing whatever it was one oversaw when it came to being in charge of a large estate. That would be almost as bad as having people defer to him just because of his title.

As loath as he was to admit it, Henrietta was right. He was ill-suited to such a role and the title should go to someone who was born and bred to such responsibilities, someone who was happy to have servants and could take the expected paternalistic approach to the welfare of the estate tenants. And that simply was not him.

But for now, there was nothing more to be said on the matter, so he bid the lawyer farewell and headed out of his office.

He strolled down the bustling London streets and tried to come to terms with a situation that would delight most men, but instead filled him with dismay and not a little despondency.

As much as he loved getting the better of his half-sisters, he could only hope that Henrietta and Priscilla did find a way of challenging this absurd situation and for once would be victorious over their unwanted older brother.

Chapter Two

Adelaide reached out and stroked her son's head. As he always did when they travelled by carriage, Joshua was kneeling on the leather bench and staring out of the window. He turned around and smiled at her, then went back to watching the passing carts, carriages, and men on bicycles.

Her son was no longer a duke. It was unexpected, but did it really matter? He was well provided for. She was well provided for. Her family had prospered since her marriage. Felicity was happily married. Her brother's estate was now profitable and he was able to support their mother in the style she had come to expect.

And now Joshua would be able to grow up without being burdened by the privileges that came with a title. Already people had started to treat him differently and she had worried he might grow up to become a self-indulgent, self-entitled scoundrel, just like the old Duke.

Now he could make his way in the world and choose

what he wanted to do with his life and hopefully grow from a sweet and loving boy into an admirable, caring and kind man.

She tousled his hair and smiled at him. This was perhaps all for the best, but it had certainly been an interesting morning and nothing like the one she had expected.

She sat back in the leather bench and shook her head slightly in disbelief. Isaac Radcliff was now the new Duke of Hartfield. It hardly seemed possible.

After her wedding, he had disappeared from her life, if not her thoughts, only reappearing at his father's funeral.

That had been somewhat of a surprise, as had been the depth of his genuine grief. The confident, almost cocky demeanour, which had annoyed her so much at her wedding, had gone, replaced by a crestfallen appearance. Dark rings had underlined his eyes and his olive skin had taken on an ashen pallor.

Despite his evident distress he had been shunned by all present, and many, including Henrietta and Priscilla, had expressed their shock and disapproval that he had dared to put in an appearance.

For the entire service, he had remained apart from the other mourners, and had stood at the back as they had gathered around the graveside. He had looked so sad and lonely. Adelaide had been tempted to go to him, to try to console him in some way, but suspected such a gesture would not have been welcome. He had made his opinions of her very clear at the wedding.

But there had been no sign of that crushed, downcast man today. Once again he had appeared buoyant and carefree. Even Henrietta and Priscilla's barbs were deflected as if they could never pierce him. Yet she wondered whether he was quite as impervious to their insults as he appeared or had he built up a protective shield over the years? Protecting one's inner self from life's trials and tribulations was something she knew a great deal about and was well aware how it could affect your behaviour.

She looked out the carriage window and smiled to herself. Hopefully she would never again have to worry about what fate had in store for her. Her late husband had left her a wealthy woman and she could now live the life she wanted, not one dictated for her to suit the needs of others.

Freedom. She had freedom. It was almost too much to believe. It would now be up to her, and no one else, to decide what she did with her life. Perhaps she would travel with Joshua. See all those places she had only ever read about. She could visit Paris, stroll along Les Champs-Élysées, explore the Louvre, or maybe attend an opera in Rome and ride in a gondola in Venice. Whatever she did it would be glorious because it would be her decision to do so.

For the first time since she had been told she needed

to marry to save the family, she felt something akin to contentment. Only one worry lurked at the back of her mind. Isaac Radcliff.

The Dowager's Cottage was on the Hartfield estate, which was now owned by him. Would that mean she would be forced to interact with him and, more to the point, how did she feel about that?

How would he cope with the management of the estate? Would it return to the state of neglect it had been in when she had married his father? How was this going to affect the servants, the tenants, the people in the nearby village? All those people's livelihoods depended on the estate being managed efficiently.

Those were questions she would inevitably have to face, just not today. Today she would just rejoice in the potential for happiness that her and Joshua's futures held.

The carriage pulled up in front of the Mayfair town house and Adelaide looked up at the four-storey brick home she had come to love and said a silent thank you to the old Duke for leaving it to her in his will.

It was surely no more than she deserved after all she had endured. She tried to push that memory to the back of her mind. Those times were over. She was now an independent woman who would never again be forced into an unwanted marriage.

The footman opened the carriage door. The moment the stairs were lowered, Joshua jumped down from the carriage, ran up the path, reached the tiled entrance and looked back at his mother, those big eyes urging her to hurry. She walked as quickly as she could up the path and, as was their routine when they arrived home, lifted him up so he could grab the brass lion head knocker and give it several hard bangs.

Another footman opened the door and bowed to both of them. 'Your mother and Lady Felicity are waiting for you in the drawing room,' he said.

'Thank you, Baxter.' She lowered a squirming Joshua to the ground and braced herself for what was going to be an uncomfortable conversation with her mother.

Joshua raced ahead to see his grandmother and aunt, but Adelaide paused in the entranceway and took a moment to look around at what was now her London home.

My home.

She smiled at the dappled light coming in through the stained-glass windows, sending colours dancing over the marble floor, then looked up at the grand staircase with its wrought-iron balustrade leading up to more than enough rooms for herself, Joshua, her mother, her entire family and anyone else who wished to visit.

'This is mine,' she whispered.

Smiling to herself, she walked down the hallway and through the double wooden doors leading to the drawing room. Pausing once again, she looked at the elegant room as if seeing it for the first time. It was her favourite in the town house. Delicate cream silk wallpaper etched with tiny pink roses gave the large room a light, feminine ambiance. The ornate, carved wooden fireplace, the gilded mirrors and artwork adorning the walls, and the lushly upholstered chairs and sofas in rich red velvet all added to the sense of comfortable refinement that Adelaide loved.

The two women looked up from making a fuss over Joshua, with matching expressions of curiosity.

'I take it from your smile that the will was all as you expected?' her mother asked.

'I am happy with the outcome, yes,' Adelaide said placidly. 'The Duke has left me this house, the Dowager's Cottage on the Hartfield estate and a substantial annuity.'

'Oh, that's lovely,' Felicity said. 'The old Duke had his flaws, no one could deny that.'

That was certainly an understatement, but now was not the time to list the litany of flaws he'd possessed.

'But he was certainly generous,' her sister continued. 'And it is good that he thought of providing so well for you, although so he should after all you had to endure.'

Felicity was the only person she had confided in as to what it had been really like to be in a loveless marriage. She had done so only to make sure her sister knew the importance of marrying for love, but even then, she had not revealed the true extent of her ordeal. It had been hard enough to smile and flirt through the Season and pretend she was enjoying the Duke's attentions, but surrendering her body to him in the marriage bed was something she had not been prepared for.

Fortunately, she had become pregnant almost immediately, after which the Duke had left her alone. When she gave birth to a son, he'd seemed as relieved as she that, with her duty done, they could now live separate lives. She blushed slightly at the memory of overhearing the Duke telling one of his friends that having a son had made him exceedingly happy as he never had to bed that cold fish ever again.

Felicity took her hand and gave it a small squeeze. 'After all the sacrifices you have made for the family, now you can finally think of your own happiness.'

'You know I never begrudged helping my family.'

'I know, but you never have to worry about any of us again. You can think about yourself for once, and now you'll finally be able to marry for love.'

Adelaide stifled a sigh. She was pleased her marriage to the Duke had given Felicity the freedom to marry a man of her own choosing, but another marriage was not the fate she wanted for herself. She would not be giving up her freedom to any man. But that, too, was not a discussion she wanted to have now, or at any time with her family.

'So what did he leave Lady Hampton and Lady Henrietta?' her mother asked, still cuddling her grandson.

Joshua broke from his grandmother's arms and sat down in the middle of the Oriental rug, opened his box of soldiers and lined them up for yet another battle.

'Look at the little Duke.' Her mother smiled fondly. 'He's already showing signs he is born to command.'

'He might be showing signs he's a born leader, but I'm afraid he is not a duke.'

Mother and sister tilted their heads in matching looks of interest. 'What do you mean?' her mother asked.

Adelaide took a seat on the sofa across from her mother's chair, while her mother continued to watch her with that quizzical expression, her calm demeanour making it obvious she had no idea what Adelaide was talking about.

'The lawyer informed us that the Duke of Hartfield had married Isaac Radcliff's mother prior to marrying the mother of Lady Henrietta and Lady Hampton. That first marriage was never annulled. Therefore, Isaac Radcliff is the legitimate first-born son and now the new Duke of Hartfield.'

Felicity covered her mouth to stop either a gasp of shock, or a laugh, it was difficult to tell, while her mother tittered lightly, as if Adelaide was making a silly joke. When Adelaide said nothing more, her mother's face collapsed into a disbelieving scowl while

Felicity's expression grew more curious at this unexpected development.

'What?' her mother finally asked through clenched teeth, in a manner much as Lady Henrietta had on receiving this news. She looked down at Joshua, happily tossing soldiers at each other. 'No, this cannot possibly be right.' She looked back at Adelaide and lowered her voice. 'That…that man cannot be the new Duke of Hartfield. His mother was an actress. He works in the theatre.'

'Be that as it may, he is the first-born son and now the rightful Duke.'

'But what of Joshua?' she gasped out.

'He is the second son, the spare, as people so callously refer to the second-born boy.'

Her mother grasped the lace at her collar. 'No, that can't be.'

She waited for Adelaide to say something more, to make this situation go away, but there was nothing more to be said.

'But I assume the old Duke left Joshua well provided for?' Felicity asked.

'Yes, he, too, will receive a generous annuity for the rest of his life and will also inherit this town house from me, so his future is safe.'

'Oh, well, no harm done, then,' Felicity added.

Their mother scowled at Felicity. 'No harm done? No harm done? How can you possibly say that?'

Felicity shrugged one shoulder. 'And what of Lady Henrietta and Lady Hampton? What did he leave them?'

Adelaide winced. 'Well, as the old Duke was not legally married to their mother when they were born, it means they are not his legitimate children so they've been left nothing.'

Her mother's face went white and her hands shot up to cover her mouth. 'If he wasn't married to their mother, that means they are…they are…'

'Yes. It was a serious blow to them, as I'm sure you can understand,' Adelaide said in what was surely yet another understatement.

'Those poor, poor girls,' her mother said.

Adelaide gave a slight nod in acknowledgement of their unfortunate plight, although, while she had some sympathy for the sisters, part of her could not help but see a certain poetic justice in this outcome. The two women had often regaled Adelaide with tales of all the mean tricks they had played on their half-brother whenever their father had invited him to stay at Hartfield Hall. They had gleefully described persecuting him as if it was almost their duty to do so. They believed he needed to know he was the lowest of the low who did not belong and any mistreatment of him was seen as completely justified.

'They plan to challenge the will and the legitimacy of the Duke's first marriage in court,' Adelaide added.

'Surely they're not going to drag this through the courts and make it all a public scandal?' Felicity asked, looking as shocked as her mother had been about the announcement of the real Duke.

'I'm afraid so.'

Her mother slowly nodded. 'Yes, challenging it in court is an excellent idea and that is what we should do as well. This cannot possibly be true and I'm sure any judge in the country would agree. It must be some nefarious scheme concocted by that Isaac Radcliff. The man is a rogue, a charlatan, a rascal, and this is nothing less than I would expect from a man of his dubious background.'

'Dubious background?' Adelaide asked drily. 'The man is a duke.'

Her mother swatted her hand in front of her face in dismissal of that appalling idea.

'And I suspect the new Duke of Hartfield was even more surprised to hear of his elevation to the peerage than anyone else in the room,' Adelaide added.

Isaac Radcliff's expression when the lawyer had said his parents were legally married appeared in her mind's eye. She had sneaked a look and seen those dark brown eyes grow wide and his mouth momentarily fall open in surprise. Then he had given a sly smile, as if this was all just a trick being played on them by his father and he was the first to realise it.

'Nonsense,' her mother shot back. 'And don't call

him that. Of course he's up to something. Men like him can never be trusted and you'd do well to remember that.' She sat up straighter and folded her hands in her lap. 'No, he could never be a duke. He simply does not have the aristocratic bearing, the nobility or the genteel breeding that marks a man out as a member of the aristocracy.'

Felicity and Adelaide exchanged incredulous looks.

'One's birth *is* the only thing that makes you an aristocrat, Mother,' she said, pointing out something her mother surely must know, but was choosing to ignore. 'It has nothing to do with your personality or any superior qualities you may or may not possess.'

Once again her mother waved her hand in front of her face as if to wipe away that statement. Adelaide could also mention that many of the aristocrats she had met, including her late husband and his friends, frequently exhibited behaviour that was far from noble or genteel. But those times were in the past and the sooner she forgot about them the better.

'No, we'll take this to court,' her mother continued. 'And make sure that upstart does not get his hands on what is rightfully Joshua's.'

At the mention of his name, Joshua paused in his battle and looked up at his grandmother, smiled and resumed tossing soldiers at each other.

'Mother, sometimes one just has to accept things the way they are.' That was a lesson Adelaide's mother had reiterated almost daily when she was being forced into a marriage she did not want. Adelaide had been forced to accept what fate had dealt her. It was time her mother followed her own advice and did the same.

'Nonsense. He is the real Duke,' her mother said, pointing at Joshua. 'You are the mother of a duke. I am the grandmother of a duke,' she stated emphatically, as if saying so made it true. 'In the meantime, we'll carry on as usual as if none of those facts are under dispute, which they most certainly are not.'

With that her mother crossed her arms as if that was all that needed saying on the subject.

'So, is Isaac Radcliff still as dashing as he was when he attended your wedding?' Felicity asked, causing her mother to frown in disapproval. 'At the time I thought he was a pirate, with that windswept black hair and those dark eyes. I don't think I'd ever seen a more handsome man, until I met my Victor, of course.'

'Yes, he looks much the same,' Adelaide said, keeping her voice as dismissive as possible.

'Pirate is right,' her mother muttered, while Felicity looked at Adelaide with renewed curiosity as if reading far too much into her casual statement.

'And until all this unfortunate business is settled in court, we should put that frightful rogue completely out of our minds,' her mother added.

Adelaide agreed that was indeed a very good idea. She only hoped it was one she could abide by.

* * *

Isaac wandered around the busy streets as if in a dream, trying to take in his situation. It was ludicrous, like one of the farces performed at the Elysian Theatre. Anyone less suited and more unwilling to being a duke he could not imagine.

Somehow he would have to get out of this. He could not be a duke. It would be beyond absurd for him to not only be a member of the aristocracy, but to be of such a high rank he was only one place below Queen Victoria's children on the social hierarchy. Ridiculous.

His wandering took him past the Eldridge Club and, despite it being only midday, he felt a desperate need for a drink. He laughed to himself. Now that he had become a duke, was he starting to adopt the behavioural patterns of his father? Was that what happened when you had endless amounts of money and nothing pressing to do with your days? He hoped not. But today he would make an exception. He deserved it after such a terrible shock.

He rushed up the stone stairs and through the highly polished black enamel door. The façade gave the appearance of a club where important matters were discussed by serious men and not a high-class drinking establishment for men who were determined to have a good time. Today he needed more than usual to joke, laugh and cut himself off from the insanity of the outside world.

'Thomas Hayward and the Earl of Rothwell are taking luncheon in the dining room,' the steward said as Isaac was about to enter the bar.

'Excellent, thank you.' That was exactly what he needed. To see his two closest friends. He had no intention of telling anyone else about the strange news he'd just received, but had no objection to sharing it with Sebastian and Thomas.

He turned and retraced his steps across the plush crimson carpet into the dining area to find his friends. It was the middle of the day, but the dark wood-panelled walls, heavy curtains over the windows and soft lighting from gas lamps made it seem as if it could be any time, day or night. It created the perfect environment for men who wanted to feel as if they had stepped out of their ordinary world into one where they could leave their troubles behind.

'You had the reading of the will this morning, didn't you?' Seb said, pausing from slicing up a large piece of steak as Isaac sat down at their table. 'How did it go? Did the old Duke leave you anything?'

'A pittance, perhaps,' Thomas said, before putting some Yorkshire pudding into his mouth.

'Some crumbs from his table,' Seb added.

'The time of day, maybe,' Thomas joined in. 'The steam off his porridge.'

'No, he left me everything, lock, stock and barrel.'

The two men stopped eating and turned to face him. 'What?' they said in unison.

'It seems I am to be the new Duke of Hartfield.' He lifted his nose in the air in a mock-lordly gesture, choosing to make fun of what would be far too disconcerting if he focused for too long on its appalling ramifications. 'But don't worry. I won't expect much bowing and scraping, or boot licking, or forelock pulling. I certainly won't let this go to my head.'

The two friends continued to stare at him, their forks poised in mid-air.

'Oh, all right, if you insist. Feel free to bow and scrape. It is no less than I deserve now that I am a man placed at the pinnacle of society, the very epitome of British manhood, a paragon of—'

'Shut up and tell us what happened,' Thomas interrupted.

Isaac shrugged. 'The lawyer found documents that show my parents secretly got married when they were still too young to know any better. That makes me the legitimate first-born son and the new Duke of Hartfield.'

'So you're not a...' Seb paused.

'A bastard? No.'

'You're a...' Thomas said, his wide-eyed stare of disbelief matching Seb's.

'A duke? Yes. For now, at least. Henny and Prissy are going to challenge it in court, so I might only be a duke for a short while, but seeing their faces when the lawyer told them the news was worth it and the funniest thing I've seen in a long time.'

'And what of the Duchess of Hartfield?' Seb asked in horrified fascination. 'How did she take the news?'

'Who knows? She was as cool and as reserved as one would expect.' Isaac did not add that she was also more attractive than she had been on her wedding day. The last six years had matured her, made her more womanly, more enticing, but no less standoffish.

'She didn't appear to want to mount a challenge, but I suspect she will. After all, she did marry a duke who she thought had no heir. She expected to be the mother of a duke. I don't imagine she's too happy about having it snatched away from her by a lowborn creature such as myself.'

Either way, he suspected it would not be the last he saw of the Duchess, either across the courtroom or when he worked out what was to be done with the Hartfield estate. How he felt about that he did not yet know, nor was he going to waste time thinking about it.

He signalled to the steward. 'I believe this calls for champagne. Now that I'm a duke I intend to drink nothing else. Only such a gilded elixir is good enough for a man of my standing, a man who is such a sterling example of the best that Britain can produce, a social luminary, an exemplar of nobility, a—'

'It's a shame no one from our school days is here,' Seb said, cutting him off. 'It would be good to see their faces as well and actually watch them have to bow and scrape to you after everything they put you through.'

'What they put us all through,' Thomas added.

'Yes, that would make it almost worth hanging on to the title,' he said, making light of what had been a painful time. From the day he had first arrived at school at the age of seven, he had been tormented by the other boys, who'd never let him forget for a moment that he was the bastard son of an actress. Only the friendship of Thomas and Sebastian had made those years tolerable.

Outsiders themselves, the three had become firm friends. Thomas was excluded by the rest of the pupils because he was the son of a wealthy industrialist. The aristocratic boys had been trained to despise new money and they had put that training to good use, while the countless scandals in Seb's family had provided endless fodder for the bullies.

Fortunately, all three soon developed the fortitude to withstand anything sent their way, from students and masters alike. They had also excelled at both their studies and sport, but rather than it proving to the bullies that one's position in society was not a mark of superiority, it only added fuel to their resentment.

The steward popped the cork and filled three champagne flutes.

'To the new Duke of Hartfield,' Thomas said, raising his glass.

'Hear, hear,' Sebastian added.

'For as long as it lasts,' Isaac said, before downing the bubbly liquid.

Chapter Three

Adelaide paused at the entrance to the Elysian Theatre. Music halls were places of vice and depravity where no decent woman would ever step foot, or so she had been told. But she needed to talk to the new Duke and would prefer to do so without her mother knowing. She'd already had to endure enough tirades on the man's character. And what better place to have a clandestine meeting than this disreputable establishment where she was unlikely to encounter anyone she knew?

She looked up at the gaudy façade, with its turrets presumably meant to depict a medieval castle, strangely set beside Indian domes and Chinese dragons. Flamboyance was apparently more important than historical or cultural accuracy to whoever had created the entrance.

Taking a deep breath to give herself confidence, she stepped inside. The foyer was no less startling than the exterior, with plaster elephants seated next to smiling maharajas, wallpaper featuring multicoloured peacock feathers even more outrageously ostentatious than adorned the real birds and stern stone lions standing guard at the foot of the stairs.

It was overly dramatic and flashy and would shame any respectable designer, but Adelaide couldn't help but smile at its playful exuberance.

The foyer was empty and there was certainly no sign of the vices of which she had been warned. An elderly woman carrying a tin bucket and a mop walked past and nodded a greeting to Adelaide.

'Excuse me, can you tell me where I would find Isaac Radcliff's office?' she asked.

'Through that door, up the stairs, first door on the left.' She pointed to a discreet door at the opposite end of the foyer. 'But I don't think he's hiring at the moment.'

Adelaide thanked the woman and bit down a smile. Her mother would be outraged at the thought of a duchess being mistaken for a showgirl, but Adelaide found it strangely amusing.

She made her way up the narrow staircase, its plain brown walls a contrast to the bright colours of the foyer, and knocked on the door bearing the sign *Manager*.

'Come in,' the brisk voice behind the door called out.

Adelaide pushed it open and was confronted with

the messiest room she had ever seen, and a dishevelled Isaac Radcliff seated behind a desk piled high with papers, books and heaven knew what else.

'Your Grace, this is a surprise,' he said, standing and looking momentarily flustered, before he pushed down his rolled-up sleeves and pulled on his jacket.

'Please, take a seat.' He looked around and could see no vacant seat, so he removed a pile of papers from a leather couch and indicated for her to sit.

She sat down and took a moment to observe him as he returned to the chair behind his desk. He really did look the worse for wear. He was dressed in the same grey suit he had worn yesterday in the lawyer's office, but the crisp white shirt was minus its stiff collar and maroon cravat.

His black hair needed to be tamed by a brush, as tousled curls were falling haphazardly over his high forehead, and the dark shadow on his strong jaw-line suggested it had not seen a razor this morning. Strangely, this unkempt appearance accentuated rather than detracted from his magnetic charm, giving him a certain rakishness that, despite herself, she found rather attractive.

Had he gone out to celebrate his new status last night? It certainly looked like it. And with whom did he celebrate? a little voice at the back of her mind asked. With one of the showgirls? She tried to push that thought away. It was none of her business what he did and with whom he did it and it was certainly no reason for her to feel jealous, if that was what that unfamiliar stabbing sensation in her stomach even was.

'What brings you to this den of iniquity, Your Grace? You're not planning a new career on the stage, are you?' he asked with a teasing smile.

She sent him back a tight smile to let him know that she was not here to be trifled with and certainly not here to be flirted with. He could save that for the showgirls she was refusing to think about. 'No, I believe we need to discuss this new situation, what it will mean for my son, for the future of Hartfield Hall and for the running of your father's estates.'

He shrugged his broad shoulders. 'Isn't that something you should discuss with the lawyer? I'm as much in the dark as you are, especially as the entire thing is going to end up in the courts.'

'No, you're not in the dark,' she stated. 'And we both know Lady Henrietta and Lady Hampton's court case is destined to fail. You now own everything that previously belonged to your father. It's all rather simple.'

'Simple is not the word I would use,' he said, running his hand along the stubble on his jaw as if suddenly aware of his unkempt appearance. Her gaze followed those long fingers, and she momentarily wondered what those bristles would feel like against her skin, before she snapped herself back to the more important matter at hand.

'What I wish to know is when do you expect me to move out of Hartfield Hall and into the Dowager's Cottage?' she said in her most matter-of-fact voice. 'Do you intend to take over running the estate? And if so, when will that happen?'

She looked around at the office and wondered just how much of a mess he would make when he did take over. Hopefully he would not be as useless and neglectful in the role as his father had been, although this office and his present appearance gave every indication that he might well be.

'It might look like a disaster area, but there is method to my madness,' he said, as if reading her mind. 'And I manage to run five other theatres throughout London, all rather successfully.'

'So when do you intend to take up running your father's estates?'

He sat back in his leather chair. 'I haven't given it much thought. In fact, I've given it no thought at all and would rather not. Who runs it now? I strongly suspect my father didn't spend much time poring over ledgers and account books or worrying about the purchase of livestock and the maximising of crop yields.'

'No, he didn't,' Adelaide said and tried not to sigh with annoyance. 'Things were in, shall we say, a state of disarray when we married. I hired an extremely competent estate manager and have also kept an eye on the books myself, along with the management of the estate.'

'You've been managing my father's estate?' He raised one eyebrow in question.

'Yes,' she said, unaccountably insulted by the assumption that she would be incapable of doing so. Although she had to admit she, too, had been surprised at how successful she had been. But over the last six years under her management the estate had improved dramatically, as had the standard of living of the tenants. There was still room for improvement, though, and she would hate to see things go backwards.

'Then would you be happy to continue to do so?' He waved his hands at the piles of papers awaiting his attention. 'As you can see, I'm rather busy here.'

And you'd presumably rather spend time with actresses and showgirls, just like your father, rather than take on the mantle of your responsibilities. That was what she could have said. Instead, she gave a small nod and said, 'As you wish,' in a detached manner, not wanting him to know just how much she had thrived under the responsibility.

'Good. And you can rest assured I have no intention of moving to Hartfield Hall. You and Joshua should go on living there for as long as you like.'

'That is very kind of you, Your Grace.'

'Please, no, not Your Grace. I beg you, call me Isaac.'

'In that case, it would only be right if you called me Adelaide,' she responded before she had fully taken in the meaning of her words. It was rather informal, but then it would be ludicrous for the Duke to be the only one not expecting the honorific.

He smiled at her and she wished he wouldn't. It was such a devilish smile, as if designed to entice her into immorality.

Immorality? Where did that thought come from? She moved uncomfortably on her seat, trying to ignore the strange feelings deep inside her and the sudden heat consuming her body.

'Adelaide,' he whispered, almost like a sigh.

She briefly closed her eyes, not wanting to think of how seductive her name sounded on his lips or how it had caused a fluttering inside her chest.

Pull yourself together. He is a practised rake. He knows exactly what effect he is having on you and is no doubt laughing at how easy it is to unsettle you.

Her eyes snapped open and she stared unflinchingly into his. 'I am willing to continue the management of the estate, but will you be wanting to oversee what I do, now that the estate is yours?' she asked, her crisp voice masking the turmoil taking place within her.

'Did my father do that?' Those dark eyebrows drew together and he frowned. 'Or did he leave it all up to you?'

'It is something I am more than capable of doing

without a man's supervision,' she shot back, insulted
that he would think that because she was a woman
she couldn't cope with such responsibilities, although
also aware she had been the one to ask whether he'd
wished to supervise. But snapping at him definitely
felt better than thinking about the way his presence
was affecting her.

He held his hands up in mocking surrender. 'I'm
sure you are. You strike me as a very capable woman
and if you are happy to continue managing the estate
without this man's supervision then please do so. You
do have a vested interest in it remaining in a good financial state, as one day your son will inherit it.'

She frowned at him. Did he not understand the rules
of primogeniture or was he deliberately choosing to ignore them? 'Only if you don't have a son of your own.'

'There is very little danger of that. I would have to
marry first.' He gave a dismissive laugh as if such a
thing were an absurdity. 'And I have absolutely no intention of fathering any by-blows the way my father
did.' He laughed again as if making a joke, but the
laughter did not move to his eyes, which were suddenly cold and hard.

'I'm sor—'

'So our lives will continue on as if your son really
did inherit the dukedom,' he continued, cutting her
off before she could say she was sorry for any unfair
suffering he might have endured over something that

was no fault of his own. It must have been hard for a young boy being subjected to the cruelties of others because he had been unfairly stigmatised from birth. She imagined Joshua enduring such anguish and felt the unfairness hit her stomach like a physical blow.

'And you will continue to manage what will one day be his birthright,' he added.

'That is very gracious of you.'

'Not at all. I'd much rather stay here, where I belong, among my own type of people.'

She looked around the room, at the walls adorned with posters from various shows, including several featuring Shakespearean plays and even one depicting Bizet's opera *Carmen*. These were certainly anomalies, which contrasted starkly with the rather unsophisticated surroundings she had seen below.

'It's not all vaudeville and showgirls, you know,' he said, registering her surprise. He sat up straighter and adopted a facetious prim and proper look. 'I'll have you know I manage some respectable theatres that put on some right proper shows that even quality folk such as yourself would not be averse to attending.'

She ignored the implied insult. 'You just prefer to be among showgirls and vaudevillians?'

'Call me a sentimental old fool if you like, but this was where my mother started out and where I spent a lot of my early childhood. She went on to perform in more respectable theatres and had a rather stellar career, but, well… I have such happy memories of my time here. This has always felt like home, so I have my office here.'

He waved an airy hand as if dismissing the insight he had unintentionally revealed as nothing more than a joke. 'And some, like Henny and Prissy, would say it's where I belong and where I should stay.'

It was becoming increasingly obvious that his self-deprecating humour hid something deeper, something painful he was determined not to expose.

'But you're right,' he continued. 'My place is here in the theatre, among people for whom I have the utmost respect. They work hard and there is a vitality to them you'd never find in a stuffy drawing room, and they really know how to enjoy themselves.'

Was that an implied criticism? Did he see her as a stuffy member of society? Did he think she did not know how to enjoy herself? Was he right?

'I believe your father felt the same way,' she said quietly.

He sent her an assessing stare and she coloured slightly, aware that she, too, might have revealed more than she'd intended.

'And can I assume you spent last night enjoying yourself among vital people who know how to enjoy themselves?' she added, resuming her disapproving tone. 'And celebrating your elevation to the peak of that stuffy society you claim to despise?'

Not that she cared one iota what he did last night or with whom. Did she?

He smiled at her, that annoying roguish smile that suggested he had indeed enjoyed himself, perhaps way too much.

'I went to my club after leaving the lawyer's office, just to clear my mind following that decidedly peculiar meeting.'

Clear his mind? That was an interesting excuse for self-indulgence.

'Two friends from school were there and I insisted we celebrate my good fortune, if good fortune is what you can call it, with champagne. And well, one thing led to another and one bottle led to a second and a third.' He shrugged as if that explained everything.

'So it was all the fault of the lawyer's meeting and your school friends?' She knew she was sounding like a schoolmarm chastising a naughty schoolboy, but was seemingly incapable of stopping.

'Nobody's fault but my own,' he said with a mockingly contrite bow of his head. 'And only Seb stayed on to celebrate, or commiserate with me, depending on how you look at it. Thomas is recently married and he's become infuriatingly responsible.'

'And stuffy?'

'You could say that. Although he looks damnably happy about it, but anyway, that was how I spent my evening. I take it you disapprove?'

'It's got nothing to do with me whatsoever and I couldn't care less how you spend your evenings.'

That roguish smile grew wider and she knew what he was thinking. If it had nothing to do with her and if she did not care, why was she interrogating him?

She lifted her head slightly higher to signal to him she was completely above this conversation. 'But I'm not here to discuss your night-time antics,' she said primly as if he was the one to raise the subject, not her. 'I merely wanted to discuss how we were to proceed now that you are the new Duke of Hartfield.'

'We will proceed exactly as we would if I was not the Duke of Hartfield.'

She nodded and stood up. 'And for that I thank you.'

He stood, came around the side of the desk and opened the door for her. 'I'll escort you out.'

As he moved past her to the door, she was suddenly aware of how small and cluttered the office was and how close they were standing. His size, at over six feet, seemed to dominate and overwhelm her. The scent of his cologne, a heady mixture of spice and musk, filled her senses and she could almost feel the warmth of his body. There was something so intoxicatingly masculine about him that was impossible to ignore, especially in the confines of such a small space.

'There is no need to escort me out. I can find my own way,' she said, embarrassed at the slight croak in her voice.

'I insist. I wouldn't want you to be accosted by any of those terrible theatre people.'

'I never said—'

His laughter cut her off. He was teasing her and once again she had fallen into his trap.

She passed him as he held the door open for her and attempted to ignore the way her shoulder nearly brushed against his jacket.

The narrow stairway seemed even narrower than when she had walked up and she was far too conscious of the man behind her. When they entered the foyer she released a held breath as if she'd just escaped from a perilous situation.

'Isaac, darling,' a young woman immediately called out.

Adelaide looked across the room to see a group of pretty women who were watching a man hang a poster on the wall advertising an upcoming performance, while one was signalling to Isaac.

'This is appalling,' the young woman protested. 'I'm the star and my name is no bigger on the poster than any other member of the cast.'

'It's an ensemble performance,' another woman said, glaring at the first speaker.

'Ladies, ladies, I'll be with you in a moment.'

The group of actresses all turned towards them and eyed Adelaide as if summing up a rival, then went back to arguing about the poster.

'I take it these are some of those vital, fun-loving people who know how to enjoy themselves,' she murmured.

'I never said they were perfect. Now, if you'll excuse me, it looks as though I have some ruffled feathers to smooth.'

She looked over at the other women. Knots gripped her stomach, which she strove to ignore, along with any thoughts of exactly how he might be smoothing their feathers.

'Goodbye then,' she said with a small curtsy, giving those pretty actresses another quick look and placing her hand over her twisting stomach, refusing to believe this feeling could possibly be jealousy.

She walked out of the theatre to her waiting carriage, leaving him to his world and returning to her own. Their worlds could not be more different and were never likely to collide again. He had left her to manage the estate and Joshua would not have to move out of the place he considered his home. That was the best outcome she could have hoped for and it would now presumably be the end of her dealings with the new Duke of Hartfield.

She should be pleased, so why did she suddenly feel such a sense of loss?

Chapter Four

Days and weeks passed and Isaac heard no more from the Duchess, and his half-sisters remained suspiciously quiet.

His life returned to normal. Well, as normal as the frenetic life of a theatre manager could be. No one outside the family and his close friends knew of his new status and that was exactly how he intended to keep it for as long as possible.

Gossip had it that Adelaide, as she had granted him permission to call her, had returned to Hartfield Hall. As he had no desire to ever revisit the site of so much misery as a child, it was unlikely their paths would ever cross again.

She would stay in her world. He would stay in his and everybody would be happy. Although he'd be happier if she didn't keep invading his thoughts at the most inopportune times. Why he should think of her so much he had no idea. He doubted he could meet a woman who was less his type. She was the epitome of an aristocrat: judgemental, aloof and superior. He liked his women warm, friendly and the more open-minded the better.

He would admit she was lovely to look at, with that thick brown hair streaked with red and gold, those big brown eyes, surrounded by long, dark lashes, and those inviting, full red lips, but that should not affect him. He was constantly surrounded by celebrated beauties who were feted throughout the land and hardly noticed their abundance of charms.

Was his attraction to her simply because she despised him and therefore a challenge? Surely not. He enjoyed the company of women, the more the merrier, but did not see seduction as a sport the way some men did. No, that couldn't be the reason his mind kept wandering to thoughts of her.

He sat back in his swivel chair and placed his feet up on the desk.

Was it because he had misjudged her so harshly that he couldn't get her out of his mind? The way she had so easily relinquished the title for her son as if it meant nothing to her had taken him completely by surprise. Hadn't that been one of the main reasons why she had married his father, to produce the son and heir, to become the wife of one duke and the mother of another?

That was certainly what he had thought on the day he had seen her standing beside his father at the altar. He had dismissed her as merely another title-seeking debutante who had struck lucky and bagged the richest duke available. And her superior demeanour on that day had only confirmed his preconceptions.

She still conducted herself in a superior manner, but had relinquished the dukedom for her son without as much as a bat of those long black eyelashes.

And it was even more of a surprise that she was running the estate. Not that he would have expected his father to have taken a hand in such matters. With all the time he spent in London, there would have been little left to devote to his responsibilities. So his young, pretty wife had stepped into the breach and taken over the work and appeared to be happy to continue doing so. Intriguing.

There was no doubting there was a lot more to her than he had realised when he first saw her on the arm of his father on their wedding day and he couldn't help but wonder what other hidden depths there were to discover in the lovely Duchess of Hartfield.

Not that he had any intention of trying to find out. He was grateful that she would continue to run the estate so he could get on with his life as if none of this duke nonsense had ever happened. Eventually her son would inherit and all would be right with the world.

She was out of his life, so now all he had to do was get her out of his mind. He looked down at the neglected letters piled up on his desk. Would any be from her? Had she sent him some documents that needed his ducal signature? Was she seeking a decision that needed his careful consideration? Would she be requesting his urgent presence at Hartfield Hall? He hoped not. Didn't he? Of course he did.

He shuffled through the pile. None bore the Hartfield crest. That was good, wasn't it? He had a new show in production and that should be getting his full attention.

He reached the bottom of the pile of correspondence and found a crisp white envelope, slit it open with his letter opener and saw the address of a law firm at the top. This was it. Henrietta and Priscilla were going ahead and legally challenging the marital status of his parents.

With resignation, he read the contents. His feet slid off the desk and hit the ground with a loud thud. He sat up straighter and reread the letter, then read it for a third time.

'She lied to me,' he announced to the empty office, then looked back down at the letter clasped in his hands, then over at the leather couch, once again piled high with papers.

She'd come to his office, sat across the desk from him on that very couch and lied to him, and like a fool he'd believed every word that came out of that pretty mouth, just because he found her damnably attractive.

He reread the letter one more time. As expected, it still stated that the Countess of Hampton and Lady

Henrietta Westleigh were mounting a challenge to his claim to the title of Duke of Hartfield. But what had almost left him gasping for air was the third plaintiff listed: Adelaide FitzWilliam, the Duchess of Hartfield.

He gripped the letter even tighter, almost tearing the crisp white paper in his indignation.

His initial low opinion of her had been correct. He had not misjudged her at all. What he had done was underestimate her. She was not, as he had first thought, some little chit who had succeeded in marrying well. And she certainly was not the admirable woman who cared nothing for status and titles that he had come to believe. She was a conniving, manipulative, grasping aristocrat determined to take what she considered rightfully hers.

He should have known that all along. Had all those years at school surrounded by members of the so-called elite taught him nothing? The aristocracy did not give up titles or property without a fight and they certainly didn't surrender what they considered to be their entitlements to a man such as himself.

Yet he had forgotten all those hard-earned lessons, simply because he was dealing with a beguiling woman, one who, he now realised, was a consummate actress. He must remember to tell her that when she lost this court case and the lawyer's fees had swallowed up her fortune. With such talents for deception and with her looks, she could make plenty more money on the stage.

He folded up the letter and placed it back in the envelope. He didn't want the title, didn't want the estate, but he was not going to throw up his hands and surrender to those grasping, high-and-mighty prigs without giving them a good run for their money.

'Gerrard,' he called out to his assistant.

The young man entered, carrying a large pile of scripts. 'Yes, Isaac, what's the problem? Is it that leak in the main dressing room? I've already called for someone to fix it. They should be here later today.'

'No, it's not that, but well done. I shall be away for a few days, or maybe a week or so, perhaps longer. Do you think you can step in and run things for a while?'

The young man stood up straighter. 'Yes, definitely. And take as long as you like.'

'Good. But if there are any problems I can be reached at Hartfield Hall.'

Gerrard tilted his head. 'Your father's estate?'

'Indeed.' For the next few days, weeks, or however long it took, he intended to reside on his estate and make it his own.

He'd see how the disingenuous Duchess liked that.

Adelaide stood at the window, watching a carriage roll up to the front door of Hartfield Hall. It came to a halt and Isaac Radcliff jumped out. He stood in front of the house, hands on hips, and looked around, giving every appearance of a satisfied man survey-ing his own domain, then turned to the servants and instructed them to carry his trunks into the house. This was not the behaviour of a man who considered himself a guest. This was a man displaying a sense of ownership.

Isaac Radcliff had lied to her. He was arriving un-invited at the home he had said she could continue to live in as if it was her own. One that he obviously now thought of as his possession.

She sighed to herself. It seemed her mother was correct. He was not a man to be trusted. Saying one thing and doing the complete opposite appeared not to present a problem for him. Why had she expected otherwise?

It seemed the son was not that different from the fa-ther after all, but he was about to find out she was not the same woman who had been forced up the aisle at the tender age of eighteen. He had given his word that she could continue to live in this house, the house that Joshua considered his home, and had said the estate was hers to manage. She was not about to let an in-competent man step in and ruin all the hard work she had put into making the estate profitable, not when so many people depended on it being run efficiently.

She placed her hands on her hips, in much the same

manner as he had, then her hands dropped to her side. Would he now be living at Hartfield Hall?

She looked towards the door of her room. It was certainly big enough for them to occupy their own wings and rarely see each other. That was how it had been when the old Duke was in residence. Perhaps it could be the same with the new Duke of Hartfield. But did she want to share the house with Isaac Radcliff, a man who caused her to have unexpected and unwanted reactions at the most ill-timed moments?

The Duke looked up at the window and, for some unaccountable reason, she jumped back as if caught doing something she should not. What in heaven's name was wrong with her? Of course her attention would be drawn to the sound of carriage wheels crunching up the drive. Yet that was how he made her feel. Every time she was in his presence it wasn't long before she felt as if she was doing something illicit and slightly wanton.

She could not continue to hide up here. She had to go downstairs and greet him. If he had seen her looking out the window and she did not go outside to meet him, he would think she had been spying on him. If she went downstairs now it would appear as if that was what she was planning to do all along. That would explain her sudden disappearance from the window.

She released a gasp of exasperation. This was all too ridiculous. She should not let that man affect her in this manner. They now had a problem that had to be sorted out, that was all. She merely needed to know what his plans were. There was no need for her to get quite so flustered.

Mustering all her dignity, she walked down the hallway and stairs at a measured pace. When she reached the entrance she found Joshua chatting to the Duke as if greeting a welcomed guest, while his nanny looked on affectionately. The Duke was laughing at something Joshua was saying and Adelaide used that distraction to do a mental inventory to ensure she was completely composed and nothing of her previous agitated state was revealed. Adopting her most self-assured stance, she descended the outdoor steps, her head held high.

'Your Grace, this is a surprise,' she said, those few words speaking volumes.

'I'm sure it is.' He looked up at her. The smile he'd been giving Joshua died. 'And I thought you agreed to call me Isaac, or did you lie about that as well?'

Adelaide swallowed a gasp of outrage. 'I don't believe *I* am in the habit of lying, *Isaac*,' she replied, placing an emphasis on his name. 'So what has brought you to Hartfield Hall, *Isaac*?' She looked at the trunks the servants were carrying inside the house. 'And how long do you plan to stay?'

'That's up to me, isn't it?' He looked around at the gardens, his hands once again on his hips. 'I thought

I'd spend a bit of time at *my* estate and get the lay of the land, as it were. *My* land.'

'I see,' she responded, keeping her voice even and refusing to react to what was apparently a provocation. 'And do you intend to move in permanently? Did you not say you preferred to remain in London? Among your own people?'

'Things have changed,' he said, his voice and look a challenge. 'You more than anyone else must realise that.'

She tilted her head in question, but he gave her no further explanation.

'Well, whatever has changed, you are of course most welcome.'

'How kind of you to welcome me into my own home.'

She sent him a tight smile. 'I'm afraid that as you did not give me notice of your intended visit, no rooms have been prepared for you.'

'Don't worry. I'm used to roughing it.' He looked up at the three-storey house, its grand entrance and main block flanked by two extensive wings that surrounded the courtyard. It was one of the largest houses in the country, and certainly the largest in Kent, and nothing about it could ever be described as rough.

'I'm pleased to hear that,' she said, not rising to the bait. 'I'll instruct the servants to prepare a room for you.'

'No need. *I* will instruct *my* servants to prepare a room, but I'll do so after I've decided which one of my rooms I want.'

She eyed him warily. 'As you wish. Do I take it you are revoking your offer to allow me and Joshua to remain in this house?'

He gave her a long, studied look. 'No, not yet,' he said slowly. 'Let's see how things work out before we start making any further arrangements, shall we, *Adelaide*?' The use of her name and the way he had drawn it out felt almost like a taunt.

She swallowed down her outrage. She would not react to his goading. 'That is very gracious of you, *Isaac*,' she responded.

'Yes, it seems us Graces can be gracious on occasion. Even if some people think we don't deserve such a title and believe a more colourful description best describes our position in society.'

She looked at Joshua, who had become bored with the adults' conversation and was distracting himself by moving gravel around with his boots. 'If you are referring to the derogatory term used by Lady Henrietta and Lady Hampton, then I can assure you I believe the status of a child's birth cannot possibly be the fault of the child. It is how that child develops, how he acts in later life that is proof of the man's true character.'

'And how a woman acts is surely proof of her character as well.'

She had no idea as to the implication of that statement, but whatever it was, his scornful expression made it clear he was not intending to compliment her.

Joshua pulled on his sleeve to draw his attention. 'So are you going to live here with us?'

That was the question to which Adelaide was also seeking an answer.

'Are you going to be my new father?' Joshua added.

'Joshua,' Adelaide snapped, louder than she intended, startling her son and causing his lower lip to quiver. 'I'm sorry, darling, I didn't mean to be so abrupt, but that is not a question you ask anyone. Isaac has come to look at the house, his house, and his estate and we must make him very welcome.'

Joshua's brow furrowed. 'No, this is my house. But I don't mind if you share it with me.'

Isaac laughed, a genuine laugh, that caused his brown eyes to sparkle and for crinkles to form at the edges of his eyes, as if laughing was something he often did. 'That's very kind of you, Joshua, and, no, I'm not going to be your new father, but I can be your brother.' He pulled a mock frown as if this arrangement seemed rather peculiar to him.

'Really?' Joshua jumped up and down at this prospect. 'Good, you can play with all my toys if you like. My soldiers are my favourites and you can play with them as well if you're very, very good.'

'Then I will endeavour to be especially good at all

times,' he said, as Joshua took his hand to lead him inside.

As Adelaide followed them up the steps and into the house, she suspected that being good was something else the new Duke merely said but had no intention of doing.

Chapter Five

It was not quite the reaction Isaac had hoped for. He'd expected to see some cracks in that imperturbable demeanour. He thought she'd be outraged at him daring to occupy a home she considered her own. He had been prepared for the sort of arguments Henrietta would have thrown his way. Instead, she'd remained her usual composed, detached self as if nothing or no one would disturb that unflappable countenance.

Well, an extended period of time in his company should put paid to that. He was about to have a great deal of fun ruffling the smooth feathers of the stoic Duchess of Hartfield.

Joshua led him up the stairs, or rather dragged him up the stairs, so eager was he to show off the house to what he considered to be his new playmate. 'This staircase is the best one to slide down as it's wide and curvy,' he informed Isaac as if passing on the most important piece of knowledge about the grand house.

'Yes, I know, I slid down it on occasion when I was a boy as well.'

Behaviour that had resulted in his half-sisters responding, 'What else would you expect from a guttersnipe who has no knowledge of how to behave?' Which had only encouraged Isaac to find ever more outlandish things to do to prove them right.

They reached the top of the stairs and Joshua ran ahead. 'This room is mine,' he announced proudly, throwing open the door.

Joshua peeked inside and saw a small brass bed under the sash window covered in a patchwork quilt and littered with a menagerie of fabric toy animals. Books were piled up on the bedside table, a large dappled grey hobby horse stood in the middle of the room and armies of soldiers were lined up on the washstand, ready for battle.

It reminded him of his own childhood room in his mother's home, full of all the things that made a child happy, the room he was forced to leave when his father sent him away to that damnable school when he was not much older than Joshua.

'It's right next to Mama's room,' Joshua said, once again pulling on his hand and leading him out into the hallway. 'I'll show you that if you like.'

'I'm sure Isaac does not want to see my room,' the Duchess said, placing her hands on her son's shoulders and turning him around. 'He needs to select a bedchamber that he finds acceptable.'

Isaac smiled as she blushed slightly. A faint crack had appeared in that implacable façade. Good.

'Perhaps Joshua can pick a room for me,' he said, turning back to the little boy. 'No one knows a house better than a young boy who likes to explore.'

Joshua frowned in concentration, as if tasked with an enormous responsibility. 'Father's bedroom was in the other wing and that's the best room in the house, but it's ever such a long way away. He wasn't here very often anyway so I don't know why he had to have the best room. And when he did visit he filled up that wing with lots of people who never wanted to play with me or my soldiers.'

Isaac tried not to react to that piece of news. Did that mean he had not shared a room with his wife? He looked down at Joshua. Obviously they had shared a bed at least once during their married life.

Isaac also knew what his father's friends were like. They were rowdy, licentious and dissolute, not unlike his father had been. It was hard to imagine how an eighteen-year-old had coped with living among such bedlam. That combined with dealing with the shrewish sisters was an ordeal he would wish on no one.

Had she coped by adopting the same distant, superior manner she was presently displaying?

It mattered not. He would not feel pity for her, not if

it undermined his determination to let her know that, despite his lowly birth, he would not be treated with disdain by a self-entitled aristocrat.

'But the room next to Mama's is very nice,' Joshua continued. 'Not as nice as mine because it doesn't have any toys in it, but you can have some of mine if you like.'

'That's very kind of you,' Isaac said as Joshua led him into the neighbouring bedchamber.

The first thing he noticed when he entered the room was the door adjoining Adelaide's. This was obviously the room the man of the house was expected to occupy, not a room in the other wing. It was much bigger than Joshua's and contained a large, intricately carved four-poster bed, draped with deep blue damask curtains. Tapestries depicting hunting scenes adorned the walls and large jewel-hued rugs covered the polished wooden floor. The floor-to-ceiling sash windows gave a view of the entrance and out on to the estate, so the man of the house could survey all he owned from the comfort of his bedchamber.

'Yes, I believe this will do perfectly,' he said.

Did she look nervously towards the adjoining door as he said this? What was she worried about? Did she think the ruffian would break in and ravish her in the middle of the night?

Isaac wanted this to increase his indignation at her low opinion of him, but perhaps she had a right to be nervous. She was a woman living in this house with a man she barely knew.

He winced. Damn, he had not come here to frighten her. 'Or maybe Joshua can show me another room, one in the west wing, perhaps.'

Joshua frowned at him. 'But that's miles and miles away. No, you have to sleep here.'

Isaac hesitated and looked towards the adjoining room. 'Can I assume that door remains locked and you have the key?' he asked quietly.

She nodded and he was pleased to see the tension in her shoulders release slightly. 'And perhaps you'd like to join me for tea in the drawing room while the servants are making the room ready for you,' she said.

Joshua raced ahead and Isaac followed the Duchess down the stairs and into the ladies' drawing room at the front of the house. He had only been in this room once before, when he was presented to Henrietta and Priscilla's mother, Winifred, the Duchess. She had returned home unexpectedly during one of his visits to his father and was far from pleased to find the bastard child of her husband's mistress in her home.

When his father introduced him, she had looked at Isaac as if he was something unpleasant she had found on the bottom of her shoe, a look that had been matched by her daughters. Isaac had reacted by deliberately brushing up against a small, flimsy table and sending a tea set crashing to the ground in an apparent act of clumsiness. If they were of the opinion that he couldn't behave in polite company, then he was determined to show them just how impolite he could be and do as much damage in the process.

Needless to say, Winifred had informed her husband that the little urchin was to never enter the ladies' drawing room again. Now here he was, back in that room, and he was the owner of all he could see. And this time, while he had no intention of acting like a bull in a china shop, he still intended to create some mayhem.

The Duchess pulled the bell to summon a servant, then took a seat on the sofa, sitting up straight and staring at him in the same manner as her predecessor had done before her.

A footman entered and bowed to the Duchess.

'Please bring tea for myself and His Grace and some lemonade for Joshua.'

The footman bowed. 'Yes, Your Grace.'

Isaac stifled a sigh of exasperation at this stuffiness which he abhorred, stood up and approached the footman. 'I'm Isaac Radcliff and I'm pleased to make your acquaintance.'

The footman stared back at him as if he'd suddenly grown another head, then sent the Duchess a panicked look.

'And your name is?' Isaac asked.

'Baxter,' the man mumbled.

'I'm pleased to meet you, Baxter,' he said, lifting up the man's limp hand and shaking it.

'I'll arrange for the tea, Your…' Colour tinged the man's cheeks and he rushed out of the room before finishing his sentence, in a manner most unlike that of the usually unflappable servant.

'If your intention was to make me feel uncomfortable with that display of egalitarianism, then I'm afraid you've failed,' the Duchess said as Isaac took his seat. 'The only person you made feel uncomfortable was Baxter. He will now be fretting that he has done or said the wrong thing and is in danger of losing his job. As the man is dependent on the income he receives as a footman, it might be best if you reassure him that this is not the case.'

Damn it all, she was correct. His intention had been to make her see that he considered no one in this house above anyone else. But she was wrong in her assumption that Baxter was the only one now feeling uncomfortable.

'I like Baxter,' Joshua added, causing him to cringe. 'He won't lose his job, will he?'

'No, of course not,' the Duchess assured her son. Then she inclined her head in Isaac's direction. 'Although that, of course, is now up to Isaac. As he has been at pains to point out, the servants are all now in his employment.'

'Baxter's job is perfectly safe,' he responded, feeling even more gauche than he had when Winifred had looked down her contemptuous nose at him.

A maid entered the room, placed the tea tray on a small table beside the Duchess and handed a glass of lemonade to a smiling Joshua.

'Thank you, Polly,' the Duchess said. 'No doubt Baxter has told you that the new Duke of Hartfield is currently in residence.'

'Yes, Your Grace,' Polly muttered. She turned to Isaac and with her eyes lowered made a nervous curtsy.

Isaac thought it wisest to merely nod in acknowledgement rather than make another show of camaraderie. 'Please apologise to Baxter for my somewhat bizarre behaviour and inform him it will not happen again,' he said, feeling like a scolded schoolboy.

'Yes, Your Grace.'

'Thank you, Polly. I will pour the tea, but can you please take Joshua downstairs with you.'

'But—' Joshua pleaded.

'And see if Cook has any biscuits or cake for him,' the Duchess added.

With that a smiling Joshua took hold of Polly's hand and started pulling her towards the door, while she attempted to give another quick curtsy.

The door closed behind them and Isaac braced himself for the expected rebuke, a lesson on correct etiquette, or even a look of disapproval, and was determined to give as good as he got.

'Milk and sugar?' the Duchess asked politely. Isaac almost wished she would criticise his behaviour in the same manner as Winifred had. Then he would be on firmer ground and know exactly how to respond. But when in the Duchess's presence, the ground under his feet was never particularly firm. She was unlike any woman he had ever met, as was the effect she had on him. As a man who prided himself on knowing women, this was a decidedly unsettling situation.

'However it comes. I don't care.'

She poured a spot of milk into each cup, picked up the silver sugar tongs and placed six sugar cubes in one cup and held it out towards him.

He took the cup. Her cool fingers lightly touched his and a jolt of heat rushed up his arm.

Hell! He did not want to be attracted to this woman. He was here to let her know that, despite the way he was brought up, despite not mixing in so-called high society, despite not actually wanting the dukedom, he was not about to lie down and let her walk all over him in her embroidered silk shoes.

Damn. Damn. Damn. Now he was thinking about well-turned ankles and feminine feet encased in delicate ballroom slippers. He took a large gulp of his tea. The sickly sweetness exploded in his mouth, making him wince and his teeth ache.

As he fought to compose his face, a small smile curled the edges of the Duchess's lips. She was enjoying torturing him. He could only hope that over-sweetening his tea was the only way she intended to do so. Judging by the effect of the brief touch of her fingers on his, she had the power to torture him in a manner that would make him forget all about the lawsuit, the estate and the title, and to roll over and willingly give her whatever she wanted.

'May I be so bold as to ask how long you intend to stay at Hartfield Hall?' she asked and took a sip of her tea.

'That depends on you, Henny and Prissy,' he said, placing the frightful cup of tea on a nearby table.

'Am I to assume you have changed your mind about taking charge of all that you have inherited?'

She really was playing it cool, but then he'd expect nothing else from such an imperious woman. 'Let's just say a recent change in circumstances has led me to seeing the advantage of taking what is now rightfully mine.'

'I see.' She placed her teacup on a small side table. 'I assume you are referring to the lawsuit.'

'Yes, that lawsuit.' Of course he was talking about the lawsuit. What else would bring him to this house? He wasn't here to take tea. He wasn't here to admire the Duchess's beauty, or to fantasise about her feet. He was here because of that letter she must know he had now received.

'It's not my place to make suggestions,' she said,

'but if I was in your position, I would offer a substantial settlement. That would hopefully nip this in the bud before it reached the courts.'

He looked at her delicate hands, at the soft, flawless skin, the long fingers with their manicured nails, and suspected she had never nipped a bud in her privileged life. With a start he also noticed she was no longer wearing her wedding ring. Did this mean she was already on the hunt for another husband? She'd already bagged a duke. Who could she be after now? A prince?

She was also out of widow weeds, although the plain dark grey dress was not a dramatic change from black. Most women out to capture a man would be dressed in eye-catching colours and sparkling with gems. Not that she needed to. She was effortlessly beautiful, with her creamy skin that was calling out for the stroke of a man's finger, that thick dark brown hair that would no doubt look magnificent when freed from its restricting bun and those full, lush lips that would cause any man to think about what kissing her would feel like.

He coughed lightly and reminded himself of why he was here as his gaze returned to those cool brown eyes. 'Would you now? And what sort of settlement do you think would satisfy the plaintiffs?'

'One generous enough to encourage them to not take this to court and expose all the Hartfield family secrets to the public.'

'So that's all this is about, is it? Filthy lucre? I'd

have thought the plaintiffs all had more than enough of that, but I suppose for some people there will never be enough property or enough money.'

She already had a substantial cottage large enough to house several families, a town house in London and a generous annual annuity, but obviously wanted more. Her own estate, perhaps, or why settle for one when she could demand two or more? With a sinking feeling deep in his stomach, he wondered how he could have ever thought she was different from his grasping half-sisters. Or was it simply that he wanted her to be different, wanted her to be the beautiful, composed and admirable woman who had visited him at his office?

'Possibly, but a settlement might soften the blow and give your half-sisters the impression they have not been defeated entirely,' she said. 'That is perhaps the gentlemanly thing to do.'

'But that would require me to actually be a gentleman and not the cur my half-sisters, and others, clearly believe me to be.'

She made no response, merely raised an eyebrow.

'And even if I suddenly did start acting like a gentleman, I doubt if even the most generous of settlements would satisfy Henny and Prissy. They've spent their lives looking down their noses at their bastard half-brother. Nothing other than proof that they are the legitimate children will satisfy them.'

'At the moment no one outside the family knows

they are illegitimate. Once it goes to court, once the newspapers get wind of a salacious story involving an aristocratic family, everyone will know, from the members of society down to your sisters' servants. That is in no one's best interest, least of all Lady Henrietta and Lady Hampton.'

He looked at her dubiously. 'So you accept that I am the real Duke of Hartfield.'

She gave a small nod. 'Given the dramatic nature of the revelation and the effect it has had on so many, I have no doubts that the lawyer checked and re-checked the validity of the marriage certificate, and that everything possible was done to find proof the old Duke was legally married to Lady Henrietta and Lady Hampton's mother. As none was found, we can assume that your parents' marriage was legal.'

Isaac remained unconvinced. 'And you don't care that your son will not inherit the title?' She had married for money and a title and, despite her claims to the contrary, he doubted she would give up either without a fight. The letter in his pocket proved that.

She picked up her cup and took another sip of her tea, leaving Isaac to wait for her response.

'I'm sure you know as well as I do that the rules that govern our society are well defined and everyone is expected to conform to those rules.'

Isaac sat back in his chair. Here it came, the expected lecture on the way the world was and how people should accept their place in it, including bastard sons who should not rise above their station.

'Is that what you are doing? Accepting your place? Or are you fighting hard to keep it for yourself and your son?

'I am a woman, Your Grace. I mean, Isaac.'

Isaac was tempted to give a snort of disbelief. As if he could forget for a single second that she was a woman.

'Like all women I have been taught from a young age to accept what fate has in store for me.'

This time he really did snort with laughter. 'Every woman except Henny and Prissy.'

'They are daughters of a wealthy duke. They were born and raised to stand at the very pinnacle of society, or so they thought. I suspect that makes you see the world in a slightly different light.'

'And that is a position you now hold, at the very pinnacle of society. Does that make you see the world differently?'

Does it make you think you are more entitled to take what is not yours to have, including my title and estate for your son?

She tilted her head slightly as if considering this. 'Perhaps being a widowed duchess does make me see the world differently. It gives me some choices I've never had before and ones that few other women possess.'

'Lucky you.'

'Lucky is not how I would describe my life up until now,' she said candidly, looking him firmly in the eye. 'Like many women I was told whom I should marry and in my case it was a man old enough to be my father. And he was…'

She paused. Isaac did not need her to continue. He knew exactly what his father had been like. 'I'm sorry,' he murmured.

'I'm not seeking your pity, merely letting you know that sometimes one unfortunately has to accept the things one cannot change. And in this case I have accepted that Joshua has not inherited the title of the Duke of Hartfield.'

'Are you saying you don't intend to challenge the will, or take this matter to court?'

Or are you just trying to get me off guard?

'That is exactly what I am saying. It is what I have always said.'

Unbelievable. She was still lying directly to his face. He was right. She was trying to get him off guard. Well, it would not work. With a theatrical flourish he removed the letter from the pocket inside his jacket and handed it to her. 'So how do you explain this?'

Once again her fingers lightly touched his as she took the letter from his outstretched hand. This time he was prepared, but that did not stop an even more powerful swell of attraction rising up inside him.

While he tried to rein in his unwelcome impulses, she scanned the contents, then looked up at him, those brown eyes meeting his. He crossed his legs and continued to stare at her as if she was his adversary, one who had no effect on him whatsoever.

She folded up the letter and handed it back to him. He carefully took hold of the edge of the envelope, not wanting to further lose his advantage by subjecting his body to another lustful surge should their fingers make contact.

'I can see why this would have angered you, but I believe—'

'Shall we drop this charade? he said, taking refuge in indignation. 'That letter proves you still have an interest in securing the dukedom for your son, or is it simply money that you are after and this is some form of blackmail?'

He waited with a sense of satisfaction for her to defend herself.

She drew in a deep breath and slowly released it, drawing his gaze to the rise and fall of her chest.

Stop this. Look at her eyes. Only her eyes.

He reluctantly followed his own mental command and once again looked into those big brown eyes.

'As I was trying to say before you interrupted me, I believe my mother is behind this. She still thinks I am under her control, just as I was before I married. But now I am under no one's control.' She held his gaze, giving him a glimpse of the formidable woman under the polite exterior.

'I shall contact my mother's lawyer immediately and tell him I have no interest in pursuing this case and let him know that if he does not drop my and my son's names from the list of plaintiffs I will be taking action against him.'

'I see,' Isaac said, suddenly feeling deflated.

'And hopefully Lady Henrietta and Lady Hampton will soon see sense and realise it is not in their best interest to expose such scandals to a newspaper-reading public eager for salacious gossip about the aristocracy.'

'And I suppose you wouldn't want your own reputation tarnished and have everyone think you were the wife of a philanderer,' he said with a renewed sense of disapproval.

'I *was* the wife of a philanderer,' she replied, once again taking the wind out of his sails. 'But you are right. While everyone in society knew what my late husband was like, it was never a subject discussed in public. If this lawsuit goes ahead, it will be common knowledge that my son's father was a bigamist and it will be a topic of discussion for everyone from the servants up to the highest ranks of society. My innocent son does not deserve that.'

Isaac was suddenly lost for words. So what should he do now? Apologise? For himself? For his father?

For the way the world treated women? For all that she had suffered? For the way he had judged her so harshly?

Instead, he picked up his tea, went to take another sip, then remembered the previous sugary torture and put it back down on the table.

Should he now take his leave? He could return to London, leave her to her quiet life here in the countryside and concentrate on his coming court case with Henrietta and Priscilla.

'And you think I should make Henny and Prissy a generous settlement?' he asked, not really caring about the answer, but strangely not wanting to end this conversation, and, if he was being entirely honest, not wanting to leave Hartfield Hall quite so soon.

'It might soften the blow somewhat. It must have been a devastating shock to hear that you are not the daughters of a duke, but his illegitimate children and therefore entitled to nothing.'

'One gets used to it.'

She inclined her head in acknowledgement.

'To be honest, I couldn't care less if they did win the court case,' he added.

Her eyebrows rose slightly and he knew what she must be thinking. If that was the case, why did he rush down here and start acting like the lord of the manor? He knew the reason why, but wasn't about to tell her he'd spent his entire life being looked down on by people from her class and that letter had brought back memories of every taunt, every snide comment, every disgusted look as if a bad odour wafted around him everywhere he went. It was something he'd had to endure as a child, but he would not do so now he was an adult.

He was saved from explaining himself by Joshua, who burst into the room waving a piece of paper in the air and clutching several others in his hand, along with his case of toy soldiers that seemed to travel everywhere with him. 'I've drawn a picture,' he announced, thrusting it towards Isaac.

It depicted two large circles with sticks poking out of them, one small similar circle with sticks and a tiny circle with a long line curving above it.

'That's marvellous,' Isaac said, hoping he was holding it up the right way. 'Worthy of being hung in the National Gallery.'

'That's what Polly said. She said it was the best one I've done so far.' He climbed up next to Isaac and pointed a finger at the paper. 'That's you, that's me, that's Mama and that's Whiskers.'

'Who's Whiskers?'

Joshua frowned at him. 'Everyone knows Whiskers. He's the tabby cat who keeps the mice out of the stables.'

He pushed another piece of paper into Isaac's hand. 'I did this one without Polly's help.'

'I see. It's just as wonderful.'

He held up the painting so the Duchess could see, hoping for some help in deciphering the different-sized blobs.

'Is it another one of Hartfield Hall?' she said, smiling warmly at her son.

'Yes, that's the trees, there's the drive and that's you, Isaac, driving up in your carriage.'

Isaac smiled his thanks to the Duchess and went back to admiring the drawing. 'And that's the lake.'

Joshua looked at him as if he was a bit simple. 'No, that's the garden. See, there are the flowers.'

'Of course, how foolish of me.'

'That's all right,' Joshua said graciously, before thrusting yet another picture into his hands.

Isaac settled back into the chair for what he suspected was going to be a protracted period of art appreciation as Joshua described another portrait of the famous Whiskers whom everyone supposedly knew.

The Duchess walked over to the bell pull. 'I believe another pot of tea is called for,' she said. 'Although I don't believe we will be needing any more sugar.'

They exchanged knowing smiles.

It looked as though the battle between them was over before it had hardly begun and for that Isaac was grateful. She had not lied to him. She was not in league with Henrietta and Priscilla. Good. Why it had knocked him off balance so much he did not know, but that hardly mattered now. He would just enjoy this moment of peace and hope that it would last.

Chapter Six

Adelaide expected Isaac to announce he was returning to London immediately, back to his own people,
away from the stuffy drawing rooms he professed to
hate so much and away from people who did not know
how to have fun.

But he settled back into his chair, Joshua perched on
the arm, as if he had no intention of moving anytime
soon. His belief that she was challenging his right to
the title had brought him here. That now had hopefully
been settled. Presumably he also had no intention of
reneging on his offer that she and Joshua could continue to live in Hartfield Hall. But did that mean he intended to stay as well, and how did she feel about that?

She watched him chatting and laughing with her
son. Joshua had warmed to him and his patience with
the young boy was more than she would have expected
from that arrogant man she had met at her wedding.

'Tomorrow, I can show you around the gardens, if

you like,' Joshua said. 'We can go down to the river. That's the best place on the whole estate.'

'I'm sure the Duke, I mean, Isaac has commitments back in London,' she said. And, no doubt, as his father had said at their wedding, he had some beauty impatiently waiting for his return. She kept her face impassive, determined to neither show nor acknowledge the tight sensation in the centre of her chest at the thought.

'But there might be tadpoles in the river. Isaac can help me catch them,' Joshua said, a look of outrage on his face.

Adelaide couldn't help but feel guilty. Joshua was so happy and was obviously enjoying having male company. He often trailed around after the male servants. They were all very accommodating, but had work to do and could not devote themselves fully to the demands of a small, energetic boy.

'When I was staying here as a boy, I once caught a frog down at the river,' Isaac said. 'And I put it in Henrietta's bed.'

Joshua's eyes grew wide with admiration. He jumped off the chair and waved his hands around in the air. 'Let's do that. Let's catch some frogs,' he cried out. 'Can we?'

Isaac looked in her direction. 'I think you'll need permission from your mother as to whether us men can go on a hunting expedition tomorrow.'

Joshua puffed himself up, enjoying being seen as

one of the men, and smiled at his mother, obviously expecting her to agree. 'Can we—can us men go hunting frogs tomorrow?'

'Yes, of course you can,' she said. 'But if you catch any frogs, I don't want them turning up in anyone's bed. It's not fair to the frogs.'

Joshua and Isaac exchanged sly grins.

'So can I assume you are still planning on staying the night,' she continued, remembering Isaac's sarcastic comment when he first arrived, about her being gracious in welcoming him into his own house and wondering how he would take this enquiry.

'If that is not an inconvenience,' he said, looking somewhat abashed, presumably also remembering the same comment.

'Not in the slightest,' she replied with equal politeness.

Oh, they really were behaving themselves now, weren't they? She had not lied to him before, not when she said she had no intention of challenging his right to the title, not when she said she was unconcerned that Joshua would not be a duke, but she suspected she was lying to him now.

While it would not be an inconvenience, she was unsure whether spending more time with him was such a good idea. She gripped her hands in her lap, remembering the touch of his skin when he had passed the lawyer's letter to her. It had been impossible to ignore the raw desire that had pulsed through her as she felt his fingers against hers.

This man affected her in a way that was disconcerting and decidedly unsettling. That alone made it unwise to spend more time in his company than was absolutely necessary. But it *was* his house, despite his agreement to let her live here, and he *was* making Joshua happy. As long as she could keep these ridiculous sensations under control it would surely do no harm for him to stay the night.

'Thank you,' he said.

She gave him a brief smile and he turned his attention back to Joshua and their discussion of frogs and tadpoles.

Of course she could keep herself under control. All she had to do was remind herself of the type of man he was. He might look harmless now, chatting away to Joshua, but he was, after all, his father's son: a rake, a seducer, a man who knew exactly how to elicit such responses from every woman he met.

All that was required was for her body to behave as logically as her mind. That was surely possible. She squeezed her hands tightly together, as if wringing out any memory of that touch, then looked up from her traitorous hands to her son and Isaac. They were now standing in the middle of the room, demonstrating what they considered the best methods of catching tadpoles.

And even if she failed, which she was determined not to do, with Joshua present there was no danger of her doing something foolish and revealing the effect Isaac so easily had on her.

'I've got a new net,' Joshua said as he swung his arms around in imitation of tadpole catching. 'We can try it out tomorrow. Those tadpoles won't stand a chance against us.'

'Indeed they won't,' Isaac said. It would be remiss of him to not stay the night, not when it would mean disappointing young Joshua.

That was the only reason he was still intending to stay. Wasn't it? It had nothing to do with Adelaide. Yes, she was beautiful and, yes, she was affecting him, but he would be a fool to act on any feelings he had for her. When it came to women, he had never been a fool and wasn't about to become one now.

His gaze continued to linger on her, on that exquisite face, on her soft, creamy skin and those full red lips. He could see why his father had been so attracted to her. But he was not like his father, not entirely. When it came to women, what his father wanted his father took. Isaac was not like that.

He looked away and turned back to Joshua. Their discussion moved on from the best way to catch those elusive tadpoles to the important issue of which cake was their favourite, then to the antics of Whiskers and whether Isaac had any pets, and the vital topic of which toy soldiers had the smartest uniform, the red ones or the blue ones.

Joshua was adorable and to his surprise Isaac was enjoying himself immensely. The non-stop prattle had the added advantage of almost distracting him from thinking about the woman seated across the room.

Not that he didn't continue to cast the occasional glance in her direction. She had taken up her embroidery, but the small, Madonna-like smile that kept crossing her lips showed she was listening to the conversation.

It was quite the domestic scene, worthy of the best sentimental painting. Isaac almost laughed at this absurdity. He was not a domesticated man and never would be. The thought of him married to the Duchess and being a father to Joshua was a joke. And not a particularly funny one. No one in their right mind would see him as an ideal parent and he was definitely not the marrying kind. Never had been, never would be.

He enjoyed his freedom too much and, like his father, had never been a man to settle for one woman, but unlike his father he had no intention of becoming a man with a wife, a mistress or two, and who knew how many children born on the wrong side of the sheets.

'What do you think?' Joshua asked.

'About what?'

'About going into battle?'

Before Isaac could ask what sort of battle, Joshua started to unpack his toy soldiers.

'Isaac might be tired after his trip,' Adelaide said, causing her son to frown at his mother, several toy soldiers clasped in his hands.

'I'm never too tired for battle,' he said instantly, turning Joshua's frown back into a cherub-like smile.

He lay on the floor and helped Joshua set out the two armies in military formation. If Winifred could see him now, she would be rolling over in her grave, mortified that the ladies' drawing room was the site of such unmannerly behaviour. She would be outraged that a rapscallion such as he was daring to sully her elegant room in such an indecorous manner.

'Right, let battle commence,' Isaac announced once the soldiers were all lined up.

A serious Joshua pushed a battalion of red soldiers towards his blue infantrymen. It was all a bit chaotic, but could almost be seen as a pincer movement and Joshua certainly looked pleased with himself.

'A cunning tactic, General,' he said. 'I think it's time for the blue army to make a strategic retreat.'

It didn't take long for them to get fully immersed in their game and the afternoon passed in this pleasant manner, until Adelaide announced it was nearly time for dinner.

'I think we're going to have to declare a draw,' Isaac

said, although he wasn't sure such an outcome existed on the battlefield.

'We can continue tomorrow,' Joshua said as he carefully packed up his soldiers. 'After we've finished tadpoling and frog catching.' He grimaced at Isaac. 'But now we have to dress for dinner.'

Isaac returned the grimace.

He had detested those seemingly endless formal dinners he'd had to attend when he visited Hartfield Hall. Henrietta and Priscilla had always tried their best to make him feel as uncomfortable as possible. While he had taken a certain satisfaction in responding in kind to every insult they threw his way, he had also found it dispiriting to be constantly reminded of his lowly status.

Despite being in the same room, his father had remained oblivious to the antics of his daughters and the more glasses of brandy he consumed the more uncaring he became.

It was even worse on the odd occasion when Winifred was in residence. No matter how straight he sat up, he was always told off for slouching and she seemed to think using the correct knife and fork was something he would never master. At the beginning of every course, she would hold up the correct pieces of cutlery, much to the sniggering enjoyment of her daughters, and slowly inform him as if he had difficulty understanding English, 'This is for the fish course, this is for cheese and this is for the fruit course.'

On one particularly fraught occasion, when he had finally reached the end of his tether, he had burst out, 'It's just cutlery, for God's sake. If I can get the highest marks at school in ancient Greek and physics, I can remember which bloody knife and fork to use for the fish.'

His father had laughed off his outburst, but not Winifred. She had insisted he never again take his meals at the dinner table if he could not conduct himself like a gentleman. That was a happy outcome for all. From that day onwards he took his meals with the servants, a group that loved to gossip and laugh over their meals and who had always made him feel welcome.

'You can always take your meals with nanny in the nursery if you prefer, then you won't have to dress for dinner,' Adelaide said to her son in a teasing tone.

'I'll race you to the top of the stairs,' Joshua announced. 'And I bet I'm dressed for dinner before you are.' He took off out the door at a cracking pace, before Isaac had even risen from the floor, causing his mother to laugh.

'I hope Joshua is not being too demanding,' Adelaide said as he stood up.

'Not at all. I think I enjoyed our battle even more than he did and there's nothing I like better than muck-ing about on the banks of a river, so I'm happy to take him tadpoling.'

'You're very kind,' she added, causing him to feel absurdly flattered and even more ridiculously pleased with himself.

'Come on,' Joshua called out, poking his head round the corner. 'If you're too slow, you'll have to eat in the nursery.'

'All right, all right, I'm coming,' he said and joined the young boy as they raced up the stairs and along the hallway towards their rooms.

'Another draw,' Joshua declared as they reached their respective doors. 'But I'll beat you tomorrow night,' he added as he disappeared into his room.

Isaac called for a bath to be run. Once the servants departed, he lay back in the warm water, whistling to himself and surprised that the day had turned out to be so enjoyable. And it was even more surprising that he was looking forward to dining with Adelaide and Joshua, and in the very room that had always filled him with such dread as a child. He was unsure if it was Joshua's joyfulness or the thought of spending more time with Adelaide that was causing this lightness of spirit, but it was a feeling he'd never had before at Hartfield Hall.

When the water started to cool, he dried himself off, dressed in his formal dinner suit, applied some cologne and ran a brush through his hair. Before leaving, he inspected himself one last time in the full-length looking glass with uncharacteristic vanity, then, still whistling, headed down to the dining room.

At the door he paused as that familiar sense of dread rushed through him. But he was not a child any more. His clashes with Winifred were all over. He was no longer the despised bastard child, but an adult and a duke to boot, of all things.

With a flourish, as if this room held no fear for him and never had, he opened the door and found Adelaide and Joshua already seated at the table. Joshua was, not unexpectedly, chattering away to his mother, and there was nothing stuffy about the scene before him. It was the very image of a happy, loving family. That is, if the loving family was headed by an angel.

Adelaide looked divine, there was no other word for it.

In the soft light of the table candelabra, her alabaster skin was almost translucent, her brown eyes sparkled like shimmering jewels and her red lips looked soft and enticing. Her hair was no longer in a tight bun at the nape of her neck, but had been swept up on to the top of her head and was intricately styled, with several curls cascading down her neck. Ringlets, he thought they were called. Surely he could not be blamed if his gaze followed those ringlets down her neck, to the exposed skin of her naked shoulders, and lower, to the agonisingly tempting hint of cleavage on display above the neckline of her burgundy gown.

Perhaps divine wasn't the right word, not when she was stirring up such wicked impulses in him.

A slight blush tinged her cheeks and he wondered—hoped?—she had dressed this way to please him. And pleased he most certainly was.

He moved forward towards the table, drawn magnetically to Adelaide and aware that he was staring like some love-struck adolescent.

'Sit next to me, Isaac,' Joshua called out, indicating a chair, which the footman dutifully pulled out.

He did as commanded, and smiled when he looked over at Joshua's place setting. Along with the line-up of the dreaded silver cutlery with which Winifred had attempted to humiliate him was a row of his beloved toy soldiers. If Winifred wasn't already turning in her grave, she certainly would be now at such impropriety at the dinner table.

Another footman entered carrying the soup tureen and Adelaide signalled for him to serve the first course.

'I see your soldiers have decided to dine with us tonight instead of in the mess hall,' Isaac said to Joshua.

Joshua looked at his mother in confusion.

'The mess hall is where soldiers take their meals,' she explained.

'Well, this can be their messy hall,' Joshua responded, causing Isaac and Adelaide to laugh.

'I'm afraid Joshua and I tend to dine rather informally,' she said. 'I hope you don't mind.'

'Not at all. I think dining rooms should always be like messy halls where everyone enjoys themselves.'

'Me, too,' Joshua agreed, plunging his spoon into his soup and instantly launching into one of his monologues. Isaac was grateful for the young boy's chatter, otherwise he was sure he would find himself tongue-tied in Adelaide's company. He doubted he had ever seen a woman who was more tempting, but more out of bounds, and it was having a strange effect on him.

When had he ever been tongue-tied with a woman? He was sure the answer to that question was never. Having grown up around actresses and showgirls, even as a youth a young woman's beauty had never intimidated him. But something about the Duchess was stopping him from resorting to the usual playful patter he used when in the company of a desirable woman.

As Joshua continued to babble on through several courses, with the occasional input from the adults, he was able to observe Adelaide. He had been wrong about her on so many counts and not just her attitude to his inheritance of the dukedom. He'd been wrong when he'd dismissed her as just another beauty. There was something about her that elevated her above every other woman he had ever met. It wasn't just her physical charms, alluring as they certainly were. Was it her calmness, her dignity, her grace?

She turned from smiling at her son and they caught each other's eye. Their gazes locked. He should look away, but he couldn't do so. As if held prisoner, he continued to stare into those brown eyes.

By God, she was beautiful and he wanted her. Badly. Would it be so wrong to give in to his desires? Having her in his bed, writhing beneath him as he took pleasure in that exquisite body would surely be worth any unwanted consequences. Would that be something she, too, might want? Whether it was or not that was something he would never discover. To do so would be to open up a world of complications, something he did not want and she did not deserve.

'Isaac, are you listening to me?' A small voice broke through the swirling mist of desire that had wreathed itself around him.

Both adults turned to face Joshua and he wondered if she was as grateful to the young boy as he was for breaking the spell that had suddenly frozen them.

'Sorry, Joshua, what were you saying?' he asked.

'I said, tomorrow I think we should swap armies.'

'Why's that?'

The little boy commenced a long explanation about fairness, which Isaac attempted to concentrate on, while fighting the temptation to look back in Adelaide's direction.

'I think that's very noble of you, Joshua,' she said, when the boy's explanation finally came to an end.

Out of politeness he turned to smile at her and forced himself not to focus on her full lips or imagine what it would be like to kiss them. Then he did his best to stop his gaze from stroking her body and wondering what her skin would feel like under his touch. Using more control than he thought he possessed, he did not let his eyes move to that hint of cleavage, temptingly exposed at the neck of her gown. To do so would cause him to wonder what it would be like to free her from her constricting clothing and take those full breasts in his hands and kiss the waiting tips.

Coughing to clear his throat, he looked around the room. He focused on the stern portraits of the ancestors lining the room, looking at him with apparent disapproval, which in this instance was probably well-deserved.

He'd thought dining with Winifred had been agony, but it was nothing compared to the anguish of sitting across the table from a bewitching woman who was and had to remain untouchable. She was not his type, he reminded himself sternly. She was an aristocrat, that class of people who had always excluded him, had always looked down on him.

Feeling somewhat more in control, he went back to eating his meal, even though he could hardly taste the food in front of him.

After what was an agonisingly long dinner, the dishes for the final dessert course were taken away and Adelaide interrupted her son, who had just launched into another involved story about which of his soft toys was his favourite and why.

'It's time you got ready for bed,' she said, which was received with a look of affront.

'You need to get a good night's sleep so you can show Isaac the tadpole stream tomorrow,' she added persuasively before her son had a chance to argue.

This distracted the young boy as it was intended to do. He turned to Isaac, his face glowing with excitement.

Isaac could see he was about to start chatting about catching tadpoles, so he gave a loud yawn and stretched, something else that would have appalled Winifred. 'Yes, I think I should get some sleep as well, so I'm nice and rested for tomorrow's hunting adventure.'

Adelaide sent him a small smile of thanks, and warmth flooded through him.

'Come along, then,' she said, standing up and holding out her hand to Joshua. 'There's brandy and port in the decanters on the sideboard, please help yourself,' she added, looking in Isaac's direction.

'Will you be joining me?' he asked, not sure whether that would be a good idea or not.

She hesitated, a slight blush tinging her cheeks. 'No,

once I've put Joshua to bed I think I'll retire myself. So I'll say goodnight.'

'Goodnight, Isaac,' Joshua called out as his mother led him out of the room.

He took his seat and looked over at the grandfather clock ticking away in the corner. It was only eight o'clock. Back in London the theatres would be filling up with excited patrons. The actors would be nervously pacing in their dressing rooms or going through their various rituals to prepare for the performance. His night would have only just begun and he would not be in bed until the early hours of the following day, if not later.

So how was he supposed to entertain himself, all alone in this enormous house?

He looked at the crystal decanters and was tempted to have a drink or two or three. That was certainly what his father would have done. He'd seen the old Duke empty those decanters on many an evening. But regular drinking to excess was one of the few vices of his father's that Isaac had not inherited and he wasn't about to adopt that destructive behaviour now. He certainly did not want to risk following his father's bad example and marrying while under the influence and having no recollection of it the next day, as he'd presumably done with Isaac's mother.

What he needed was another method of getting

thoughts of the desirable Duchess out of his mind and to pass the remaining hours safely.

He wandered down the hallway and passed the library.

An early night with a good book. That should do the trick. He entered the room and scanned the shelves full of leather-bound tomes, looking for one that would keep his interest through the long hours, or, alternatively, be so boring it would put him to sleep.

He pulled out a random selection and, with a pile under his arm, walked up to his bedchamber and settled into a chair by the large windows. An early night with a good book, he thought with self-deprecating amusement. He really was becoming the epitome of respectability.

His attention turned from the words in front of him, to the door that separated his room from Adelaide's. Had she retired already? Was she at this moment taking off that burgundy gown, unlacing her corset, rolling her silk stockings down her legs?

He coughed and turned back to the book. Dinner had been difficult enough. He did not need to increase his suffering with thoughts of her, just behind that door, perhaps disrobing at this very minute.

He looked back at the door and wondered whether it was locked. Of course it would be. And even if it wasn't, that did not mean it would be an invitation for him to enter. He returned to his book and tried to focus. His eyes were soon drawn to that door again and, as if under the power of an irresistible force, he stood up, crossed the room and turned the handle. It was locked. He released a sigh that was a curious mix of relief and disappointment.

She didn't want him in her room. Of course she didn't.

Now that his curiosity had been satisfied, he returned to his chair and opened his book. He could forget all about her. He could stop speculating as to how that lovely body looked when freed from the restraints of whalebone and laces.

He bent the spine of the book and stared hard at the words to drive those thoughts out of his mind.

This really was ridiculous and proof that he needed to get out of Hartfield Hall. He'd spend one more day here, then return to his own world, away from the temptation of the delectable Duchess.

And, more importantly, away from the danger of doing something he knew he would live to regret.

Adelaide never went to bed this early, but she would not return to the dining room. She could not stay in the same room with Isaac a second longer. Dinner had been an ordeal and she had been so grateful for Joshua's presence and the ability of a five-year-old to chatter away, oblivious to whether he had the full attention of the adults or not.

She settled her son into his bed, picked up his favourite book and reread it for what must be the twentieth time. He snuggled in beside her, thumb in mouth, and followed the story until his eyelids started to flicker and he quickly fell asleep.

It had been such an exciting day for him. Isaac was surprisingly good with children. Who would think that a rake, a man who spent his days surrounded by scantily clad showgirls, would happily join a young boy in a mock battle with toy soldiers or offer to take him tadpoling?

She kissed her son on the top of the head, tucked the cover closely around him and entered her bedchamber.

Flicking open the small fob watch she kept by the bed, she could see it was not long after eight o'clock. With a sigh, she picked up her book and settled herself into the armchair beside the window. After reading a few sentences and not understanding a word, she placed the book back on the small table and stared out of the dark window.

It had been such a strange day. If anyone had seen them at dinner tonight they would assume they were watching an innocent domestic scene, with a happy child and two loving parents.

But if they'd known what was going on beneath the surface they would not think the scene so innocent. The intensity of those occasional looks she had exchanged with Isaac felt almost sinful and the ferocity of her physical reaction some would describe as downright immoral.

Each time his gaze had stroked over her, it had felt as if he was undressing her with his eyes. She should have been outraged. That was how the respectable, virtuous woman she presented to the world should have reacted. But Isaac made her feel things that were neither respectable nor virtuous.

Instead, every inch of her skin had seemingly come alive, yearning to feel the touch of his caressing hands. When his gaze had lingered on her breasts, she had even leant forward, her heart pounding hard, her breath caught in her throat, as if she was offering herself to him.

She pulled at her dress. Hadn't that been the reason why she had picked this gown to wear this evening? It had been pushed to the back of her wardrobe and not worn since her debut Season. Her mother had insisted she wear daring colours and styles back then, knowing it would draw the attention of every eligible man. Since her marriage she had chosen to wear plain clothing in dull colours, yet, tonight, despite her protestations that she had no interest in Isaac, she had picked that gown, as if inviting his admiration.

And it was an invitation she still ached for him to accept, even though she knew it would be so wrong if he did.

She looked towards the door that joined her room

to his. What was wrong with her? This was not like her. Why was she behaving like this and with him, of all men? She knew exactly what sort of man he was. A rake. A man who had pleasured countless women. A man who, even now, probably had a woman waiting for him back in London.

She once again picked up her book and tried to concentrate, then looked back out of the window. But he was also a man who wanted her. That much was obvious. The desire in his eyes when he looked at her tonight was undeniable and only a blind man would have missed the effect he was having on her. And Isaac Radcliff was definitely not blind.

He must know it would not take much for her to succumb completely, to put all morality to one side and give herself to him.

The tempo of her heart increased at the thought of him opening the adjoining door, coming into her room and leading her over to her four-poster bed.

She stood and walked over to the door. All she had to do was turn the key, open it and invite him in.

Her hand shot to her mouth, as if she had said those words out loud. Could she do such a thing? Could she be so obvious?

She looked back down at the brass key sticking out of the lock, her heart beating ever more fiercely in her chest. She placed her fingers tentatively on the key, then quickly pulled back as if the metal had seared her skin.

No, of course she would not invite him into her room. To even think such a thing was insane.

Turning around quickly before she could do something she knew she would come to regret, she walked back to her chair and sat down.

For the first time in her life she had exactly what she wanted. She was a mother and an independent woman of means. Why would she upset that by becoming entangled with a rake? He lived in a world she would never inhabit, an easy-going one where people openly took lovers and moved from one to the other without a backward glance.

But would it really be so bad to give in to temptation? She'd finally discover what it was like to make love to a man she was intensely attracted to. Her life would remain the same, but she would have the chance to experience something she wanted so badly.

She frowned. What on earth was the matter with her? That was not who she was. That was not the world in which she lived and the sooner Isaac Radcliff returned to London so she could put all these foolish thoughts behind her, the better.

With that, she forced herself to open the book again, nearly breaking the spine, and did her utmost to concentrate on the words that had an unfortunate habit of swirling around on the page.

Chapter Seven

After a restless night's sleep, Isaac woke the next morning with a determined resolve. He would keep his promise to Joshua, then he would leave. There was no real reason for him to stay here any longer and there was no point subjecting himself to the agony of being in the company of a woman he both wanted and did not want, and one he knew he most certainly could not have.

As they assembled for breakfast he went over and over in his mind the simple list of things he would do this day. He would go tadpoling, say goodbye to Joshua and Adelaide, then take the train back to London late this afternoon and that would be that. End of agony. End of frustration. Perfect.

First on the list, he should tell Joshua and Adelaide about his plans and breakfast provided the perfect opportunity to do so. He served himself a plate of smoked salmon and scrambled eggs from the porcelain terrines lined up on the sideboard, all the while mulling over his determination to leave. After consuming the meal, and drinking several cups of strong black coffee, he still had not uttered those simple words.

'I've got my tadpole net all ready,' Joshua announced as they rose from the breakfast table. 'And I can show you around my estate as well if you'd like.'

'That would be delightful,' Isaac responded. 'And I hope your mother will accompany us.'

Isaac and Joshua turned to Adelaide and waited for her answer.

'Yes, all right. I do need to inspect some of the tenants' cottages. The estate manager has mentioned that several of them are in need of repair.'

'Goody,' Joshua said. It wasn't how Isaac would have expressed it, but it was certainly how he was feeling.

After they had changed into suitable clothing, they assembled in the hall, Joshua bearing his tadpole net and a bucket in anticipation of his catches and Adelaide dressed in a grey skirt and lacy white blouse. Unlike last night, her clothing was once again modest and unadorned and eminently suitable for a walk in the countryside, but she still looked enchanting.

Joshua raced ahead, waving his tadpole net, and Isaac offered Adelaide his arm.

'I assume you do not need Joshua to act as your guide and are familiar with the estate,' she said as they walked down the gravel path passed the formal gardens. 'I believe you came here often as a child?'

'No, only occasionally. My father would sometimes invite me during the school holidays, but he had the decency to do so only when Winifred was away. Although she did on a few memorable occasions return unexpectedly.'

'Did you enjoy your time here?'

He looked around at the precision of the formal gardens, with their lined up and carefully pruned roses and box hedges, out towards the groves of oak, beech and yew trees growing without restraint, and down towards the river, where Joshua's tadpoles roamed free, and he pondered that question.

'When I first came here I was probably about Joshua's age. I thought it was paradise after living all my life in smoky London and I loved running wild in all this space and greenery. When I got older and had a better understanding of my parents' relationship, it rather put a damper on my enjoyment.' He laughed so she would know he was now amused by what had been a rather painful realisation at the time.

She neither laughed nor smiled back at him. 'And what of Lady Henrietta and Lady Hampton—how did they react to your visits?'

'Let's just say it was not a cordial time and the bonds between siblings my father was misguidedly hoping to achieve never eventuated.'

'I imagine it was difficult for them.'

He turned and looked at her. Was she serious? Was she feeling sympathy for the tormentors and not the tormented? Was it because they were from the same class as she and were therefore the ones more deserving of understanding?

'They seemed to enjoy themselves immensely when I came to visit,' he said, remembering those cruel smiles and constant sneers.

'It was obvious from the moment I met you that you were the favoured child,' she said. 'And that your father loved you far more than his daughters. If I could grasp that within a few minutes of seeing the two of you together, they would have been painfully aware of it, even if as children they couldn't articulate it to themselves.'

Isaac shrugged off this claim. 'If he was showing a certain camaraderie with me at your wedding, then I believe it was more to do with, shall I say, our being more like-minded in the way we chose to live our lives and that gave him more in common with me than he had with Henrietta or Priscilla.'

'Perhaps,' she said, the note of scepticism in her voice suggesting she did not agree with him. 'But when he talked of you there was always pride in his voice. He chose to be with your mother and support both you and her. Men such as him are under no obligation to do so, yet he did. Whereas I believe his marriage to Winifred was merely one arranged by the two sets of parents and I suspect there was no love between them.'

Isaac stared at her, unsure what to make of her words.

'Winifred was expected to provide him with an heir and she failed to do that,' she continued. 'It must have been hard on her to know that the woman she thought was her husband's beloved mistress was the one to provide him with the much-wanted son.'

He looked straight ahead, considering all she had said. Images of the constant taunts, the sneering, the mocking comments about how his birth made him inferior to his half-sisters in every way entered his mind. That could not all be explained away by the pain that Henrietta, Priscilla and Winifred had suffered. Could it?

'I think perhaps you are being a bit kind to the shrewish sisters and their wicked mother.'

'I'm not saying it justifies treating anyone badly, especially a small child, but it might explain it, that is all.'

They walked on in silence for a moment or two.

'Were they very cruel?' she finally asked, her voice quiet.

'They tried their best, but unfortunately for them I'd had lots of practice dealing with members of the aristocracy who enjoyed the sport of harassing the bastard child of an actress,' he said, keeping his voice light. 'Father sent me to an exclusive school, although most of the other pupils did not think it exclusive enough if it could accept someone like me, and nothing Henny and Prissy did to me equalled their cruelty.

'That's terrible and not something you need to turn into a joke.'

Was that what he did, made light of those times so they would not cause him pain?

'I could not bear the thought of Joshua enduring such torment.'

They looked towards her son who was now swatting at a dandelion with his net. Isaac had been not much older than Joshua when he was sent off to that boarding school. It was now hard to believe he had been so young.

'No child should suffer in that manner,' she said, almost in a whisper.

'No, but it did make me the man I am today. Although that's hardly a recommendation for the British public school system.'

She looked over at him, her eyes full of concern and warmth.

He had built up an immunity to the taunting of his half-sisters and that of his fellow school pupils, but he had no resistance to the sympathy in her gaze. So he looked straight ahead, refusing to succumb to the strange emotions welling up inside him.

'And what of you?' he asked, changing the subject. 'While I was off supposedly learning how to be a gentleman, what sort of education did you have?'

'I was taught embroidery, how to play the piano, how to make polite conversation and little else. In other words, I, too, had an education to make me the woman you see before you today. One who made an ideal wife for a titled man.'

He turned to face her, seeing a woman who was so much more than that. 'And yet you are managing this estate. Somehow along the way you've picked up the skills to do that.'

'That was a case of necessity. Someone had to do it. The Duke was absent so much of the time and the estate was being neglected. The estate manager was obviously stealing funds and avoiding his duties, so I dismissed him and hired the one we now have. He was the one to teach me financial management, farming practices, land laws and all I needed to know so we could work together in managing the estate.'

'I hope my father appreciated all that you did.'

'Of course,' she said, a note of pique entering her voice. 'That is, he appreciated that I provided the son and heir and did it so quickly he could return to the women he really loved. In other words, I did my duty, what I had been trained for. If he appreciated what I did on the estate he never said, although I'm sure the extra income was appreciated when he was indulging himself and his countless friends and their mistresses in all the best that life can offer.'

Before Isaac could think of any response to this revelation, she broke from his arm and rushed off towards her son. 'Joshua, we need to visit the cottages before we go to the river.'

Joshua turned towards her and frowned.

'I have to talk to Mrs Cooper.'

At the mention of that woman's name Joshua smiled and Isaac knew how he felt. He'd also enjoyed visiting Mrs Cooper when he was a boy. She always had some fresh baking hot out of the oven and a hug for him when he visited.

They neared the cottages, where a group of women were sitting out in the sunshine, chatting and spinning wool. They all stood up as they approached and made low curtsies.

'Is that Master Isaac?' It was Mrs Cooper who had asked. She had aged somewhat, but still had that warm smile he would never forget.

'It is. It's lovely to see you again, Mrs Cooper,' he said, giving her a warm embrace.

'I think you can call me Agnus, now that you're all grown up.'

'And how are your sons, Agnus?' he asked, wondering about the boys who were more than happy to include him in their games when he was a child.

'Out working in the fields. Bert's married now, with

another little one on the way. Will is to wed in a few months.' She leaned closer and lowered her voice. 'Also with a little one on the way. And my Freddie is a bit like you, one for the ladies and unlikely to settle down any time soon.' He smiled.

She quickly looked over at the Duchess. 'Begging your pardon, Your Grace.'

'The estate manager says there are cottages in need of repair,' the Duchess said, her voice all business.

'Yes, if you'll come this way,' Agnus said, once again on her best behaviour. 'There's scones and jam in the kitchen,' she added to Joshua who did not need to be told twice and quickly disappeared inside the cottage.

'Is there enough for me?' Isaac asked, remembering those fluffy scones from his childhood, the jam made from the raspberries grown in Agnus's garden and the cream from her dairy cow.

'Of course. You boys help yourself while us women do all the work.'

He, too, did not need to be told twice and dashed into the cottage to join Joshua.

'Such a lovely boy,' Mrs Cooper said as she led Adelaide to the cottages that needed repairing. She smiled back at the older woman, always delighted when someone complimented Joshua.

'A bit wild, mind, but that was to be expected given

the way he was treated,' Mrs Cooper added and Adelaide realised it was not her son who was being discussed. 'But a heart of gold, he had.'

Her own heart missed a beat. 'So, what needs to be fixed?' Adelaide asked briskly as they entered a cottage.

Mrs Cooper escorted her through the small but tidy building, pointing out the damage to the thatched roof from the recent storms, the repairs necessary to the windows to keep the draughts out and the bricks that needed repointing.

Once she'd made a list of the repairs, they joined Joshua and Isaac, who, having consumed their fill of scones and jam, were seated with the women outside the cottage, Joshua's mouth still bearing the red and white signs of his recent indulgence.

'Right, tadpoles,' her son said, standing up and waving his net again.

'Say thank you to Mrs Cooper for the scones first.'

'Thank you, Mrs Cooper,' Isaac and Joshua chorused together, causing the older woman to smile indulgently.

'Be off with the two of you,' she said, waving them away.

Joshua ran ahead and once again Isaac took Adelaide's arm.

'Is the problem with the cottages sorted?' he asked.

'Yes, I just need to get the thatcher out to fix the

roof and a builder to do some repairs. So you used to visit Mrs Cooper when you were a boy?' she asked, knowing the answer, but wanting to hear something from his childhood that was happier than the time he'd spent with his half-sisters.

'Yes, she and her sons made my visits a joy, along with the other tenants and the servants. They never looked down on me and never gave it a second thought whether my parents were married or not.'

'As it should be. A child should never be blamed for the sins of the parents.'

He sent her a sideways glance. 'So you think my parents were sinners, do you?'

She was unsure whether he was teasing her or not. 'It's just an expression and I certainly do not blame your mother. I suspect she had little choice regarding the life she lived. Women seldom do.'

'Including you.'

She turned to face him to see if he was making sport of her, but she could see no sign of that in either his expression or his words.

'Few debutantes have a choice in who they marry. I was no different. From the moment you have your coming out, you have to present yourself in the best possible light, or at least, in the best light in the eyes of the available men, and see who responds. Then your parents weigh up the offers of marriage and make a decision on who will best advance the family's position, or, in my family's case, who will best dig them out of the deep financial hole in which they had found themselves.'

'Your family must have been over the moon when the wealthy Duke of Hartfield offered for your hand.'

'Yes, my mother was.' She sighed heavily, remembering the day when she was told her fate. 'My mother was a recent widow and my father had never been good with money. When he died, my brother discovered the estate was so heavily in debt he could see no way out of our troubles. But Mother did. She scraped together enough money for one Season, but I had to marry a man who did not want a marriage settlement. He also ideally had to be one who was happy to support his wife's family. The Duke of Hartfield's offer was far too good for my family to refuse.'

'I'm sorry, that's terrible, it's as bad as—'

'It's the life of a woman from my class,' she interrupted, not wanting his sympathy and certainly not wanting to hear any comparisons he might make. 'And believe me, it could have been much worse.'

'I'm sorry—'

'Joshua is trying to get your attention,' she said, once again cutting short his apology. 'While you are off tadpoling, I believe I'll return to the house.'

She released his arm, turned and walked in the other direction.

Why had she revealed so much of herself to him? Was she trying to make him understand why she was the woman she was? Why she was not like those actresses she'd seen at the Elysian Theatre, those fun-loving theatre people he liked and admired so much? Or was it simply because she wanted him to know why she had married his father?

She had seen the way he looked at her on the day of the wedding, as if she was a social climber who had caught the best man available that Season. That was not who she was, but why should she care how he saw her? He would be leaving soon and they were unlikely to spend any more time together.

She stopped and drew in a deep breath. But she did care what he thought of her, didn't she? She liked it when he smiled at her, had warmed at seeing the admiration in his eyes when she'd told him about managing the estate and especially liked it when she saw that spark of attraction, even desire, in his eyes.

She resumed walking, turned the corner and headed back up the path that led to the house, then came to another abrupt halt. Several carriages were parked at the top of the drive. She glimpsed the occupants of the carriages and released a long, exasperated sigh.

She had more visitors and suspected these new arrivals were not going to be pleasant house guests.

No tadpoles were caught, despite their energetic attempts, but neither Isaac nor Joshua were disappointed. They'd had fun. That was all that mattered.

While Joshua discussed the ones that got away and what they should do next time they embarked on a wild game hunt, a small shadow of disappointment crept over Isaac's happiness. There was now no reason for him to delay his departure from Hartfield Hall. He had responsibilities back in London and the reason for his visit had been adequately dealt with. That was what he'd wanted, wasn't it? He did not belong here. And yet?

They turned the corner and headed for the house and were greeted by the sight of servants unloading carriages.

'Henny and Prissy,' he hissed under his breath, recognising the crest of Priscilla's husband on the side of one carriage.

Henrietta emerged from the house, her hands firmly planted on her hips. 'Don't think you can get away with this,' she called out as soon as he was within earshot. Even from this distance he could see the rage on her face.

'Take the tadpole net down to the servants, there's a good boy,' he said to Joshua, not wanting to subject the young child to the inevitable argument. 'I'm sure they'll be waiting with bated breath to hear all about the ones that got away.'

Waving hello to Henrietta, Joshua rushed up the stairs and down the hallway, throwing his tadpole net over his shoulder in a somewhat haphazard manner that put the vases, statues and other ornaments under more threat than the tadpoles had ever been.

'Whatever it is you are up to, it won't work.' Henrietta said, her voice still raised even though he was close enough for such shouting to be unnecessary. 'I suppose you think moving in here will give you a better chance of keeping this estate. Well, it won't. This is our family home and I will not let you occupy it.'

'How did you know I was here?' Isaac asked. 'Did one of your pet bats let you know? Or did you send out one of your familiars to report back? Maybe you've been flying your broomstick over the estate again?'

Isaac waited for the expected reaction and was not disappointed. Her lips pursed as if pulled together by a drawstring and furious colour exploded on her cheeks.

'I knew you'd be up to something, so I sent a servant round to that house of harlots you call a theatre. He reported back that you were now in residence here, in my family home.'

'I take it both you and Prissy are planning on moving in as well? Won't that be jolly. We can all live together as one happy family.' There was no point in telling her he had intended to leave later this afternoon. Where would be the fun in letting her think she had already won this latest battle before it had even begun?

'Yes, we intend to stay for the time being. Although, unlike some people, my sister and I have responsibilities. We have husbands and estates to run.'

Isaac laughed at her unintended slip, thinking of those poor husbands the sisters had to run.

'But this is our home and we will not stand for you living in it,' she added. 'I want you gone. Now.'

'Until it's settled in the courts, I believe you'll find it is *my* home.' He walked away, heading back up to his room to change. Henrietta had given him no choice. He would not be leaving Hartfield Hall today and for that he sent a silent thank you to his sharp-tongued sister for giving him an excuse to remain a little bit longer.

Chapter Eight

The sooner this ridiculous feud between the siblings was over and Adelaide could get on with her life, the happier she would be. But under the bluster and brow-beating, it was obvious Henrietta and Priscilla were still reeling from the shocking revelation at the reading of the will. So for now she would endure their presence and, though hard as the sisters sometimes made it, show them a bit of compassion.

While the sisters bustled around the house as if they owned it, Adelaide headed downstairs to the servants' area. With an extra three people in residence, two of whom she knew to have extremely high standards, Adelaide would have to speak to Cook.

She entered the busy kitchen and found everyone hard at work, as usual.

'Four adults for dinner tonight, I assume, Your Grace,' Cook said, pausing in supervising the kitchen maid who was adding vegetables to the stock-pot.

'Yes. Lady Henrietta, Lady Hampton and the Duke

of Hartfield will be staying for…' She paused and turned her hands up to indicate that the cook's guess was as good as hers.

Cook frowned, then nodded. 'That will be no problem, Your Grace. I know exactly what the three children like to eat, although Isaac, I mean the Duke, has always been easy to please. I'd best serve Lady Hampton and Lady Henrietta their favourites, as they're a lot more particular.' Her nostrils flared slightly in silent criticism.

Cook grabbed a pencil and quickly scribbled down a menu, then handed it to Adelaide. It was certainly grander than what was usually served when only Joshua and herself were there.

'Please don't go to any additional trouble,' she said to Cook as she handed back the menu.

'Begging your pardon, Your Grace, but I believe it will be less trouble to ensure their ladyships are served what they like. If they don't get their own way, they are inclined to voice their objections.' Cook tapped her pencil against the table. 'I best order in some extra fois gras, truffles, lobster and caviar and Mr Baxter will need to look at how much champagne and burgundy there is left in the cellar.'

'Well, I'm sure you know best,' Adelaide said, knowing Cook was right. There was no point adding any extra fuel to the fire and stoking the sisters' rage.

'Shame not everyone is as easy as Isaac and young Joshua.'

'Do you remember the new Duke from when he was a child?' she asked, trying not to sound too interested. Was he a cheeky child as she suspected? Did he always have a devil-may-care attitude? Was he always so good-looking, so charming? They were questions she would also like answered, but was hardly likely to ask anyone, particularly a servant.

The cook raised her eyebrows slightly and Adelaide feared she had failed in her attempt at nonchalance.

'Yes, all the older servants remember him. He often took his meals down here when he visited the Hall. He was such a delight and kept us entertained with tales of what was happening upstairs.' She smiled in affectionate remembrance. 'He was a born mimic, that one, and often had us all reeling with laughter.' She immediately looked more serious and her naturally florid cheeks turned a darker shade of red. 'Begging your pardon again, Your Grace.'

Adelaide sent her a polite smile. It was no news to her that the servants discussed and sometimes mocked their employers. Her only regret was the cook's discomfort would mean she was unlikely to get any further information on what the young Isaac Radcliff was like.

'Well then, I'll leave you to your work.' She looked around the large basement kitchen, bustling with busy servants chopping vegetables, kneading dough and washing dishes.

Joshua also liked to spend time down here in a room always warm from the cooking stove and full of the delicious aroma of food, and he especially loved being indulged by Cook and the kitchen staff and scullery maids.

She could imagine it had also provided a wonderful retreat for Isaac, particularly if he was unwanted upstairs.

'Will there be anything else, Your Grace?' Cook asked, pulling her out of her reverie.

'No, no, that's all,' she said, reluctant to leave the cosy kitchen and return to the inevitable turmoil upstairs.

She looked around the room one more time. A few servants briefly looked up from their work and she suspected they had kept one ear open to her conversation with Cook and this exchange would be dissected for every scrap of meaning the moment she left. They would certainly all be speculating on her interest in Isaac Radcliff.

'Right, well, I'll leave it all in your capable hands, Cook,' she said and left the kitchen and climbed the narrow stairs back up to the main part of the house.

Hearing Lady Henrietta's raised voice as she approached the drawing room, she chose to leave them to their arguments and instead headed to Joshua's room.

Joshua was the youngest member of the household, but his behaviour was mature in contrast to the childish antics of the old Duke's other offspring.

She found her son in the nursery, where he was describing to Nanny his adventures down at the river. With her entry it seemed he had to re-tell the story from the beginning, starting with their quest to find where the tadpoles were hiding.

She settled down to listen to her son and that was where she spent the remainder of the day. When it came time for dinner, she knew she could avoid the rest of the family no longer.

After changing into a dinner gown, she collected Joshua and headed down to the dining room to find the siblings arguing over the seating arrangements.

'You have no right to sit there,' Lady Henrietta stated, glaring at her exasperated brother who was standing behind the seat at the head of the long mahogany table.

'Perhaps for tonight we can leave that place vacant,' Adelaide said tactfully, hoping that would appease the warring factions.

'An excellent idea,' Isaac said, moving to another seat. 'Or perhaps Joshua might like to sit there,' he added, cutting off whatever it was Henrietta was about to say.

She closed her mouth, narrowed her eyes as if trying to ascertain what trick this was, then nodded. 'Yes. Good, that's as it should be.'

'Are Henrietta and Priscilla going to live with us now as well, just like Isaac?' Joshua asked as he walked around the table and took his seat at the head.

'No,' Adelaide said rather definitely, causing three sets of eyebrows to raise. 'They're just here for a visit.' And hopefully a very short visit, she wanted to add.

'Well, you can all stay in my house for as long as you like,' Joshua said generously.

'Thank you, Joshua,' Lady Henrietta said with a tight smile. 'And it is *your* house, never forget that.' She turned towards Adelaide, still wearing that pinched expression. 'I'm so pleased you've decided to join the lawsuit. We need to present a united front and you have even more to gain from winning than we do.'

Adelaide signalled for the footmen to serve the lobster bisque and braced herself for a conversation she knew Lady Henrietta was not going to like. 'I'm afraid it was not me who consulted a lawyer. It was my mother. She went behind my back and presumed too much. I won't be contesting the outcome of the will or anything else that was mentioned at the lawyer's office.'

Henrietta's lips grew even thinner. 'I can see what you're up to.'

Adelaide frowned, unaware that she was up to anything.

'I noticed the moment I arrived that you were no longer wearing widow weeds, even though Father is not long in his grave, and that you've removed your wedding ring.'

Adelaide could inform them that while she still wore black in public out of respect for the family, it would be hypocritical to remain in a state of mourning at home for a man she had been forced to marry and whom during her six years of marriage she barely saw, but suspected that would only further anger an already fuming Henrietta.

'You set your cap at Father so you could drag yourself out of poverty and become a duchess,' Henrietta continued. 'And I saw the way you looked at Isaac when you entered the dining room. It's obvious you're now out to capture the man you think is the new Duke.'

Isaac jumped to his feet. 'Now see here, Henny, you can keep your—'

'Baxter, please take Joshua upstairs,' Adelaide said before this argument got out of hand and her son heard things that were not suitable for his young ears. 'He can have his meal with Nanny.'

Isaac looked towards her son and had the decency to appear embarrassed, which was more than she could say for his two half-sisters.

'Yes, that's a good idea,' Isaac said to Joshua. 'You don't want to be bored by the silly things adults always talk about at dinner. And you'll need to get a good night's sleep so you've got your wits about you tomorrow when we go after those sneaky tadpoles.'

Joshua's face had been poised for an argument, but the thought of another day down at the river turned his frown into a smile. 'Yes. Let's see if we can catch some frogs as well.'

He looked towards Lady Henrietta and wriggled his eyebrows up and down, causing Isaac to laugh.

If it was his plan to repeat Isaac's bad behaviour and place a frog in Henrietta's bed, Adelaide would be making sure that never happened. There was enough childish behaviour in this house already and, up until now, Joshua was the only one still behaving himself.

Joshua said goodnight to everyone and Baxter led him out of the room.

'Now see here,' Isaac repeated as soon as the door closed.

'You do not need to defend me,' Adelaide interjected once again. 'I have no intention of justifying my marriage to your father, but I will say that I have no intention of marrying again.'

Henrietta huffed out her disbelief.

'I don't believe you,' Lady Hampton said, speaking for the first time. 'You're young and, well, men obviously approve of your appearance.' She looked towards her half-brother, frowned, then back at Adelaide. 'How else would a penniless earl's daughter bedazzle my father? You're bound to want to marry again and to marry well, to a man who'd make it worth your while giving up the very generous annuity Father left you.'

Adelaide couldn't help but give a humourless laugh. 'Believe me it was not difficult for a young woman to bedazzle your father. A lot of women can make that claim.'

Lady Henrietta puffed herself up with moral outrage and glared at Adelaide. 'I'll have you know my father was—'

'A womaniser,' Isaac said.

'A philanderer,' Adelaide said at the same time. 'If he wasn't, we wouldn't have found ourselves in this present situation.'

'Well, yes, he was a weak man, I'll admit that, and a certain type of woman did turn his head,' Henrietta said, sending a scornful look at both Adelaide and Isaac. 'But he knew right from wrong. He might have had his dalliances, but he would only ever *marry* a respectable woman. He would never have married an actress.'

'And yet the legal documents say otherwise,' Isaac pointed out.

'That's nonsense,' Henrietta snapped. 'As if a man like my father would ever stoop so low. He was a peer of the realm. He dined with royalty.'

Isaac rolled his eyes at his half-sister's deliberate naivety. 'And royalty never consort with actresses, do they? No, I'm wrong,' he said, looking up as if in thought. 'Wasn't Lillie Langtry one of Prince Albert's mistresses?'

'But he didn't marry her, did he?' Henrietta shot back, her voice rising. 'No one from the aristocracy ever marries an actress.'

Isaac and Adelaide exchanged incredulous looks.

'Now, let me see,' Isaac said slowly. 'Aristocrats who married actresses? There was the Duke of Belmont, the Earl of Thornfield, Lord Brightwell—'

'But our family is better than those,' Henrietta all but shrieked. 'Father should never have even acknowledged your existence. He should have just paid off your mother and kept you as a guilty secret. That's what any other man in his position would do. Then none of this would ever have happened.'

She looked to Priscilla for support, who vigorously nodded her agreement.

'Yes, it was a shame our father wasn't a hypocrite like virtually every other member of the aristocracy. Your class has such an enviable ability to ignore what they don't want to see, to pretend that everyone is ever so respectable even if they're living depraved lives that would shock any self-respecting harlot.'

Adelaide could point out that as a duke, they were *his* class, too, now, but instead signalled to the footmen to remove the untouched and now cold bowls of soup and serve the next course.

'Sending you off to that school was a big mistake,'

Lady Henrietta muttered, as she inspected the duck à l'orange. She stopped frowning at her food and glared at Isaac. 'It gave you notions above your station. The way you used to swagger around this house when you were a child, it was disgusting. Even then you acted as if you were better than the rest of us. And Father expected us to treat you like a brother. As if we would be willing to associate with a…with a…'

'A bastard is the word I believe you are grasping for,' Isaac said, not in the slightest bit perturbed by the insult. 'But don't worry. I intend to treat you with the same level of respect I always have, despite discovering the unfortunate circumstances of your birth.'

'Don't you dare,' Henrietta said, standing up and throwing her napkin onto the table. 'My sister and I were born ladies. We are now respectably married women with husbands who are the very model of propriety. That is the way the world is supposed to be and your disgraceful attempt to grab our father's title will not change it.'

She turned to leave. 'Come, Priscilla.'

Priscilla stopped eating her duck, frowned, then also stood up and tentatively threw her napkin onto the table. She then followed her sister out of the room.

'Baxter, will you please arrange for meals to be sent up to Lady Hampton's and Lady Henrietta's rooms,' Adelaide said, then gave a resigned sigh.

'I'm sorry about that,' Isaac said. 'I'm used to their

bad behaviour, but you and Joshua should not be subjected to it.'

'They're upset. Their entire world has been turned upside down. It's not surprising they're behaving in such an unpleasant manner.'

'That is no excuse for accusing you of having bedazzled Father.'

She shrugged one shoulder. 'Wasn't that exactly what you thought I had done when we first met?'

'Yes, I apologise. I did judge you rather harshly at the wedding. I'm sorry.'

She nodded slightly in acknowledgement of his apology.

'But it wasn't entirely my fault,' he said with a teasing smile. 'You looked so beautiful on your wedding day I could see how you would be capable of bedazzling any man.'

A flush of heat burned Adelaide's cheeks, which she attempted to ignore. 'As I said to Henrietta, it did not take a lot to attract your father. He married me because he believed he needed a young wife to give him a son and heir. I fulfilled my duty almost immediately, freeing him to return to the women he really was attracted to, women who knew how to have a good time away from the stuffy drawing rooms of society.'

Once again she watched him squirm in his chair as she repeated the words he had said to her when she'd come to visit him at the theatre.

'Then he was more of a fool than I thought him,' he said quietly. 'But if you hadn't been forced into an unwanted marriage, if you could have chosen the life you wanted to live, what would it have been like?' he asked as the footman removed his plate and began serving the watercress and endive salad.

'That's a pointless question. I couldn't choose the way I lived and to speculate about what I could have done with my life would only make me more aware of all the options that were not available to me.'

'But you can do whatever you like now.'

'Yes, I can.'

'And so?'

She shrugged. 'I've always dreamed of seeing Paris, Rome, Venice.' A lightness lifted her spirits. Now that dream was within her grasp.

'Are the shrewish sisters correct? Will you marry again?'

She shook her head. 'I married because it was what my mother needed me to do. I am now an independent woman of means. Why would I surrender that? I've been left with an annuity that I'll lose if I marry. As you said, I can make choices. Why would I give that up by marrying again?'

He nodded. 'That makes perfect sense to me.'

'What about you?' she asked.

'Lord, no, I have no intention of marrying,' he said, cutting up his food with determination.

'I meant what would you have done with your life if things had been different, if you had known that your parents were married and you had been part of the aristocracy?'

He paused, his knife and fork suspended in mid-air. 'That's a terrible thought. I suspect I would have run off and joined the circus at a young age and probably found myself exactly where I am now, managing a series of theatrical establishments and horrifying the likes of Henny and Prissy.'

Or you'd be just like your father. You'd spend your time consorting with actresses. In other words, living exactly the life you presently do.

She released a small sigh.

'This fighting between those two harpies and me must be very difficult for you,' he said, misinterpreting her sigh.

She signalled to the footman to serve the baked Alaska and to remove her untouched plate.

'And I don't think we'll be getting rid of the scolding sisters any time soon.' He looked towards the doors through which they had departed. 'I imagine right now they've got their heads together and are plotting their next move. Or perhaps they've gone into the garden to collect some newts' eyes or frogs' toes so they can cook up a witch's brew and curse me back to the hell they believe I came from.'

Despite herself Adelaide gave a small smile at the

thought of the sisters dancing around a cauldron and reciting incantations under a full moon.

'It's where they grew up, they still see it as their family home,' she said, pulling her face into a more serious expression. 'But I do hope they don't intend to stay until the court case is settled. I believe such things can take an age and you're right, their presence is rather upsetting.'

'From the look of all those carriages laden down with trunks, I suspect that is their intention,' he said, digging his fork into his dessert.

Adelaide sighed again. 'Perhaps until this is settled Joshua and I could move into the Dowager's Cottage.'

'No, don't do that,' he said with surprising force, the dessert fork clattering into the bowl. 'Don't let the spiteful sisters drive you out of your home. You and Joshua have more right to be here than they do.' He frowned. 'Leave it up to me. I know exactly how to drive them away and no newt will have to give up its eyes, or frog surrender its toes in the process.'

'So, are you going to tell me this plan?' she asked, still contemplating what needed to be done to enable her to move to the cottage as quickly as possible.

'By morning all will be revealed,' he said grandly, putting down his fork and waving his arms in the air like a magician about to perform a conjuring trick. 'And soon those harpies will be disappearing, as if in a puff of smoke.' He clicked his fingers, smiled again and went back to eating his dessert.

She swallowed a sigh. He might have a plan, but his obvious enjoyment suggested it was something just as upsetting for the sisters as finding a frog in their bed. First thing in the morning, she would make arrangements to move into the cottage and leave the siblings to their ongoing rivalry.

Chapter Nine

As soon as dinner was over, Isaac drafted a telegram and handed it to his father's valet, who had now, under his own volition, taken over the role as Isaac's valet.

The man looked down at the words, his otherwise imperturbable eyebrows momentarily rising before he suppressed his surprise at what he was reading.

'Very good, Your Grace. I'll arrange for it to be sent immediately.'

Isaac had abandoned his attempts to stop the servants calling him Your Grace. After his exchange with Baxter it was obvious he had gone a step too far in trying to get them to treat him as an equal. He had suggested his valet call him Sir, but even that had not lasted long and the man had almost immediately slipped back to using Your Grace. Isaac hoped to change that eventually, but while his sisters were present, he would have no objection to the title, not if it riled them even further.

* * *

The next morning when he joined Adelaide and Joshua at the breakfast table Henrietta and Priscilla were nowhere in sight.

'Are the sharp-tongued sisters still sulking?' he asked Adelaide. 'I can only hope they are and that they'll continue to punish me by taking all their meals in their rooms and never speaking to me again.'

'I saw them going up to the attic,' Joshua said, as he dipped his toast soldier into his soft-boiled egg.

'The attic? Why on earth would they want to go to the attic?' Isaac asked.

Adelaide shrugged one shoulder, but Baxter gave a small cough. 'I believe the ladies went in search of old letters and documents,' he said.

'It's probably the best place for the two of them, especially if it keeps them out of my way,' Isaac said as he served himself a hearty breakfast.

Just as he had finished his meal, Henrietta burst into the room, followed by Priscilla, their matching triumphant smiles warning him that they had not come bearing good news for him. Instead, they clutched a pile of letters tied up with pink ribbons.

'We've got it,' Henrietta said, waving an open letter under his nose. 'Our lawyer said we should look for proof that your parents never married and that is what we've found.'

'You've got spiderwebs in your hair,' Isaac said, picking one long thread from her coiffeur.

She swatted his hand away. 'Just listen to this.' She looked around the room, her face gleeful. 'It's from your mother to our father, written before he *legally* married our mother.

'"*My dear, darling Henry...*"' Henrietta scowled. '"*I appreciate your tender words of love, which I return to you tenfold, and your expressions of deep remorse, which I fully appreciate. I understand, my love, that you have to do what your family expects of you. I am sorry that you are being forced to marry Miss Winifred Drummond against your will, but take heart that you will always be loved by me...*" It goes on with some rather sickeningly sentimental talk, but the important thing is she has said nothing about being his wife. She knows he is single and that he is entering into a legal marriage. As did our father.'

She smiled in satisfaction at everyone in the room.

'It's just a letter,' Adelaide said quietly. 'I doubt if it's enough to counter legal documents. The only thing that would counter it was an official document showing the marriage had been annulled.'

'Balderdash,' Henrietta all but shouted. 'Any court in the land will know that this...' she tapped the letter '...proves everything.'

'Does that mean you'll now be leaving?' Isaac asked hopefully.

'You'd like that, wouldn't you? To drive my sister and me out of our own home.'

Isaac didn't answer those rhetorical questions as everyone present, except perhaps Joshua, knew the answer was a decided yes, of course he would like to drive them out of this house, out of his life and as far away from him as it was possible to go.

'Well, that's not going to happen any time soon.' Henrietta sent him a self-satisfied smile, then her attention, along with everyone else in the room, was taken by the sound of carriage wheels on gravel.

'Who are they, Mama?' Joshua asked, staring wide eyed out of the large windows that overlooked the drive and gardens as heavily laden carriages came to a halt at the entrance and the colourful occupants disembarked.

Isaac looked at the three women and was pleased to see the expected looks of horror on his half-sisters' faces, while the Duchess remained her usually unperturbed self.

Joshua rushed to the window and pressed his nose against the glass. 'Is it a circus? Where's the elephant?'

'They're actors,' Henrietta said with such contempt one would suspect she'd prefer to see elephants trampling the formal gardens and pulling up the oak trees with their trunks.

Joshua raced out the door, followed at a more measured pace by Isaac and Adelaide.

'Am I to assume this is part of your plan?' Adelaide asked placidly as they walked down the hallway.

'It is and just you wait. The sinister sisters will be gone before nightfall.'

He stopped at the top of the outdoor stairs and smiled down at the troupe of actors being ordered around by their director, dressed for the occasion in a royal blue frock coat, blue-and-red-checked trousers, a long, teal-coloured scarf around his neck and a homburg hat perched at a jaunty angle on his head.

It was a flamboyant style of dressing anyone who worked in the theatre would be used to, but one he was sure would further outrage his half-sisters.

'Dear boy, there you are,' Peregrine said, rushing up the stairs, taking hold of Isaac's shoulders and kissing him on each cheek. 'You are correct.' He waved his arms around, taking in the house and gardens. 'This is the perfect place for rehearsals and it is so good to be out of that smoggy London air and finally clear my lungs.'

He breathed in deeply, expanding his chest.

'Adelaide, may I present Peregrine Flambert, the director of the Starlight Theatre? Peregrine, Adelaide FitzWilliam, the Duchess of Hartfield.'

He took Adelaide's hand and bowed low. 'Charmed,' he said, before adding a kiss to the back of her hand. 'May I be so bold as to say, Duchess, that a beauty such as yourself would shine on the stage, simply shine?'

Adelaide sent him a confused look, seemingly un-sure whether that was a compliment or not.

'And who is this handsome gentleman?' Peregrine continued, looking down at Joshua.

'I'm Joshua FitzWilliam. Isaac's brother.'

Peregrine said nothing as he bowed to Joshua, al-though the raised eyebrows held a multitude of ques-tions.

'Where's the elephant?' Joshua asked.

'Elephant? There's no elephant in *A Midsummer Night's Dream*, but in my production we do have a magician and a fire-eater. I'm sure I can get them to perform their tricks for you.'

Joshua looked up at his mother, his eyes enormous with expectation. 'Please, Mama, a magician.'

'Off you go then, but don't—'

Joshua didn't wait for her to finish, but raced off down the stairs towards the colourful throng.

'Get in anyone's way,' she finished saying, even though the boy was long gone.

'It looks as though my invitation to go tadpoling has been topped,' Isaac said as he watched Joshua in-troduce himself to a group of actresses, who smiled down at him as if he was the sweetest thing they had ever seen.

Crew members quickly set to work, unloading props, scenery and musical instruments which had been piled high on the top of the carriages.

'Be careful with that ass's head,' Peregrine shouted out to a workman. He turned back to Isaac. 'Where do you want us to set up?'

'The ballroom will be big enough, if that is all right with you, Adelaide?'

'Yes, I suppose so,' she said, her expression baffled.

They all looked back at the house. Faces were peering from every window. The servants bore expressions of fascination, while Henrietta's and Priscilla's outraged faces loomed from the breakfast room window.

'Or, better still, while this weather holds, perhaps you can set up in the garden,' Isaac said, unable to suppress a devious grin.

'Splendid,' Peregrine declared. 'The garden will be perfect.'

Isaac looked back at the sisters. The garden would be perfect in more ways than one. In the ballroom one might be able to forget the presence of the actors, but it would be impossible to miss them when so many of the rooms overlooked the garden.

'I hope you don't mind,' he said to Adelaide.

'A warning would have been appreciated, but, no, I suppose not.'

Isaac would have preferred a bit more enthusiasm for his plan, but she was not objecting and had made no further reference to retiring to the Dowager's Cottage. That had to be a good sign.

He looked down at Joshua, who was now staring in

fascination as a crew member unloaded swords and shields, torches and lamps, and an array of fairy wings.

'I don't think Joshua would forgive you if you moved out now,' he added slyly.

'Hmm,' came her noncommittal answer.

'What is the meaning of this?' Henrietta bustled out of the entrance, her body fluffed up like an irate pigeon about to launch into combat. 'What are these… these people doing in my father's house?'

'My house, until the court decides otherwise,' Isaac said smoothly. 'Would you like me to introduce you to the cast and crew of the Starlight Theatre, Henny? They'll be here for the next month while they rehearse their upcoming play, but I'm sure you'll hardly notice their presence.'

'Mind those bleeding lamps. You break 'em and I'll have your guts for garters, you clumsy oaf,' a stage-hand shouted out, causing Henrietta to shudder with disgust.

'No, I most certainly do not want you to introduce me to these people,' she said, her nostrils flaring as if she could smell something unpleasant.

As if on cue, an actress walked past and winked at Isaac, causing Henrietta and Priscilla to gasp and clutch the lace around their necks.

'I will not have my father's house filled with women like that,' Henrietta said, pointing to the actress who was now sauntering into the house.

'Actresses, do you mean? Women like my mother, who by right should have taken the title of Duchess?' he said, goading his half-sister. 'Don't you approve of actresses, Henny?'

'Of course I don't approve. These people are an abomination and have no right to be here.'

'Hey, ducky, who are you calling an abomination?' a heavily made-up ageing actress said as she puffed her way up to the top of the stairs. When she reached them, she looked Henrietta up and down, sniffed her disapproval, threw her feather boa around her neck and strode into the house as if she owned it.

'Well, I'm not going to stay here and watch my family home turned into some sort of brothel.'

'You're familiar with what brothels look like, are you, Henny?'

Her red face turned a shade closer to purple. Isaac watched in fascination, certain he had never before seen a human being look as if they were about to spontaneously combust and secretly hoped that she might.

'Come on, Priscilla, we're leaving. We've got what we came for; we will not degrade ourselves a moment longer by staying in this…this bawdy house.'

With that the two sisters turned and marched back into the house.

Isaac turned to Adelaide and smiled. 'I told you my plan would work, although I admit I didn't expect it to be quite this easy.'

'Hmm,' she said, and he could not tell whether that was a sound of approval or disapproval. 'I suppose I should inform the housekeeper that we have...' She looked at the people milling around beneath them. '...how many guests?'

'The theatre company consists of twenty people when you include both the cast, crew and the musicians.'

She looked back down and he knew what she was thinking. With such pandemonium whirling beneath them, it looked like much more than a mere twenty guests.

'Right, I will inform the housekeeper to prepare twenty bedrooms and that we will have that many guests for at least a month.'

'And that you will no longer be moving to the Dowager's Cottage?' he asked hopefully. 'You wouldn't want Joshua to miss out on all the fun.'

She turned back to face him. 'And I'll cancel my plans to move,' she agreed. 'For the time being.'

Isaac rubbed his hands together. Excellent. All in all, his plan was a complete success.

He accompanied her back into the house and found the actress who had winked at him, talking, or rather flirting, with Baxter. And from the expression on the footman's face and the way he was leaning on the banister in such a casual manner, he was obviously immensely enjoying being flirted with.

When he saw them, Baxter immediately stood to attention, his head high.

'Ooh, you've gone all stiff,' the pretty actress said. 'I do like that in a man.'

Baxter blinked and tightened his lips in an obvious attempt to stifle a smile. It was also apparent that until rehearsals were over, there were going to be some interesting times at Hartfield Hall, to say the least.

As soon as the crew had unloaded the props and scenery, Henrietta's and Priscilla's carriages pulled up in front of the house.

Isaac returned to the doorstep to assure himself that they really were leaving.

'This won't be the last you hear of this,' Henrietta warned as she and her sister rushed past and headed towards the waiting carriage. Isaac did not doubt that for a moment, but he was free for now and there would hopefully be no more talk from Adelaide about moving out. And while the theatre people were in rehearsals, he also had a good reason to remain at the house for another month.

That, too, was decidedly satisfying.

He watched as the sisters' carriages disappeared around the corner at the end of the drive and smiled to himself.

Still smiling, he re-entered the house and was stopped in his tracks, his smile dying.

'Isaac, darling. I have missed you so,' Genevieve cooed. The actress was leaning up against a marble pillar, her hip thrust out in a deliberately suggestive pose.

Perhaps there was one small flaw in his plan. He'd got rid of the snarling sisters, but had unintentionally invited his ex-lover into his home. And her greeting suggested she had every expectation that they were going to continue where they'd left off.

'So this is where you've been hiding yourself,' another woman said from the top of the stairs. He looked up to see Marigold walking down towards him, her hips swinging seductively from side to side.

He stifled a groan. He and Marigold had been lovers, when? Two years ago? They were friends now, or more accurately, friends who occasionally relived their amorous times together. But that was all. There had been no commitment at the time, there wasn't one now and he was most certainly not expected to inform her when he was going to be out of town.

'Yes, you are a naughty, naughty boy,' Imogen added, emerging from who knew where and pouting at him. 'I've been feeling so neglected since you left London and I expect you to make it up to me.'

This time he did groan. It had been so long since he and Imogen had been lovers that he couldn't remember exactly when it had been that they had parted. All he did know was although they were also still friends, she had never hitherto expected them to resume their relationship.

Why on earth were these women, with whom he had remained on such amicable terms, suddenly expecting to renew past relationships with him?

He looked around the entrance, from the three women smiling at him to the grand entrance hall flooded with light from the glass dome two storeys above their heads, at the black-and-white marble tiles under their feet and the precious artworks and tapestries adorning the walls.

The answer became obvious.

They knew that he was a duke. They knew he was now fabulously wealthy. The visit from Henrietta and Priscilla's servant sniffing for evidence must have let the cat out of the bag.

Genevieve entwined her arm around his waist and kissed him on the cheek, her lithe body pressed up against him. Not to be upstaged, Marigold and Imogen moved in close for their own kisses, their lips pursed provocatively.

At that moment, over their heads, he saw Adelaide emerge from the stairs that led to the servants' area. Her eyes momentarily grew enormous before a scornful expression crossed her face and she turned and walked off down the hallway.

He had to follow her. He had to explain, although explain exactly what he was unsure. He removed Genevieve's arm from around his waist and Imogen's from around his neck, but like the tentacles of an amorous octopus, more arms immediately entangled him.

'Looks as though the drama is not going to be restricted to the stage, dear boy,' Peregrine said as he strode past, eyeing the three flirtatious actresses still wrapped around him. 'Just don't wear out my actresses. I want them to mount a play, not you.'

This caused the three women to giggle and Isaac to hope and pray that Adelaide had not heard the ribald comment.

I'm not like my father, he wanted to shout up the stairs.

He looked down at the three women cooing at him, then back up the stairs.

Not any more.

Chapter Ten

Adelaide quickly skirted around the corner at the top of the stairs and stopped, her hand on her chest to still her rapidly beating heart. She was such a coward, fleeing from the sight of Isaac with another woman, well, three other women. It was ridiculous. She was being ridiculous. If she was to continue to live in this house, to share it with Isaac and this theatrical troupe, she needed to show some fortitude.

It wasn't as if she didn't know what sort of man he was. A womaniser. A philanderer. Just like his father. When they had been alone together she had momentarily forgotten that fact, but the exhibition she had just witnessed had clearly reminded her.

Thank goodness for that. It had shattered all her delusions and brought her back to reality.

And if she ever again started to forget the type of man he was, all she had to do was remember the scene she had just witnessed. That would provide the necessary antidote to his charms.

But she had never been a coward before and was not about to become one now. She would not hide away as though she was the one who had done something to be ashamed of.

To prove to herself, and to Isaac, that she would not be flustered by the sight of him with another woman, she turned and walked back down the stairs, her head held high, her posture upright.

'Isaac, I need to talk to you,' she said in her most resolute voice, letting him know that it was a matter of some importance and, unlike the other women, she had no intention of flirting with him to gain his attention.

'Of course,' he said, disentangling himself from the arms of the three women.

'But first let me introduce you to the Misses Genevieve Thornton, Marigold Bennett and Imogen Winslow. Genevieve, Marigold, Imogen, may I present Adelaide FitzWilliam, the Duchess of Hartfield.'

As one, the three women looked her up and down as if assessing a rival, then all three curtsied, their expressions suggesting they saw such deference as ironic rather than what was owed to a woman with a title.

Adelaide performed her own curtsy, aware that she, too, had assessed the three women and was astounded by how they were even more glamorous up close. A blonde, a redhead and one with hair as black as onyx, each with perfect features, full lips, high cheekbones, tiny waists, rounded hips and ample bosoms.

Their flattering clothing was of the latest fashion and Adelaide suddenly felt very dowdy in her plain brown dress which had been made last year, or maybe the year before that, and her hair tied back in a sensible bun at the nape of her neck.

Forcing herself to ignore all that, she turned to Isaac. 'As I said, I need to have a word with you.'

'Of course, if you'll excuse me, ladies.'

Each one sent him a coquettish smile, then watched their departure while talking quietly together. Adelaide refused to speculate on what their conversation might be about as she led Isaac down the hallway and out onto the terrace at the top of the outdoor stairs. Although she suspected their twittering might be about her.

Isaac pointed towards the large oak doors leading back into the house. 'I'm sorry about—'

'I have a son of an impressionable age,' she cut him off, not wanting to hear any empty apologies. She had seen how much he was enjoying the attentions of the three actresses and doubted he was sorry in the slightest.

'I hope I can rely on you to ensure he is not exposed to any behaviour that might confuse, upset or embarrass him.'

He frowned. 'I can assure you that everyone in the cast and crew knows how to conduct themselves and will do nothing to upset or embarrass a child.'

'I'm merely thinking of Joshua.'

A squeal of delight drew their attention to a group of actors cavorting in the formal gardens. One had hoisted Joshua up onto his shoulders. Her son had thrown up his arms high above his head, like an acrobat who had just performed a death-defying trick, while the other actors applauded. He looked as though he was bursting with happiness, raising the question— was it really the effect the theatre people would have on Joshua's delicate sensibilities she was concerned about, or her own?

'I would never do anything to upset Joshua,' he said and she could hear the hurt in his voice that she would think otherwise.

'It's just…' Adelaide came to a halt, unsure what it was she wanted to say.

'I'm sorry I invited these people into your home without asking you. I was only thinking of how to get rid of Henrietta and Priscilla. But you have my guarantee that I and the rest of the cast and crew will respect any rules you wish to impose on us while we are here.'

But can you guarantee that no one, particularly you and those three beauties, will do anything that causes my heart to feel as if it is being squeezed within my chest?

'Good, that is all I ask,' she stated instead, in her most authoritative voice.

'And do you have any rules you wish me to pass on to the others?'

I don't want you paying attention to any other women. I don't want you flirting with actresses. I don't want you taking any other woman to your bed.

'No, there are no rules. I have your guarantee, I'm sure that will be enough. So, I'll let you get back to your...friends.'

Isaac looked towards the door. 'Yes, about those three... I'm afraid theatrical people can get a bit, well, theatrical at times.'

'You all seem rather familiar.'

Damn. Why did she have to say that?

She did not want him thinking she cared whether one or other of those actresses was his current lover. She did not care. She simply did not care. She placed her hand on her stomach to ease its churning and repeated one more time that she did not care.

'Rumours have obviously started to spread at the theatre that I'm now a duke and it is like flames and moths for some women, irresistible.'

That and being outrageously handsome, decidedly masculine and having an intriguing wildness about you, she thought ruefully. Any one of those qualities would catch the attention of most women, but together they were a lethal combination. She could hardly blame the three actresses.

She looked back towards the entrance and wondered

how long it would be before one of those actresses, or some other equally seductive woman, managed to secure the title as the next Duchess of Hartfield.

'Yes, dukes do tend to have their pick of women,' she said, fighting to keep the bitterness out of her voice. 'Your father certainly did.'

His eyes softened as he looked down at her. 'And he chose you,' he said, quietly.

'He chose me to marry, that is all,' she shot back. 'But in the eyes of men like your father, the marriage vow to forsake all others means nothing.'

And it was obvious the apple did not fall far from the tree when it came to licentiousness. If she ever doubted that fact again, she'd just have to remember the look on Isaac's face as those three actresses fawned over him. He gave every appearance of a satisfied cat being offered a selection of three delicious bowls of cream. It was obvious that for him, the more women the better. Well, she for one would not succumb to his charms, join his harem and become just another one of his conquests.

'You hardly need to remind me of my father's vices. If he had been an upstanding man who honoured his vows, my childhood would have been very different.'

She clenched her teeth tighter, determined to not let him distract her from her anger. Yes, the old Duke's behaviour had also made things hard for Isaac, but that did not excuse his present conduct. She would not let thoughts of his difficult childhood allow her to forget that and lower her guard.

'Well, *you're* not married, so you can do whatever you please. Just don't do it in front of my son,' she said, her voice terse.

He pointed back to the entrance. 'We're not—'

'It's none of my business.'

'We're not—'

'I said, it's none of my business,' she repeated, her voice getting louder. 'Now, if you'll excuse me, I have a household to run and guests who need accommodating.' With that she turned and strode back into the house, not waiting for his attempt to explain, justify, or, worse, lie about what she had seen with her own eyes.

She stormed in through the entrance and was pleased to see it free of waiting actresses, then paused at the bottom of the stairs and drew in a long, slow breath.

He had said they'd be in rehearsal for a month. Somehow, she would have to control her feelings for a full four weeks. It would be so much easier if she *could* just run away to the Dowager's Cottage, but it would be cruel to deny Joshua all this fun and revelry. Instead, she would have to ensure she revealed nothing of how Isaac affected her and put on a brave face.

Surely that would not be too hard. She had been

putting on a brave face for most of her life. She could continue to do so for another month, couldn't she?

She looked back over her shoulder and grimaced. When it came to Isaac, all those traits that had served her so well for so long—bravery, stoicism, composure—seemed in short supply. Just when she needed them the most.

Chapter Eleven

Three beautiful women vying for your attention was surely every man's dream come true, but for Isaac it was a nightmare. He was almost tempted to invite Henrietta and Priscilla back, as coping with the stern sisters was much less taxing.

The three actresses had almost come to blows over who was to sit where at the dinner table. Isaac had taken his seat at the head of the table, which meant only two of the three could sit next to him. After much jostling, Imogen had taken the seat on his right, Marigold to his left, and a disgruntled Genevieve had been relegated to the seat next to the man who was sitting next to Imogen. But that did not stop her from leaning forward to focus her attention solely on Isaac.

The women had all dressed to impress and outdo each other. Isaac doubted if he'd ever been confronted with so much powdered cleavage or brighter smiles. As they talked over each other and tried to drown each other out with their gaiety, he was subjected to an array of subtle and not-so-subtle advances, much to the amusement of the man seated between Imogen and Genevieve.

When Isaac did manage to get a word in, everything he said was either greeted with serious nods as if he had somehow become wise beyond his years, or peals of laughter that a vaudevillian comedian would be more than pleased with.

It was all so tiresome. This presumably was what he would have to put up with now that he was a duke. He hated to think what was going to happen when the next edition of *Debrett's* was printed and the desperate debutantes and their mercenary mothers got wind that there was a young, eligible, unmarried duke roaming free. He shuddered.

He looked down the long table, past the ornate displays of flowers, the large candelabras with flickering candles and all the other fripperies that were deemed essential when one dined, to where Adelaide was seated.

If she could see the expression on his face, she did not respond to his call for help and chose to ignore him. When he finally caught her eye, she quickly looked away. He was tempted to stand up and call down the table, over the sound of twenty people all chattering and laughing and the clatter of cutlery on fine china, 'I've done nothing to encourage this attention. It's all the fault of that damn title I didn't even want!'

And it was true. Despite what she might think, he had done nothing wrong. Well, other than making the mistake of inviting his ex-lovers into her home.

Joshua looked in his direction and sent him a quick wave. The little boy looked completely happy with so many people to talk to. The cast and crew had accepted him as one of their own, joking with him, listening to his stories and causing him to laugh loudly and often.

He could only hope Adelaide's desire to see her son happy would counteract the offstage theatrics of the three actresses and stop her making good on her threat to move out of the house and into the Dowager's Cottage. He would hate it if his plan backfired and she moved. Apart from not wanting her to leave, it would be so wrong for her to be driven out of what should be her home.

After dinner the noisy party adjourned to the drawing room. The guests walked down the hallway in a chaotic manner that bore no resemblance to the usual orderly parade insisted on by members of the aristocracy, where everyone's position was determined by their rank and age.

Three women vied to take his arm, but by making a hurried excuse and moving quickly he avoided what could have turned into an embarrassing fracas. Instead, he strode down the hallway, desperate to talk to Adelaide.

When he caught up with her, he found himself suddenly lost for words. He felt compelled to try to explain away the antics of the three beauties, but what could he say? While he was trying to formulate the words, Joshua rushed up to them, smiling fit to burst.

'May I, Mama? May I? Peregrine says I can, but I have to ask you and get your permission.'

'I can't give you my permission until I know what you're asking me,' Adelaide said, smiling at her son's enthusiasm. 'So slow down and tell me what you want.'

'Peregrine says I can be one of the fairies while they rehearse the Summer Night play if you say it is all right. Please say it's all right, please, please, please.'

'Oh, all right,' Adelaide said.

Isaac was unsure whether she was merely trying to halt the barrage of begging or agreeing to what he was asking, but Joshua took it as permission and immediately turned and ran back down the hallway towards the director.

'She said yes. I'm going to be an actor,' he called out, which was met by applause by everyone who heard.

'I suspect I've just horrified Lady Henrietta and Lady Hampton even more than having actors in their father's home ever would,' she said with a wicked gleam in her eye. 'They'd be mortified if they knew the person they consider the rightful Duke was about to take to the stage.'

'Yes, what would their lawyers make of that?' he

added, watching Joshua twirling around in what was presumably a fairy-like manner.

'I don't know what the lawyers would say, but I know exactly what Lady Henrietta would.' She adopted Henrietta's prim demeanour. 'No judge in the land would ever believe an actor could be a duke.'

'I think Peregrine is right. You should be on the stage. You captured her perfectly.'

She smiled at him. It was such a mesmerising smile. No wonder she was causing him all this consternation.

They entered the drawing room, where the rugs had been rolled back. Musicians had set up in the corner and were already playing a lively tune while several couples danced in the middle of the floor.

Imogen, Genevieve and Marigold stood up, all three sets of eyes firmly fixed on him. Then, like an approaching army, they began their advance. That was, if an army ever sauntered, swung their hips seductively and pursed their lips.

'Dance with me, Adelaide,' he said, taking her arm. 'If you don't, you'll be throwing me to the hounds and you'll have to watch the unsightly spectacle of a poor man being fought over like a piece of meat by three hungry animals.'

She rolled her eyes, and he wasn't sure whether it was his absurd imagery or the thought of dancing with him that was responsible.

'Please,' he repeated, sounding not unlike her son.

'Oh, all right.'

He led her into the middle of the room, placed his hand on her slim waist and took her hand in his. Then he spun her around the room in time to the lively polka. It felt so good to have her in his arms, and not just because it had saved him from being pulled every which way by the ambitious actresses. She was so light, so graceful, and dancing with her was a joy. But it wasn't just her proficiency on the dance floor that felt so good. It was being this close to her, so close he was enveloped by her delicate scent of rosewater and lilac, so close he could feel the warmth of her body.

He moved in towards her. He was now a few tantalising inches from that desirable body. She did not move away as he feared. In fact, she closed the gap further, until their bodies were almost touching, and he swallowed a groan of desire. Another inch and he would know what it was like to have her breasts pressed against his chest, her thighs touching his.

As if she could read where his inappropriate thoughts were taking him, she quickly stepped back, widening the gap between them, her body now stiff in his arms.

Did he apologise? But for what? For his thoughts?

'I see you continue to be greatly sought after tonight,' she said, her voice once again prim and proper.

'Hmm, but I don't believe Joshua was aware of the antics at my end of the table. Antics, I might add, I have done nothing to encourage.'

She said nothing, but her silence spoke volumes. No matter what he said, she was not going to believe him. And why should she? Under normal circumstances he would not be averse to the attentions of three desirable women, but not tonight.

'Joshua is certainly happy,' he said, hoping to move the conversation away from the intense feminine interest he had not sought and did not want.

'What child wouldn't be happy with all this attention?' They both looked over at Joshua, who was laughing as the magician pulled coins from behind his ear.

'But after this dance I'm going to have to try to get him to bed or else he's going to be a cranky little boy tomorrow.'

'What?' he gasped in mock horror. 'You're not going to leave me to the trio vying to be the next Duchess?'

'I'm sure you'll cope,' she said, not smiling at his attempt at a joke.

'None of those women is my lover, I hope you realise.'

She raised her eyebrows, but once again said nothing.

'Oh, all right. Yes, at one time or another I've been involved with all three, but that is in the past.'

Those disbelieving eyebrows remained raised.

'It's just the thought of becoming a duchess that has rekindled their interest in me,' he continued, desperate for her to understand. 'It's amazing what a woman will do to get her hands on a title and immense wealth.'

Her lips turned into a frown and she became even more rigid in his arms.

Damn, why did he say that?

'Not that I'm suggesting you ever did anything—'

'If you'll excuse me, I need to put Joshua to bed.'

With that she stopped dancing and stepped away from him.

'I didn't mean…' His words came to a halt as she walked across the room, leaving him exposed to the attentions of three women he did not want but could easily have, while the woman he did want, but shouldn't, had turned her back on him.

'Come on, Joshua, time for bed,' Adelaide said, wanting to escape this room as much as needing to put her son to bed.

Joshua's brow furrowed.

'No argument, darling.' The last thing she wanted was to have to deal with a difficult child in front of all these guests.

'But, Mama—'

'Time for bed, little man,' Isaac said as he scooped Joshua up into his arms. 'I can see the fairy dust in your eyes and you can barely keep them open. If you're going to be an actor you need to get your rest. Isn't that right, Peregrine?'

'Yes, exactly,' the director said with a nod. 'Off you go, young man. We only want bright-eyed fairies at rehearsals tomorrow.'

'And a good actor always does what his director says,' Isaac added. 'You want to be a good actor, don't you?'

'Yes,' Joshua said reluctantly.

'So let's get you into bed.' He hoisted the boy up above his shoulder. 'Now say goodnight to everyone in your best, booming actor voice. One that will reach even those up in the highest stalls at the back of the theatre.'

'Goodnight, everyone,' Joshua called out.

'Goodnight, Joshua,' the cast and crew chorused back.

With that Isaac carried him out the room and Adelaide followed on behind. Despite her annoyance with Isaac, she could not deny he was good with her son. Neither she nor Joshua were used to a house full of guests and getting her excited boy to bed was going to be a trial, but Isaac had managed it so well, making Joshua almost think it was what he wanted to do.

'Thank you for that,' she whispered as they walked up the stairs. After so much excitement, Joshua was already starting to doze off in his arms.

'My pleasure,' he whispered back.

They entered Joshua's room. She quickly changed her sleeping son into his pyjamas, and Isaac gently lowered him onto the bed, picked up his stuffed rabbit and placed it under his arm.

'I don't think I've ever seen him so excited.' She brushed back a lock of hair from Joshua's forehead. 'I suspect this is going to be one of the most memorable occasions of his young life.'

She looked up at Isaac and smiled.

He smiled back. The smile faded. He held her gaze, his eyes soft.

'And not just in Joshua's life,' he said, his voice barely audible as if talking to himself.

Her breath caught in her throat. She should look away, but how could she not stare into those dark eyes, appearing almost black in the dim light? Despite her animosity towards him, he was truly the most magnificent man she had ever seen and it was not surprising he caused her to act in such an uncharacteristic manner.

Her gaze moved to his mouth. Her own lips parted as she stared at his full lips, at the natural curve of the upper lip and the softness of the lower one. What would it be like to run her finger along the etched line at the edge of his mouth? What would it be like to feel those lips pressed against hers?

Her lips tingling, she leant towards him. As if pulled by the same magnetic force he moved towards her, just as he had when they had danced together. Across the bed, she could feel the warmth of his body radiating from him. His musky, intoxicating masculine scent caused shivers to ripple down her spine and she moved slightly closer, so close she could almost feel his mouth on hers, could almost taste him.

She closed her eyes, her heart pounding, her breath caught in her throat and waited, her body throbbing with anticipation.

Joshua snuffled in his sleep. Her eyes sprang open. She looked down at her innocent son. What on earth was she doing? She had almost kissed Isaac! For one treacherous moment she had wanted him to kiss her back. And yet the last thing she should want to do was to kiss Isaac Radcliff, the notorious rake!

'Well, I think I'll get an early night as well,' she said hastily as if she had not just made a complete fool of herself.

'Goodnight,' he replied and before he could say any more, or she could make herself look even more ridiculous, she hurried out of the room and down to her bedchamber.

Closing the door behind her, she leant against the wall, her heart still pounding hard inside her chest.

She had done it again. She had forgotten everything she knew about him. And once again she had fled like a frightened rabbit. This was not the woman she was.

But then, she had never faced a situation like this before, so did not really know what sort of woman she was. How was one supposed to act when in the impossible position of both wanting and not wanting Isaac Radcliff?

While her mind knew he was a man any sensible woman should avoid, her body was not being the slightest bit sensible. When she was with him some primal instinct seemed to take control and all she wanted was for him to kiss her, for his caressing hands to explore her body, and to experience what it would be like to be made love to by such a captivating man.

And every time her body came close to yielding to these desires, her sensible mind took over, and sent her running for cover.

She released a long, slow sigh. But surely that was something for which she should be grateful? If she did give in to what her body wanted, she had no idea where it would take her. She was used to being in control of her emotions. She liked being in control of her emotions. It was that control which had enabled her to endure the life that had been thrust upon her. She did not want to give up control to anyone, least of all a man like Isaac Radcliff.

She filled her lungs with a deep breath and exhaled slowly. Perhaps an early night *was* what she needed. Joshua wasn't the only one who had experienced an exciting day, although tumultuous would be a more apt description in her case. After a good night's sleep surely she would see things differently. Once again she would be able to think logically and not be confused by all these tempestuous emotions.

Rather than calling for her lady's maid, she undressed herself, changed into her nightdress and climbed into bed, but sleep would not come.

She turned to one side, then the other, tried sleeping on her back, then on her stomach, fluffed up her pillows, pushed off the quilt then pulled it back again. Nothing worked.

As she lay awake, she heard others retiring for the night and the house slowly settling, but still she was lying there, eyes wide open, staring at the ceiling.

Climbing out of bed, she pulled on her robe and quietly opened the door. She would check on Joshua. Once she had reassured herself that her son was sleeping peacefully, then hopefully sleep would also come for her as well.

Walking as quietly as possible down a hallway lit only by the light of the moon streaming in through the windows, she made her way towards her son's bedroom. The sound of footsteps coming her way caused her to quickly conceal herself behind a large suit of armour.

Why she was hiding in her own home she did not know. Was it simply because she did not want anyone to see her in her nightdress or was it curiosity over who else was prowling round the house at this late hour?

The red-headed actress quietly passed her by, paused

at Isaac's door, looked both ways and turned the door handle. Adelaide's hand shot to cover her mouth and stop the gasp from escaping that would have revealed her presence.

Holding her breath, she watched as the redhead disappeared behind the closed door. None of the actresses was his lover, that was what he had said to her. It was a lie, a blatant lie, and he had made that lie straight to her face.

Slowly, quietly, she emerged from behind the armour, and tiptoed down the hall to Joshua's room. He was deep in sleep, still cuddling his rabbit, his chest rising and falling with each peaceful breath. She crossed the room and kissed him lightly on the cheek.

He, at least, was having a restful night.

As silently as she had entered, she left the room and tiptoed back down the hallway. Once again, she heard footsteps coming along the darkened hallway and once again she quickly secreted herself, this time behind a large sideboard bearing an enormous Venetian urn bedecked with cascading dried flowers.

The blonde actress passed by, and like the redhead, walked up to Isaac's door, turned the handle and walked in, as bold as brass. She, too, had obviously been invited to spend the night in his bedchamber.

Two women.

It was outrageous!

Perhaps he hadn't lied to her when he'd said that not

one of those actresses was his lover. He wasn't making love to one, but to two at once.

Drawing in a furious breath, she returned to her room. He was worse than she could possibly have imagined. He was a lecher, a dissolute rakehell and thank goodness she had not succumbed and kissed him across the bed of her innocent son.

Her angry heart still pounding out a furious drumbeat, insults and recriminations circling in her head, she climbed back into bed and fought not to listen for sounds coming from the room next to her.

Despite her determination not to do so, she leant towards the door that joined her room to his, her head tilted, her ears straining. She could hear nothing and was both grateful for and annoyed by the thick door that muffled all sounds.

But what she did see was the light of a lamp and the shadow of feet under her door that led to the hallway.

Another one?

Surely not.

To either prove herself wrong or right, she crept over to the door, opened it a crack and peeped out. As expected, the raven-haired beauty passed her by. She did not need to poke her head out to see where she was going. Instead, she listened, and heard the undeniable sound of Isaac's door handle being turned.

All three of them were in there now and she did not

think for a moment they were discussing the play in which they were acting.

Unable to return to bed when her mind and body were in such an agitated state, she began pacing the room.

It was disgusting. He was disgusting. The lowest of all men. The man she had almost kissed. The man she had wasted time fantasising about.

And he was going to be in this house for at least another month, spending every night in the room next to hers with his three lovers.

It was more than she could endure. She had to get away from him. She would move into the Dowager's Cottage tomorrow and leave him to his debauchery. No, better still, she would toss them all out and send them back to London. She sighed and stopped in her pacing, and looked towards Joshua's room, remembering his excited face when she'd said he could be a fairy.

She could not do that to her son. She could not deprive him of something that would be a cherished memory of his childhood, but the next month was surely going to stretch the stoicism that had got her through many a trial in the past, possibly to breaking point.

Isaac had hardly slept a wink and he was exhausted. Convincing one woman after another that he did not want her in his bed was surprisingly tiring, as was trying to keep them quiet so as not to draw the attention of the woman sleeping in the next room.

Was it his fatigue that made breakfast the next morning seem particularly tense?

'I hope everyone got a good night's sleep,' Peregrine said, standing at the end of the breakfast table. 'I expect everyone to be in their best form for today's rehearsals.'

Isaac looked around the table. Four women glared back at him, all with lips pursed in disapproval. He could understand why the actresses were annoyed with him. They were not used to rejection, but why was Adelaide sending him a cross look? Had she seen something? Heard something?

'Marigold, Imogen, Genevieve, I take it you all did as I requested and got a good night's sleep.'

'Yes, Peregrine,' they chorused, shooting daggers at each other, obviously assuming one of the other three was the reason for their rejection.

Peregrine's eyebrows remained arched dramatically as he looked down the table at Isaac.

'Before you ask, yes, I, too, slept the sleep of the virtuous and got a full eight hours,' Isaac said, looking towards Adelaide and hoping she would believe that, despite what she might or might not have seen or heard last night.

'Your performance, dear boy, has never been called into question,' Peregrine said, making Isaac wince. 'I just don't want it interfering with the performances of my actresses.'

Isaac looked towards Adelaide, whose lips were now even more tightly pursed. She *had* seen or heard something. But if she had, she would have been the only one to do so. His night-time visitors could not possibly have disturbed Joshua.

After Imogen had left he had checked on the boy and found him sleeping peacefully, oblivious to other people's night-time wanderings. Joshua had most certainly not been confused or embarrassed by anything that had happened, or in this case, not happened.

Adelaide's reaction could only mean one thing. Despite her standoffish behaviour towards him, she did not want him taking a lover because she was jealous.

He had not misinterpreted that look she had given him last night. For a brief moment she had wanted him. Even if she had then turned away from him and fled from the room.

Was that what was wrong now? Was the green-eyed monster causing her to look at him with such contempt? Despite rejecting him herself, she still did not want him to be with another woman.

And what did he think of that? There was no denying he wanted her. He was a man and she was an eminently desirable woman. But while the part of his body that was incapable of thinking wanted her desperately, his sane, sometimes rational brain knew that would be an enormous mistake.

Last night he had been so grateful when she had walked away before he did something they would both regret, because with her lips looking so alluring his rational brain did not stand a chance.

It was such a dilemma. He doubted he could trust himself, so he needed her to not want him, or else they were in danger of going down a path that could lead them heaven knew where, or more likely, hell knew where.

'Right, everyone, I want you all out at the front of the house, ready to work hard,' Peregrine said, clapping his hands together and causing a rush towards the dining room doors.

Neither Isaac nor Adelaide was needed for rehearsals, but they followed the troupe out into the garden and settled on the stone bench at the bottom of the outside stairs, to watch Peregrine put the actors through their paces.

Adelaide's body was tense beside him and he suspected she was here, in his presence, only because Joshua had taken his place among the actors. There could be no other reason because she certainly did not look happy to be at his side.

'Joshua looks excited,' he said, trying to get a polite, uncontroversial conversation started.

'Yes,' she stated bluntly.

'Some of the cast are worried he might upstage them,' he added in a mock-jovial manner, then grimaced at how desperate he was starting to sound.

'Oh, did one of your mistresses tell you that?' He felt her flinch beside him, and suspected she wished she could take that back, but as she had raised the subject he decided it was time to clear the air.

'I have already told you I do not have a mistress.'

She gave a small huff of disapproval. 'No, not one. But it's none of my business whether you do or do not have a mistress and I simply do not care how many actresses you have in your bed.'

He turned slightly on the bench to observe her. 'I don't know what you think you saw or heard last night, but I did not share my bed with anyone. I slept alone, chaste as a vestal virgin.'

Again she made that huffing noise.

'Whatever you think you saw, you are wrong.'

'Oh, so it's my eyes that are at fault, is it?'

He looked into those usually composed dark eyes, flashing with anger, the raw intensity and passion setting his blood on fire. He wanted to take her in his arms, to kiss away her rage, but knew that would not be welcome right then.

'Imogen, Genevieve and Marigold came to my room last night, but each one was turned away.'

'I don't believe you.'

'You have to believe me. Last night I made it clear

to all three I did not wish to resume our relationship and that none of them would be the future Duchess of Hartfield.'

'It's none of my business and, as I said, I couldn't care less how many women you have in your bed.'

'It looks as though I'm not the one lying here.'

She turned to glare at him, her lush red lips pulled into a frown, those big brown eyes simmering with indignation.

'I'm not my father,' he said gently. 'I know he behaved appallingly his entire life. He was a selfish man who cared only about his own gratification and assumed that was his right. I'm not like that.'

Her eyes narrowed, then she resumed looking straight ahead.

'Yes, I've sown a few wild oats in my time, but I saw how my mother was treated and, yes, as you have pointed out, how Winifred was also treated and how I suspect you were treated as well. I'm like my father in many ways, unfortunately, but I would never want to cause the harm he did. The actresses want the title of Duchess. That's what they are after, not me. I would never take advantage of that in order to bed them. Nor would I hurt any other woman.'

She scowled at him and he braced himself for what was probably a deserved onslaught, but instead she suddenly sighed.

'I suppose I can hardly blame them,' she said, her voice quiet.

He waited for further explanation.

'As you have said, I, too, chased after a title.'

'No, no, I should never have said that, Adelaide,' he said, his voice beseeching. 'I judged you so harshly and I was so wrong. I know you had no choice. You should never have been forced into a marriage and you were just another victim of my father's selfishness.'

She shrugged, but the softening of her face suggested she had finally accepted his apology and believed he was telling the truth.

Thank goodness for that. It was more important to him than he would have thought possible that she not see him as being entirely like his father, a man who took what he wanted without care for whom he might hurt. If he was just like his father, he would have been hellbent on getting her into his bed as quickly and as often as possible and damn the consequences.

But it would be dangerous to think of what it would be like to take her to his bed and he needed to get that out of his mind. He turned back to the production and forced himself to think of something, anything else.

Joshua danced onto the stage, his hand held by the actor playing Puck. Adelaide sat forward, a beauteous smile on her lips as her focus turned entirely to her son.

Joshua spotted her and waved vigorously, something Isaac was sure was not in the script.

Adelaide waved back and Joshua did a little jig, still beaming with happiness.

Several servants who were setting up a table in the gardens for luncheon also stopped in their work. Joshua spied them watching him and sent them a wave, which they returned, then he waved vigorously to the house.

Isaac looked over his shoulder. At windows on every floor, servants were looking out, watching the action below and waving back.

'I think this play, and Joshua's performance, is going to cause a lot of disruption in the running of the household,' he teased.

Adelaide turned to where he was looking and the heads quickly disappeared.

'I certainly can't blame them. This really is the most exciting thing that has happened at Hartfield Hall since I've been in residence. It would be unfair to stop the servants from watching.'

'But if no meals are cooked and no beds are made I suspect you'll have a lot of disgruntled guests in the house.'

'Excuse me,' she called out, standing up and signalling to Peregrine.

The director walked over towards her, a cordial

smile on his lips. 'Yes, Your Grace, how may I be of assistance?'

'I've had an idea regarding the performance.'

The cordial smile became strained. 'I'm all ears, my dear. There's nothing a director likes better than to have someone from outside the industry giving him advice on how to mount his production.'

If she had caught his sarcasm, she made no acknowledgement of it. 'Perhaps, before you return to London, you might stage a full production here at Hartfield Hall and I'll invite the tenants, the village people and all the servants to make up the audience.'

'Excellent idea, my dear. We'll stage a full dress rehearsal,' Peregrine enthused. 'Actors perform so much better if they have an audience and it will be a perfect opportunity to iron out any pesky little flaws before our premiere on the London stage.'

'Good,' she said with satisfaction, sitting back on the bench. 'There's no reason why everyone can't enjoy this wonderful event, just like we are.'

She angled her head in thought. 'In fact, Hartfield Hall is such a perfect venue it would be wonderful if it became a regular event. If we hosted theatrical productions here at the hall, it would bring lots of people into the area. That would benefit all the local inns, shops and tradespeople. It could bring much-needed prosperity to the village. What do you think, Isaac?'

'I agree with Peregrine. I think it's an excellent

idea,' he said, not sure if it was just the merits of her idea he was approving of, or the way she had said, *we* could host theatrical productions here at the hall.

Chapter Twelve

For the next month the house settled into a routine, if you could call a state of constant noise and commotion a routine. The three actresses appeared to have accepted they were not going to become the next Duchess of Hartfield. They were now cordial rather than flirtatious with Isaac. Adelaide was becoming increasingly confident that this was no subterfuge and Isaac had not been lying when he'd insisted that none of them, and certainly not all three, was his lover.

Despite believing him, for the first week, each night after she retired, she strained her ears, attempting to hear if there were any night-time visits to the adjoining room. Eventually she accepted she was being overly vigilant and started having restful sleeps.

Not that this meant there wasn't plenty of flirting taking place among the cast and crew, and, she suspected, the rest of the household. It would be hard to miss Baxter's constant smile and she had heard him whistling as he went about his work on more than one occasion. Although that might have been merely due to the infectious laughter and chatter that seemed to fill every inch of the large house.

With the constant high spirits of the cast and crew and the musicians playing each night, the drawing rooms of Hartfield Hall could never be described as stuffy and she could see why Isaac much preferred the world of the theatre to the starchy conventions of society.

All in all, having the cast and crew as guests at Hartfield Hall was a great success and Isaac had been right that their behaviour had been entirely respectful, certainly more so than the friends of the old Duke had been when they had invaded the house for one of their riotous weekend parties.

Soon Isaac along with everyone else would be departing. He would be going back to his own world and leaving her behind. She wanted her independence, had craved it for so many years, but independence without him in her life, without the colour and excitement he brought with him, suddenly seemed like an empty prospect. And how Joshua was going to cope with their quiet little world when all this excitement was over she preferred not to dwell on.

When the night of the final dress rehearsal came around, it suddenly became something she would have to think about. Tomorrow the entire cast and crew would be returning to London for their premiere and Isaac would be going with them.

But she would worry about that tomorrow. Tonight she would enjoy the show.

Just as night began to fall, along with Isaac, the villagers, tenant farmers and the servants, she took her seat on the terrace in front of the house and looked down at the garden, which had been transformed into an enchanted fairy forest.

Strategically placed lanterns cast light and shadows that swirled in the gentle breeze, creating an enchanted scene where one could believe anything could happen. Twinkling lights in the surrounding trees appeared to join with the stars above them, evoking a dream-like atmosphere.

Everyone assembled was dressed in their finest clothing and the excitement among the audience was almost palpable as they waited for the show to begin. Adelaide had also made a special effort, dressing in a light yellow gown that she hoped reflected the happy mood, an embroidered green silk shawl draped around her shoulders and a string of pearls around her neck.

When the Duke of Athens emerged from the darkness to announce his wedding to the Queen of the Amazons in his booming voice, a hush fell on the audience. Like Adelaide, they were immediately captivated and it was hard to believe the commanding man she saw on stage was the same one who had been helping himself to a second serving of kippers just this morning at breakfast time.

The silent awe in which the audience watched the performance soon turned to laughter as the play proceeded and everyone was caught up in the tale of love potions and mistaken identities.

When Joshua came on stage in the second act holding Puck's hand, Adelaide gasped at the sight of him transformed into a fairy. Dressed in a doublet embroidered with flowers, gossamer wings on his back and wearing shimmering cosmetics that gave him a luminous appearance, she could hardly recognise him.

She had watched him rehearse this scene again and again over the last month, but still her heart was in her mouth as her little boy stood in the middle of the stage.

'That's Lord Joshua,' she heard Mrs Cooper exclaim and this statement rippled in repetition through the audience. A ripple that soon turned into spontaneous applause, interrupting the performance.

Puck whispered something in Joshua's ear and gave him a little nudge forward. Joshua stepped to the front of the stage and with a wide sweeping motion of his hand made a low bow. But that did not appear to be enough for his audience, who continued to applaud through several bows before they finally settled down and the play could recommence.

Adelaide found tears had sprung to her eyes and she was smiling like the proud mother she was.

'I believe the boy is a natural,' Isaac said beside her and, before she realised what she was doing, she took his hand and gave it a small squeeze.

'Thank you so much for this, Isaac,' she said. The happiness this moment had given her son was simply priceless and it was one she knew he would remember even when he was an elderly man.

'If he decides he now wants a career on the stage, I doubt if you'll be thanking me,' he whispered back.

'If it makes him as happy as he is tonight, then that will be exactly what I wish for him.'

He smiled at her, gave her hand a squeeze in response and she was sure it was not possible to feel more joyful than she did right now.

The play continued and it wasn't until they were near the final act that she realised she was still holding Isaac's hand. How on earth had that happened? And how was she expected to extricate her own now? The answer to that question came when the performance ended and the cast assembled in front of the audience.

Adelaide joined in the standing ovation, sure that she had seen the best production of *A Midsummer Night's Dream* that had ever been staged and not just because her son had played a small part.

Finally, after countless bows, the applause died out. Servants rushed off so they could organise food and drink for the audience and cast, and Joshua ran forward into his mother's waiting arms.

'Did you see me? Did you see me?' he called out as she gave him a hug and kissed the top of his head.

'I did and I think you were magnificent.'

'Did you see me, Isaac? Did you see the dance I did around Genevieve—I mean Titania.'

'I did and I don't think I've ever seen a better fairy dance,' Isaac said, smiling at both Adelaide and Joshua.

'Yes, that's what Peregrine said. He said my performance was simply sub-slimy, dear boy.'

Isaac laughed. 'I think he meant sublime.'

'Yes, that. And Marigold, I mean Hermia, said such a talent should never go to waste and I should consider becoming an actor.'

'Did she?' Adelaide said with a smile, not wanting to let any remaining animosity towards those actresses taint what was a wonderful night.

'There's Mrs Cooper,' Joshua said, breaking from her arms. 'I must tell her all about it.'

With that he rushed off into the crowd, where he was instantly surrounded by his admiring audience.

'Oh, dear, I think he really will have the acting bug now,' Isaac said.

'Is that what happened to you?' she asked, still watching her son, who was now re-enacting the dance he'd performed around Titania.

'No, my first time on the stage was a disaster,' he said with a laugh. 'With a mother as talented as mine, everyone thought I'd be a natural, but I fluffed my lines, missed my cues and could never stand in the right spot on the stage.'

'That's not what Cook said. She told me you used to regale the servants with impersonations of Winifred and her daughters.'

'She did, did she? I think I had a rather sympathetic audience, but when I got on to the proper stage my lack of talent was impossible to ignore.'

'But it's still a world you love?'

'Yes, I think it's like an addiction and once you've had a taste you can't let it go.'

Several actresses walked past them, still dressed in the diaphanous gowns they'd worn on stage, and she wondered whether there were other aspects of working in the theatre that were equally addictive. Then she smiled, refusing to allow any pettiness to ruin what was such a glorious evening.

'Your son was a triumph,' Peregrine said, joining Isaac and Adelaide. 'He should join us on the London stage.'

Adelaide beamed an even brighter smile. 'Thank you, but I think...' she directed her smile at Isaac '...tonight he had a very sympathetic audience.'

'And he made full use of it. That's what a good actor always does. He's a natural.'

'It is such a shame you'll be returning to London tomorrow. You've made a lot of people happy,' she said, looking around at the audience, which was now mingling with the actors. They, too, would be remembering this night for many years to come.

'I haven't forgotten your excellent suggestion, Your Grace,' Peregrine said. 'I can see endless possibilities for this wonderful setting. The three of us are going to have to get together soon to discuss forthcoming performances.'

Adelaide's heart did a small skip within her chest. It was not over. Tonight would not be the last time she would see Isaac. If they did mount ongoing performances here on the estate, would that mean they would spend a considerable amount of time together, year after year?

'Oh, Your Grace, thank you so much,' Mrs Cooper said. 'Tonight has been such a treat and Lord Joshua is a real treasure.'

Adelaide realised she had been neglecting her guests and, after conversing briefly with Mrs Cooper, she circulated among the audience, cast and crew, accepting countless compliments on Joshua's behalf, sure she could never get enough of hearing how marvellous her son was.

The night wore on, people continued to chat, laugh and partake in the refreshments on offer, with no sign that anyone was planning to leave any time soon. She could see Joshua talking to the chambermaid, once again doing his little dance, but this time without as much enthusiasm and with eyes that were becoming hooded with tiredness.

'I think it's time for a little fairy to disappear into his fairy mound and get some sleep,' Isaac said.

'I was thinking the same thing, but I don't believe it's going to be easy to drag him away from his adoring public.'

'Leave this to me. I might not be any good on stage, but I am a theatre manager and know how to deal with temperamental actors.'

'Good luck,' she said as she followed him across the grass to her sleepy son.

Isaac placed his hand gently on Joshua's shoulder. 'Did Peregrine ever tell you the most important thing about being an actor? The secret that separates an ordinary actor from one who is truly a star?'

Joshua looked up at him, his sleepy eyes suddenly wide. 'No? What is it? Because I really, really want to be a star.'

'Always leave your audience wanting more.'

'Oh,' Joshua said, digesting that information. 'How do you do that?'

'You can do it right now.'

Isaac clapped his hands for silence. Everyone stopped talking and turned in his direction. 'Ladies and gentlemen, I give you Joshua FitzWilliam, a star of unparalleled talent, a future luminary of the theatre and the finest fairy to ever tread the boards.'

Applause erupted and Joshua once again performed his flamboyant bow.

'Right, now it's time to leave while they're desperate for more,' Isaac said, taking the boy's hand and leading him back to the house.

Joshua turned and waved a few more times to his applauding audience before Isaac scooped him up in his arms and carried him into the house.

'Yes, that was an impressive bit of management,' Adelaide murmured when she caught up with them. She looked down at her son who was already drifting off to sleep in Isaac's arms.

When they reached Joshua's bedroom Adelaide gently wiped off his face paint, removed the sleepy boy's fairy costume, dressed him in his pyjamas and placed him in his bed with his favourite rabbit tucked under his arm. Then they left and shut the door behind them.

'So will you be going back to London tomorrow, along with the rest of the cast and crew?' she said, asking what she already suspected to be true.

'Yes, I suppose so, unless Henny and Prissy make an unexpected reappearance, but they have been suspiciously quiet of late.'

'You must be missing London.'

'Not really. It has its attractions, but so does the countryside.' Was his voice a husky whisper because he was trying not to wake Joshua in the room behind them? She looked up into his dark eyes. And was that longing she saw, or merely her own emotions reflected back at her?

'You must be missing all those fun-loving women,' she said with a forced laugh.

'There's no one I miss.' His gaze moved slowly from her eyes, down to her mouth. A soft sigh escaped her parted lips.

'What, no one?' she whispered.

'There's no one I want.' With each word, the tempo of Adelaide's heartbeat increased, pounding out a vigorous rhythm in her chest as the pulse of desire throbbed deep inside her.

'No one at all?' she pressed, as desire surged up within her, sending feverish heat rushing through her body.

'Only you,' were the last words she heard before his lips were on hers. Like an addict finally given the drug they craved, she returned his kiss with a wildness and passion she didn't even know she possessed.

Following a primal need that had taken her over, she melded herself into his body, her breasts hard against his chest, one of her thighs in between his, her arms wrapped around his neck. She kissed him with a hunger she was desperate to satisfy.

His hands moved down her sides, cupping her buttocks and pulling her in even tighter. Shamelessly she arched her back and rubbed herself against him, letting him know what she wanted, what she needed, as she continued to devour his masculine taste.

Her mouth tingled as he ran his tongue along her bottom lip. Reeling with desire, she opened up, granting him entrance, his taste intoxicating her. His kisses deepened, became wilder, hungrier. He wanted her, wanted her as desperately as she wanted him. He had to have her, just as she had to have him.

With reluctance she broke away from his kisses and took a step backwards.

'I'm—' he started to say.

She placed a finger on his lips. This was not a time for words. She took his hand and led him down the hallway towards her bedchamber.

'Are you sure, Adelaide?' he asked urgently as she turned the door handle.

Right now, Adelaide had never been more certain of anything in her life. She might feel differently tomorrow, but she would deal with that in the light of day, when this enchanting night was over.

Chapter Thirteen

The darkened room was lit only by the moon coming in through the large sash windows as Adelaide led him towards the bed. Isaac was tempted to light the lamp, desperate to see her clearly, but equally keen not to break the mood.

She turned towards him, and her lips were back on his, the intensity between them shooting erotic heat through his body and straight to his groin. God, he wanted her, wanted her right now, but he had to strip her of those layers of clothing first.

He was still kissing her as his fingers moved to the buttons running up the front of her gown. She stepped back a little, making it easier for him. Her chest rising and falling rapidly with each gasped breath, she watched as he undid the seemingly endless number of ridiculously tiny pearl buttons. When enough buttons were finally released, he pushed her gown off her shoulders and feasted himself on the sight of her.

The alluring mounds of her breasts were pushed up

by her corset and temptingly swelled above her chemise. He leant down and kissed a line along the soft creamy skin. Her hands encircled his head, holding him to her breasts, fingers thrust into his hair. How many times had he fantasised about doing this? More than he could remember, and now his fantasy was coming true.

Wanting more, so much more, he stood up, pulled down her chemise and exposed her breasts to his appreciative view. Full and perky, the dark nipples pointed up at him as if waiting for his kisses. He looked into her eyes, to see if she held any objections. Her mouth was slightly parted and her breath came fast and shallow, causing those glorious breasts to rise and fall, and her eyes were closed.

There was no disputing that look. She was as enraptured by the intoxicating power of desire as he was.

He kissed her lush lips as his hand encased one rounded breast, loving the feel of the nipple tightening under his touch as he ran his thumb over it. Still teasing that furled bud, he slowly trailed kisses down her neck. Her body writhed against him and he loved the way her sensuous movements were urging him on, loved the way she wanted him, was ready for him. His kisses went lower, across her naked shoulders and over the swell of her breasts.

A loud gasp escaped her lips when he took the hard waiting bud in his mouth, his tongue swirling around the sensitive tip. With each stroke of his tongue her gasps grew louder until she was moaning. He cupped her other breast, his caressing fingers increasing her arousal, until he heard that satisfying final groan and felt her body give a small shudder.

Before she could recover, his lips were immediately back on hers, kissing her with increased fervour as he led her closer to the bed. It was deliriously tempting to lift up her skirt, pull off her drawers, bury himself deep inside her and take her hard and fast. But he also wanted to savour this moment, take her slowly and enjoy every pleasure her glorious body could provide.

'Turn around,' he ordered, his rampant desire making him incapable of more poetic language.

She did as he asked. He undid the buttons of her skirt, pushed it over her rounded hips and let it drop to the ground. Kissing her naked shoulders, he loosened the laces of her corset, then pulled it down over her hips, reached for her drawers and quickly pushed them low enough for her to step out of them.

'Lift up your arms,' he whispered huskily in her ear and she shivered.

Once again, she did as he asked. In one movement he pulled her chemise over her head and tossed it across the room.

She turned to face him. Standing in front of him, dressed only in her silk stockings and with a string of pearls around her neck, she looked him boldly in the eye.

'My God, you are beautiful,' he said fervently, his eyes caressing those wondrous breasts, her small waist, the feminine curve of her hips and that glorious dark mound between her legs.

'Sit down,' he said hoarsely, his voice thick with emotion. She sat on the edge of the bed and he knelt before her, undoing the laces of her shoes and tossing them to one side. Then he did what he had often imagined doing, lifted up one leg, then the other, pulled down her garter belts and slowly rolled her stockings down those long, lovely legs.

She lay back in the bed and Isaac savoured the glorious, erotic sight of her naked body laid out before him, waiting for him.

'Your turn,' she murmured, her hooded eyes holding his gaze. 'Take off your clothes.'

He did not need to be ordered twice. With more haste than finesse, he tore off his shirt, ripping off several buttons in the process, unbuttoned his trousers and threw them all across the room.

She lay back on the pillows watching him, her long hair falling out of its confining bun, those magnificent breasts rising and falling with each breath. Her eyes ran down his body and halted at his erection and he groaned in torment as her legs parted in invitation.

As much as he wanted to take his time to fully enjoy

the glorious sight before him, he could wait not a minute longer. But he was still determined not to rush this, determined to receive and give maximum pleasure. To that end, he joined her on the bed. Lying at her side, he ran his hands slowly over her breasts, down the curve of her waist and to the cleft of her legs.

Her legs parted more widely, allowing him to tease his fingers along her feminine folds, parting them and feeling her wet heat.

Determined to drive her wild, he took one nipple in his mouth, licking, sucking, nuzzling, as his hand moved over the sensitive bundle of nerves between her legs. Her back arched up as he stroked her, harder, faster, loving the sound as her gasps became moans, then unconstrained growls. Still stroking, his fingers entered her, her sheath gripping him tightly, and a shudder immediately rippled inside her as she released a long cry and collapsed back onto the bed.

Before she recovered, while she was still gasping, he covered her with his body and placed himself at her entrance. She was more than ready for him, but if he'd harboured any doubts, when she wrapped her legs around his waist, opening herself up for him, they would all have been chased away.

He slid inside her in a skilful glide and moaned as the sensation of soft, velvet heat encased him.

'Oh, Adelaide, my darling,' he whispered, before kissing her eager lips and pushing himself deeper inside her.

Her hands clasped his buttocks. She moved her legs higher up his back, allowing him to enter her fully. With her moans urging him on, he thrust firmly inside her, then pulled almost completely out and thrust in again, harder, faster, deeper.

Her moans matching his rhythm, he wrapped his arms around her, lifting her up, holding her tightly as he surrendered himself to the pleasure of being inside her.

When her inner muscles fluttered along his length, he quickly pulled out and reached his own climax, before sinking onto her body, completely satisfied, utterly spent.

Slowly, his frantic heartbeat subsided to a less furious pace and he lightly kissed her still panting lips. He had wanted her so badly, had thought about, imagined making love to her for so long, but nothing had prepared him for the intensity of how he'd felt in that moment. Now that he'd had her, he knew once was never going to be enough for him. She did not want marriage. He did not want marriage either, but he hoped and prayed she, too, wanted to experience more of this passion between them, because he certainly had a lot more to give.

He pulled her in close and she cradled her head on his shoulder. Adelaide could hardly believe what had just happened. Not the part that she had finally succumbed to her desire and they had made love. She certainly believed that, especially as she had been the one to instigate it. It was the sheer intensity of what she had experienced that she could hardly believe. Even now, residual shivers were still vibrating inside her most feminine of places, as if reliving the exquisite rapture of having him deep inside her.

This was exactly how lovemaking was supposed to be. This was what she had missed out on by marrying a man she'd had no feelings for. And it was certainly something she wanted to experience again and again. Neither of them wanted to marry, so this closeness would likely be transitory. He intended to leave tomorrow so she would have to make the most of tonight. Now that she had put aside the warnings of her mind and surrendered to what her body wanted, she had nothing more to lose and so much to gain.

She ran a finger slowly down the middle of his chest, loving the touch of his warm, naked skin. She traced a line over the sculpted muscles, relishing their powerful hardness. Wanting to touch every part of his magnificent body, she continued down to his stomach, her fingers exploring the ridges and ripples of his abdomen under the surface of his skin. His body was even more impressive than she had imagined and this potently masculine man had just made love to her and shown her what ecstasy felt like.

Leaning over, she kissed each of his nipples, just as

he had done to her earlier. Her tongue stroked across his chest muscles, loving the salty taste of his skin, slick with perspiration from their lovemaking.

He moaned softly. She looked down and saw he was stirring again. Good. That was what she wanted. That was what she had to have, again and again, until he had to leave.

Lifting herself up, she straddled him, rubbing her feminine cleft against him, feeling him grow firmer and longer under her stroking.

'My God, you're insatiable,' he said with a groan, as he reached up and cupped both her breasts.

'Then you'll have to see trying to satisfy me as a challenge,' she said, surprised at her boldness.

'Or perhaps this time you can focus on satisfying me,' he said, a wicked smile curling his lips and a glint in his eyes.

'If you wish.' Her heart pounded faster as trembling excitement shivered over her skin. 'What do you want me to do?'

'Release your hair.'

She reached up and pulled out the few remaining pins holding her bun in place and tossed them to the floor. Her hair tumbled around her shoulders. He picked up one lock and curled it around her nipple, causing her to moan with erotic anticipation.

'That is how I often imagined you,' he said, looking from her breasts and up to her eyes. 'That constraining

bun set free and your hair circling your naked breasts.'
He grinned. 'But my imagination was obviously lacking. I never imagined you would look like such a voluptuous temptress.'

His eyes moved over her body, leaving trails of heat in their wake, and she had never felt more beautiful as his gaze stroked her.

He cupped both breasts. She closed her eyes and inhaled a breath,as his fingers lightly pinched each sensitive tip.

She opened her eyes and looked down at him. 'I thought I was supposed to be pleasuring you, not the other way around.'

'This gives me pleasure. Looking at your stunning body gives me a lot of pleasure.'

She sent him a seductive smile. 'As much pleasure as this?'

She lifted herself up, positioned herself over his arousal and slid down with a sinuous wiggle, taking him inside her to the hilt.

An animal growl escaped his lips and she smiled.

'Was that a yes?' she whispered. 'Is this what you want?'

'Yes,' he said, the word hardly distinguishable from his primal moans.

He placed his hands on her hips and she moved up and down on his shaft, in time to the call of her own body's needs. The fire within her burned hotter and hotter with each stroke, taking her higher and higher.

His fierce growls matched her cries of ecstasy, growing louder and louder, as the tension in her body wound tighter and tighter. Just as she thought she was about to crash over the apex, his arms took possession of her, spun her on to her back, and he pushed himself even deeper within her. Losing herself completely, as wave after wave shuddered through her, she cried out his name and sank back onto the bed, exhausted but replete.

Once again they lay together, both breathing hard, hearts pounding furiously.

'So is the insatiable woman finally satisfied?' he said as he rolled off her.

'For now.' She gave a small giggle. 'But the night is still young.'

He laughed, wrapped her in his arms and kissed her neck. 'You are completely right.'

It had been a joke, but not entirely. She hoped he had plenty of energy, because she wanted much more of him, and if tonight was to be their only night together she was not going to let him sleep, not for one single minute.

Chapter Fourteen

'You need to go.' Isaac was shaken awake from his brief sleep following another energetic and particularly enjoyable bout of lovemaking.

'Go?' He blinked heavy eyes and rolled over to see Adelaide now wearing her nightdress and furiously pulling a brush through her tangled hair. They'd made no commitment to each other, but he had expected to spend more than just one night together. If a lover had ever before told him to leave the next morning he would have counted himself a lucky man, but for some reason he did not want to leave Adelaide's bed.

'Joshua sometimes comes into my room in the mornings. He can't see you here.'

Relief washed through him.

'Here, let me do that,' he said, reaching out for her hairbrush.

'No.' She snatched it away. 'You need to leave. Please. Joshua is an early riser and I don't know how I would explain this to him.'

Isaac jumped out of bed and pulled on his trousers. 'I understand. We wouldn't want to confuse or embarrass the young boy.'

She raised an eyebrow of grudging acknowledgement on hearing her words reflected back at him, then paused in her brushing, her avid gaze moving over his still naked chest.

'I *have* to go, remember,' he said drily, pulling on his shirt.

'Yes, yes, of course.' She went back to vigorously brushing her hair. 'But, well, perhaps we need to talk about what happened.'

'Of course.'

'Before you leave.'

'Now? I thought you said I had to go before Joshua arrived?'

'I mean before you leave Hartfield Hall and go back to London with the rest of the cast and crew. Perhaps we should make some time later this morning.'

'I like the sound of that,' he said suggestively, licking his lips.

'I mean so we can *talk* before you go,' she said, flicking the hairbrush in his direction and laughing.

Did she really expect him to leave today, after last night? How could he possibly go now? How could he walk away after what they had shared together? That, too, was a new sensation for him. Something very strange was happening to him.

'I'll tell Peregrine I'm staying a bit longer.' He looked at the bed, with its tousled sheets, the bedclothes fallen on the floor, and at her abandoned clothes tossed carelessly around the room. 'We need to have that conversation, don't we? Although I can think of much more enjoyable ways to spend our time together than talking. Can't you?'

That had to be the reason for this unfamiliar state in which he found himself. He needed more of that glorious body, wanted their lovemaking to continue until they had fully gratified themselves. It couldn't be anything deeper than that. Could it?

She gave him a smile that was decidedly flirtatious. 'Yes, but not now.' She placed the hairbrush on the dressing table and waved both her hands towards the door in a shooing motion.

He quickly kissed her lips, then turned the key in the connecting door, hoping it would be the last time it would be barred to him, then shut it behind him.

He pulled the bell cord to summon his valet and looked out of the window at the estate, at the newly risen sun sending a golden light over the gardens and woodlands. He had never before seen Hartfield Hall look more serene, more idyllic, more perfect. He could hardly believe this was the same place where he had endured so much misery as a child.

The valet entered, bearing a pitcher of hot water, a bowl, towels and his shaving gear.

'Good morning, Your Grace,' the valet greeted him as he placed his instruments on the washstand. 'You're up bright and early this morning.'

'Yes, it's such a glorious morning I couldn't stay in bed a moment longer.'

Did Isaac notice a barely perceptible raise of his eyebrows? Did the man cast a quick look in the direction of his carefully made bed? No matter. The man presumably suspected he had spent the evening in the arms of one of the actresses—that was certainly what his father would have done.

While the valet sharpened the razor on the leather strop, Isaac washed himself in the warm water.

'Last night was a delight,' the valet said, as he used the shaving brush to lather Isaac's face.

'It was, wasn't it?' he agreed, remembering the power of his feelings when he made love to Adelaide. It wasn't just the physical intimacy that had left him feeling so fulfilled, nor was it the surprising intensity of her passionate nature, it was also the closeness he had felt when he held her tight. It was ridiculous, he knew that, but at the same time it was almost as if it wasn't just their bodies that were joined, but their souls. He had never felt like that with a woman before and, while it was exhilarating, he had to admit it was also very unnerving.

'I'm sure it's a night Lord Joshua will never forget.'

'What?' Isaac sat up and only the quick actions of

the valet prevented his chin from being nicked with the razor. 'Oh, yes, I'm sure he won't,' he added, lying back down. Of course the man was talking about the play. No one knew anything about the even more delightful performance that had taken place between himself and Adelaide in private and that was how she presumably wanted to keep it.

And how he wanted to keep it as well, he added to himself. Later today they would discuss what this meant for both of them.

From his perspective, he only ever wanted uncomplicated relationships with his lovers. He most certainly wanted Adelaide to continue to be his lover and nothing else.

Didn't he? Wasn't that what he wanted?

Of course he did. What was the other option? Marriage? That was ridiculous. She knew he was not the marrying kind and hadn't she also insisted she had no desire to marry, ever again?

The valet finished shaving him, wiped off the remaining soap and placed a warm towel over Isaac's face.

But if she expected him to marry her, would it be so bad? Marriage would mean going to bed with her every night, waking up every morning with her in his arms, and there would be no fleeing her room in a hurry as if they had done something shameful. It would mean spending his days and nights in her company. That could never be considered a hardship.

He removed the towel and sat up in shock. What the hell was he thinking? One night with a woman, albeit the most enchanting, intoxicating woman he had ever met, and he was already tempted to change the habits of a lifetime? He was getting way ahead of himself. He would have the conversation with Adelaide and see what she expected of him. If she wanted marriage, then he would bite the bullet and agree. Yes. He would accept his fate like a man and make the best of it.

With that he began whistling a jaunty tune as his valet helped him dress for the day.

Adelaide's worries had all been for naught. Once she had dressed for breakfast she entered Joshua's bedchamber to find her son still fast asleep. The late night and the excitement of the play had obviously exhausted him.

Just as she was about to leave he opened his eyes and smiled at her. Within a few seconds he was out of bed and immediately chattering.

'I think I'll wear my fairy costume again today,' he said, picking up his wings.

'No, that has to be saved for the play,' she said, removing the diaphanous wings from his hands. 'Now get dressed so you can join the other actors at breakfast. I'm sure you'll all have a lot to talk about.'

Thankfully he made no further fuss and they were soon heading down the stairs.

'Why are you doing that, Mama?' Joshua asked just as they reached the door of the breakfast room.

'Doing what?' She looked around to see what he was alluding to.

'You're humming.'

'Am I?' She hadn't noticed. 'I suppose I'm still happy after last night's performance.' Her hand covered her mouth as if she had revealed something she shouldn't, then she gave a little laugh.

They entered the breakfast room and everyone exuberantly greeted Joshua, then said a polite hello to her.

'Mama was so pleased with last night's performance she was humming all the way down the stairs.'

Adelaide caught Isaac's eye. She tried not to smile and hoped her cheeks had not turned a tell-tale red, although she could not help but notice Peregrine looking from her to Isaac and back again.

Fortunately, the rest of the cast and crew were busy eating substantial meals and chattering and laughing among themselves.

Adelaide discovered she was much hungrier than she usually was and served herself a generous plate of eggs, smoked kippers and several slices of toast, which she smothered with generous amounts of butter and marmalade.

Voices swirled around her as Adelaide contentedly

ate her meal, catching Isaac's eye on occasion and exchanging a secret smile.

'The moment breakfast is over we have some packing to do, if we're to be back in London on time,' Peregrine announced to the table. 'Isaac informs me he won't be joining us immediately as he has some loose ends to tie up here at Hartfield Hall.' He cast another look in Adelaide's direction, his eyebrows raised, and this time she did feel heat rush to her cheeks.

Adelaide knew she had to say something—she was, after all, the hostess—so, hoping everyone would think her blushes were due to shyness at talking in front of a large group, she rose to her feet.

'I think I speak for everyone in the household and the village when I say your visit has been simply marvellous and last night was unforgettable.' She made a point of not even glancing at Isaac, sure it would cause her blushes to burn even brighter. 'Hopefully, we will be able to make performances on the Hartfield estate a regular event.'

'Hear, hear,' Isaac said.

'I believe making it a regular event is the loose end that Isaac has to tie up,' Peregrine added, his eyebrows still raised, a knowing smile on his lips. 'Thank you, Duchess, for being such a gracious hostess and welcoming this band of players into your glorious home.'

That was greeted with a 'hear, hear' from everyone around the table.

'Now, come on, people, your adoring public wait for no one,' Peregrine added, clapping his hands together.

'Can I go with them?' Joshua asked his mama in a quiet voice.

'Not today,' Adelaide answered. 'But perhaps we'll go down to London soon and we can visit the Starlight Theatre.'

'Where you will, of course, be honoured guests,' Peregrine said over the sounds of chairs being pushed out and people leaving the room.

Joshua followed them, chattering away to Peregrine, leaving Adelaide and Isaac alone at the breakfast table.

She looked over at the footmen clearing the table and sideboard of discarded dishes. 'Perhaps we should adjourn to the morning room while the others are busy packing so we won't be in the way.'

They needed to have that talk and the sooner the better, although what she was going to say she was not entirely sure.

He followed her from the breakfast room and, as they passed through the doorway, his hand lightly touched her wrist, sending shivers rippling up her arm. They entered the morning room and the door had barely shut when she was in his arms and he was kissing her.

It was not what they were here for, but it felt good, very good. She was sure if she could spend an eternity being held by him, kissed and caressed by him, she would know complete happiness.

'Having you back in my arms was all I could think about from the moment you walked into the breakfast room,' he said when their lips finally parted. 'You don't know how much self-control I had to exercise to not touch you, to sit there and act as if I was not remembering you naked, recalling the touch of your skin, the feel of your lips, your lovely legs wrapped around me.'

He kissed her neck and she all but purred under his touch.

'We said we should talk,' she said, her eyes closed as she turned her head to the side, exposing her sensitive skin to his lips and trying to remember what they had intended to discuss.

'We also said there were much better ways we could make use of our time than talking.'

'Yes, but before we, well, make better use of our time, we do perhaps need to talk about what happened.'

'Then let's sit. I for one can't think straight with you in my arms.'

Taking her by the hand, he crossed the room and they sat on the nearest sofa.

She drew in a breath. 'Last night was, well, it was rather...'

'Yes, it was, wasn't it?' he said with a mischievous smile.

'But I want you to know it meant nothing.'

His smile died and she immediately regretted her words. 'I don't mean it meant nothing to me. It was the most wonderful experience of my life; it was, well, it was nothing short of divine.'

That smile returned, much to her relief. 'It was, rather, wasn't it?'

'I just meant that I have no expectations of you. I certainly don't expect a proposal of marriage or anything like that.'

'I see.'

She had expected to see relief on his face, but instead his expression was carefully blank. Did he not believe her?

'I'm not a debutante. I don't have to remain chaste until my wedding night, so no harm has been done.'

'Of course.'

'You don't seem pleased,' she said rather hesitantly.

'No, no, of course I'm pleased. As I said, I'm not exactly the marrying kind and I fully appreciate your desire to keep your independence. But, well, where does that leave us?'

She shrugged. 'This is all rather new to me, but as long as you're at Hartfield Hall my bedroom door will always be open to you.' She blushed slightly at the formality of that statement.

'I hope it's not just your bedroom door that will be open to me,' he said with that roguish smile she was coming to love.

She shifted in her chair, attempting to relieve the sudden coiling tension deep inside her, but knowing there was only one way, and one man, who could do that.

'I believe that would also be agreeable,' she replied. 'More than agreeable.'

The sound of carriages drawing up outside the house drew their attention to the window.

'I think before you make good on that promise, we need to say goodbye to our guests,' he said, standing up and offering her his hand.

She placed her hand lightly in his. Tremors rippled up her arm and she wondered how she was going to get through the farewells without revealing to everyone present just how intense her desire was for this exceedingly handsome man.

Chapter Fifteen

With a great deal of noise, the caravan of cast and crew, laden down with props and scenery, finally made its way down the drive, out onto the country lane and disappeared into the distance.

The house and gardens suddenly felt very quiet and Adelaide expected Joshua to be bereft.

'So, would you like to go tadpoling, or perhaps we can restage that battle?' Isaac said, anticipating the boy's regret at seeing all his new friends disappear. He looked up at her and mimed the word sorry.

He had nothing to apologise for and she was grateful for his concern over Joshua's well-being.

'No, not today. I'm afraid I'm going to be very busy,' her serious son announced. 'Peregrine said I would also make a sub-slimy director. So I'm going to write, direct and star in my own production, then put it on for everyone on the estate and in the village.'

'That's very enterprising of you,' Isaac said approvingly. 'Is it to be a one-man show? I can't wait to see it.'

'No, last night I invited some of the village children to come over to the Hall. They'll be arriving soon, so I'll be busy with my production and I won't be able to play with you and Mama today.'

Adelaide bit her bottom lip to stop herself from smiling at the earnest little boy. 'Oh, that's all right. Isaac and I will just have to find other ways to pass the time.'

'Perhaps you two can play together while I'm at work,' Joshua said, looking between Isaac and Adelaide. She had to bite even harder on her bottom lip to prevent a delighted laugh from escaping.

'Yes, I'd be more than happy to play with your mother,' Isaac said with a straight face and this time she couldn't hold in her laughter.

'You can have your rehearsals in the garden,' she said, adopting a more serious expression. 'I'll ask Nanny to supervise and arrange for Cook to have some refreshments sent out to you and your friends.'

'Cast,' Joshua corrected. 'My fellow actors are called the cast.'

Happy with those arrangements, Joshua stood at the top of the stairs and awaited the arrival of his new cast of actors.

'Now that I've been given permission to play with you, I can think of lots of new games we could try,' Isaac said wickedly.

'Really? There's more than what you showed me last night?'

'I'm sure I can come up with a few interesting games that I think you'll enjoy,' he said as they walked towards the stairs that led them back to their rooms.

'And once we've played as many as you can think of,' she said, anticipation throbbing through her entire body, 'then we can go back and play the same games over and over again, as I doubt I'm going to get tired of them any time soon.'

Once they reached the top of the stairs, they both looked around to make sure there were no servants in sight, then raced down the hallway like giddy children and into his bedchamber. Once the door closed behind them, they had their clothes off faster than Adelaide would have thought possible and all but threw themselves onto the bed and into each other's arms.

The rest of the day was spent in bed together, exploring each other's bodies, talking, laughing, then once again making love. When she became a wealthy widow, Adelaide had imagined what she could do with her new-found freedom, but never for a moment had she considered taking a lover. If she had known what ecstasy was possible in the arms of a man, it would have been top of her list.

She knew it was unrealistic to hope this could last for very long, so for now she would not allow herself to think of the future, but to just enjoy the moment.

As the morning moved into afternoon, they forgot

all about luncheon, preferring to feast on each other, until they finally slipped into a drowsy sleep.

The sound of a carriage crunching up the drive dragged Adelaide out of her slumber. Naked, she walked across the room and peeped around the curtain. Were the actors returning? Had they forgotten something? Whatever it was, she hoped the servants would be able to deal with it, as nothing or no one could draw her away from this room, this man, and her fervent anticipation of continued passionate exertions.

'Oh, no,' she squealed, throwing herself away from the window and up against the wall, suddenly completely awake. She raced across the room, pulled on her chemise, picked up the rest of her clothes and quickly rushed through the connecting door to her own room, leaving a baffled Isaac lying naked in the middle of his bed.

'What brings you to Hartfield Hall?' Adelaide asked as she kissed her mother on each cheek, then tucked a stray lock back into her bun and did a quick check to make sure her blouse was correctly buttoned and her skirt was straight.

'I've got something important I need to discuss with you,' Lady Wentworth said as the maid helped her out of her travelling cloak.

'If it's about the letter Henrietta and Priscilla's lawyer sent, then I think my letter to you made my feelings on that very clear.'

Her mother held up both hands to halt her daughter's words. 'Yes, yes, I know you have, my dear, but I've had a chance to think about things and I believe we should not give up entirely. We just need to reassess our approach.'

Adelaide stifled a sigh. She should have known. Just like Henrietta and Priscilla, her mother would not be willing to give up without a fight, even if the battle had been lost before they'd even started.

'Would you like to take tea, Mother, or would you prefer to rest after your journey?'

'Yes, tea would be lovely, then we can have a nice long chat.'

Adelaide signalled to the maid and led her mother through to the drawing room.

'I don't know what you are planning, but you won't succeed,' Adelaide said bluntly as she took her seat. 'Isaac Radcliff is the new Duke of Hartfield and the sooner you, Henrietta and Priscilla accept that fact, the better. They've got it in their heads that they now have proof that the marriage was invalid, but they are grasping at straws. If they thought about it at all logically, then they would realise that for themselves.'

Adelaide braced herself for the expected arguments, but her mother merely sighed. 'Yes, I'm afraid I agree. I have had another meeting with our family lawyer and he has convinced me that pursuing a case against Isaac Radcliff would be a very expensive waste of time and the only people likely to benefit from it are the lawyers through their exorbitant fees.'

Thank goodness her mother had finally seen some sense. 'Good, so we can put that all in the past.'

'Hmm,' her mother said as the maid entered and began serving the tea. 'Not entirely. Your son is still second in line for the dukedom.'

'Yes, I know. That has never been under dispute.'

'And if Radcliff does not have any children then Joshua will eventually inherit the dukedom.'

'That, too, is correct.'

'Well,' her mother said, with a smile that could only be described as self-satisfied as she picked up her teacup. 'If you married Isaac Radcliff, and denied him any legitimate children of his own, then your son would definitely inherit the title.'

Adelaide stared at her mother, hardly able to believe what she was hearing. 'You want me to—'

'Don't look so shocked. It's a perfectly sensible solution. Or if you feel it's morally wrong to not perform your wifely duties and you do provide him with a son, it won't be so bad, since that boy will be the next Duke of Hartfield. Either way, we'll keep the dukedom in our family where it belongs. That's so much better than him marrying some trollop he meets at the theatre and fathering a child with her.'

Her mother sat back in her chair and took a sip of her tea, looking decidedly pleased with herself.

Adelaide was aghast. She was expected to marry, yet again, not because she wanted to, but for other people's benefit. Adelaide did not care about the title, she did not care whether Joshua became a duke—in fact, she was sure her son would be much happier if he didn't inherit the title. But it was important to her mother, so Adelaide was expected to once again sacrifice herself on the marriage altar.

The fact that it was Isaac she was expected to marry, the man whose bed she had just left, was neither here nor there. She had married once because she was told to and she would not do it again. She would not marry someone just to suit other people's ambitions. She would not give up her independence, not for anyone.

'No, Mother I will not do it,' she said firmly.

'Don't be so hasty, dear. The man is not entirely repugnant. He does move in rather vile circles, but that should not affect you. It's not as if you're not already used to turning a blind eye to your husband's peccadillos with women of a certain class, is it?'

A sudden pain gripped Adelaide's chest. Not because of her late husband's so-called peccadillos. They had never affected her in the slightest and not because accepting his constant infidelities was what was expected of her, but because she simply didn't care. Yet the thought of Isaac with another woman was like a dagger in her heart.

'Don't look so shocked, Adelaide,' her mother continued as Adelaide tried to drag in a steadying breath. 'It's not as if I'm expecting you to do something you haven't already done and surely this time it will be far more agreeable than your last marriage.'

Before Adelaide could formulate any words from the ones whirling round in her head, the door flew open and Joshua burst in. 'Grandmama, I'm going to be an actor and a famous director when I grow up,' he announced, climbing up onto the seat beside his grandmother.

She laughed indulgently and kissed her grandson's cheek. 'I thought you intended to become a soldier, like your toys.'

'That was before the Summer's Dream came and I got the bug.'

'Oh, no, you've been unwell?' She looked to Adelaide for clarification. 'Why did you not tell me?'

'No, Mother, he means the acting bug. We had members of the Starlight Theatre staying recently and they put on a performance of *A Midsummer Night's Dream*. Joshua played a fairy and now he wants to be an actor.'

'You had actors? Here? At Hartfield Hall?' she said, drawing out each word as if they were leaving a bad taste in her mouth.

'Yes, the Duke invited them here to rehearse and

they kindly staged a performance in the gardens in front of the tenants, servants and everyone in the village.'

'Oh, I see,' her mother said, trying to take in this information. 'So where are these…actor people…now?'

'They returned to London today.'

Her mother visibly relaxed.

'You should have come yesterday, Grandmama, and you would have seen me playing a fairy.' Joshua jumped off the sofa and performed his small dance, much to his grandmother's delight. 'But don't worry, I'm writing and directing a play and we should be ready for our full dress rehearsal soon and you can watch that instead.'

'That's lovely, dear. There's nothing wrong with amateur dramatics, but remember members of the aristocracy do not take to the professional stage.'

'I believe the new Duke of Hartfield is involved in the professional stage, is he not?' Adelaide added, drawing her mother's attention to something she would once have seen as unacceptable in a potential husband.

Her mother sent her a pinched smile. 'No one is perfect, Adelaide, and sometimes we all have to make sacrifices for the greater good.'

'And sometimes we have had enough of making sacrifices and we don't want to make any more,' she shot back.

'Don't be silly, dear,' her mother said dismissively.

'Women always have to make sacrifices for others, from the moment they are born until the day they die. That is something I should not have to point out to you.'

Adelaide clenched her teeth tightly together to stop herself from shouting in front of her son. Once her temper was under control she looked her mother firmly in the eye. 'I did what was expected of me once before, but I will no longer be used as a pawn in other people's games.'

That was something her mother would have to accept, along with anyone else who wanted to use her for their own advantage.

After Adelaide's sudden, frantic departure, Isaac had crossed the room, looked down to the entrance and seen the reason for her panic. Lady Wentworth's servants were unloading her carriage at the front of the house.

He released a long sigh of exasperation and pulled on his clothes. It seemed the idyll he was hoping for, the days and nights spent in bed with Adelaide, had come to a sudden, untimely end.

Instead, he would have to endure being subjected to Lady Wentworth's snobbery and contempt. Thank goodness he was well practised in deflecting the insulting barbs fired at him by the aristocracy.

He entered the drawing room, curious to see how

Lady Wentworth's ability to insult him would compare with Henrietta, Priscilla, Winifred and all those others he'd had the misfortune to encounter growing up.

'Oh, you're here,' Lady Wentworth said as he entered, looking suspiciously pleased to see him. 'You didn't tell me the Duke was still in residence,' she said to Adelaide.

The Duke? In residence?

This was new.

'Yes, I'm still here and, yes, you are most welcome to stay in *my* home, Lady Wentworth,' he said in a deliberate act of provocation as he took his seat, then waited for the inevitable fireworks.

'That's very kind of you,' came her confusing answer. 'I was just saying to Adelaide—'

'My mother was just saying she agrees with me that the legal case against you is a waste of time.' Adelaide grimaced at her mother. That, along with her rigid posture and tense expression, made it obvious there was a lot more the two women had been discussing that neither was revealing.

'Yes, I was just telling Adelaide that I was foolish to ever think we had a right to contest the will or your right to be the new Duke of Hartfield,' Lady Wentworth continued, her expression still strangely benign. 'I do hope you can forgive me for my momentary lapse. I should never have let Lady Henrietta and Lady Hampton talk me into joining them in that folly.'

Isaac looked at Adelaide for an explanation, but she was too busy scowling at her mother.

'There's nothing to forgive,' he said, guardedly. 'You were just looking out for your daughter and grandson.'

Her head bobbed in acknowledgement. 'That is so kind of you. I was also just telling Adelaide it is time she thought of remarrying. Under the circumstances, nobody would find it odd that she doesn't wait until her year of mourning has passed before she takes another walk up the aisle. Don't you agree?'

Adelaide glared at her mother, obviously not happy about the direction the conversation had taken.

'That's up to Adelaide, surely,' he said, looking from smiling mother to glowering daughter.

'Oh, how modern of you... Your Grace.' The smile faltered slightly as if the honorific was uncomfortable in her mouth, then returned as bright as before.

'Please, call me Isaac. Your Grace always makes me feel as though I've turned into my father.'

'How kind of you. Yes, your father was quite the character, wasn't he? And I'm sure you'll also be able to admirably live up to the prestigious Hartfield dukedom.'

Isaac stared at her, waiting for her to laugh at what surely was a joke. She didn't laugh, just continued to beam that forced smile at him.

'I'll do my best,' he said with some irony. 'Did Adelaide tell you we just had a troupe of actors staying at Hartfield Hall? I'm sure that's something my father would have approved of. My mother, his first wife, certainly would have.'

As expected, the older lady's smile faltered again. 'Yes, Adelaide mentioned it. How delightful. What a shame I missed them. You do mix with such interesting and colourful characters.'

'Just like my father.'

'Yes,' she said and took a sip of her tea.

Isaac resisted the temptation to shake his head in disbelief. When he was the bastard son, nothing he could do or say had earned the approval of the aristocracy, so he'd given up trying at an early age. Now that he was a duke it seemed nothing he could do or say would give any offence. He was above reproach. Would that make misbehaving lose its appeal? Only time would tell, but he had no intention of changing the habits of a lifetime. Not yet anyway.

'So, as I was saying before you arrived, Isaac...' that obsequious smile returned '... Adelaide really does need to think about marriage. She is only four and twenty and still a lovely young woman, one any man would wish to have as his bride.' She looked down at Joshua sitting on the floor at his mother's feet. 'And she has already proven she can produce sons.'

He looked cautiously at Adelaide. She had already made it clear to him she had no intention of marrying again, but it seemed she had not made that equally clear to her mother.

'I believe I have already said that is surely up to Adelaide. Should she choose to marry again, that will be up to her, as will her choice of husband.'

'I believe I can speak for myself,' Adelaide said, frowning at both of them. 'And what I wish to say is that I intend to remain a widow. The former Duke left me very well provided for and I do not need another man in my life.'

Isaac sent her a sideways glance. Only moments before she'd been making it exceedingly clear to him just how much she did want a man, if not in her life, then certainly in her bed. She blushed slightly, possibly thinking the same thing.

'If you remain single, you'll be a target for every fortune hunter in the country,' her mother protested, looking in appeal to Isaac. 'Don't you agree?'

'I think—'

'They can hunt as much as they like,' Adelaide interrupted. 'But they'll soon find, just like you, Mother, that they are wasting their time.'

'Isaac, I'm sure you'll agree that a woman as beautiful as my daughter will soon have a string of suitors at her door desperate to marry her.'

The fact that she was beautiful was something Isaac could not dispute. Every time he looked at her she seemed to grow more stunning. Her skin appeared more flawless, her eyes seemed to sparkle more brightly. She became more captivating and he was certainly falling hopelessly under her spell.

But right now, that captivating woman was looking as if being called beautiful was the worst insult that could be levelled at her.

'And that imaginary string of suitors will be disappointed,' she said coolly. 'Just as you will be, Mother.'

'So how long do you intend to remain at Hartfield Hall, Isaac?' Lady Wentworth asked, abruptly changing the subject.

That was a question he should be asking himself, yet was one he had been avoiding. 'I'm not sure. I do have work commitments back in London I have been neglecting, so I must return to them at some time.' He looked at Adelaide. 'But not just yet.'

'Commitments?' Lady Wentworth echoed, as if this was a foreign concept. 'Surely now that you are the Duke of Hartfield, and, dare I say it, a man of substantial means, other people can take care of these commitments for you so you can remain here.'

'And what would I do with my time? I'm not one for taking endless long walks in the countryside. I don't shoot or ride to hounds and have no intention of taking up either of those activities.'

Although the prospect of being here was now seeming a lot less distasteful, especially after Adelaide's suggestion that the estate could be used to stage theatrical productions and such events would benefit everyone connected to the estate. Including him. It would certainly give him a good excuse to return to Hartfield Hall. Often.

'Oh, I believe there are other things that could keep you amused.' She looked from Isaac to Adelaide and back again, her expression decidedly smug.

He caught Adelaide's eye. She blushed slightly, then turned his attention back to Lady Wentworth who was sipping her tea.

She knew.

And if she knew that there was something between her daughter and him, what was she likely to do with that knowledge? The glint in her eyes answered that question.

She wanted her daughter married. To him. How could he have missed what this conversation had really been all about? Dukes were not only forgiven any transgression, including working in the theatre, but it was not just actresses who suddenly saw them as eligible husbands. They were also enthusiastically pursued by ambitious mothers looking to marry off their daughters.

Lady Wentworth was astute enough to discern that he was attracted to her daughter, but what would she think and do if she found out that Adelaide was already his lover? He knew the answer to that—she would bring as much pressure as possible to bear to get them up the aisle. Adelaide had just made it clear how she felt about marrying again. But for him, the most important question was, how did he feel about it?

Chapter Sixteen

Days passed and her mother settled in for what appeared to be a long visit. Adelaide found herself in the bizarre situation of fending off her mother's attempt to foist a man on her, trying to pretend she was not in the slightest bit interested in him, while at the same time spending every moment she could in that same man's bed.

She was tempted to tell her mother outright that Isaac Radcliff was now her lover, but they had no intention of marrying. The thought of shocking her mother certainly had its appeal, but once she had recovered from the initial shock, Adelaide knew exactly what would happen. The pressure to marry Isaac would increase to an unbearable degree.

It would be like her debutante days all over again. Her mother would give no consideration as to what Adelaide wanted, only what would benefit other people, and would pass that off as Adelaide doing her duty as a good daughter should. She would not put it past her mother to attempt to pressure Isaac into making an 'honest' woman of her daughter and that Adelaide would never allow. She did not want to be made to marry against her will and nor did she want Isaac to suffer the same fate.

No, things would stay exactly as they were and she would continue to deflect her mother's futile match-making. She loved being an independent woman, and every time she entered Isaac's bedchamber, or he came to hers, she was reminded of that fact. She was now able to take a lover if she chose. That was something she would once have thought an impossibility, but the freedom of it gave her more happiness than she could ever have imagined.

Each time they made love it was even more wonderful than the last. She had discovered so much about his body and he had taught her a lot about her own. But it wasn't just his prowess as a lover that was filling her with such happiness. As much as she adored every moment of their lovemaking, she also cherished the times they spent together lying in each other's arms, talking the night away, sharing stories from their past, laughing over funny incidents and comforting each other over the tribulations they had both endured.

While she knew their time together had to come to an end eventually, Isaac appeared to be making no immediate plans to return to London. She thought he might return for the opening of *A Midsummer Night's*

Dream, but he stayed. Instead, he was content to read what the critics had to say in the daily papers, especially as the production was showered with unanimous praise. He received constant updates from his assistant on what was happening at his other theatres and sent back regular letters. He often laughed that he was becoming increasingly redundant and his staff would soon forget he even existed, but still he stayed.

He'd even taken an interest in the running of the estate, asking questions about the tenants, the villagers, and the changes she had made since taking on the mantle of making it more profitable.

He really was becoming the country gentleman. Maybe he would soon be taking long walks in the countryside, shooting, or riding to hounds, although somehow she doubted it. She also hoped he would not change that much or become too domesticated. She loved the wildness about him, the way he was so different from any other man she had ever met or was likely to meet in society.

But two weeks into her mother's visit, while they were having breakfast, a letter arrived that changed everything.

'What is it?' she asked, seeing his expression darken.

'It's from Henrietta and Priscilla's lawyer, notifying me that a date has been set for the first hearing into the legality of my parents' marriage. Their lawyer says my half-sisters are insisting that the letters found in this house are proof that my parents never actually wed and are insisting the court case go ahead.'

'Letters? What letters?' her mother asked with sudden interest.

'When Henny and Prissy—I mean Lady Henrietta and Lady Hampton were staying here, they found some love letters in the attic where Isaac's parents discussed his coming marriage to Winifred,' Adelaide informed her. 'They believe that proves both Isaac's parents knew they were not legally married.'

'I see,' her mother said, dragging out those two words. Adelaide could almost see her mind working. This development opened up yet another way she could ensure she was the grandmother of a duke.

'I suppose I'm going to have to return to London to consult with my lawyer,' he said, folding up the letter and setting it beside his plate.

Adelaide could hear the reluctance in his voice. She shouldn't feel so pleased, but she did. He did not want to go back to his world. He wanted to stay here, in hers. With her. But she always knew this day would come.

'How long do you think this will all take?' She tried to ask the question in a detached manner, not wishing to give any more fuel to her mother's burning desire to see them wed, but not entirely sure if she succeeded.

She flicked a quick look in her mother's direction and saw her failure to keep her emotions in check was abundantly clear. Her mother had placed her teacup back in the saucer, abandoned her toast and marmalade and was watching the two of them with avid interest.

This, and a desire not to cause Isaac to think she was seeing more to their relationship than actually existed, stopped her from asking the other question she really wanted an answer to. *Will you be coming back to me or will the pull of the excitement of London be too much?*

'Who knows?' he said. 'I believe these things can drag on for years.'

'Years?' she blurted out, all pretence at detachment lost in that one word.

'Yes, but that does not mean I'd have to stay in London all that time. I suppose I could return on the weekends to Hartfield Hall.'

'Yes, of course, if that is what you wish,' she said, her voice straining with forced composure. She did not want her mother to know the extent of how much she wanted Isaac to return to her, nor for him to know how much the thought of them being apart was like a physical ache.

'Or you could come to London with me,' he said, his voice suddenly brightening. 'There's nothing to keep you here, is there? And I'm sure Joshua would love to see London. Didn't you promise him a visit to the Starlight Theatre?'

'Yes, please,' Joshua piped up. 'I want to see Peregrine again and tell him all about my new play.'

A weight she didn't know had been pressing down on her shoulders suddenly lifted.

'It might be nice to visit London, I suppose,' she said with as much false indifference as she could.

Nice didn't begin to describe it. They would not be apart. They could continue to spend all their time together, in and out of his bed. And more than that. He still wanted her. He was not being lured away from her by the attractions of London.

She looked over at her mother who was adopting that unfortunately familiar smug manner again.

'Yes, you two young people go off to London together,' her mother urged. 'See the sights, have fun together, and don't worry about that silly lawsuit thing. No matter the outcome, I'm sure it will all work out satisfactorily.'

She tousled Joshua's hair, causing Adelaide to sigh. Her mother obviously thought she now had two ways of securing the dukedom for her grandchild, either through the loss of the lawsuit, or through the gaining of the new Duke as a son-in-law.

Adelaide was tempted to say no, on second thought she'd remain at Hartfield Hall while Isaac was in London, so she could prove her mother wrong, but that really would be cutting off her nose to spite her face. She wanted to spend more time with Isaac, longed to do so with all her heart and soul and the thought of being away from him for possibly years with only visits at the weekends was more than she could bear. And Joshua was so looking forward to it and she would not disappoint her son.

'I suppose I could also use the time to order some more clothes.' She looked down at the drab dress she was wearing, one that Isaac had seen her in so many times. It would be nice to purchase the latest fashions and for him to see her, in private of course, in something new and more flattering than all her old gowns.

'That's settled then,' her mother said, reaching across the table and patting her hand. 'The three of you go off to London, like a happy little family. You can attend a show or two, take walks in Hyde Park, go to art exhibitions, all the things that couples like to do when they're courting.'

'Mother!' Adelaide said, her voice loud.

'Sorry, a slip of the tongue. Of course you're not courting.' She sent the two of them a victorious grin. 'But now that you're a respectable widow you won't need a chaperon. That will give you a lot more of that independence you seem to value so highly. I'm happy to remain behind and I'll look forward to the outcome.'

Her mother's grin grew wider and she was all but vibrating with self-satisfaction. 'Of the court case, I mean.'

Chapter Seventeen

The last time Adelaide had been in London it had been for the reading of the will. If anyone had told her then that in a few short months she would be back in the city and Isaac Radcliff would be her lover she would have laughed at such a preposterous idea. Now it seemed so right, almost inevitable that they would find each other.

It was agreed that they would stay in her town house, telling her disbelieving mother that it was for convenience's sake as it would be far easier for Isaac to travel to the courts and his lawyer's office from there. Her mother had mentioned slyly that Mayfair was rather a distance from the courts, but Adelaide chose to ignore her.

After their train journey they arrived at the town house full of excitement, as if on an adventure and not in the city to settle an annoying legal case.

'Please instruct the servants to make up the guest

room for the Duke,' she told the footman as he carried their luggage from the carriage and into the house.

'Very good, Your Grace,' the footman said.

She exchanged a smile with Isaac. Neither of them really expected him to sleep in that room, at least not alone.

'I've never been here,' Isaac said as they moved through to the drawing room, while Joshua rushed up to his bedroom to help Nanny unpack his toys.

'This house holds no memories of my childhood, neither good nor bad.' He sat down on the sofa in front of the window and looked out at the tree-lined street, obviously pleased by that observation.

'Did your father never bring you here?'

'No, when he was in London he always stayed with my mother and me. I didn't even know of this house's existence. It was the one he kept for his legitimate family, or, as it turns out, his illegitimate family, or whatever Henrietta and Priscilla really are.'

She sat beside him. 'Do you think there's any chance that they might win? They've both got influential husbands and it's obvious they're not going to give up until they've exhausted every possible means of proving you are not a duke.'

He shrugged. 'I never wanted the dukedom in the first place.' He smiled at her and lightly stroked her cheek. 'Although becoming the Duke of Hartfield has had one rather pleasant outcome. It brought you into my life. I can't imagine we would ever have met again if I hadn't inherited the title.'

'You know that it means nothing to me whether you are a duke or not, don't you?'

He smiled at her. 'Ah, you say that now, but how will you feel if I'm pushed off my ducal pedestal and relegated back to being a no one?'

'You'll never be a no one to me and I care naught for titles.'

His fingers continued to stroke her cheek and she sighed softly.

'But if I lose, you'll be a wealthy woman, the guardian of all that Joshua will inherit when he comes of age and I'll be a poor working theatre director with barely a penny to my name.'

'And that won't matter a fig to me,' she said, gasping as his hand travelled down her neck and his fingers ran along the collar of her blouse.

'I could become your kept man. You could set me up in an apartment in London and come and visit me whenever the mood took you.'

'I rather like the sound of that,' she said with laughter in her voice. 'I would have you all to myself whenever I wanted you. All you'd have to do is wait for me and make sure you looked as attractive as possible when I arrived so I didn't tire of you and move on to someone else.'

He laughed, his hand moving lower and slowly, teasingly, opening her top button. 'You are so wicked. And what else would you expect of me so your attention didn't wander?'

'Well, you could keep doing what you're doing now,' she responded, that now familiar delicious tension stirring deep within her body.

'More of this?' He undid several more buttons, slid his hand inside her blouse and cupped her breast. 'Is this what madam requires?'

She gasped as his thumb ran over the tight, sensitive nub. 'Yes,' she said on a sigh. 'I believe that will hold my attention.'

'Or would madam prefer it if I did this?' He lifted up the edge of her skirt, his hand sliding up the inside of her leg, over her silk stockings until it reached the naked skin of her thighs.

She gave a small moan. 'Oh, yes, I think that will definitely keep me coming back for more.' With great reluctance she pushed down his hand and with unsteady fingers did up her buttons.

'Have you tired of me already?' he said, with mock petulance.

'Of course not, but we can't do this here,' she said, her voice raspy. 'Anyone could come in.' She smiled at him. 'I want you to go up to your bedchamber and make yourself ready to do my bidding when I arrive.' Their game had made her feel decidedly brazen.

'Believe me, I've been ready to do your bidding from the moment I touched your beautiful breast.'

She looked him up and down and could see he was not lying.

'Off you go then. I expect you to earn your keep, you know.'

He touched his forehead in a deferential manner. 'Yes, madam, it will be my pleasure.'

And mine, too, Adelaide thought as he left the room. She knew it would be more in keeping with the game if she delayed going to him for a few minutes, but she just couldn't wait any longer. Instead she rushed out the door and, joining in his laughter, she overtook him on the stairs as they raced each other to the guest bedroom.

Isaac could happily spend all his time in London in bed with Adelaide, but after they'd made love he reluctantly dragged himself out of bed and pulled on the clothes he had so frantically discarded.

'So, do I pass your test?' he asked, as she remained lying in bed looking just how he liked to see her, naked, exhausted and thoroughly satisfied. 'If I lose my case, will you take me on as your kept man?'

She sent him a slow, lazy smile. 'Are you hoping I'll flatter you?'

'Yes,' he said with a laugh.

'Well…' She tapped her chin as if considering. 'I

think I might need a repeat performance to really be able to judge whether it is up to the standard I've come to expect.'

He leant over the bed, gave her naked buttocks a playful pat and kissed her. 'I've said it before and I'll say it again, you are insatiable, which is all well and good because I certainly cannot get enough of you.'

The temptation to climb back into bed with her was all but overwhelming, but he had arranged to meet with his assistant before his appointment with his lawyer. The sooner he got all that business out of the way the sooner he could get back to Adelaide.

'I have to go,' he said, kissing her one more time. 'But I'll be back as soon as I can for that promised repeat performance, or several repeat performances if that is what you demand.'

'Mmm…' she said, and moved sensuously on the bed.

He groaned. 'Don't do that or I'll never leave this room and Henny and Prissy will win their case through my forfeiture.'

She sat up in the bed, and to his regret pulled the sheet around her. 'Good luck with the lawyer,' she said.

He shrugged. 'Either way I win, or, at least, I don't lose.' With that he took one final kiss and headed out the door.

After visiting his office at the Elysian Theatre and discovering his assistant was doing an admirable job without his presence, Isaac took a cab to the meeting with his lawyer.

Usually, when he visited Archibald Worthington it was to discuss such things as the contract for a new theatre he was purchasing or something else connected to the world he loved. On such occasions, he'd race up the carpeted stairs that led to the office with a spring in his step, excited by his new enterprise. Today he walked slowly, his hand on the polished wooden banister as if he needed its support. This was all so tiresome and the sooner it was over the better.

He had grown up thinking and accepting that his parents weren't married, so finding that they were made no difference to him at this age. If he could, he'd allow Henrietta and Priscilla to win their legal battle, but it was not up to him. The law would decide.

The secretary greeted him and told him to go straight through to the office, where Archibald was waiting for him, standing behind his large desk which, as usual, was cluttered with files, fountain pens, blotters and inkwells.

'Isaac, or should I say, Your Grace, how good to see you again,' Archibald said, shaking his hand and gesturing to a seat in front of the desk.

'Isaac will do just fine. I never want to be addressed by that title.'

'I'm afraid you are going to have to get used to being called Your Grace,' the lawyer said matter of factly, taking his seat, untying the ribbons holding together a pile of papers and opening a file.

'No, I will always be Isaac, whatever the outcome of this lawsuit.'

'Unfortunately, the laws of primogeniture say otherwise,' he said, looking down at the document in his hand, then back up at Isaac.

'So my half-sisters still intend to take me to court.'

'Yes, I'm afraid Lady Henrietta and Lady Hampton are—how shall I put it?'

'As stubborn as mules.'

'Precisely. It has been drawn to their attention, repeatedly, how much gossip such a court case would generate, how it would negatively impact on them and their husbands, and how they have no chance whatsoever of winning.'

'And still they won't back down. Typical. What happens next?'

'That is what I wish to discuss with you. I have had several meetings with the ladies' lawyer and their husbands to find a solution to this problem that does not involve going to court and can keep the publicity and gossip to a minimum.'

'And?'

'Lady Henrietta's husband has offered to take up a military posting in India—Calcutta, I believe—and Lady Hampton's husband has agreed to accept a diplomatic posting in Russia, in St Petersburg.'

'That is excellent news. When do they leave and, more to the point, how long will they be away? And how does this affect the court case?'

'That, I'm afraid, is up to you.'

'Me? I might be a duke now, but I hardly have control over the British military or the diplomatic service.'

'No, but you do have the ability to minimise the scandal that will inevitably erupt when word gets out about your sisters' circumstances. Their husbands, not surprisingly, do not wish to put their wives through such a humiliation and that is why they want to take them out of the country.'

The lawyer paused as if gathering his resources. 'In exchange for doing so, the husbands have requested that you marry the Duchess of Hartfield.'

Isaac stared at him, unsure he had heard correctly. 'They what?'

'I appreciate this is a rather unusual and unexpected request, but marriages for the sake of the family, or to avoid scandal, or for some other reason of convenience, are certainly very common among the aristocracy.'

Isaac continued to stare at him as he digested what the man was saying.

'I also appreciate that the Duchess is not officially out of her period of mourning yet, but needs must. As soon as you place an announcement of your intended nuptials in the paper, Lieutenant Colonel Westleigh and Lord Hampton will make arrangements to move overseas. Their wives will have no choice but to go with them.'

'And how will this prevent the scandal of their illegitimacy?'

'It won't, not entirely. But the husbands are confident they can convince their wives that such a marriage will definitely distract society from focusing on them and hopefully by the time they return, if they return, the gossips will have moved on to another scandal.'

'And there's always plenty of those to go around.'

'Indeed. The husbands also have another request.'

'Besides arranging my marriage?' Isaac said drily.

'Yes. They ask that you do not discuss your half-sisters' unfortunate situation with anyone and, should they return to England, that you never, ever mention it to them. The husbands believe this will allow their wives to maintain the illusion that they remain legitimate.'

'All right,' Isaac said slowly. 'I can see some merit in this idea, but there is one thing no one seems to have considered. The Duchess. She also has to agree to this. Why do you think she might?'

'I believe the Duchess will also see the great advantages of this arrangement. She, too, is, I'm sure, not keen for her late husband's scandalous deeds to be aired in public. Such a marriage will also mean she will not have to worry about another woman becoming the next Duchess of Hartfield and ousting her from her home. She will continue to live at Hartfield Hall, and, of course, if you choose to have a marriage in name only, there will be no other offspring, so Lord Joshua will eventually inherit the dukedom. That is certainly to her benefit, as would having another son with you. Either way, she remains the mother of a duke.'

Isaac did not wish to point out to the lawyer that he and Adelaide were already lovers and, while they were taking every precaution against having children, there was no real guarantee in such matters. There were plenty of people who could put their existence down to precautions not working. Including himself.

But in all other matters the lawyer was right. Such an arrangement would mean no lawsuit and while he felt a great deal of animosity towards his sisters, he had no desire to humiliate them, nor did he wish to embarrass their husbands, who were blameless in all this. And what would marriage to Adelaide really change? Nothing. They were already living in the same house and sleeping together.

'All right. I'll do it. I'll get married.'

'Good. What we decided would be best was that the announcement go in the paper immediately, then you marry quickly and go abroad on an extended honeymoon. While you are away the husbands will arrange the overseas postings, convince the wives of the wisdom of dropping the case and accompanying their husbands to their new positions. And that will be the end of the matter.'

'You make it all sound so easy.'

'Not easy. Just logical. Your sisters can pretend their leaving was merely because their husbands were advancing their careers by taking up prestigious posts in places where the Empire most needs men of their high standing and ability.'

'And you think all this will contain the scandal?'

'Not entirely. News will inevitably leak out about your elevation to the peerage, but none of the people affected by the gossip will be present in England to endure it. Believe me, Your Grace, the sisters' lawyers and I have explored every avenue and we believe this is the best option for you all.

'We are certain the sisters know deep down they will not win this case and it will cause them and their husbands a great deal of harm. Despite this, they seem incapable of conceding to you, but this way, they are allowed to save face and they will be out of the country when news of your inheritance becomes well known and they can pretend none of it ever happened, and that your presence at Hartfield Hall is because you are married to the Duchess.'

Isaac nodded slowly. He could see the logic in all the lawyer was saying. Now all he had to do was convince Adelaide that this could work—that it was indeed the most sensible option for everyone.

* * *

Adelaide had no reason to be nervous, yet she found herself pacing up and down, waiting for Isaac's return with news from the lawyer.

When he finally arrived, she rushed up to the door and the questions flowed out of her before he'd even removed his hat and coat.

'What did the lawyer say? Is the case still going to go to court? Have your sisters come to their senses? How long will you have to stay in London?'

Without replying, he placed his hand on the small of her back and led her through to the drawing room and towards the sofa. His solicitous manner and awkward smile did not suggest good news.

'To answer your questions, Henny and Prissy are still intending to go ahead with the lawsuit. That is despite concerted efforts by my lawyer and their lawyer to make them see sense, but seeing sense is not Henny's or Prissy's strong suit. Even their husbands have tried to persuade them against this folly, but to no avail.'

She released an exasperated sigh. 'So it will have to go to court. Has anyone explained to them the potential damage this will do to their reputations and their husbands'? When they lose, they will likely all be shunned by society.'

'Oh, yes, that has been explained, repeatedly. Put it down to innate stubbornness or, as you said, their anger towards me for being the so-called favoured child, or some sort of loyalty to their aggrieved mother, but they will not budge.'

Adelaide was pleased he was starting to have some sympathy for his half-sisters' plight, but could not deny her disappointment at this outcome.

'So you will be remaining in London and have to spend your days at the Court of Chancery.'

'Perhaps.' His expression grew somewhat sheepish. 'Although you might be able to call a halt to the legal proceedings.'

'Me? What on earth can I do?'

His gaze dropped to his hands and he removed an invisible piece of lint from his trouser leg, his brow furrowed. It was not like him to be nervous. She prepared herself for the worse.

'The lawyer suggested it would be a good idea if you and I were to marry.'

She stared at him, unsure if she had heard him correctly. 'He said what?'

'He said the best way for us to avoid a lawsuit and to save Henny's, Prissy's and their husbands' reputations is for us to get married.'

'Your lawyer wants us to marry?' she repeated incredulously, beginning to wonder if Isaac or the lawyer, or both, were a bit touched in the head.

'I know, I know, I was as shocked as you, but thinking about it, it does make sense.'

'How could me being forced into another marriage possibly make any sense?' Adelaide said, outrage welling up inside her.

'Don't get emotional. Let's just discuss this sensibly.'

'Don't tell me how to react,' she said, seething.

Isaac sighed, walked over to the mantelpiece and leant on it, as if this was a casual conversation and he was not asking her to completely change her life. Again.

'The lawyer had a meeting with the sisters' lawyer and their husbands and they came up with a scheme. We put an immediate announcement in the paper that we are to wed, have a quick wedding, then disappear overseas on our honeymoon.'

'We do, do we?'

'Yes. Then the husbands take overseas postings and Henny and Prissy will go with them. Gossip inevitably erupts when everyone gets wind that my father was married to my mother, not the mother of Henny and Prissy, which is why I'm the Duke instead of Joshua, but we're all out of the country. By the time we get back someone else will have done something equally scandalous and the wagging tongues will have moved on to destroy some other poor blighter. Henny and Prissy can tell themselves that I'm living at Hartfield Hall because I'm married to you, not because I'm the Duke. It's all a bit ridiculous, but then, as you well know, my sisters are nothing if not ridiculous.'

'But we will be married.'

'Yes. But it won't make any difference.' He smiled at her. He actually smiled!

'It will make a lot of difference to me,' she said slowly to keep her fury under control.

'How? We are already living like a married couple, are we not, and I promise you, you will still have complete freedom to do whatever you want, just as you do now.'

'And you will kindly grant me this freedom?'

'Yes.'

'The freedom that I already have, the freedom that I will surrender by marrying you? You will kindly let me keep what I already possess, unless of course at any time you change your mind and take it off me?'

He crossed the room, sat down beside her and attempted to take her hands, which she snatched away. 'I know it's not ideal, but if we don't agree to this scheme, it will involve a long, protracted, unpleasant, not to mention expensive court case.'

'So this marriage will save both time and money?'

'Yes. And it will also save Henny and Prissy from being ridiculed. Everyone has tried to get the sisters to drop the case and they won't, but this might work.'

'So, let me get this completely clear,' she said, turning to face him. 'You want to marry me to prevent your sisters from taking you to court, to save time and money and the reputations of two stubborn women who are more than capable of acting like mature, sensible adults and calling off this lawsuit themselves?' Adelaide stated each word clearly to make sure he understood the extent of what he was asking of her.

'I know, I know, it's ludicrous, really, but the lawyers can think of no other way around it. Henny and Prissy are so blinded by their anger over me inheriting the title they're incapable of doing what's in their own best interest. So, what do you think?

'I think it is the most outrageous thing I have ever heard.'

'What? Why? It changes nothing between us. Not really.'

She stared at him in disbelief.

It changed nothing?

How could he possibly say that? It changed everything for her.

'And if nothing else it will make your mother happy,' he said with a laugh.

Heat rushed to Adelaide's cheeks, her throat suddenly tight and dry. Did this man not know her at all?

'Your mother has made no secret of the fact she wants you married again,' he continued. 'And I'm now the Duke, which is all she cares about. But think about it, Adelaide. If we were married, we wouldn't have to creep around the house the way we've been doing. That alone has to be a good reason for putting our heads in the parson's noose.'

'How romantic,' she said under her breath, wondering if she had ever really known this man either.

'So, what do you think? Will you become the Duchess of Hartfield for the second time?'

Adelaide took a moment to compose herself, her anger making it hard to get the words straight, but she was determined that Isaac would know exactly what she thought of his offensive proposal and why.

'You are going to need another meeting with your lawyer, because I will not be putting my head in any noose, the parson's included,' she said, stating each word slowly. 'I will not be giving up my freedom. I will not be marrying you to avoid a lawsuit. I will not be marrying you because your half-sisters would rather drag their good names through the courts than let go of a childhood grievance.' She paused to get her breath under control, which was coming in angry gasps now. 'And I most certainly will *not ever* be marrying you to make my mother happy.'

He stared back at her, his stunned expression almost comical, but nothing about this warranted laughter.

'In case I have not made myself completely clear,' she continued icily, 'I will not marry you under any condition. So you and the lawyers are going to have to find some other way of avoiding going to court, because I will not be used in this manner.'

'But—'

'I would appreciate it if you left my town house immediately. This is still my property, left to me legally by your father, and that is how it will remain. I will arrange for your luggage to be sent on to wherever you decide to reside while you are in London and I will also make arrangements to move into the Dowager's Cottage when I return to the Hartfield estate. My cottage.'

'But—'

'I said… I want you to leave.'

'But, Adelaide, can't you see—?'

'Now.'

He continued to stare at her mutely as if his entire world had just been shattered. Good. Now he would be able to experience something of how she felt after receiving that insulting marriage proposal. No, it could not be called a marriage proposal. Proposition, one that merely proved he knew nothing about her and that he was not the man she had thought him to be.

Chapter Eighteen

'Adelaide, please, see reason,' Isaac called out to her retreating back as she stormed out of the drawing room.

What in God's name was wrong with her? Nothing between them would change. They would just be married instead of secret lovers. And everyone would be happy. Well, everyone except Adelaide, it would seem.

Despite it being a sensible arrangement, she had made it very clear she did not want to marry him. She did not want to make their relationship permanent. She had been happy enough to be his lover, but not his wife.

Yet she had married his father. A tight knot twisted in his stomach. Was that what this was really about? Was this why she was acting so illogically, so unlike her usual calm self? Was it that she did not want to marry a man who had been raised in a theatre by an actress, a man whom society was never likely to truly accept as the real Duke of Hartfield?

He would not have believed it of her, but what else was he supposed to think?

And now she didn't even want him in her house. Well, if that was what she wanted, that was what she would get.

'I'm leaving, right now,' he called up the empty stairs.

'Very good, Your Grace,' the footman said from behind him, the only person who appeared to be interested in his plans.

He looked back up the stairs, clenched his teeth tighter when no reply came, strode out the house and marched down the street, as incoherent words of frustration and annoyance swirled in his head.

When he reached the end of the street, he looked around, wondering where he was going and what he was doing. A hansom cab passed by and he signalled for it to stop.

'The Eldridge Club,' he called out to the driver.

That was where he needed to be. He would not return to his rooms at the Elysian Theatre. He would stay at his club, a world populated only by undemanding men and away from all irrational, emotional, irritating women. He would not have to deal with frustrating lovers, half-sisters, scheming mothers or ex-lovers. He'd be able to relax.

Still steaming with annoyance when the cab pulled up in front of his club, he paid the driver, then marched up the stairs towards those welcoming solid oak doors, doors thick enough to keep out all frustrating females.

'A brandy, please, Arthur,' he said to the steward the moment he entered. 'A large one. And could you prepare a room for me,' he added. 'I'll be staying here for the foreseeable future.'

'Very good, sir,' Arthur said with a bow of his head before heading off to get Isaac that much-needed drink.

He walked through to the billiards room and was greeted by the murmur of male conversation and the quiet clicking of ivory balls striking each other. Excellent. Knocking coloured balls around the green baize while discussing manly subjects like the state of the nation, technological advances or the prowess of various sporting heroes was just what he needed. He spotted his two closest friends, Sebastian and Thomas, standing beside a table in the far corner, billiard cues in hand.

Even better.

His drink arrived, but he no longer needed it. Spending time in the company of his level-headed friends would have a more beneficial effect than alcohol ever could.

He crossed the room, placed the drink on a nearby table and gave his friends a hearty greeting, determined to put all thoughts of this vexing day out of his mind.

'I hear you've been hiding yourself out in the countryside,' Thomas said as he lined up a shot. 'Staying at Hartfield Hall.' He took the shot, then frowned as the red ball failed to go down its designated pocket. 'With the Duchess of Hartfield,' he added, standing up and sending Isaac a questioning look.

'I had no choice,' he said quickly as if defending himself. 'I thought she was mounting a legal case against me.'

'And was she?' Seb asked as he walked around the table, eyeing up his next shot.

'No. It was just her mother causing trouble. The Duchess has no interest in the case.'

And no further interest in me, it would seem.

That knot curling inside his stomach tightened, so he took a drink of his brandy in an attempt to drown it.

Seb rubbed chalk on the end of his cue. 'And yet you stayed?'

'Well, first Henny and Prissy turned up so I couldn't leave and let them think they had driven me out of what is now my home.'

There was no need to mention he had actually wanted to stay and had been grateful to his half-sisters for giving him an excuse. 'They were being their usual troublesome selves, so I came up with a scheme to drive them out. I invited a troupe of actors to the house and they left immediately.'

'And after that there was no reason for you to stay, so I take it you returned immediately to London?'

Seb's question was followed by the thwack of ivory hitting ivory, as the white ball connected with the striped red-and-white one, sending it firmly down the pocket.

'Good shot,' Thomas said, moving a peg along the brass scoreboard.

'No, I stayed on for a bit longer.'

Both men looked over at him.

'I had to. I'd invited the cast of the Starlight Theatre to Hartfield Hall for rehearsals. I could hardly just leave them all there, could I?'

'So once rehearsals had finished you came back to London?' Thomas asked.

'Yes.'

Isaac flinched slightly. That was not entirely the truth. If he hadn't heard from Henrietta and Priscilla's lawyer he'd probably still be at Hartfield Hall. But his friends did not need to know about that. Nor did they need to know about all the time he had spent in bed with Adelaide, or the times they had lain in each other's arms, talking and laughing together, or when they had merely been silent together, just content being in each other's company.

He coughed to drive out that memory. No, he would not be telling them any of that. Nor did they need to be told that he had thought those times meant something, something special. They certainly had to him, but apparently they had meant nothing to her, not if she could just throw him out of her house so unceremoniously.

'What?' he asked his two friends, noting that they were still staring at him. They exchanged a look that Isaac could not decipher, then went back to their game.

'And now that you're back in London...' Seb sent the white ball across the table and sank the yellow-and-white one in the far pocket '... I assume you have once again immersed yourself in the world of theatre and lovely actresses.'

'Well, yes and no. To be honest, I haven't spent much time at the theatres yet. I had to come back to London because I had a letter from Henny and Prissy's lawyer. They're still going ahead with that ridiculous lawsuit, so I had to consult with my lawyer.'

Both men nodded, as if they were not surprised by such imprudent behaviour from the spiteful sisters.

'And the Duchess remained at Hartfield Hall, did she?' Thomas asked with an ironic smile.

Damn, he would, of course, know all the London gossip. His sister, Georgina, somehow knew everything that everyone was up to and had no compunction in sharing it with whomever she met, including her brother.

'No, we came here together and, before you ask, yes, I was staying at her town house.'

'I suspect there are many other questions we need not ask,' Thomas said. 'Oh, bad luck,' he added, as Seb's shot went awry. 'And as a gentleman you would not answer if we did,' he added, looking in Isaac's direction.

Isaac merely gave a small shrug in agreement.

'But now she's kicked me out.' The desolation he had been hoping to avoid moved over him like a dark cloud. He suddenly felt very tired and disillusioned and slumped onto a nearby stool.

It was unbelievable. His time with Adelaide was over. It had been so wonderful, more wonderful than he would have imagined possible, and now she had made it clear she wanted him out of her life.

'What did you do wrong?' Thomas asked.

'I didn't do anything wrong.'

Once again they both paused and exchanged disbelieving glances, then went back to their game.

'Unless you call proposing marriage doing something wrong.'

The cue ball skittered across the table, hitting nothing and randomly bouncing off the cushions.

'You did what?' the two men asked as one.

'I asked her to marry me.'

'I take it she said no?' Thomas asked, stepping back so Seb could take his shot.

'Yes, she said no, then she told me to leave.'

Seb sent the white ball spinning across the table. A blue-and-white ball just missed the pocket. 'Damn.'

'Exactly. Damn her and damn all women. They can be so irrational. It was such a sensible proposition.'

Annoyance started to well up inside him, filling up the empty hole of desolation. He was grateful for it. The fire of infuriation was much easier to deal with than cold sorrow and regret.

'It was a plan devised by my lawyer, my sisters' lawyers and their husbands. It's such a sensible idea, too. All Adelaide and I had to do was get married and that would bring an end to the court case.'

Thomas watched him, eyebrows raised. 'And that's what you said to the Duchess, was it? That you wanted to marry her because you thought it was a sensible idea?'

'Yes, more or less. I explained what a logical solution it was and how it would solve everyone's problems.'

'How romantic of you,' Thomas added drily, as he lined up his next shot. 'I'm surprised she didn't fall into your arms immediately and tell you what a clever fellow you are.'

'It's not like that,' he protested, not sure what it was like, but surprised that his friends did not appear to be seeing things the way he did. Did they not realise that he was in the right? He had been only thinking of others and that unselfishness had been thrown back in his face.

A few more balls were sent down pockets, and pegs were moved along the scoreboard as Isaac considered their unexpected response.

'So do you think I should have phrased the proposal differently?' he asked as much of himself as his friends. 'Perhaps I shouldn't have put so much emphasis on the logic of the situation?'

'Don't ask me,' Seb said. 'I've never wooed a woman in my life, nor have I proposed, and hope it will be a long time before I'm expected to do so.'

Isaac turned to his married friend. 'Well, what should I have done to make her see reason?'

Thomas sent him a long appraising look. 'Before I answer that, I believe you need to think carefully about what it is you really want,' he said.

'I want this damn court case to go away.'

'Good shot,' Thomas said to Seb, as another ball disappeared down a pocket, then he turned back to his friend. 'And is that the only reason you wish to marry the Duchess?'

'Yes, of course. You know I am not the marrying kind, never have been, never will be.'

'Then her rejection should not matter to you.' Thomas moved the scoreboard peg to register Seb's successful shot.

'But the court case,' he said, suddenly feeling on slightly unsteady ground. 'Our marriage would have put an end to it.'

'Yes, that is unfortunate, but the only people who are really going to suffer as a result of the continued court case are Henrietta and Priscilla and there's never been much love lost between you three.'

'No, I suppose not.'

'If they take you to court and win, then you've lost a dukedom you don't want. If they lose, then they have to deal with the consequences of their actions.'

'Yes, that's true.'

'So you proposed marriage to the Duchess. She said she did not see this as an acceptable solution to the problem and turned you down. Nothing has changed.'

The turmoil in Isaac's stomach, the sense of despair he was fighting off, the crushing weight that had descended onto his shoulders, didn't make him feel as if nothing had changed.

Thomas eyed him shrewdly. 'Has it?'

Isaac did not answer. What could he say? From the moment he met Adelaide something had changed and changed so dramatically it had turned his life upside down. He did not usually react like this. He did not usually feel like this. Yet here he was, struggling against a feeling of despair he didn't want and was sure he didn't deserve.

With every other lover, when their relationship came to an end, he merely accepted it as inevitable, knowing that another woman would soon take her place. But he could not imagine anyone replacing Adelaide. He wanted her, only her, but she did not want him.

'But if her rejection is affecting you,' Thomas continued as if reading his mind, 'and not just because it means the court case will go ahead, then perhaps you need to ask yourself why.' He took his shot, potted a ball, then looked back at Isaac. 'And when you've worked out the answer to that question, perhaps then you should think about what you intend to do next.'

Isaac once again picked up his brandy and took a long swallow. His friends were being disappointingly unhelpful. He had expected then to be entirely in agreement with him, then move on to discussing something that took his mind off the despondency he was feeling.

The one thing he did not expect was for them to suggest he analyse those damn feelings or to let his emotions determine what he was to do next.

That was something Isaac had never done before and he had no idea how he was to do so now.

Adelaide had fumed with indignation as she'd watched Isaac stomping off down the street through the window. He hadn't got his own way, but that did not give him a right to be angry. She was the one who had been insulted, not him.

The moment he disappeared around the corner she informed the servants to pack up his possessions, ready to be removed from her home the moment he sent word as to where he would be residing.

Once that was done, she looked around, trying not to wonder what she would now do with her time.

As tempting as it was, she would not be fleeing back to Hartfield Hall, nor would she make any immediate plans to leave London. Joshua was having far too much fun enjoying the sights and she would not let that man or his insulting proposal ruin her son's enjoyment. But she would send word to Hartfield Hall to ask the servants to begin packing, so she could move into the Dowager's Cottage the moment she returned.

When she did return, she would start her life anew, just as she had planned when she became a widow. She had plenty to keep her busy on the estate, so busy she was certain that irritating, insensitive, insufferable man would never enter her thoughts.

Now all she had to do was stop fuming over his outrageous proposition. Once she calmed down, she could forget all about him, about how he made her feel, of how much she had laughed when in his company and how much she liked the woman she was when she was with him.

She scowled at herself. This was exactly what she did not want to do. She didn't want to think of all she had lost when she had turned him down and told him to leave. What she wanted to do was forget all about his proposal, consign their affair to the past and get on with the rest of her life, without him.

That was something she could surely do. After all,

before she'd met Isaac again she was completely content. More than content. For the first time ever she was an independent woman of means and beholden to no man.

Adapting to circumstances that had been thrust upon her was something she'd always had to do. This time, the changes had not exactly been thrust on her, however. She had made the choice to eject him from her life, so she had even more reason to prove to herself that she was more than capable of coping without him.

Joshua arrived home and immediately raced into the drawing room. 'Mama, you'll never guess what we did today,' he cried out as his nanny attempted to help the excited boy out of his coat.

As expected, before she had a chance to guess he answered, 'We saw a lantern show.' He looked up at his mother, his eyes wide with amazement. 'We saw the Three Little Pigs' houses fall down and everything. I can't wait to tell Isaac.'

Adelaide braced herself for an uncomfortable conversation.

'Thank you, that will be all, Elsie,' she said to the nanny. Once the door closed she smiled at Joshua, hoping to soften her news. 'I'm afraid Isaac isn't here, darling, but perhaps you'd like to tell me all about the Three Little Pigs and what happened to their houses.'

'Where is he and when is he coming back?'

'I'm afraid he has moved out.'

'Why?'

Because I threw him out. Because he is an insufferable oaf. Because he hurt me more than I thought it was possible for anyone to hurt me. Because he insulted me with an offensive proposal that was even worse than the one I received from his father.

'I believe he has work to do and needs to spend time on his own so he can get it done.' She cringed, not wanting to lie to her son, but not knowing how else to explain Isaac's absence.

'But he can work here. I'll be really quiet if that's what he wants,' Joshua said with a frown. 'He doesn't have to leave us.'

'I'm sorry, Joshua. But sometimes adults need to have time to themselves. Now, bring down your soldiers and we'll have a game.'

Joshua sent her a quizzical look, no doubt surprised that for the first time she had offered to play soldiers with him, but at least he went upstairs without asking any more uncomfortable questions.

She turned and looked out of the window, her heart clenching tighter at the painful realisation that she was not the only one who would miss Isaac. He had said he wanted to marry her for the sake of his half-sisters and had even infuriatingly suggested it would make her mother happy. Neither of those reasons had convinced her to make another marriage for the convenience of others, but if he had said such a marriage would make Joshua happy, she might have weakened. Even now she wondered whether she had been selfish to deprive her son of a man in his life, one he cared about so deeply, one who was so good to him.

Joshua arrived back in the drawing room, carrying his box of soldiers. He laid them out on the floor and Adelaide sat beside him on the mat.

'So what are the rules?' she asked.

Her son looked at her as if she was a bit light-headed. 'You have to knock over all the other soldiers to win the battle.'

'I see,' she said, not really seeing at all, but happy to divert him from Isaac's departure and her mind from all its turbulent questions.

They were soon immersed in a game that appeared to consist entirely of making lots of battle noises and tossing soldiers around the floor, when the footman entered and announced that her sister had come for a visit. Adelaide declared Joshua's soldiers the victors and asked him to pack his toys away.

Felicity entered, bringing her usual sense of joy with her. Since her marriage to the Duke of Greystone, she radiated that joy everywhere she went. Her happiness usually filled Adelaide's heart with a sense of satisfaction, knowing that her own marriage had given her sister the freedom to marry for love. But today it was a cruel reminder of how happy Adelaide had been only a few hours previously.

'Joshua,' Felicity cried out, opening her arms wide. 'Don't you have a hug for your aunt?'

Joshua rushed across the room into her arms and received countless kisses on the top of his head. 'You're such a big boy now. Every time I see you, you seem to have grown a foot,' she said between kisses.

Joshua looked down at his feet and frowned. 'No, I've still only got two.'

The sisters laughed. 'And I'm pleased to hear it,' Felicity said.

The maid entered and Adelaide asked for tea to be served and for Joshua to be taken upstairs for his afternoon nap.

Once they had departed, Felicity took a seat and turned her full attention to Adelaide. 'I've had a letter from Mother. She said you had come to London, with a certain someone.' She sent Adelaide a knowing smile which only proved how little she actually did know.

'Things are not as Mother imagines or hopes,' Adelaide replied, swallowing her annoyance at her interfering mother.

'Well, she said the two of you came down to London together and that he is staying here, in your town house.' Her sister looked around as if expecting Isaac to suddenly appear.

'It's not—'

Conversation came to a halt as the maid entered and placed the tea service on the small table.

'Thank you, that will be all,' Adelaide said and, after bobbing a small curtsy the maid departed.

'And Mother said that same someone spent rather a long time staying at Hartfield Hall,' Felicity continued, before reaching over and placing several small delicacies on her plate.

'It is his estate,' Adelaide said noncommittally as she poured the tea. 'He can stay there as long and as often as he wishes.'

'So?' Felicity asked, wriggling her eyebrows several times above the rim of her teacup in what was presumably supposed to be a comical manner, but Adelaide did not feel like laughing.

'So, what?'

'That's exactly the question I was going to ask. So what is going on between you and the new Duke?'

'Nothing,' Adelaide all but snapped back.

'That's not what Mother said. Her letters were full of how close the two of you are getting and how there will soon be another wedding in the family.'

'That is what Mother wants, but it is purely wishful thinking. Once again she is hoping I will marry the man of her choosing.'

Felicity took a sip of her tea, her eyes still fixed on Adelaide. 'So Mother is wrong then, is she? There is nothing between you and the Duke?'

Adelaide shrugged one shoulder. 'Well, we had a dalliance, I suppose you could call it.'

Felicity placed her teacup on the table so quickly it rattled in the saucer. 'I knew it. I just knew it. I could tell by looking at you that something dramatic had happened in your life.'

Adelaide chose to say nothing on that matter. 'Would you care for a macaroon to go with your petit fours? Cook is rather proud of them.'

'Don't try to change the subject,' Felicity said, reaching out and placing two biscuits on her plate. 'And I don't believe what you had with Isaac was just a dalliance. My dutiful, serious sister would never do anything so flippant. If something happened between you two, then it had to mean something. I want to hear all about it.'

'You're wrong. It was a brief dalliance, nothing more.'

'Really? Well, Mother said that she heard you humming to yourself and you smiled constantly. Neither of those behaviours is like you. If it was merely a dalliance, can I assume it was a rather satisfactory one?'

'Yes, I suppose so.' She placed a small cake on her plate. She was not hungry, but had to do something to distract herself from thinking about just how satisfactory it was and how she would no longer be feeling the intense pleasure that had made her body sing and her heart soar. She had thrown him out and had been right to do so, but there was no denying she would miss having him in her bed. And not just that, she would miss having him to talk to, to laugh with, to spend comfortable hours together, enjoying each other's company.

'And?'

'And nothing. It was satisfactory while it lasted, but it's all over now.'

'Over? Why? What happened?' she asked and placed the best part of a macaroon in her mouth.

'He proposed.'

Felicity coughed on her macaroon and quickly took a sip of tea. 'He what?' she gasped out.

'He proposed and it was the most insulting marriage proposal I've ever heard. It was even more insulting than when the old Duke announced he had chosen me to be his new bride in front of Mother and I was given no option but to accept and was even expected to express how honoured I was to be the one selected. I had to swallow my outrage then. I did not have to swallow it this time.'

'So you turned him down?'

'Of course I turned him down,' she fired back. Her sister was not usually this dim-witted.

'Because you don't love him and don't want to be his wife?'

'What? No, well, yes, I don't know.'

'You don't know if you love him? You don't know if you want to be his wife? Perhaps they were questions you should have pondered before you turned him down.'

Adelaide stared at her sister. Neither of those questions were ones she had asked herself at the time and had no desire to do so now.

'I turned him down because he said he wanted me to marry him not because of any regard for me, but because it would stop this stupid court case with his half-sisters.'

Adelaide drew in a breath, the pain in her jaw registering her tension. 'I will not do that ever again,' she said, seething. 'I will not be caught up in other people's games. I will not surrender my independence. I will not sacrifice myself again and marry for the advancement of another's interests.'

Felicity looked down at her lap and her cheeks coloured slightly.

'Oh, Flick, I'm sorry.' She reached out and patted her sister's hand. 'Last time I agreed to sacrifice my happiness to help the family out of the financial mess in which Father had left us as there was no other option. And I'm so pleased that you have found the love and happiness in your marriage that you deserve. That made it all worthwhile.'

'But this time you would be marrying Isaac Radcliff. He's not his father,' Felicity said quietly.

Adelaide shrugged.

'And he is very handsome.'

'Yes.' That was something she could not deny. He was the most breathtakingly handsome man she had ever laid eyes on and his body was simply magnificent. Memories of that hard, masculine chest, those wide shoulders and the sinewy muscles of his arms invaded her mind, causing heat to rise up her body.

'And I hear he's rather charming.'

'Women definitely find him charming,' she said tersely.

'And you two spent rather a lot of time alone together.' Felicity once again wriggled her eyebrows in that silly manner that was obviously meant to be suggestive. 'And you said the dalliance was satisfactory.'

'He's certainly charming, he's handsome, and he knows how to satisfy a woman.'

Despite her attempt to dismiss those attributes, she couldn't help but draw in a shuddering breath as she remembered his kisses, the light ones, the passionate ones, the hungry ones that left her reeling. They were kisses she would never taste again, nor would she feel the caress of his hands on her body or the touch of his naked skin against hers.

'I take it from that look on your face it was more than just satisfactory, but all rather wonderful and magical.'

'Yes, I suppose it was,' she said, pursing her lips and trying to drive out thoughts of just how magical, how wonderful it was.

'Wouldn't that alone be worth marrying him for?'

'Of course not,' she shot back.

Would it? No, it most certainly would not.

'What would make you want to marry him?'

She stared at her sister for a moment, unable to think of an answer. 'I don't know. Why did you marry Victor?' she finally asked.

'Because I loved him and I knew that he loved me.'

'Exactly.'

'And the two of you don't love each other?'

'No, it would seem not. No man who loved a woman would ever insult her the way he insulted me.'

'Hmm,' Felicity replied. 'Men can be rather oblivious at times, but the important question is, do you love him?'

'No, of course not.'

Felicity tilted her head. 'You're talking to me, Adelaide, your sister. I know that is not the whole truth.'

'Well, yes. I suppose I do have feelings for him.'

Her sister's head tilted slightly more.

'I suppose they are rather intense,' she added, reluctantly.

'*Rather* intense?'

'Oh, all right, yes, they are so intense they consume me. I have never felt like this about any man before. I didn't know it was possible. With him I feel so alive, as if he brings out something in me that I didn't know existed. Everything about him makes me happy, his looks, his laugh, the way he talks, the funny things he says, everything.' She realised she was smiling and immediately arranged her face into a more serious expression.

'That sounds like love to me.'

'But he can also be so infuriating, so annoying and can vex me so much. I mean, that proposal was unforgivable. If he loved me even a little, he would have known how badly he was insulting me. He would have known I'd refuse him.'

Felicity nodded slowly. 'Yes, I know. Even the most lovable of men can sometimes be incredibly clueless, I'm afraid.'

On that she was in total agreement with her sister.

'But what you need to ask yourself is—do you really want to live the rest of your life without him?'

Adelaide went to pour another cup of tea and discovered her cup was still full. 'No, the question I need to ask myself is—how do I live my life now that Isaac Radcliff is no longer in it?'

And that was a question to which she was going to have to find her own answers, because it was obvious Felicity was going to be no help whatsoever in that regard.

Chapter Nineteen

Isaac was loath to admit it, but his friends had been a severe disappointment to him and he would not be taking their advice. He was not about to start analysing his feelings. As for the suggestion that he had done something wrong—well, that most certainly did not require any further consideration.

Yes, he would admit that Thomas was correct on one count. Adelaide's rejection had affected him more than it should have. He should not be going over and over everything she'd said to him and everything he'd said to her. He should just be accepting that he'd offered for her, she'd said no and that should be the end of it. As for her tossing him out of her house—that, too, should not be affecting him the way it was.

This was all so new. He did not ever feel this way about women. His ex-lovers didn't remain constantly in his mind, but thoughts of Adelaide were always there, from the moment he woke up in the morning until he fell asleep at night, and even then he did not get a reprieve. Last night she had invaded his dreams in a rather delightful way. The woman simply would not leave him alone.

It was all too much. What he needed was the distraction that his friends had failed to provide. And he would get that by burying himself in his work. So, the next morning he returned to the Elysian Theatre.

His assistant went through everything that had been happening, but unfortunately there were no disasters that needed his immediate attention, no chaos that had to be set right and no crisis that required his urgent intervention.

'Excellent work,' he informed his assistant dourly. 'I can see I left the theatres in good hands.'

Damn it all, his presence was hardly needed. Gerrard had even tidied up his office and he could now see clear spaces on his desk. 'Yes, truly excellent work. I can see you are deserving of a generous raise in your salary.'

The happy assistant wandered off and Isaac stared at the four walls and sighed. He picked up a new script that had been sent in, read the first page, then stopped. He had not taken in one single word. He held the pages tighter, stared at the words more intently and tried to concentrate, but the words continued to swirl in front of his eyes while his mind wandered off yet again to reliving Adelaide's response to his proposal.

He threw down the script onto the now tidy couch

and grabbed his jacket. This was not working either. He needed action, people, noise, not this quiet office.

If he watched a rehearsal, maybe that would do the trick. Surely the sight of a bevy of pretty girls high-kicking their way across the stage would be enough to take any man's mind off his problems. He headed downstairs and into the empty auditorium and was surprised to see Peregrine from the Starlight Theatre seated in the stalls, watching the performance.

'Slumming it, are you, Peregrine?' he said as he took a seat next to the director. 'Vaudeville is a long way from Shakespeare.'

'I'm aware of that, dear boy, but there's a young actress I wanted to watch. I believe she would make an excellent Kate in my next production of *The Taming of the Shrew*.'

They turned and watched the two comedians on stage and he could see what the director meant—the young actress's comic timing was perfect.

'So, you're back in London,' the director stated the obvious as the duo left the stage and a line of high-kicking beauties entered. 'And where is the lovely Duchess?'

Isaac gritted his teeth together. Would he never be allowed to forget about that woman, even for a second?

'She also came to London, but we have since decided to part ways.'

Peregrine turned in his seat and faced Isaac. 'Do tell, dear boy—what did you do to encourage her wrath?'

'I did nothing wrong. Why does everyone assume it's my fault that she kicked me out?'

One arched eyebrow rose up Peregrine's forehead.

'If you must know, I proposed marriage to her and that's what, as you said, encouraged her wrath.'

'Oh, my poor, poor boy, that's frightful.'

Good, someone was finally on his side.

'You bared your soul, declared your undying love for the woman who has captured your heart and she spurned you. You must be devastated.'

Isaac cringed at Peregrine's misreading of the situation. 'Well, I didn't exactly bare my soul or declare my undying love.'

'But you said you proposed.'

'Yes, it was a scheme my lawyer presented to me. He said it would be the best way to put a halt to my half-sisters' lawsuit.'

Peregrine stared at him and for once the director was seemingly lost for words.

'I see,' he finally said, drawing out those two words as if they constituted a long speech. 'So what you were actually proposing was a marriage of convenience that would make your life easier and stop you from having to go through an unwanted lawsuit.'

Now Isaac was the one who was lost for words.

When he put it like that it did sound rather selfish, but that was not how he had meant it. Not entirely, anyway.

'Not just me,' he mumbled. 'My half-sisters would be able to drop the lawsuit without losing face.'

Peregrine continued to stare at him, that annoying eyebrow still arched.

'And her mother was keen on the idea of us marrying,' he added, then winced as he heard how pathetic that sounded.

'I take it you did not propose because you are in love with her.'

He stared at Peregrine, not knowing how to answer that question, so he merely shrugged his shoulders.

'Well, do you love her?' the other man pressed.

It was such a bold question and one Isaac had not thought to consider before. 'Well, I, er, I love being with her. I'm never happier than when I'm in her company. I can't get her out of my head, no matter what I do. I think she is the most beautiful, wonderful, enchanting woman I have ever met. Is that love?'

Peregrine did not answer, but a second raised eyebrow joined the first.

'And since she tossed me out, I've had this excruciating pain in my stomach and a gripping sensation in my chest that won't let me go, no matter how much bicarbonate of soda I take.'

'I see,' Peregrine said, once again stretching those two words to their maximum. 'It's perhaps not the most poetic description of love I've ever heard, but it certainly sounds as though that is the affliction from which you are suffering.'

'But it hardly matters now. I asked her to marry me, and she said no, so that's the end of it.'

Peregrine slowly shook his head. 'For a man who has an enviable reputation with women, you really are—how shall I put it?—an idiot who knows nothing about women, aren't you?'

'Well, I've never been in love before.' Isaac stared at the director, realising that he had just admitted it. He was in love. In love with Adelaide. And more to the point, he had no idea of how to cure himself of this devastating condition.

'Yes, unfortunately love does make fools of us mortal men. But hopefully all is not lost. So, my next question is, do you really want to marry her?'

'Yes,' Isaac answered immediately. 'Yes, I do want to marry her and not just because of that lawsuit. Hang the lawsuit. I want to marry Adelaide because I love her. I can't live without her. I don't want to live without her.'

Finally, those arched eyebrows lowered.

'But she's never going to believe me now,' Isaac continued. 'I've ruined everything, haven't I? You're right, I'm a complete idiot.'

'Yes, but perhaps you could try making another proposal, this time a proper one.'

'How? I've got as much experience at proposing as I have at being in love.'

'You need to woo her, to make her swoon with the depth of your feelings for her, to make her see that no man has loved a woman more than you love her.'

'Well, that is all true, but how on earth do I convince her that I'm not an unromantic clod but a clueless man in love? How can I, of all people, convince her of the depth of my feelings when I hardly understand them myself?'

He looked to the director for help. Peregrine said nothing.

'I might have, as you say, an enviable reputation with women, but I've never been in love before. I've never wanted to marry anyone before. How do I convince Adelaide that I'm in love with her? I can hardly tell her I love her so much it's giving me indigestion.'

He continued to stare in appeal at the director.

'I believe, dear boy, when it comes to matters of the heart, you cannot go wrong with Shakespeare.' Peregrine stood up and adopted a theatrical pose. 'The Bard knew best how to capture that most powerful of all emotions.' He lifted his arms wide, as if addressing an invisible audience. 'Perhaps you could say, *"Doubt the stars are fire, doubt that the sun does move, doubt truth to be a liar, but never doubt I love you."'*

'Hmm, didn't Ophelia say that to Hamlet before he

cast her away? And didn't everyone die a violent death at the end of that play?'

'Yes, well, sometimes love can be a bit fraught.'

A bit fraught? That was an understatement.

'In that case…' Once again, Peregrine lifted his arms and moved them in a sweeping gesture. 'Perhaps you could say, *"But I do love thee, and when I love thee not, chaos is come again."'*

'Um…didn't Othello say that to Desdemona, but then later he killed her out of misplaced jealousy?'

'Well, no one ever said the course of true love ran smooth.'

'Yes, I think the Shakespeare was right about that.'

'Of course he was, dear boy, the Bard is always right. Well, I hope I've been of some help and I look forward to attending the wedding.'

With that Peregrine wandered off, having been no help whatsoever, leaving a bewildered Isaac convinced that the whole thing was hopeless.

Chapter Twenty

Isaac had no idea what he was going to say to Adelaide, but one thing he knew for certain. He had to make amends for what was perhaps the worst proposal a man had ever made. He had insulted the woman he loved and for that he had to atone. Even if the outcome was him making a complete fool of himself, it had to be done.

To that end, he left the Elysian Theatre and hailed a hansom cab to take him to Adelaide's town house. Throughout the journey he practised what he was going to say. Lines from Shakespeare ran through his mind, but despite what Peregrine claimed none seemed quite right. They were undeniably poetic, but did not match his situation and sounded contrived and false to his ears.

Still trying to get his thoughts straight, he climbed out of the cab, walked up the path and stopped at her door. This was so important. The most important thing he had done in his entire life, yet he was hopelessly ill-prepared. He did not know how he was going to apologise. He could not even begin to think how one convinced a woman that you were not a buffoon, but merely a man in love. And he certainly did not know how to tell her he wanted to marry her and to spend the rest of his life with her.

But he could not be a coward. He had to try, even if he failed miserably, as he suspected he was about to do. He drew in a series of long, calming breaths, lifted the lion door knocker and knocked with more decisiveness than he felt before he had a chance to turn tail and run.

The footman greeted him politely, led him through to the drawing room and announced his arrival. Good, at least he hadn't been banned from the house and the servants hadn't been given orders to throw him into the street should he ever dare to show his face again. That had to be a good sign. Didn't it?

Adelaide looked up from her embroidery. Her expression was surprised initially, then it turned to that same fierce expression he had seen when she had tossed him out. One that was anything but welcoming.

'Adelaide,' he said.

Merely saying her name was not a great start, but it was better than standing in the middle of the room completely mute.

'Adelaide,' he repeated, causing her to tilt her head and give him a sideways look.

'Adelaide,' he said for a third time. 'I want to marry you.'

Damn. There was nothing poetic in that declaration even if it did express precisely what he wanted.

He waited, his breath caught in his throat, his heart seemingly pausing in its beating, as if also waiting to see whether it was about to break into a thousand pieces or expand with joy.

She continued to look at him, her head still tilted, then calmly went back to her embroidery.

He waited, watching the needle go in and out of the fabric.

She had not rejected him, but nor had she accepted his proposal. She had said nothing. Was still saying nothing, leaving him standing in the doorway. Was that good? Bad? He suspected the latter, unfortunately.

He took a step forward. 'I said I—'

'I heard what you said. You want to marry me. You made that clear the last time you were here and I gave you my answer. You're going to have to find some other way to put an end to your half-sisters' court case than placing our heads in the parson's noose, as you so eloquently phrased it.'

Peregrine was right. He knew nothing of women, nothing of romance, nothing of love. Except that he felt it, deeply.

'No, no, I don't care about the court case,' he said, taking another step towards her, his hands held out, pleading. 'Oh, God, Adelaide, I am so sorry I made that stupid proposal. If I could take it back, I would. It was insulting and you were perfectly right to throw it back in my face.'

She stopped in her embroidering again, looked up at him, but said nothing.

'And you were right to give me my marching orders after I behaved like such a cad. When the lawyer said we should wed I thought, yes, that would solve everyone's problems. I would not have come to that conclusion if marriage to you wasn't something I already wanted, wanted so desperately I immediately leapt into it, without a second thought.'

She just stared at him, as if not believing a word he was saying.

'There's no excuse for my behaviour,' he continued, 'but I think at the time I was under the illusion that if I framed our marriage as a logical solution to a problem, you might put aside your objections to giving up your independence and see it as a viable proposition.'

'After all that I've been through, you thought I would see sacrificing my independence and marrying once again for the benefit of others as a viable proposition?' she scoffed.

'I know. I'm sorry. No one could ever accuse me of being sensible or sensitive.'

'You'll get no argument from me there.'

'I should have known better. I should have been more sensitive to what had happened to you in the past. After being forced into your first marriage to save your family, I should have realised that you would never want to make a marriage like that ever again. I am such a fool.'

She huffed. 'Again, you'll get no argument from me on that score.'

He sighed, knowing that he was once again making a total mess of things. But as this might be the last time he was likely to see her, he needed to say everything that was in his heart. Hopefully, this time he would be able to express his true feelings with a modicum of eloquence.

'I do want to marry you, but I can understand why you would not want to marry a fool who would make you such an appalling offer. But before I go, I just want to tell you that I love you.' It was only a simple phrase, but it would have to do and it summed up everything he was feeling. 'I love everything about you: your smile, your laughter, your strength, your warm heart, your beautiful soul.'

She looked back at him, her needle paused, her eyes wide.

'I never really believed that love existed until I met you, but now my love for you consumes me night and day. When I first met you all I saw was a beautiful woman, but I've come to see that you are so much more than that. Your beauty is more than just your face, and, well, your body. You're a beautiful soul, a beautiful spirit.'

He drew in a deep breath, knowing he just had to get the words out. 'I love you more than I can possibly express, but I also respect and admire you. I know you are a woman who cherishes her independence and it is no less than you deserve, and I fully understand why you would never want to marry again. Or to marry a man such as myself. I insulted you when I proposed and for that I am deeply sorry.'

Still, she said nothing, merely stared at him.

'I know my words must sound empty to you. I just wish I was a poet and could say in verse how much I love you. I wish I could tell you how you have awakened something in me I did not know existed, how you have shown me it was possible to love another with all my heart and soul.'

He stood before her, aware that his words had failed to convince her, but it mattered not. He had said his piece, that was all he came for and now he could leave.

But before he could do so, she put down her embroidery, crossed the room and kissed him.

It was his turn to be taken by surprise, but it was a surprise that lasted only a fraction of a second before he was kissing her back passionately, hungry for all that he had missed, all that he thought he had lost.

Holding her closely in his arms, he tasted her sweet lips and hoped this was not a kiss goodbye, but a kiss of forgiveness, a kiss of second chances and redemption.

When they finally broke apart she smiled at him. 'I believe you are indeed a poet and those words were more than adequate.' She smiled up at him, still encased in his loving arms, and euphoria washed through him. She believed him. She had forgiven him.

'But your kisses are even more eloquent than your words,' she added with a cheeky smile. 'And if you wanted to make me another offer, I believe I might be more receptive this time.'

He was instantly down on one knee, Adelaide's lovely hand in his.

'Adelaide FitzWilliam, would you do me the greatest honour in the world and consent to be my wife?'

She inclined her head, and lightly tapped her chin, teasing him. He was happy to be teased if it gave him an opportunity to express all that was in his heart.

'Adelaide, will you marry me and give me the opportunity to prove myself worthy of being your soulmate? I want to spend my life with you, showing you every day how much I love you, making you smile, making you happy, making you feel loved and cherished as you deserve. Will you allow me to do that?'

She smiled down at him, and whispered, 'Yes.'

All tension floated out of him, his heart expanded

in his chest, as a lightness took hold of his being. He smiled up at her, hardly able to believe that she had said that one, wonderful word.

'Yes, I will marry you,' she repeated.

'Oh, Adelaide, my darling Adelaide,' he breathed, rising to his feet and taking her in his arms. 'I promise you will never regret this, not for one second of the rest of your life.'

'If you don't give me another of those eloquent kisses soon I might start to have regrets,' she said with a beaming smile.

He didn't need to be asked twice. His lips were immediately on hers and his kiss expressed all the happiness that was flooding his body. This wonderful, independent, resourceful woman was to be his wife. He doubted he deserved such good fortune, but he would be true to his word and spend the rest of his life ensuring she did not ever regret making him the happiest man in the world.

Chapter Twenty-One

Tears of pure joy filled Adelaide's eyes as she walked up the aisle on her brother's arm towards her husband-to-be. She was in love with the most wonderful man in the world and that man loved her in return. Once she would not have thought such a thing was possible, not for her.

As agreed with Henny's and Prissy's husbands, the notice of their intention to wed had gone into the newspapers immediately, the banns had been read and within three weeks she was once again about to become a duke's wife.

Despite the haste, everything about this wedding had been a joy to prepare, from choosing her flowing gown to organising the white lilies that decorated the small stone church near Hartfield Hall. This time she could also share her happiness with Joshua, who was her pageboy, and Felicity, her matron of honour.

Joshua couldn't be more delighted with his role. Wearing a morning suit of dove grey that matched

Isaac's and the other men in the wedding party, he took his job of carrying her train seriously, even if he did drop it on occasion to smile and wave at guests he recognised.

He had been somewhat disappointed when told he could not give another performance of his fairy dance during the ceremony, but Isaac had assured him there would be plenty of time for that at the wedding breakfast.

He was also ecstatic to learn that his original wish had come true, that Isaac was to live with them and he was to be Joshua's father. It was something she now suspected she had always secretly wished for as well, even if she hadn't known it at the time.

She drew closer to the altar and smiled at her mother seated in the front pew. At her last wedding, her brother's and sister's smiles had been sympathetic—now she knew they were joyful. Her mother's was equally jubilant, although Adelaide strongly suspected that was because she thought she had once again successfully arranged an advantageous marriage for her daughter.

'You look enchanting,' Isaac whispered as she reached the altar, his love shining in his eyes. He looked so handsome dressed in his frock coat with a white rose in his lapel, standing beside his best man and groomsman, Sebastian and Thomas.

The vicar recited the marriage ceremony and every word rang true. They did love each other, of that there was no doubt, and they would cherish and honour each other, until death parted them.

When the vicar finally said, 'You may kiss the bride,' Isaac lifted her veil and lightly kissed her lips.

'Is that it?' she said quietly, unable to stop smiling.

'We're in public in case you haven't noticed, so that little kiss will have to do for now,' he whispered back, also smiling from ear to ear. 'My insatiable wife will have to wait until tonight if she wants more than just chaste kisses.'

A shiver of delightful expectation rippled down Adelaide's body, from her heart to her toes curling inside her silk shoes, and back up again. Tonight would be their first night as husband and wife, no more sneaking around, and she could hardly wait.

The bells chimed out their happy tune as Isaac took her hand and led her out of the church. Everyone beamed smiles back at them, basking in their happiness, aware that they had just witnessed two people declaring their true love and commitment to each other.

When they reached the steps of the church, Isaac and Adelaide were instantly surrounded by well-wishers, shaking Isaac's hand and kissing her on the cheek, and Adelaide was delighted to be able to share their joy with family and friends.

Lady Henrietta approached, one of the few who was not smiling, followed by an equally sullen Priscilla.

'I hope you two receive all the happiness you deserve,' she said, a begrudging note in her voice. 'But I am afraid I will be unable to attend the wedding breakfast.'

Then she did smile. 'I don't know if you are aware, but my husband has been appointed to the position of District Commander in Calcutta and we have much to do before our departure.'

'Of course,' Adelaide said. The guests included a large number of theatre people and Adelaide suspected that was one reason why Lady Henrietta wished to leave early, but whatever it was, Adelaide was happy to see the last of her.

'Congratulations on your husband's appointment. It is a great honour,' Adelaide said diplomatically, maintaining the charade. 'And I believe Lady Hampton and her husband are soon to depart for St Petersburg?'

'Yes. When the Empire calls, men of such exalted positions as our husbands must do their duty.'

'Most noble of you.'

Lady Henrietta nodded her head as if graciously accepting Adelaide's tribute, then left, followed by her sister and their husbands.

Isaac squeezed her hand gently, a squeeze that spoke volumes. With the sisters' departure, they could now celebrate their nuptials with people who really did want to share in their happiness and good fortune.

And that was exactly what they did. Although the wedding breakfast had been hastily arranged, it had been done with such love and that showed in every bouquet of flowers the servants had placed around Hartfield Hall, the banquet Cook and the other servants had prepared and the happiness that radiated in the faces of their guests.

Adelaide laughed and cried through the speeches and was sure her happiness was complete when Isaac took her hand and they danced the night away.

Finally, guests started to leave in their carriages, or made their way up to their bedchambers in Hartfield Hall, and Isaac and Adelaide were able to retire.

'I believe you promised me an ecstatic wedding night,' Adelaide whispered, as Isaac took her hand and led her up the stairs.

'Tonight, I plan to achieve the impossible,' he said. 'I'm going to try to finally sate my insatiable wife.'

'Never,' Adelaide said, as the bedroom door closed behind them and his lips found hers.

Isaac had been almost true to his word. Her wedding night had been ecstatic, but in one area he was wrong—she knew she was never going to get enough of her wonderful husband.

When she awoke the next morning, she would have loved to remain in her marriage bed for ever, but they had no choice but to rise early.

While they breakfasted, trunks were loaded on to carriages and it was all but impossible to get Joshua to eat anything, he was so excited to be off on their journey. Throughout the train trip he chatted constantly about what he intended to do and see during what he kept referring to as 'our honeymoon in Europe.'

They arrived at the London docks and Adelaide felt as giddy as Joshua as she took in all the activity, the rushing here and there of passengers, crew, officials and sailors from seemingly every nation. A cacophony of sounds and foreign languages filled the air, along with the scent of the ocean and the smell of coal from the steamships.

They quickly boarded their ship and Isaac lifted Joshua up to the top of the rail so he could watch all the activity below them. When the steam whistle gave a loud blast, the engines began to churn and they were soon travelling out of London and into the open seas. As they watched the land disappear behind them, Adelaide was sure her excitement rivalled Joshua's.

The arrival at Calais was no less thrilling, and Adelaide could hardly believe she was actually here. In France. She now had the freedom she had always wanted, the happiness she had always dreamed of.

As if caught up in a glorious whirl, their months away from England seemed to fly past. Just as she had always promised herself, she strolled down the Champs Élysées, explored the Louvre, travelled by gondola in Venice, attended an opera in Rome and so much more.

* * *

When they took the steamship back to London, they had so many memories to cherish and Joshua was debating with himself whether he would become a world-famous actor or an intrepid world traveller.

'Now we have to face the music,' Isaac said with fortitude as they docked in London.

'And I believe that is exactly what we will do,' she replied.

He raised his eyebrows in question and waited for her to explain.

'I think we should host a ball at Hartfield Hall, our home, and let society know that the Duke and Duchess of Hartfield have nothing to be ashamed of and care nothing for what the gossips have to say.'

'A ball? Invite the aristocracy? Into our home?'

'Don't look so shocked. Yes, the aristocracy. People like me, my brother and sister, your friend Sebastian, Joshua—we're all members of the aristocracy. We're not all bad, you know, and you're not going to be able to avoid us now that you're a duke.'

'If you think that's a good idea,' he said, his expression suggesting he was not entirely convinced.

So that was what they did. From the moment they were back at Hartfield Hall, Adelaide threw herself into arranging what she hoped would be a memorable event, for all the right reasons.

While Isaac was visiting the theatre, checking on

the work of his highly competent assistant and putting into motion the first of what they hoped would be many theatrical events on the Hartfield estate, Adelaide enlisted the help of her sister, her mother and Grace, the wife of Isaac's friend Thomas, to organise a ball. With much laughter and chatter, they busied themselves organising the enormous bouquets of flowers to decorate the ballroom, enlisting an orchestra, choosing the lavish buffet, the champagne and other refreshments essential for the success of the evening.

Every single invitation that had been sent out had been accepted, although whether that was through curiosity, or a genuine desire to meet the new Duke, Adelaide was unsure, and on the night of the ball she had to admit to feeling a few nerves.

'You have nothing to worry about,' Felicity whispered to her, as she stood beside her in the line-up to greet their guests. 'I hear the Prince of Wales has taken another mistress and I believe she is a French actress. That has far surpassed the gossips' interest in discovering the old Duke had actually married Isaac's mother after all.'

The footman announced the arrival of the first guests, Thomas and his wife Grace, followed by Thomas's sister, the Duchess of Ravenswood, and her husband. They were soon followed by everyone who was anyone in society. Isaac greeted them all with his usual easy charm and she could see they were falling immediately under his spell.

She had never doubted otherwise. After all, if she had been unable to resist her handsome, magnetic husband, how could anyone else be immune to his charisma?

Introductions over, the orchestra began playing the music for the first dance. Isaac bowed formally in front of her. 'May I have this dance, Your Grace,' he said, with that roguish smile she had never been able to resist.

'I believe you may, Your Grace,' she replied with a curtsy,and he led her out on to the floor in front of everyone, before being joined by other swirling couples.

As much as she'd like to spend the entire night dancing with her husband, Adelaide knew she had to circulate. She danced with numerous other men and chatted with as many of the ladies as she could, discovering they were all more interested in hearing about her extended trip to Europe than any scandal that might surround the family.

If people were still gossiping about her, Isaac and the sisters, she did not care. This ball meant they had made their mark on society and let the world know they were above it all. That was all she had wished for.

Eventually, a little fatigued from so much dancing and chatting, she joined her husband, who was waiting for her at the edge of the dance floor with a much-needed glass of punch.

'I've just been watching Sebastian,' he said, nodding his head discreetly in the direction of his friend, who was talking to a pretty blonde woman. 'Those two have been trying to ignore each other all night.'

'They don't appear to be doing a very good job of it,' Adelaide said, observing the way the woman was waggling her finger at Sebastian and the frown he was giving her in return.

'No, they've been failing dismally. As the Bard said, as well I know, the path of true love never did run smooth, and it looks as though Sebastian and that young lady are already well and truly on that path. I suspect it won't be long before we are attending another wedding.'

'Oh, I do hope so,' she said, handing her drink to a passing servant. 'In the meantime, I have found my second wind and now I want to continue dancing with my husband.'

And with that, he once again swept her into his arms and they danced around the room, oblivious to everyone but each other.

* * * * *

MILLS & BOON®

Coming next month

THE TAMING OF THE COUNTESS
Michelle Willingham

'What did Papa want to talk with you about?'

James hesitated a moment before answering, 'He wants me to marry you.'

She blinked a moment, as if she hadn't heard him correctly. 'He what?'

'He believes I should marry you and offer the protection of my title.' He took the remainder of the brandy and finished it in one swallow. 'It would be quite difficult to arrest a countess.'

Evangeline's disbelief transformed into dismay. 'That's a terrible idea. You and I are not suited at all.' But there was a faint undertone in her voice, as if she were trying to convince herself.

'I agree.' Though he hated the idea of hurting her feelings, he couldn't let her build him up into the man she wanted him to be. 'We both know I'll never be the right man for you.'

Her eyes grew luminous with unshed tears, and she nodded. 'You made that clear enough when you sailed half a world away.'

'You could have any man you desire, Evangeline,' he murmured. 'Just choose one of them instead.' He wanted her to find her own happiness with someone who could give her the life she deserved.

The very thought made his hands curl into fists. And that was the problem. Every time he tried to do the right thing and let Evie go, he kept imagining her in someone else's arms. And the idea only provoked jealousy he had no right to feel.

Continue reading

THE TAMING OF THE COUNTESS
Michelle Willingham

Available next month
millsandboon.co.uk

Copyright © 2025 Michelle Willingham

COMING SOON!

We really hope you enjoyed reading this book.
If you're looking for more romance
be sure to head to the shops when
new books are available on

Thursday 24th
April

To see which titles are coming soon, please visit
millsandboon.co.uk/nextmonth

MILLS & BOON

LET'S TALK

Romance

For exclusive extracts, competitions
and special offers, find us online:

- **f** MillsandBoon
- **X** @MillsandBoon
- **⬤** @MillsandBoonUK
- **♪** @MillsandBoonUK

Get in touch on 01413 063 232

For all the latest titles coming soon, visit
millsandboon.co.uk/nextmonth

FOUR BRAND NEW BOOKS FROM
MILLS & BOON MODERN

The same great stories you love, a stylish new look!

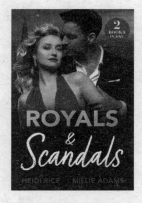

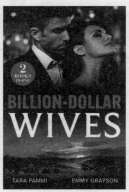

OUT NOW

Eight Modern stories published every month, find them all at:

millsandboon.co.uk

afterglow BOOKS

Afterglow Books is a trend-led, trope-filled list of books with diverse, authentic and relatable characters, a wide array of voices and representations, plus real world trials and tribulations. Featuring all the tropes you could possibly want (think small-town settings, fake relationships, grumpy vs sunshine, enemies to lovers) and all with a generous dose of spice in every story.

♪ @millsandboonuk

⊙ @millsandboonuk

afterglowbooks.co.uk

#AfterglowBooks

For all the latest book news, exclusive content and giveaways scan the QR code below to sign up to the Afterglow newsletter:

SCAN ME